THE DEMOCRACY CLOCK
EVENT LOG

THE DEMOCRACY CLOCK EVENT LOG

VOLUME I, JANUARY 2025 – JULY 2025

JIM VINCENT

VINCENT PRESS

Copyright © 2026 Jim Vincent

All rights reserved.

No part of this book may be reproduced, stored in a retrieval system, or transmitted in any form or by any means—electronic, mechanical, photocopying, recording, or otherwise—without prior written permission of the publisher or author, except for brief quotations used in reviews, scholarship, journalism, or news reporting.

This volume is a contemporaneous public record of governance actions affecting democratic institutions in the United States during Weeks 1–26 of the Democracy Clock project (January 20–July 18, 2025). It is intended for historical, journalistic, scholarly, and civic reference.

The events documented herein are drawn from publicly available sources, including government records, court filings, legislative actions, executive orders, and contemporaneous reporting. Inclusion of any event does not imply endorsement of any individual, institution, or viewpoint.

Every effort has been made to ensure accuracy at the time of publication. Given the evolving nature of public records, corrections, clarifications, or supplemental volumes may be published separately.

The author asserts the moral right to be identified as the author of this work.

First edition.

ISBN 978-1-7642233-2-4 (Hardback)

ISBN 978-1-7642233-3-1 (Paperback)

Published by Vincent Press: https://thedemocracyclock.com

Printed and distributed by IngramSpark and BookVault.

Available through Amazon, Barnes & Noble, and international distributors.

CORRECTIONS NOTE

This volume is part of an ongoing public record.

Every effort has been made to ensure factual accuracy at the time of publication. Events documented in this book are drawn from publicly available primary sources and reputable contemporaneous reporting, and are recorded as they were known and verifiable at the time they occurred.

If a factual error is identified, corrections or clarifications may be issued in accordance with The Democracy Clock's Corrections & Amendments Policy. Where corrections are made, they are documented transparently and without erasing the original historical record.

Disagreements of interpretation, emphasis, or perspective do not constitute grounds for correction. This volume preserves what was recorded, when it was recorded, and why it mattered at the time.

The integrity of the record depends not on unanimity of interpretation, but on the stability and traceability of facts.

CONTENTS

Volume I Scope	1
Introduction	3
Source Basis and Verification	5
1. Week 1 (20 Jan 2025 – 24 Jan 2025): Emergencies as Operating System	7
2. Week 2 (25 Jan 2025 – 31 Jan 2025): Law and Memory as Weapons	23
3. Week 3 (1 Feb 2025 – 7 Feb 2025): Systems as Spoils	41
4. Week 4 (8 Feb 2025 – 14 Feb 2025): DOGE as Parallel Statecraft	55
5. Week 5 (15 Feb 2025 – 21 Feb 2025): The State as Personal Instrument	73
6. Week 6 (22 Feb 2025 – 28 Feb 2025): Bureaucracy as Patronage Engine	89
7. Week 7 (1 Mar 2025 – 7 Mar 2025): Tools As Habit, Not Exception	109
8. Week 8 (8 Mar 2025 – 14 Mar 2025): Citizenship and Service as Leverage	123
9. Week 9 (15 Mar 2025 – 21 Mar 2025): Emergency Powers as Routine Governance	139
10. Week 10 (22 Mar 2025 – 28 Mar 2025): Voter Rolls as Leverage	157
11. Week 11 (29 Mar 2025 – 4 Apr 2025): Chaos as Methodical Governance	173
12. Week 12 (5 Apr 2025 – 11 Apr 2025): Emergency Powers as Routine Governance	187
13. Week 13 (12 Apr 2025 – 18 Apr 2025): Loyalty as Daily Governance	209
14. Week 14 (19 Apr 2025 – 25 Apr 2025): Universities and Borders as Levers	227
15. Week 15 (26 Apr 2025 – 2 May 2025): Emergency Rule as Routine Governance	245
16. Week 16 (3 May 2025 – 9 May 2025): Stratified Rights as Routine Governance	263
17. Week 17 (10 May 2025 – 16 May 2025): Citizenship as Leverage	277
18. Week 18 (17 May 2025 – 23 May 2025): Inequality as Operating System	293
19. Week 19 (24 May 2025 – 30 May 2025): Institutions as Instruments of Loyalty	309
20. Week 20 (31 May 2025 – 6 Jun 2025): Surveillance as Everyday Governance	325
21. Week 21 (7 Jun 2025 – 13 Jun 2025): Emergency Powers as Routine Governance	343

22. Week 22 (14 Jun 2025 – 20 Jun 2025): Citizenship as Sorting Mechanism ... 359
23. Week 23 (21 Jun 2025 – 27 Jun 2025): Secrecy as War-Making Method ... 375
24. Week 24 (28 Jun 2025 – 4 Jul 2025): Hardwiring Inequality as Governance ... 395
25. Week 25 (5 Jul 2025 – 11 Jul 2025): Immunity as Architecture of Power ... 411
26. Week 26 (12 Jul 2025 – 18 Jul 2025): Data and Force as Governance ... 429
    Archival Closure Note ... 445

VOLUME I SCOPE

This volume includes the first half of The Democracy Clock: Events Log, covering the period from January 20, 2025, to July 18, 2025. It records the first twenty-six weeks, starting with the constitutional transition date and ending at the midpoint of the first year. The first week, from Monday, January 20 to Friday, January 24, is shorter than the following full Saturday–Friday weeks; all later weeks in this volume follow the standard weekly format.

INTRODUCTION
HOW TO USE THIS RECORD

This volume serves as a public record. Between January 20, 2025, and July 18, 2025, the United States underwent a notably intense series of governance actions. These actions impacted democratic institutions, civil liberties, administrative norms, and the balance of power within the government. Many of these actions were lawful on their face. Some faced challenges. Others were unprecedented in their scale, speed, or scope. What made this period distinctive was not any single event but the cumulative pattern created by hundreds of individual decisions made over weeks and across agencies. This book is intended to preserve that pattern.

The Democracy Clock: Events Log is not an argument, manifesto, or forecast. It is an archival document—a contemporaneous, week-by-week record of verifiable actions taken by public officials and institutions, based on primary sources and reputable reports. The record begins on the constitutional transition date of January 20, 2025; hence, the first week covers events from that date to Friday, January 24, 2025, and is shorter than the subsequent full Saturday–Friday weeks. Each following week is treated as a distinct historical unit. Each entry details what happened, when it occurred, who was involved, and why it was significant for democratic governance at the time.

Readers should understand what this volume is—and what it is not. It does not assign intent beyond what is explicitly stated in official documents or credible reports. It does not speculate about future outcomes. It does not score, rank, or compare events. Interpretation, synthesis, and evaluation are covered in companion volumes. This book's role is narrower and more demanding: to ensure that the factual record exists, intact and usable, before memory fades or narratives harden. The log's structure is deliberately consistent. Each week starts with a brief summary providing context and orientation. Events are grouped under stable governance categories—power and authority, institutions and governance, civil rights and dissent, economic structure, and information and memory—allowing readers to follow patterns over time within and across areas. Citations are included for each event to support verification and further research. This consistency is not stylistic. It is methodological.

Democratic erosion rarely announces itself in a single dramatic moment. It accumulates through normalization, fragmentation, and repetition. Emergency powers invoked once become routine. Administrative exceptions harden into precedent. Oversight weakened in one domain reappears weakened elsewhere. The only reliable way to see such processes clearly is to record events as they occur, without retrospective compression or selective hindsight.

This volume is therefore designed for use, not persuasion.

Researchers may examine it longitudinally to observe institutional change. Journalists may refer to it to place breaking news within a larger context. Legal scholars, historians, and civic groups might use it as a reference when assessing claims, defenses, or reforms. General readers may follow it week by week to understand how significant shifts arise from seemingly ordinary actions.

No conclusions are imposed here. The record speaks for itself.

If this book succeeds, it will do so quietly—by making it more difficult in the future to say that no one noticed, no one recorded, or no one could have known.

This volume is part of a two-book series.

The Democracy Clock is the analytical companion to this record. It interprets the same events through a structured framework designed to evaluate democratic resilience and decline over time. While this book preserves the weekly factual archive, the companion volume explores the meaning of these events when viewed cumulatively—how patterns form, accelerate, or reverse, and how democratic norms are reinforced or undermined across weeks and institutions.

Readers can use the two volumes independently or together. This book is meant to stand alone as a primary source record. The companion volume assumes the existence of this log and expands upon it. Together, they separate evidence from interpretation—ensuring analysis remains rooted in a clear, transparent historical record.

SOURCE BASIS
AND VERIFICATION

Events documented in this volume are based on contemporary public records and reports produced during the covered period. These include official government documents, court filings and rulings, agency releases, legislative records, executive actions, and verified accounts of institutional activity provided by established news organizations and watchdog groups. Individual events are identified by the date they entered or could be confirmed to have entered the public record. Dates indicate when an action was publicly documented, reported, or corroborated—not necessarily when the action itself took place. This reflects the log's purpose: to keep a chronological record of observable governance actions affecting democratic institutions, rather than to reconstruct undocumented or inferred timelines of internal decision-making.

Events are included only if their occurrence could be verified at the time through primary documents, corroborated reports, or institutional records. As reporting evolved, entries were either conflicted or clarified over time; they reflect what was verifiable within the specified weekly interval. Multiple dates indicate independent confirmation or sustained documentation across sources, not repeated or ongoing actions. No event is included solely on speculation, inference, or unverified claims.

Sources are not listed with each entry. This is a deliberate design choice that reflects the log's role as an archival record rather than an argumentative or narrative text. The absence of inline citations does not imply a lack of sourcing; it reflects a separation between evidence collection and analysis.

Readers seeking original documents, contemporaneous reports, or additional context should consult public records and reports corresponding to each entry's documented date or dates. Analytical interpretation of these recorded events is addressed separately in the companion volume, The Democracy Clock.

CHAPTER 1
WEEK 1 (20 JAN 2025 – 24 JAN 2025): EMERGENCIES AS OPERATING SYSTEM

In Trump's first week back in office, overlapping emergencies, purges, and decrees turn the presidency into a central engine of unilateral rule.

This week marks a severe blow to the American democratic system, driven by a series of Trump executive orders, personnel purges, and symbolic actions that together threaten to cause a constitutional crisis. The greatest pressures are on executive limits, equal citizenship, the rule of law, and the nonpartisan civil service. Trump declares multiple national emergencies, militarizes the border, and openly defies laws and Supreme Court rulings (TikTok delay), while re-implementing Schedule F and dismissing inspectors general and senior career officials, effectively placing the bureaucracy under personal loyalty. At the same time, he seeks to rewrite the Fourteenth Amendment by decree, categorizing citizenship based on parentage, and launches a broad anti-immigrant campaign: CBP One is shut down, asylum and refugee programs are halted, expedited removals are increased, and sanctuary jurisdictions face prosecution threats. Mass pardons for January 6 and FACE Act offenders, along with a temporary halt on Foreign Corrupt Practices Act enforcement, signal that violence and corruption aimed at supporting the regime will be tolerated. Parallel efforts dismantle DEI initiatives, revoke long-standing anti-discrimination orders, and politicize abortion and gender policies, while fossil-fuel and crypto directives reinforce crony capitalism. Courts, states, civil society, and some Republicans do push back—blocking birthright changes, suing DOGE and Schedule F, and organizing opposition

—but they are reacting to a coordinated, rapid consolidation of presidential power.

Power and Authority

1. President Joe Biden commuted Leonard Peltier's life sentence to home confinement. The commutation for Indigenous activist Leonard Peltier addressed long-criticized prosecutorial misconduct and raised expectations that executive clemency can be used to correct historic injustices in politically sensitive cases. (20 Jan 2025)

2. President Joe Biden issued protective pardons and commutations for family members and Trump critics. Biden's end-of-term pardons for relatives, January 6 investigators, and officials like Milley and Fauci used clemency power pre-emptively to shield perceived political targets from anticipated prosecutions by the incoming administration. (20 Jan 2025; 21 Jan 2025)

3. President Joe Biden and Vice President Kamala Harris publicly declared the Equal Rights Amendment to be law despite lack of ratification. The administration's inaccurate claim that the Equal Rights Amendment was already law blurred constitutional procedure and highlighted how symbolic assertions by top officials can misstate the status of formal rights protections. (20 Jan 2025)

4. President Donald Trump was inaugurated for a second term and delivered a populist inaugural address. Trump's second inauguration, framed as a "liberation day" and laced with false claims about elections and government weaponization, set a confrontational tone for executive-legislative relations and public trust in institutions. (20 Jan 2025)

5. President Donald Trump declared a national emergency at the US-Mexico border and ordered military involvement. Trump's border emergency declarations enabled troop deployments and wall construction while bypassing Congress, normalizing emergency rule for routine policy disputes and expanding presidential control over immigration enforcement. (20 Jan 2025; 21 Jan 2025; 22 Jan 2025; 24 Jan 2025)

6. President Donald Trump issued an order redefining and restricting birthright citizenship. Trump's executive order to deny automatic citizenship to many US-born children directly challenged the Fourteenth Amendment, testing whether a president can unilaterally narrow constitutional membership in the political community. (20 Jan 2025; 21 Jan 2025; 22 Jan 2025; 23 Jan 2025)

7. President Donald Trump issued sweeping pardons and commutations for January 6 defendants and related offenders. By pardoning or commuting

sentences for more than 1,500 January 6 participants and ordering pending cases dropped, Trump used clemency to erase accountability for an attack on the transfer of power and to reward loyal offenders. (20 Jan 2025; 21 Jan 2025; 22 Jan 2025; 23 Jan 2025; 24 Jan 2025)

8. President Donald Trump ordered investigations into alleged weaponization and censorship by the prior administration. Trump's directives for DOJ and intelligence leaders to probe supposed censorship and political targeting under Biden repurposed investigative powers toward retribution, risking politicization of law enforcement against former officials and critics. (20 Jan 2025; 23 Jan 2025)

9. President Donald Trump reinstated and expanded Schedule F to reclassify policy-influencing civil servants. Recreating Schedule F and removing protections for thousands of career officials allowed Trump to purge perceived disloyal staff and replace expertise with political loyalists, weakening bureaucratic independence from presidential will. (20 Jan 2025; 21 Jan 2025)

10. President Donald Trump terminated federal diversity, equity and inclusion programs and offices. Trump's orders abolishing DEI structures across the federal government reversed long-standing anti-discrimination efforts and signaled that equity work by civil servants could trigger discipline, reshaping who feels protected in public employment. (20 Jan 2025; 21 Jan 2025; 22 Jan 2025; 23 Jan 2025)

11. President Donald Trump issued an order redefining gender in federal policy as strictly male or female from conception. By mandating binary, conception-based sex definitions in federal law, Trump's gender ideology order curtailed recognition of transgender and non-binary people and embedded fetal personhood language with potential implications for abortion law. (20 Jan 2025; 21 Jan 2025; 23 Jan 2025)

12. President Donald Trump declared a national energy emergency to accelerate fossil fuel development. The energy emergency declaration empowered agencies to fast-track drilling, pipelines and export approvals, using crisis framing to override environmental safeguards and entrench executive discretion over long-term energy choices. (20 Jan 2025; 21 Jan 2025)

13. President Donald Trump withdrew the United States from the Paris climate agreement. Trump's renewed withdrawal from the Paris accord removed federal commitment to multilateral climate targets, weakening international coordination and signaling that major climate policy can be reversed by unilateral executive action. (20 Jan 2025; 21 Jan 2025)

14. President Donald Trump ordered US withdrawal from the World Health Organization. By initiating US exit from the WHO and halting contri-

butions, Trump used executive authority to pull the country out of a key global health body, reducing multilateral oversight over US health policy and pandemic cooperation. (20 Jan 2025; 21 Jan 2025)

15. President Donald Trump directed DOJ not to enforce the statutory TikTok ban for a fixed period. Trump's order pausing enforcement of a congressionally mandated TikTok divest-or-ban law, despite a Supreme Court ruling, asserted presidential discretion over statutory execution and raised questions about selective obedience to judicial decisions. (20 Jan 2025; 21 Jan 2025)

16. President Donald Trump signed an order restoring the federal death penalty and urging reversal of limiting precedents. Restoring federal executions and instructing DOJ to seek reversal of Supreme Court limits on capital punishment expanded executive influence over life-and-death criminal sanctions and signaled a more punitive federal justice posture. (20 Jan 2025)

17. President Donald Trump revoked security clearances of dozens of former intelligence officials and John Bolton. Targeting former officials for clearance revocation over alleged 2020 election interference used classification authority to punish critics and could chill future intelligence professionals from publicly challenging presidential narratives. (20 Jan 2025)

18. President Donald Trump issued an order ending US participation in international environmental and climate finance agreements. By revoking US climate finance commitments and prioritizing domestic fossil interests in environmental treaties, Trump centralized foreign-economic climate decisions in the presidency and weakened external checks on US emissions policy. (20 Jan 2025; 21 Jan 2025)

19. President Donald Trump suspended the US Refugee Admissions Program and halted most refugee resettlement. Suspending refugee admissions by executive order allowed Trump to unilaterally override congressionally supported humanitarian programs, concentrating control over who may seek refuge in the US in the White House. (20 Jan 2025; 21 Jan 2025; 22 Jan 2025; 23 Jan 2025)

20. President Donald Trump ordered construction of additional border wall segments. Resuming border wall construction by executive order reallocated federal resources toward a contested security project without new legislation, reinforcing presidential control over physical border policy and land use. (20 Jan 2025; 21 Jan 2025)

21. President Donald Trump created the Department of Government Efficiency under White House control. Establishing DOGE inside the Executive Office centralized cross-agency technology and process reforms under presi-

dential aides and outside normal agency chains, increasing direct White House leverage over day-to-day administration. (20 Jan 2025)

22. President Donald Trump issued an order making independent regulatory agencies answerable to the White House. Requiring independent regulators to submit priorities and budgets for presidential approval eroded their statutory autonomy and concentrated rule-writing power in the executive, weakening checks designed by Congress. (20 Jan 2025)

23. President Donald Trump ordered a government-wide review to rescind regulations and advisory bodies deemed inconsistent with his agenda. The directive for agencies to work with DOGE to cull regulations and advisory committees gave the president broad influence over which expert inputs and safeguards remain in place, shifting rulemaking toward political loyalty. (20 Jan 2025)

24. President Donald Trump fired Coast Guard Commandant Linda Fagan and other senior security officials. Removing the Coast Guard's first female commandant and other leaders over perceived DEI emphasis and immigration priorities signaled that top security posts depend on ideological alignment with the president, not professional norms. (20 Jan 2025; 22 Jan 2025; 23 Jan 2025)

25. President Donald Trump removed and reassigned senior Justice Department national security and criminal division officials. Trump's reshuffling of top DOJ career leaders in sensitive divisions weakened internal continuity and signaled that prosecutorial leadership would be judged by political loyalty, not independence. (21 Jan 2025)

26. President Donald Trump sidelined about 160 National Security Council career staff. Marginalizing large numbers of NSC professionals reduced expert input into foreign and security decisions and concentrated sensitive policy advice among a smaller, more politically aligned circle. (22 Jan 2025)

27. President Donald Trump fired inspectors general at at least 12 major federal agencies. The mass removal of agency inspectors general, reportedly without the statutory 30-day notice to Congress, stripped internal watchdogs across government and sharply reduced institutional capacity to investigate executive misconduct. (24 Jan 2025)

28. President Donald Trump threatened to prosecute former President Joe Biden. Publicly suggesting that his predecessor could face prosecution, Trump used the prospect of criminal law against a rival, reinforcing fears that prosecutorial power may be wielded as a political weapon. (22 Jan 2025)

29. President Donald Trump announced intent to abolish or radically shrink FEMA and condition disaster aid on politics. By floating abolition of

FEMA and tying relief funds to political considerations, Trump signaled willingness to use disaster response as leverage over states, undermining neutral federal support in emergencies. (22 Jan 2025; 23 Jan 2025)

30. President Donald Trump signed orders enforcing the Hyde Amendment and reinstating the global gag rule on abortion funding. Trump's abortion-related orders barred federal and many foreign aid funds from supporting abortion services or advocacy, using executive power to narrow reproductive access domestically and abroad without new legislation. (24 Jan 2025)

31. President Donald Trump froze disbursement of Inflation Reduction Act and Bipartisan Infrastructure Act funds. Suspending already-authorized infrastructure and clean-energy spending allowed Trump to unilally stall congressionally approved investments, shifting budgetary power from the legislature to the executive. (23 Jan 2025)

32. President Donald Trump directed the Department of Defense to deploy 1,500 active-duty troops to the southern border. Ordering thousands of active-duty troops to support immigration enforcement at the border blurred lines between military and civilian roles and expanded presidential use of the armed forces in domestic policy. (20 Jan 2025; 22 Jan 2025; 24 Jan 2025)

33. President Donald Trump issued a memorandum to reroute California water supplies under the banner of "Putting People over Fish". Trump's California water directive sought to override state and environmental constraints on delta flows, asserting federal control over contested resources and prioritizing favored economic interests over negotiated ecological protections. (23 Jan 2025; 24 Jan 2025)

34. President Donald Trump threatened to condition California wildfire aid on voter ID laws and water policy changes. By tying disaster relief to adoption of voter ID and water policy concessions, Trump used federal emergency support as leverage to influence state election rules and environmental governance. (24 Jan 2025)

35. President Donald Trump signed an order establishing a FEMA Review Council to reassess the agency. Creating a FEMA Review Council to examine the agency's impartiality and structure opened the door to restructuring or downsizing national disaster management under close presidential direction. (24 Jan 2025)

36. President Donald Trump issued a series of rapid executive orders across immigration, climate, health, and digital policy. The sheer volume and breadth of Trump's first-week orders—from asylum suspensions to WHO exit and digital-asset policy—created deliberate policy whiplash that strained

oversight capacity and consolidated agenda-setting in the presidency. (21 Jan 2025; 22 Jan 2025; 23 Jan 2025; 24 Jan 2025)

Institutions and Governance

1. US Senate and House of Representatives passed the Laken Riley Act mandating detention of certain undocumented immigrants. The Laken Riley Act, soon to reach Trump's desk, expanded mandatory detention and empowered state attorneys general to sue the federal government, shifting immigration discretion away from agencies and raising due-process concerns. (20 Jan 2025; 23 Jan 2025)

2. US Senate confirmed Marco Rubio as Secretary of State. Rubio's near-unanimous confirmation as Secretary of State quickly filled a key foreign-policy post, signaling Senate willingness to endorse Trump's "America First" diplomatic agenda despite broader institutional tensions. (21 Jan 2025)

3. US Senate advanced Pete Hegseth's nomination for Secretary of Defense despite serious allegations. The Senate's movement toward confirming Pete Hegseth, amid affidavits and reports of aggression, extremism, and mismanagement, highlighted how partisan loyalty can outweigh vetting norms for control of the Pentagon. (22 Jan 2025; 23 Jan 2025; 24 Jan 2025)

4. House Republican leadership created a new select subcommittee to re-investigate January 6. Forming a new January 6 panel under GOP control, shortly after mass pardons, positioned Congress to challenge prior factual findings and potentially recast an attack on certification as victimization of Trump supporters. (22 Jan 2025; 24 Jan 2025)

5. Mississippi State Representative Justin Keen introduced a bill to create an Illegal Alien Certified Bounty Hunter Program. The proposed Mississippi bounty-hunter scheme would pay civilians per deportation, formalizing vigilante-style enforcement and raising risks of abuse and racial profiling under color of state law. (23 Jan 2025)

6. Representative Andy Ogles introduced a constitutional amendment to allow a third presidential term for Donald Trump. Ogles's resolution to relax the 22nd Amendment specifically for Trump signaled an organized effort inside Congress to weaken presidential term limits and personalize constitutional rules around one leader. (23 Jan 2025)

7. House DOGE committee chaired by Marjorie Taylor Greene began work with a mandate seen as targeting federal agencies and safety nets. The new House DOGE committee, criticized for excluding Republican women

and aiming to dismantle agencies and social programs, illustrated how oversight structures can be designed to advance ideological downsizing rather than neutral review. (21 Jan 2025)

8. National Treasury Employees Union sued the Trump administration over the Schedule F reclassification order. The NTEU lawsuit argued that reclassifying thousands of civil servants as at-will political appointees violated due-process protections, using the courts to contest executive attempts to politicize the federal workforce. (21 Jan 2025)

9. National Security Counselors and other plaintiffs filed lawsuits challenging the legality and transparency of the DOGE program. Litigation claiming DOGE functions as an unregulated federal advisory committee sought to force balanced representation, record-keeping, and public access, testing whether new White House-centric structures must obey transparency law. (20 Jan 2025; 21 Jan 2025)

10. California and a coalition of states and cities sued to block Trump's birthright citizenship order as unconstitutional. State and local governments challenged Trump's attempt to narrow birthright citizenship, asserting that only Congress and the Constitution can define national membership and that the order would harm residents and state systems. (23 Jan 2025)

11. Federal district courts issued temporary restraining orders blocking Trump's birthright citizenship order. Federal judges in Washington and Washington State halted implementation of Trump's citizenship order, calling it blatantly unconstitutional and underscoring the judiciary's role as a check on unilateral constitutional reinterpretation. (22 Jan 2025; 23 Jan 2025; 24 Jan 2025)

12. Federal Election Commission scheduled a closed Sunshine Act meeting on enforcement and compliance matters. The FEC's closed meeting to discuss enforcement, personnel, and litigation highlighted ongoing but opaque oversight of campaign-finance compliance at a moment of heightened concern about money and influence in elections. (23 Jan 2025)

13. Ohio legislature enacted a law allowing high fees for access to police body-camera and video records. Ohio's new law permitting departments to charge up to $750 for body-cam footage erected financial barriers to obtaining police records, weakening practical transparency and public oversight of law enforcement. (24 Jan 2025)

14. US Election Assistance Commission corrected a notice regarding the National Mail Voter Registration Form. The EAC's correction to its Federal Register notice on the national registration form clarified its information-collection process, supporting procedural accuracy in federal guidance on voter registration. (22 Jan 2025)

15. Federal courts and Purdue Pharma oversaw a $7.4 billion settlement restructuring Purdue Pharma over the opioid crisis. The Purdue–Sackler settlement, requiring family members to relinquish control and fund remediation, illustrated how mass-tort litigation can impose accountability on powerful firms for public-health harms, albeit via negotiated compromise. (23 Jan 2025)

16. Federal district court barred Stewart Rhodes and other Oath Keepers from entering Washington DC without permission. Release conditions restricting Rhodes and other January 6 defendants from entering the capital without court approval aimed to protect Congress and the city while balancing post-conviction liberty interests. (24 Jan 2025)

17. Federal agencies including EPA, FCC, OSHA, FDA and DEA issued multiple routine regulatory approvals, corrections, and information-collection notices. A series of Federal Register actions on air quality plans, disaster reporting, product safety labs, and controlled-substance manufacturing showed core regulatory machinery continuing to function despite broader political upheaval. (21 Jan 2025; 22 Jan 2025; 23 Jan 2025; 24 Jan 2025)

Civil Rights and Dissent

1. President Donald Trump ended use of the CBP One app and canceled tens of thousands of asylum appointments. Shutting down CBP One and voiding scheduled border appointments abruptly cut off a key lawful pathway for asylum seekers, stranding many in dangerous conditions and undermining predictable access to protection. (20 Jan 2025; 21 Jan 2025; 22 Jan 2025; 23 Jan 2025)

2. President Donald Trump suspended asylum processing and refugee resettlement at the southern border. Orders halting asylum claims and refugee resettlement, framed as responding to an "invasion," sharply curtailed protections for people fleeing persecution and tested statutory and treaty obligations toward refugees. (20 Jan 2025; 21 Jan 2025; 22 Jan 2025; 23 Jan 2025)

3. Department of Homeland Security under President Donald Trump reinstated the Migrant Protection Protocols requiring asylum seekers to remain in Mexico. Reviving "Remain in Mexico" forced many asylum seekers to wait in unsafe border cities with limited legal access, weakening practical ability to pursue claims despite formal rights on paper. (21 Jan 2025; 22 Jan 2025)

4. Department of Homeland Security under President Donald Trump expanded expedited removal and detention authority nationwide. Nation-

wide expedited removal and directives to detain migrants without release increased the risk of deportations without full hearings, eroding due-process protections for non-citizens inside the US. (21 Jan 2025; 22 Jan 2025; 24 Jan 2025)

5. Department of Homeland Security under President Donald Trump authorized ICE arrests in and around churches, schools and other sensitive locations. Ending long-standing limits on enforcement in sensitive spaces exposed worshippers, students, and patients to immigration raids, heightening fear in immigrant communities and discouraging use of essential services. (21 Jan 2025; 22 Jan 2025)

6. US Department of Justice under President Donald Trump directed prosecutors to target sanctuary officials and oppose sanctuary city laws. DOJ guidance to investigate and potentially charge state and local officials for "harboring" undocumented immigrants escalated conflict with sanctuary jurisdictions and threatened criminalization of local policy choices. (22 Jan 2025)

7. President Donald Trump announced plans for the largest mass deportation program in US history. Trump's pledge to deport millions of undocumented people, including long-term residents, signaled a shift toward large-scale, militarized removals that could separate families and chill immigrant communities' participation in civic life. (21 Jan 2025)

8. President Donald Trump revoked protections and pathways for certain nationalities with US sponsors. Ending parole programs for Cubans, Haitians, Nicaraguans and Venezuelans with sponsors closed legal avenues that had allowed them to live and work temporarily while seeking permanent status, increasing precarity for these groups. (21 Jan 2025)

9. President Donald Trump issued orders to intensify immigration enforcement and create Homeland Security task forces in all states. New task forces and directives to prioritize immigration prosecutions expanded federal enforcement presence nationwide, increasing surveillance and legal exposure for undocumented residents and mixed-status families. (20 Jan 2025)

10. President Donald Trump revoked Biden-era protections for LGBTQ+ people and targeted gender-affirming care. Orders rescinding protections against LGBTQ+ discrimination and restricting gender-affirming care for minors rolled back civil rights gains and signaled that access to health and recognition would depend on conformity to narrow gender norms. (20 Jan 2025; 21 Jan 2025; 23 Jan 2025)

11. President Donald Trump revoked Executive Order 11246 and related anti-discrimination rules for federal contractors. Repealing long-standing requirements that federal contractors avoid discrimination in hiring weak-

ened a major lever for enforcing equal opportunity in large swaths of the labor market tied to public funds. (21 Jan 2025; 23 Jan 2025)

12. President Donald Trump banned transgender athletes from women's sports and narrowed Title IX interpretations. Trump's sports order directed agencies to treat trans girls and women as ineligible for female categories, using federal civil-rights law to exclude a group from educational and athletic opportunities. (20 Jan 2025; 21 Jan 2025)

13. President Donald Trump ordered English-only policies for federal language access and certain jobs. Making English the official language and requiring truck drivers to speak English reduced language accommodations in public services and employment, disproportionately burdening linguistic minorities. (20 Jan 2025)

14. President Donald Trump issued orders to end alleged anti-Christian bias and elevate Christian claims in federal policy. Creating a taskforce to combat supposed anti-Christian bias and reorienting civil-rights enforcement toward protecting Christians risked privileging one faith in government decisions and weakening protections for religious minorities. (20 Jan 2025)

15. President Donald Trump pardoned anti-abortion activists convicted under the FACE Act. Clemency for activists convicted of obstructing clinic access signaled tolerance for coercive tactics around reproductive health facilities and may embolden future efforts to intimidate patients and providers. (22 Jan 2025; 24 Jan 2025)

16. US Department of Justice under President Donald Trump froze all civil rights division cases and barred new filings. Halting DOJ civil-rights litigation paused federal enforcement against discrimination in voting, policing, housing, and education, leaving vulnerable groups more dependent on uneven state protections. (23 Jan 2025)

17. US Department of Justice under President Donald Trump issued a memo halting new police reform consent decrees. Stopping agreements to remedy patterns of police misconduct weakened a key federal tool for enforcing constitutional policing, especially in jurisdictions resistant to local reform. (22 Jan 2025)

18. Trump administration immigration authorities conducted aggressive ICE raids causing fear and disruption in communities. New ICE operations, including raids in Newark and elsewhere, led to racial profiling concerns and depressed work and school attendance, illustrating how enforcement tactics can chill everyday civic participation. (21 Jan 2025; 23 Jan 2025)

19. Trump administration escalated deportation rhetoric and plans against undocumented people. Announcements of intensified deportations heightened fear among undocumented residents and mixed-status families,

affecting their willingness to access services, report crimes, or engage with government. (20 Jan 2025)

20. Right Rev Mariann Edgar Budde and President Donald Trump clashed publicly over a sermon urging mercy for immigrants and LGBTQ+ people. Trump's denunciation of Bishop Budde as a "radical left hater" after her call for compassion toward marginalized groups illustrated how religious advocacy for inclusion can be framed as partisan opposition. (22 Jan 2025)

21. Pro-democracy civil society organizations organized legal challenges and opposition to Trump's executive orders. Networks of advocacy groups rapidly mobilized litigation and public campaigns against new executive orders, demonstrating civil society's role as a counterweight when formal checks are strained. (23 Jan 2025)

22. Teamsters union authorized a strike against Costco over pay, leave and surveillance issues. The Teamsters' strike authorization for 18,000 Costco workers underscored ongoing labor organizing to secure fair compensation and protections, even as federal policy trends weakened worker safeguards. (20 Jan 2025)

23. National Labor Relations Board approved a union election at an Amazon warehouse in North Carolina. Authorizing a union vote for 4,300 Amazon workers advanced collective-bargaining rights at a major employer, testing whether federal labor institutions can still facilitate worker organization in concentrated corporate settings. (23 Jan 2025)

24. NC GOP and election challengers moved to overturn the election of North Carolina Supreme Court Justice Alison Riggs. Efforts to undo Justice Riggs's election raised alarms that partisan actors may normalize post-hoc challenges to judicial races, undermining confidence that certified results will be respected. (20 Jan 2025; 23 Jan 2025)

Economic Structure

1. President Donald Trump launched personal cryptocurrencies and promoted them while in office. Trump's launch and promotion of TRUMP and MELANIA coins, largely controlled by entities he owns, created a direct, opaque channel for speculative payments to the sitting president, blurring public office and private enrichment. (20 Jan 2025; 21 Jan 2025)

2. Major crypto exchanges Coinbase, Kraken and Robinhood listed and promoted the $TRUMP coin while under SEC scrutiny. By aggressively marketing $TRUMP amid ongoing enforcement risks, large exchanges appeared to bet on regulatory leniency from the Trump administration, illus-

trating how firms may seek favorable treatment by amplifying presidential financial products. (21 Jan 2025)

3. President Donald Trump ordered creation of a sovereign wealth fund and a strategic bitcoin reserve. New vehicles for national investment and bitcoin accumulation, funded partly through forfeitures, concentrated large pools of public capital under executive influence with limited detail on governance or safeguards against political use. (20 Jan 2025)

4. President Donald Trump issued orders reshaping trade policy through reciprocal tariffs and de minimis changes. Trump's tariff orders, including broad reciprocal duties and closing the de minimis loophole on Chinese imports, reoriented trade rules by executive fiat, with major implications for prices, supply chains, and foreign relations. (20 Jan 2025; 21 Jan 2025)

5. President Donald Trump suspended disbursement of major infrastructure and clean-energy funds. Freezing Inflation Reduction Act and Bipartisan Infrastructure Act spending allowed the White House to stall or redirect large, congressionally approved investments, injecting political discretion into long-term economic development programs. (23 Jan 2025)

6. House Republicans proposed $2–3 trillion in spending cuts to finance new tax reductions. The proposed reconciliation package of deep cuts, potentially affecting Social Security and Medicare, would shift fiscal burdens away from high-income taxpayers and toward social programs, reshaping the social contract. (23 Jan 2025)

7. President Donald Trump publicly pressured the Federal Reserve Chair to lower interest rates. Trump's demands that the Fed cut rates, despite inflation risks, challenged central-bank independence and suggested monetary policy should respond to presidential preferences rather than technocratic judgment. (22 Jan 2025)

8. Jared Kushner and Affinity Partners secured a $2 billion investment from Saudi Arabia's sovereign wealth fund. Saudi backing for Kushner's fund, despite internal objections, raised concerns that foreign governments were rewarding a former senior White House adviser, potentially buying influence with the president's inner circle. (22 Jan 2025)

9. Jared Kushner and the Trump Organization partnered on Trump Tower Belgrade and other foreign real-estate deals. New Trump-branded developments on government-linked land abroad, including in Serbia and Gulf states, created avenues for foreign governments to enrich the president's business while his administration sets foreign policy. (22 Jan 2025)

10. The Trump Organization expanded merchandise sales tied to Trump's return to the White House. A surge of new products on Trump's online store monetized his presidency directly, reinforcing concerns that official status is

being used to drive private revenue streams for the president's family business. (24 Jan 2025)

11. Elon Musk and SpaceX/Starlink offered "free" wildfire internet and donated Starlink kits with opaque terms and distribution. Starlink's wildfire offer required costly hardware and auto-renewing subscriptions, and the unclear distribution of donated kits highlighted how high-profile corporate relief can mask limited, poorly documented public benefit. (20 Jan 2025)

12. California state government implemented a $20 minimum wage for fast-food workers. California's new sectoral minimum wage raised pay for low-wage workers in a major industry, demonstrating how state-level policy can counteract national trends toward weakened labor protections and inequality. (22 Jan 2025)

13. Indiana General Assembly introduced a bill to revoke tax-exempt status for non-profit hospitals overcharging patients. The Indiana proposal to strip tax breaks from hospitals charging more than 200% of Medicare rates sought to tie non-profit privileges to affordability, using tax law to discipline powerful health providers. (22 Jan 2025)

14. House Budget Director Ross Vought and allies moved to challenge the constitutionality of the Impoundment Control Act. Questioning the Impoundment Control Act aimed to restore presidential power to withhold congressionally appropriated funds, shifting budgetary control from the legislature toward the executive branch. (23 Jan 2025)

15. North Carolina Republican leadership advanced budget priorities expected to favor the wealthy over struggling residents. Analyses of NC Republicans' budget plans suggested tax and spending choices that would deepen inequality, illustrating how state fiscal policy can entrench economic divides within a federal system. (23 Jan 2025)

16. US Congress and executive agencies continued implementing CHIPS Act, Inflation Reduction Act, and solar manufacturing incentives. Ongoing reshoring of semiconductor, battery, and solar manufacturing under recent laws strengthened domestic industrial capacity and reduced dependence on foreign supply chains, bolstering economic resilience and strategic autonomy. (24 Jan 2025)

Information, Memory, and Manipulation

1. President Donald Trump ordered the dismantling of the federal police misconduct database. Eliminating the national database of police misconduct removed a key transparency tool for tracking abusive officers, making it

harder for the public and policymakers to monitor patterns of excessive force and discrimination. (20 Jan 2025)

2. President Donald Trump ordered the renaming of the Gulf of Mexico and Denali and reshaped geographic naming bodies. Renaming the Gulf of Mexico as the Gulf of America and Denali as Mount McKinley, and directing changes to the Board on Geographic Names, used executive power to imprint nationalist symbolism on maps and public memory. (20 Jan 2025; 21 Jan 2025; 23 Jan 2025)

3. President Donald Trump withdrew the US from WHO, UNRWA, and the UN Human Rights Council and paused most foreign aid. Exiting key UN bodies and freezing development assistance reduced US participation in multilateral human-rights and health regimes, weakening international channels that document abuses and coordinate responses. (20 Jan 2025; 21 Jan 2025; 24 Jan 2025)

4. President Donald Trump ordered declassification and release of JFK, RFK and MLK assassination records. Mandating release of long-sealed assassination files responded to public demands for transparency and could reduce space for conspiracy narratives, while also giving the executive control over the timing and framing of sensitive history. (20 Jan 2025; 23 Jan 2025)

5. President Donald Trump repeatedly claimed the 2020 election was rigged and misrepresented Biden's clemency actions. Trump's renewed falsehoods about a stolen 2020 election and Biden "pardoning murderers" further eroded trust in electoral and justice institutions, embedding disinformation at the center of presidential communication. (20 Jan 2025)

6. President Donald Trump made false claims about California's wildfire water management and China's role in the Panama Canal. Inaccurate statements about California withholding water for fires and China operating the Panama Canal misled the public about state competence and foreign control, potentially justifying policy shifts on distorted premises. (20 Jan 2025)

7. Trump administration health agencies imposed a communications blackout and halted reports and meetings at HHS, CDC and FDA. Pausing external communications, scientific meetings, and new reports at major health agencies restricted public access to health data and expert guidance, enabling greater political control over what information is released. (21 Jan 2025; 23 Jan 2025; 24 Jan 2025)

8. Trump administration froze DOJ civil rights cases and paused civil-rights enforcement activity. Freezing civil-rights litigation not only halted active cases but also suppressed the production of official findings and records about discrimination, narrowing the documentary trail available to future investigators and the public. (23 Jan 2025)

9. Federal Communications Commission under Chair Brendan Carr reinstated Trump campaign complaints against major TV networks and entertained calls to revoke MSNBC's license. Reopening partisan complaints and amplifying threats to strip a network's license signaled potential regulatory pressure on critical broadcasters, risking chilled coverage of the administration. (22 Jan 2025)

10. President Donald Trump signed an order on "Restoring Freedom of Speech and Ending Federal Censorship". While framed as protecting speech, Trump's order to investigate past government interactions with platforms could be used selectively to intimidate agencies and partners that moderated disinformation unfavorable to him. (20 Jan 2025)

11. President Donald Trump established a President's Council of Advisors on Science and Technology and a digital-finance working group. New advisory bodies on science, AI and digital assets centralized expert input under presidentially chosen members, raising questions about whether scientific and financial advice will be filtered through ideological and industry lenses. (23 Jan 2025)

12. Ohio legislature allowed high fees for access to police body-camera footage and other videos. Ohio's new fee structure for body-cam records effectively priced many journalists and citizens out of obtaining critical evidence of police conduct, weakening transparency through economic barriers rather than outright denial. (24 Jan 2025)

13. Colorado Bureau of Investigation saw a crime lab analyst charged with falsifying DNA reports in sexual assault cases. Charges that a state analyst altered DNA values in dozens of cases exposed vulnerabilities in forensic integrity, undermining confidence that scientific evidence in prosecutions accurately reflects underlying facts. (24 Jan 2025)

14. President Donald Trump used renaming orders and DEI rollbacks to reshape official narratives about race and gender. Symbolic acts like renaming landmarks and erasing equity directives from federal websites worked alongside policy changes to recast US history and law in ways that downplay past discrimination and current diversity. (20 Jan 2025; 21 Jan 2025; 22 Jan 2025; 23 Jan 2025)

15. Popular Info and watchdog groups documented opaque or misleading aspects of Musk's disaster relief and Trump-linked business ethics. Investigations into Starlink wildfire offers, undisclosed hardware costs, and the Trump Organization's relaxed ethics statement provided independent scrutiny of elite narratives, partially offsetting official opacity. (20 Jan 2025; 22 Jan 2025)

CHAPTER 2
WEEK 2 (25 JAN 2025 – 31 JAN 2025): LAW AND MEMORY AS WEAPONS

In Trump's second week back in power, pardons, purges, and data erasure turned law, citizenship, and information into tools of loyalty and fear.

This was an acute rupture week: a sitting president used executive power to attack nearly every major democratic safeguard simultaneously, while courts and civil society mounted only partial, reactive resistance. Structurally, the heaviest pressure fell on civil service independence, oversight institutions, immigration/citizenship equality, and the rule of law. Trump's mass firings of inspectors general, DOJ and FBI officials, NLRB and EEOC leaders, combined with Schedule F–style civil service politicization and mass resignation offers, directly hollowed out neutral administration. Parallel moves—blanket pardons for January 6 offenders, closing Jan. 6 cases, and purging prosecutors—recast law as a weapon of the executive and removed accountability for regime-aligned violence. Immigration and citizenship policy shifted toward stratified status and mass detention, including Guantánamo expansion, raids in schools and churches, and attempts to end birthright citizenship. Information and memory were aggressively curated through DEI purges, climate and Jan. 6 data removal, and education orders targeting 'indoctrination.' Courts blocked some funding freezes and the birthright order, and state and civil society actors sued over raids and civil service politicization, but these were defensive brakes against a coordinated power grab.

Power and Authority

1. President Donald Trump met with New York City mayor Eric Adams amid speculation about a pardon. The meeting between Trump and indicted mayor Eric Adams, shortly before inauguration, raised concerns that presidential clemency could be used to shield political figures from federal corruption accountability. (25 Jan 2025)

2. President Donald Trump canceled flights for 1,600 Afghan refugees bound for the United States. Canceling refugee flights for Afghans who aided U.S. forces signaled a willingness to abandon vulnerable allies and use executive power to sharply restrict humanitarian admissions. (25 Jan 2025)

3. President Donald Trump declared a state of emergency at the southern border. Declaring a border emergency expanded unilateral authority over immigration enforcement and resources, normalizing emergency framing for long-running policy disputes. (25 Jan 2025; 26 Jan 2025)

4. President Donald Trump issued executive orders dismantling federal DEI and affirmative action programs. Eliminating diversity, equity, and inclusion and affirmative action initiatives across the federal government reduced institutional commitments to equal opportunity in hiring and contracting. (25 Jan 2025; 30 Jan 2025)

5. President Donald Trump disbanded the Equal Employment Opportunity Commission by executive order. Abolishing the EEOC stripped a key federal mechanism for enforcing anti-discrimination law in workplaces, weakening protections for workers facing bias. (25 Jan 2025)

6. President Donald Trump authorized ICE agents to enter schools and churches to search for migrants. Allowing immigration raids in schools and houses of worship eroded long-standing protections for sensitive spaces and increased coercive pressure on immigrant communities. (25 Jan 2025; 26 Jan 2025)

7. President Donald Trump froze almost all foreign aid except military assistance to Israel and Egypt. Halting congressionally appropriated foreign aid without statutory authority challenged legislative control of spending and disrupted U.S. diplomatic and humanitarian commitments. (25 Jan 2025; 29 Jan 2025)

8. President Donald Trump froze funding for congressionally approved infrastructure projects. Blocking infrastructure funds that Congress had already approved asserted presidential control over the purse, undermining separation of powers and delaying public works. (25 Jan 2025)

9. President Donald Trump withdrew the United States from the Paris climate accords and the World Health Organization. Exiting major climate

and health agreements weakened multilateral cooperation and signaled a retreat from shared global problem-solving. (25 Jan 2025; 26 Jan 2025)

10. President Donald Trump demanded that NATO members raise military spending to 5% of GDP. Pressuring allies to meet an unprecedented defense-spending target risked destabilizing NATO burden-sharing norms and cooperative security arrangements. (25 Jan 2025)

11. President Donald Trump directed the military to resume delivery of 2,000-pound bombs to Israel. Ordering renewed heavy-bomb shipments to Israel reversed prior constraints and deepened U.S. involvement in a contested conflict, with implications for civilian protection and regional stability. (25 Jan 2025)

12. President Donald Trump announced a proposal to relocate Gaza's population to other Arab countries. Advocating mass relocation of Gazans disregarded self-determination norms and signaled support for demographic engineering as a policy tool. (25 Jan 2025; 27 Jan 2025)

13. White House personnel teams under President Trump screened civil service job applicants for loyalty to the president. Loyalty vetting of applicants undermined merit-based hiring and moved the bureaucracy toward partisan patronage. (25 Jan 2025)

14. President Donald Trump declared an energy emergency to roll back appliance efficiency standards. Using an emergency declaration to weaken efficiency rules expanded executive discretion over long-term regulatory policy beyond acute crises. (26 Jan 2025)

15. President Donald Trump issued mass pardons and commutations for roughly 1,500 January 6 defendants. Blanket clemency for January 6 offenders signaled tolerance for pro-regime political violence and weakened deterrence against future attacks on democratic institutions. (25 Jan 2025; 26 Jan 2025; 27 Jan 2025; 28 Jan 2025; 30 Jan 2025; 31 Jan 2025)

16. President Donald Trump signed executive orders diverting California water and overriding state policies. Directing federal agencies to override California's water management and endangered-species protections asserted federal leverage over state environmental policy and funding. (26 Jan 2025; 27 Jan 2025)

17. President Donald Trump froze travel and communications at the Department of Health and Human Services. Halting HHS travel and communications constrained public-health agencies' ability to share information and coordinate responses, centralizing control in the White House. (25 Jan 2025)

18. President Donald Trump ordered a broad freeze on federal grants, loans, and financial assistance. Freezing trillions in congressionally appropri-

ated aid and grants attempted to subordinate legislative budget authority to presidential ideological review. (27 Jan 2025; 28 Jan 2025; 29 Jan 2025; 30 Jan 2025; 31 Jan 2025)

19. President Donald Trump rescinded the federal funding freeze memo after legal and political backlash. Withdrawing the funding-freeze directive limited immediate damage but underscored the administration's willingness to test constitutional limits on spending control. (29 Jan 2025; 30 Jan 2025)

20. President Donald Trump issued executive orders restructuring military personnel and DEI policies. Orders banning transgender service, abolishing military DEI offices, and reinstating vaccine-refusers reoriented personnel rules toward ideological criteria over inclusive readiness standards. (27 Jan 2025)

21. President Donald Trump invoked the Alien Enemies Act to target undocumented immigrants as a crime threat. Framing undocumented immigrants as enemy aliens responsible for a "crime wave," despite contrary data, repurposed an old national-security statute for domestic immigration crackdowns. (28 Jan 2025)

22. President Donald Trump signed an executive order ending birthright citizenship for children of noncitizens. Attempting to end birthright citizenship by executive order challenged a core interpretation of the Fourteenth Amendment and threatened to create a class of stateless U.S.-born children. (28 Jan 2025; 30 Jan 2025)

23. President Donald Trump ordered deportation flights to Colombia to resume after tariff threats. Restarting deportation flights following economic pressure on Colombia illustrated the use of trade leverage to secure foreign cooperation with domestic enforcement priorities. (26 Jan 2025; 28 Jan 2025)

24. President Donald Trump revoked deportation protections and TPS extensions for Venezuelans. Canceling deportation protections and TPS for hundreds of thousands of Venezuelans exposed them to removal despite ongoing instability in their home country. (28 Jan 2025; 29 Jan 2025)

25. President Donald Trump signed an executive order restricting gender-affirming care for minors and cutting related federal funding. Barring federal support and coverage for gender-affirming care for youth used executive power to limit access to medically endorsed treatment for a targeted group. (28 Jan 2025)

26. President Donald Trump paused approvals for new renewable energy projects on public lands and waters. Blocking new renewable leases and approvals on federal lands slowed the energy transition and concentrated discretion over climate-relevant infrastructure in the executive. (28 Jan 2025)

27. President Donald Trump eliminated federal-level AI safety require-

ments by executive order. Removing AI safety oversight at the federal level prioritized rapid deployment over risk governance, shifting responsibility away from public regulators. (28 Jan 2025)

28. President Donald Trump ordered the opening of a 30,000-person migrant detention facility at Guantánamo Bay. Expanding Guantánamo for mass migrant detention exported immigration enforcement to an offshore military site with weaker legal protections and oversight. (29 Jan 2025; 30 Jan 2025)

29. President Donald Trump issued guidance creating a new Schedule Policy/Career category to strip civil service protections. Reviving Schedule F-style rules to reclassify policy-related civil servants weakened job protections and made dismissal for political reasons easier. (29 Jan 2025)

30. Office of Personnel Management under Trump offered mass deferred-resignation deals and buyouts to federal employees. Emailing nearly all federal workers with inducements to resign by fall sought to clear space for loyal replacements and destabilized the nonpartisan bureaucracy. (29 Jan 2025; 30 Jan 2025; 31 Jan 2025)

31. President Donald Trump fired 18 inspectors general and ordered dismissal of independent anti-corruption inspectors. Removing inspectors general across multiple agencies without required notice dismantled internal watchdog capacity and reduced checks on executive misconduct. (25 Jan 2025; 26 Jan 2025; 27 Jan 2025; 29 Jan 2025; 30 Jan 2025)

32. President Donald Trump fired Democratic appointees from the NLRB and EEOC before their terms expired. Removing labor and civil-rights regulators mid-term, despite statutory protections, undermined agency independence and enforcement of worker protections. (30 Jan 2025; 31 Jan 2025)

33. President Donald Trump issued an executive order stripping many civil servants of employment protections. Curtailing statutory job protections for federal employees made it easier to purge perceived opponents and politicize the administrative state. (30 Jan 2025)

34. President Donald Trump issued an executive order on FAA staffing blaming prior diversity policies for a fatal crash. Using an air disaster to justify rolling back diversity-oriented hiring at the FAA politicized safety policy and targeted inclusion efforts without evidence. (30 Jan 2025; 31 Jan 2025)

35. President Donald Trump issued an executive order titled Unleashing Prosperity Through Deregulation. Requiring repeal of at least ten regulations for each new one and imposing a negative cost cap shifted federal rulemaking toward aggressive deregulation regardless of public-interest impacts. (31 Jan 2025)

36. President Donald Trump ordered USDA to remove climate-crisis content from agency websites. Directing USDA to take down climate-related web pages suppressed public access to scientific information and constrained agencies' ability to communicate environmental risks. (31 Jan 2025)

37. President Donald Trump ordered removal of DEI language from IRS materials and set up a DEI tip line. Scrubbing DEI references from IRS guidance and encouraging reports on such content institutionalized hostility to equity efforts within tax administration. (31 Jan 2025)

38. President Donald Trump signed an executive order renaming the Gulf of Mexico as the Gulf of America. Renaming a major body of water by decree used symbolic power to assert nationalist branding, drawing criticism as a politicization of geographic nomenclature. (29 Jan 2025)

39. President Donald Trump issued executive orders canceling federal diversity programs government-wide. Canceling diversity programs across agencies reduced institutional support for addressing discrimination and representation in federal workplaces. (30 Jan 2025)

40. President Donald Trump issued an executive order affecting treatment of transgender people in federal prisons. Mandating transfers of trans women to men's prisons and halting gender-affirming care in custody curtailed protections for a vulnerable incarcerated group. (30 Jan 2025)

41. President Donald Trump signed an executive order blaming DEI for aviation dangers after a fatal crash. Linking a deadly collision to diversity policies without evidence used tragedy to justify rolling back inclusion initiatives in aviation oversight. (30 Jan 2025; 31 Jan 2025)

42. President Donald Trump signed an executive order establishing a task force for America's 250th birthday. Creating a presidentially chaired semiquincentennial task force centralized control over national historical commemoration and revived prior monument-focused orders. (29 Jan 2025)

43. President Donald Trump signed an executive order on educational freedom and ending radical indoctrination in K-12 schooling. Linking federal education funds to school-choice priorities and defunding programs labeled as radical or anti-American increased federal leverage over curriculum content. (29 Jan 2025)

44. President Donald Trump signed the Laken Riley Act expanding mandatory detention of undocumented immigrants. Enacting the Laken Riley Act broadened ICE's authority to detain immigrants based on charges rather than convictions and empowered states to sue over federal enforcement choices. (29 Jan 2025)

45. President Donald Trump signed an executive order seeking to deport international students who joined pro-Palestinian protests. Targeting foreign

students for deportation based on protest participation linked immigration status to political expression and chilled campus dissent. (29 Jan 2025)

46. President Donald Trump signed an executive order blaming DEI for flight dangers and directing policy changes. Using an executive action to tie aviation risk to diversity initiatives reframed inclusion policies as safety threats and justified their rollback. (30 Jan 2025)

47. President Donald Trump signed an executive order on additional measures to combat antisemitism. Directing agencies to intensify use of civil-rights tools against antisemitism, especially on campuses, expanded federal scrutiny of certain speech and association in educational settings. (29 Jan 2025)

48. President Donald Trump signed an executive order on military excellence and readiness restricting transgender service and pronoun use. Recasting gender identity as incompatible with military standards narrowed who can serve and embedded cultural priorities into defense personnel policy. (27 Jan 2025)

49. President Donald Trump signed an executive order titled The Iron Dome For America to build a national missile defense shield. Mandating a next-generation missile defense architecture committed large defense resources through executive direction, shaping long-term security policy with limited legislative input. (27 Jan 2025)

50. President Donald Trump signed an executive order protecting children from chemical and surgical mutilation. Barring federal funding and coverage for gender-affirming procedures for minors used federal spending power to restrict a contested area of medical care nationwide. (28 Jan 2025)

51. President Donald Trump signed an executive order unleashing prosperity through deregulation. Imposing a ten-for-one repeal rule for new regulations constrained agencies' ability to respond to emerging risks and favored deregulatory outcomes. (31 Jan 2025)

52. President Donald Trump signed an executive order on FAA staffing emphasizing merit-based recruitment. Reframing prior diversity-oriented hiring as illegal and ordering a return to narrow merit criteria reshaped staffing rules in a key safety agency along ideological lines. (31 Jan 2025)

53. President Donald Trump signed an executive order on aviation safety rolling back diversity initiatives. Rolling back diversity initiatives in aviation under the banner of safety shifted regulatory priorities and signaled skepticism toward inclusion efforts in technical roles. (31 Jan 2025)

54. President Donald Trump signed an executive order on celebrating America's 250th birthday reinstating monument-protection orders. Reinstating prior monument-protection orders through a semiquincentennial

directive reinforced a narrative of safeguarding traditional symbols against protest or reinterpretation. (29 Jan 2025)

55. President Donald Trump signed an executive order expanding educational freedom and opportunity for families. Prioritizing school choice in federal education funding guidance shifted support toward alternative schooling models and away from traditional public systems. (29 Jan 2025)

Institutions and Governance

1. U.S. Senate confirmed Kristi Noem as Secretary of Homeland Security. Confirming a close Trump ally to lead DHS placed immigration and internal security agencies under more ideologically aligned leadership, affecting enforcement priorities and oversight. (25 Jan 2025; 27 Jan 2025)

2. U.S. Senate confirmed Pete Hegseth as Secretary of Defense by tie-breaking vote. Installing a polarizing media figure with limited conventional defense experience to run the Pentagon raised concerns about politicization of military leadership. (25 Jan 2025; 26 Jan 2025)

3. U.S. Senate and President Donald Trump advanced and supported controversial nominations for RFK Jr., Kash Patel, Tulsi Gabbard, and Pam Bondi. Hearings for key health, intelligence, FBI, and Justice posts highlighted efforts to place ideologically aligned or controversial figures atop major institutions, potentially weakening their independence. (25 Jan 2025; 29 Jan 2025; 30 Jan 2025; 31 Jan 2025)

4. Federal courts issued multiple stays and injunctions blocking Trump's federal funding freeze. Judges in several jurisdictions temporarily halted the administration's attempt to freeze grants and loans, reinforcing congressional spending authority and checking executive overreach. (27 Jan 2025; 28 Jan 2025; 29 Jan 2025; 30 Jan 2025)

5. Federal courts temporarily blocked Trump's attempt to end birthright citizenship. A federal judge's temporary block on the birthright-citizenship order preserved existing constitutional practice while litigation proceeds. (29 Jan 2025; 30 Jan 2025)

6. Federal courts issued stays related to Trump's federal grants and loans freeze and ordered funds released. Court orders requiring continued disbursement of federal funds mitigated immediate harm to state services and underscored judicial oversight of impoundment attempts. (27 Jan 2025; 28 Jan 2025; 29 Jan 2025; 30 Jan 2025)

7. Federal courts handled litigation over immigration enforcement in sensitive locations and civil service politicization. Lawsuits by Quaker congregations and civil servants challenged new enforcement and personnel poli-

cies, using the judiciary to contest executive encroachments on rights and neutrality. (27 Jan 2025; 29 Jan 2025)

8. Federal courts intervened in Trump administration handling of January 6 cases and supervised-release conditions. Judicial actions, including lifting Stewart Rhodes's DC ban after commutation and reviewing DOJ case handling, showed courts adapting to executive clemency while trying to preserve some oversight. (27 Jan 2025)

9. Department of Justice under Acting Attorney General James McHenry fired dozens of prosecutors and lawyers involved in cases against Donald Trump and January 6 defendants. Purging prosecutors tied to Trump and insurrection cases compromised DOJ independence and signaled that legal careers depend on alignment with presidential interests. (26 Jan 2025; 27 Jan 2025; 28 Jan 2025; 29 Jan 2025; 31 Jan 2025)

10. Department of Justice removed its public database of January 6 prosecutions. Taking down the Jan. 6 case database reduced transparency about accountability for the Capitol attack and hindered public tracking of outcomes. (26 Jan 2025)

11. Department of Justice launched a special project reviewing handling of January 6 criminal cases. Re-examining Jan. 6 prosecutions under new leadership raised concerns that accountability efforts could be softened or reversed for political reasons. (27 Jan 2025)

12. Trump administration closed the case against former co-defendants in the classified documents probe. Ending prosecutions of Trump's co-defendants in the documents case reduced legal scrutiny of alleged mishandling of state secrets by insiders. (29 Jan 2025)

13. U.S. Congress enacted the Laken Riley Act expanding immigration detention authority. Passing and signing the Laken Riley Act codified broader mandatory detention for certain undocumented immigrants and gave states new tools to pressure federal enforcement. (29 Jan 2025)

14. Representative Andy Ogles introduced a constitutional amendment bill to allow Donald Trump a third presidential term. Proposing to relax the two-term limit for presidents moved the idea of extended tenure from rhetoric into formal constitutional debate. (29 Jan 2025)

15. Senator Mike Lee proposed authorizing privateering against drug cartels. Reviving privateering concepts for cartel enforcement blurred lines between state and private violence and raised legal questions about delegating war-like powers. (29 Jan 2025)

16. Federal Election Commission announced a Sunshine Act meeting and adjusted campaign finance limits for inflation. Routine FEC actions on open meetings and updated contribution limits maintained procedural trans-

parency and adapted campaign finance rules to current economic conditions. (27 Jan 2025; 30 Jan 2025)

17. National Archives and Records Administration invited public comment on federal records schedules and appointed SES review board members. NARA's records-schedule notice and SES board appointments reflected ongoing institutional processes for managing federal records and senior-staff accountability. (28 Jan 2025; 29 Jan 2025)

18. Environmental Protection Agency delayed effective dates of several regulations and reopened comment periods on six actions. Delaying environmental rules under a regulatory freeze while reopening comment on others showed how executive directives can slow protections even as formal participation continues. (28 Jan 2025; 31 Jan 2025)

19. General Services Administration postponed GSAR amendments and sought comment on overseas employment and SAM notarization rules. GSA's postponement of acquisition-rule changes and solicitation of comments on employment and registration forms illustrated how regulatory freezes ripple through procurement and personnel systems. (27 Jan 2025; 31 Jan 2025)

20. Drug Enforcement Administration processed multiple applications to import or manufacture controlled substances for research and diagnostics. DEA's handling of controlled-substance import and manufacturing applications showed ongoing regulatory oversight of sensitive pharmaceuticals despite broader political turmoil. (28 Jan 2025; 31 Jan 2025)

21. Illinois Governor JB Pritzker barred January 6 participants from state employment by executive order. Illinois's move to exclude insurrection participants from state jobs used state authority to reinforce accountability norms for attacks on democratic institutions. (30 Jan 2025)

22. U.S. Congress held hearings and boycotts over Russ Vought's OMB nomination and RFK Jr.'s HHS nomination. Senate Democrats' boycott of Vought's markup and tough questioning of RFK Jr. signaled legislative concern about nominees seen as threats to budget norms and public-health policy. (30 Jan 2025)

23. U.S. Congress introduced bipartisan bills to improve pay and support for federal wildland firefighters. New House and Senate bills to stabilize firefighter pay and careers aimed to strengthen a critical public-safety workforce through legislative action. (30 Jan 2025)

24. U.S. Congress froze federal grants and loans via OMB memo without clear authorization, prompting oversight concerns. An OMB memo halting grants and loans without explicit statutory basis raised alarms about unilateral budget control and triggered talk of a constitutional confrontation. (31 Jan 2025)

25. Federal courts handled cross-state abortion and homelessness litigation. Cases over a New York doctor indicted in Louisiana and anti-camping rules in Oregon showed courts arbitrating conflicts between state policies and individual rights. (30 Jan 2025; 31 Jan 2025)

26. Federal courts oversaw settlement of high-profile defamation and First Amendment cases involving media and Meta. Settlements in defamation and free-speech litigation involving ABC News and Meta highlighted how powerful actors resolve speech disputes through negotiated payouts rather than full trials. (30 Jan 2025; 31 Jan 2025)

27. U.S. Senate Judiciary Committee held a confirmation hearing for Pam Bondi as Attorney General. Bondi's hearing, including questions on gun policy and enforcement priorities, foreshadowed how DOJ leadership might approach rights and public-safety tradeoffs. (31 Jan 2025)

28. U.S. Congress called Chicago's mayor to testify on sanctuary city policies. Republican efforts to summon Chicago's mayor for hearings on sanctuary policies used congressional oversight to pressure local choices on cooperation with federal immigration enforcement. (30 Jan 2025)

29. Federal courts indicted and sentenced high-profile political figures for corruption and bribery. The indictment of Eric Adams and sentencing of Bob Menendez to 11 years demonstrated that federal courts continued to prosecute corruption among powerful officials. (25 Jan 2025; 29 Jan 2025)

30. Federal courts issued an injunction against Trump's attempt to impound funds owed to states. A district court's injunction against impounding state-directed funds protected state budgets and reinforced that the executive cannot unilaterally withhold appropriated money. (30 Jan 2025)

Civil Rights and Dissent

1. President Donald Trump commuted the sentence and later pardoned Oath Keepers leader Stewart Rhodes. Clemency for a leader convicted of seditious conspiracy signaled leniency toward organized political violence against Congress. (25 Jan 2025; 27 Jan 2025)

2. Trump administration directed ICE to conduct large-scale raids with arrest quotas and in sensitive locations. Aggressive ICE operations with daily arrest targets, raids in churches and schools, and multi-agency sweeps heightened fear and risk of rights violations in immigrant and Indigenous communities. (26 Jan 2025; 27 Jan 2025; 28 Jan 2025; 29 Jan 2025; 30 Jan 2025)

3. Oklahoma State Board of Education required proof of citizenship or immigration status for public school enrollment. Mandating status documentation for K-12 enrollment threatened to deter undocumented families from

sending children to school, undermining equal access to education. (28 Jan 2025)

4. President Donald Trump rescinded deportation protections and TPS for Venezuelans in the U.S. Ending protections for Venezuelans fleeing crisis exposed them to removal and signaled a harsher stance toward humanitarian relief for certain nationalities. (28 Jan 2025; 29 Jan 2025)

5. President Donald Trump issued orders targeting transgender youth healthcare and transgender students' rights. Federal actions cutting funds for gender-affirming care and imposing bathroom bans curtailed protections for transgender minors in health and education systems. (28 Jan 2025; 30 Jan 2025)

6. President Donald Trump attempted to end birthright citizenship for children of noncitizens. The birthright-citizenship order, though blocked, threatened to create a hereditary underclass lacking full civic membership based on parentage. (28 Jan 2025; 29 Jan 2025; 30 Jan 2025)

7. Trump administration invoked the Alien Enemies Act and framed undocumented immigrants as a crime wave. Using an antiquated national-security law and misleading crime claims to justify crackdowns cast immigrant communities as inherent security threats. (28 Jan 2025)

8. Trump administration planned to detain up to 30,000 migrants at Guantánamo Bay. Routing migrants to an offshore military facility associated with terrorism detention raised serious due-process and human-rights concerns. (29 Jan 2025; 30 Jan 2025)

9. Trump administration expanded use of military facilities for immigration detention and processing. Allowing ICE to use Buckley Space Force Base for migrant processing blurred lines between civilian immigration enforcement and military infrastructure. (29 Jan 2025)

10. Trump administration moved to deport international students who participated in pro-Palestinian protests. Threatening deportation for campus protesters weaponized immigration status against political expression and academic freedom. (29 Jan 2025)

11. Quaker congregations and allied groups filed lawsuits challenging ICE access to churches and sensitive locations. Faith communities turned to the courts to defend religious freedom and sanctuary norms against expanded immigration enforcement in sacred spaces. (27 Jan 2025; 29 Jan 2025)

12. Navajo Nation leaders and advocates raised concerns about Indigenous people being swept up in immigration raids. Reports of Indigenous Americans questioned or detained in border sweeps highlighted risks of racial profiling and jurisdictional confusion. (27 Jan 2025)

13. ICE agents in Milwaukee wrongfully detained Puerto Rican U.S. citi-

zens during an enforcement action. Detaining a Puerto Rican family until they proved citizenship underscored how aggressive enforcement can erode rights even for citizens of color. (29 Jan 2025)

14. Judge Griffin and North Carolina litigants pursued litigation to overturn Justice Alison Riggs's election by discarding 60,000 votes. Efforts to invalidate tens of thousands of ballots in a state supreme court race echoed broader attempts to undo certified election results through the courts. (26 Jan 2025; 30 Jan 2025)

15. Common Cause NC, Emancipate, and allied groups mobilized voters against attempts to discard ballots in North Carolina. Grassroots organizing, legal advocacy, and public education campaigns sought to defend voters whose ballots were at risk of being thrown out. (26 Jan 2025)

16. Siembra NC expanded ICE watch programs to monitor immigration enforcement in North Carolina. Community-based ICE watch efforts aimed to protect undocumented residents by tracking raids and sharing information about enforcement activity. (26 Jan 2025)

17. Disability Rights Oregon sued Grants Pass over enforcement of anti-camping ordinances. Challenging camping bans that left disabled unhoused people with no legal place to sleep tested how far localities can go in criminalizing homelessness. (30 Jan 2025)

18. Federal courts blocked Kalispell, Montana, from closing a homeless shelter. An injunction protecting a homeless shelter limited local efforts to displace unhoused residents without adequate alternatives. (27 Jan 2025)

19. Louisiana prosecutors and a grand jury indicted a New York doctor for prescribing abortion pills to a Louisiana minor. Charging an out-of-state physician for telehealth abortion care tested the reach of restrictive state laws across borders and shield-law protections. (31 Jan 2025)

20. Illinois Governor JB Pritzker barred January 6 participants from state employment. Illinois's employment ban for insurrectionists used state hiring power to reinforce consequences for anti-democratic violence. (30 Jan 2025)

21. Trump administration changed federal prison policy to transfer trans women to men's facilities and halt gender-affirming care. New prison rules increased physical and psychological risks for transgender inmates by disregarding gender identity in housing and treatment decisions. (30 Jan 2025)

22. Trump administration lifted protections against immigration raids in schools, churches, and hospitals. Removing sensitive-location safeguards expanded where enforcement could occur, discouraging immigrants from accessing education, worship, and healthcare. (30 Jan 2025)

23. Trump administration used Guantánamo Bay and military bases for migrant detention and processing. Relying on military installations for civil

immigration detention blurred civilian-military boundaries and placed detainees in more remote, less transparent settings. (29 Jan 2025; 30 Jan 2025)

24. Trump administration expanded use of the Laken Riley Act to detain immigrants arrested for minor offenses. Allowing detention and deportation based on low-level charges, without conviction, broadened state power over noncitizens and increased vulnerability to arbitrary enforcement. (29 Jan 2025)

Economic Structure

1. President Donald Trump launched a personal cryptocurrency branded $Trump. Creating a presidentially branded cryptocurrency blurred lines between public office and private speculation, raising conflict-of-interest and consumer-protection concerns. (25 Jan 2025)

2. Trump administration froze and then rescinded a broad pause on federal grants and loans. The abrupt freeze and reversal of federal financial assistance disrupted Medicaid portals and other services, illustrating how executive maneuvers can destabilize core social programs. (27 Jan 2025; 28 Jan 2025; 29 Jan 2025; 30 Jan 2025; 31 Jan 2025)

3. Trump administration halted foreign aid appropriated by Congress. Freezing foreign aid programs undermined long-standing U.S. development and humanitarian efforts, potentially ceding influence to rival powers. (29 Jan 2025)

4. President Donald Trump imposed new tariffs on Colombia, Canada, Mexico, and China. Tariffs tied to deportation disputes and broader trade policy risked retaliatory measures and economic strain for workers and consumers in multiple countries. (28 Jan 2025; 30 Jan 2025; 31 Jan 2025)

5. Trump administration froze NIH funding and imposed new restrictions on health researchers. Pausing NIH support and adding constraints on fellows threatened continuity of biomedical research and the careers of early-stage scientists. (30 Jan 2025)

6. Trump administration halted approvals for renewable energy projects on federal lands and waters. Blocking new renewable projects on public lands slowed clean-energy investment and favored incumbent fossil-fuel interests. (28 Jan 2025)

7. Trump administration delayed multiple FDA and EPA regulations under a regulatory freeze. Delaying health and environmental rules shifted regulatory timelines in ways that can benefit regulated industries at the expense of public protections. (27 Jan 2025; 28 Jan 2025)

8. Jared Kushner and Affinity Partners positioned private investments to

benefit from potential Gaza redevelopment. Kushner's financial stake in Gaza-related real estate created potential conflicts between private profit and U.S. foreign-policy decisions on Palestinian displacement. (27 Jan 2025)

9. Trump Organization issued an ethics statement while pursuing Trump Tower Belgrade on Serbian state land. Pledging to avoid foreign-government business while building on government-owned land via a private partner highlighted loopholes in self-imposed ethics rules. (27 Jan 2025)

10. Trump Media and Technology Group announced a crypto-focused financial brand called Truth.Fi. Expanding a politically connected media company into large-scale crypto investments raised questions about regulatory oversight and entanglement of political influence with speculative finance. (31 Jan 2025)

11. Meta Platforms and Donald Trump settled Trump's lawsuit over his suspension for $25 million. A large settlement tied to Trump's future cooperation with Meta suggested that political leverage can shape corporate accountability and platform decisions. (31 Jan 2025)

12. Senator Mike Lee called for abolishing the Transportation Security Administration. Proposing to dismantle TSA and shift screening to airlines would significantly restructure federal responsibility for aviation security. (27 Jan 2025)

13. House Republicans and President Donald Trump discussed potentially abolishing FEMA at a Florida retreat. Entertaining abolition of FEMA signaled openness to shrinking federal disaster response, which could leave states and individuals more exposed to catastrophic risk. (26 Jan 2025)

14. Trump administration and Elon Musk's allies pressured Treasury and OPM systems, contributing to a senior official's resignation. Conflicts over access to sensitive payment systems and HR data, culminating in David Lebryk's departure, highlighted growing private influence over core financial infrastructure. (30 Jan 2025; 31 Jan 2025)

15. Texas energy sector continued rapid build-out of solar power capacity. Texas's leadership in solar deployment illustrated how market forces and state policy can drive large-scale renewable adoption even amid federal headwinds. (28 Jan 2025)

16. Biden administration pursued antitrust actions against major tech companies. Ongoing antitrust efforts against dominant tech firms reflected attempts to curb concentrated economic and political power in digital markets. (28 Jan 2025)

17. DeepSeek, a Chinese AI company released open-source large language models rivaling U.S. systems. China's release of competitive open-source AI models complicated U.S. efforts to maintain technological

advantage through export controls and proprietary development. (30 Jan 2025)

18. Trump administration halted federal grants and loans that included DEI provisions. Conditioning federal funding on exclusion of DEI initiatives tied access to public resources to compliance with the administration's ideological agenda. (29 Jan 2025)

19. Organic Consultants LLC, Aveva, Vici Health Sciences, Medi-Physics, and Catalent sought DEA registrations for controlled substances manufacturing or import. Multiple firms' applications to handle controlled substances for research and diagnostics underscored the role of federal licensing in shaping pharmaceutical and research markets. (28 Jan 2025; 31 Jan 2025)

Information, Memory, and Manipulation

1. Trump administration removed DOJ's public database of January 6 defendants and outcomes. Deleting the Jan. 6 prosecutions database obscured the public record of accountability for the Capitol attack and hindered independent analysis. (26 Jan 2025)

2. Trump administration ordered USDA and Forest Service to take down climate-crisis web content. Removing climate-related pages from federal websites limited public access to scientific information and erased official acknowledgment of climate risks. (31 Jan 2025)

3. Trump administration deleted DEI references from IRS materials and removed diversity webpages. Scrubbing diversity language and resources from IRS documents sanitized the historical record of equity efforts within the tax agency. (31 Jan 2025)

4. U.S. Air Force removed material on Black and female WWII pilots from training to comply with Trump's DEI order. Erasing Tuskegee Airmen and WASP content from training curricula diminished recognition of marginalized groups' contributions to U.S. military history. (25 Jan 2025)

5. Trump administration suspended DEI-related training materials at the State Department's Foreign Service Institute. Pulling hundreds of DEI-related courses from diplomatic training constrained efforts to build an inclusive foreign-service culture. (27 Jan 2025)

6. President Donald Trump and Elon Musk's allies used a "government efficiency" initiative to seek opaque access to personnel data and influence HR systems. Lawsuits and reports about Musk-linked data collection and system lockouts at OPM raised alarms about private actors controlling sensitive government information. (25 Jan 2025; 27 Jan 2025; 31 Jan 2025)

7. Trump administration locked EPA employees' status to probationary

and limited their job security. Reclassifying over 1,100 EPA staff as probationary increased vulnerability to dismissal and may chill internal dissent about environmental policy changes. (29 Jan 2025)

8. Trump administration removed or withheld records related to the Cop City protest killing until investigative reporting. State withholding of documents on Manuel Paez Terán's killing, later obtained by journalists, limited transparency around a controversial police operation. (28 Jan 2025)

9. President Donald Trump falsely claimed the U.S. military entered California to turn on water supplies. Misrepresenting routine water-pump maintenance as military intervention distorted public understanding of federal-state relations and environmental management. (27 Jan 2025)

10. White House Press Secretary Karoline Leavitt made misleading claims about foreign aid being spent on condoms for Gaza. False assertions about aid spending were used to justify halting foreign assistance, illustrating how misinformation can frame major policy shifts. (30 Jan 2025)

11. President Donald Trump blamed DEI policies for a fatal DC air crash without evidence. Speculating that diversity hiring caused an aviation disaster politicized tragedy and fueled narratives against inclusion initiatives. (29 Jan 2025; 31 Jan 2025)

12. President Donald Trump claimed undocumented immigrants were driving a crime wave despite data showing declines. Using inaccurate crime statistics to justify invoking the Alien Enemies Act framed immigrants as dangerous and supported harsher enforcement. (28 Jan 2025)

13. Elon Musk supported far-right politicians abroad and spread smears against foreign leaders. Musk's amplification of far-right narratives and gestures abroad raised concerns about wealthy individuals influencing democratic discourse in multiple countries. (27 Jan 2025)

14. Federal Communications Commission under Chair Brendan Carr opened investigations into NPR, PBS, and requested unedited CBS interview transcripts. Targeting public broadcasters and demanding raw interview materials risked chilling editorial independence and advantaging more government-aligned outlets. (29 Jan 2025; 30 Jan 2025)

15. Pentagon reallocated press-corps seating to favor pro-Trump outlets over legacy media. Shifting Pentagon press access away from major outlets toward friendlier media altered who can routinely question defense officials. (31 Jan 2025)

16. Elon Musk's aides at OPM locked career civil servants out of HR data systems. Blocking staff from accessing personnel systems concentrated control of sensitive employee data in the hands of political appointees and private allies. (31 Jan 2025)

17. Trump administration restored TikTok's operations in the U.S. Reversing prior efforts to restrict TikTok without clear new safeguards raised questions about data security and the platform's role in the information ecosystem. (25 Jan 2025)

18. Trump administration used executive orders and education policy to promote a 1776-style patriotic curriculum and defund "radical" programs. Reestablishing the 1776 Commission and tying funding to approved narratives sought to reshape civic education toward a narrower, state-sanctioned history. (29 Jan 2025)

19. Trump administration pressured media and tech companies through lawsuits and settlements. Legal pressure on ABC and Meta, culminating in settlements, illustrated how powerful political actors can shape media behavior through litigation risk. (30 Jan 2025; 31 Jan 2025)

20. National Archives and EPA published environmental impact statements and reopened comment periods. Maintaining public access to environmental impact statements and extending comment windows supported transparency and participation in environmental decision-making. (31 Jan 2025)

21. Trump administration used Medicaid portal messaging to attribute outages to executive orders on unallowable grant payments. Portal notices linking service disruptions to new grant rules highlighted how technical systems can be used to communicate and justify contentious policy changes. (29 Jan 2025)

22. Trump administration suspended observance of MLK Day, Holocaust Day, Juneteenth, and Pride at the Defense Intelligence Agency. Halting recognition of key civil-rights and remembrance days within a major intelligence agency signaled a retreat from institutional acknowledgment of historical injustices. (28 Jan 2025)

CHAPTER 3
WEEK 3 (1 FEB 2025 – 7 FEB 2025): SYSTEMS AS SPOILS

In Trump's third week back in office, executive power fused with private wealth, hollowing out oversight while courts and unions fought rearguard actions.

This week reveals a rapid surge in authoritarian consolidation on multiple fronts. The most urgent pressures target executive constraints, civil service neutrality, the rule of law, and information integrity. Trump and Musk's DOGE apparatus gained or solidified control over key state infrastructure—Treasury payments, HR databases, USAID, SBA, Education, NOAA, CMS, and even air traffic control—often without statutory authority or proper clearances, then partially retreated only when faced with litigation threats. At the same time, the Justice Department and FBI removed officials connected to Trump and January 6 cases, while enforcement agencies for civil rights, foreign bribery, and foreign influence were dismantled. Mass pardons for January 6 defendants, sweeping firings of prosecutors, and orders framed as "weaponization" redefined accountability. Protections for DEI, LGBTQ+, immigrants, and the environment were rolled back through broad executive orders and personnel changes, while religion was mobilized via anti-DEI and "anti-Christian bias" taskforces. Internationally, tariffs, aid freezes, UN withdrawals, ICC sanctions, and a Gaza "takeover" proposal marked a stark break from liberal multilateralism. Courts, unions, states, and Congress mounted notable resistance—blocking the fund freeze, birthright order, trans-prison policy, buyouts, and DOGE access—but these stand as defensive measures against a swiftly centralizing presidency–oligarch nexus.

Power and Authority

1. President Trump and the State Department froze most foreign aid and moved to fold USAID into State Department control. The administration halted roughly $60 billion in USAID foreign aid and began stripping the agency of independence, concentrating foreign assistance decisions in the executive branch and disrupting humanitarian programs worldwide. (1 Feb 2025; 2 Feb 2025; 3 Feb 2025; 4 Feb 2025; 5 Feb 2025; 6 Feb 2025; 7 Feb 2025)

2. President Trump imposed sweeping tariffs on imports from Canada, Mexico, and China using emergency powers. Trump used national emergency authorities to levy broad tariffs on the three largest U.S. trading partners, turning emergency economic powers into a routine tool of unilateral trade and foreign policy. (1 Feb 2025; 2 Feb 2025; 3 Feb 2025; 4 Feb 2025; 6 Feb 2025)

3. President Trump and Elon Musk's DOGE team gained de facto control and deep access to U.S. Treasury payment systems. By granting Musk's associates access to systems that move trillions in federal payments, the administration effectively outsourced core fiscal authority to a private actor with limited oversight, raising separation-of-powers and privacy concerns. (1 Feb 2025; 2 Feb 2025; 3 Feb 2025; 4 Feb 2025; 5 Feb 2025; 6 Feb 2025; 7 Feb 2025)

4. President Trump and Elon Musk's DOGE team secured broad access to sensitive federal personnel and program data across multiple agencies. DOGE operatives were allowed into OPM, SBA, Education, CMS, NOAA, Energy and other systems holding detailed employee and beneficiary data, enabling political vetting and potential manipulation of core administrative records. (1 Feb 2025; 2 Feb 2025; 3 Feb 2025; 4 Feb 2025; 5 Feb 2025; 6 Feb 2025)

5. President Trump issued executive orders and directives targeting diversity, equity, and inclusion programs across government. Trump revoked long-standing equal opportunity protections, ordered dismantling of DEI programs, and directed agencies to treat many DEI efforts as discriminatory, reshaping federal civil rights enforcement and workplace norms. (1 Feb 2025; 2 Feb 2025; 3 Feb 2025; 4 Feb 2025; 5 Feb 2025)

6. President Trump signed executive orders restricting transgender rights in healthcare, prisons, sports, and immigration. New orders sought to cut federal funds to providers of gender-affirming care for youth, purge trans service members and prisoners, and bar trans women from women's sports and related visas, using federal leverage to narrow protections. (2 Feb 2025; 3 Feb 2025; 5 Feb 2025)

7. President Trump issued blanket pardons for over 1,500 January 6 participants. Mass pardons for people charged or convicted in the Capitol attack

signaled executive willingness to shield political allies from accountability for violence against the constitutional transfer of power. (3 Feb 2025)

8. President Trump ordered a federal funding and grants freeze then quickly rescinded it after backlash and court action. The White House attempted to pause vast categories of congressionally appropriated funds, then reversed course within days under public and judicial pressure, illustrating aggressive but unstable assertions of impoundment power. (2 Feb 2025; 3 Feb 2025; 4 Feb 2025)

9. President Trump signed executive orders pausing newly announced tariffs on Canada and Mexico for one month. After announcing sweeping tariffs, Trump delayed implementation in exchange for limited border-security concessions, using rapid reversals to keep trade partners and domestic actors off balance. (2 Feb 2025; 3 Feb 2025; 4 Feb 2025; 6 Feb 2025)

10. President Trump signed an executive order establishing a U.S. sovereign wealth fund. The order directed Treasury and Commerce to design a national investment fund, potentially enabling large, centrally directed state investments that could be steered toward politically favored projects or firms. (3 Feb 2025)

11. President Trump ordered opening of two California dams against local water-management practice. Trump directed the Army Corps to release billions of gallons from California reservoirs, nearly flooding farms and undermining state water planning, then reversed after backlash, showing ad hoc intervention in complex resource policy. (4 Feb 2025; 6 Feb 2025)

12. President Trump issued an executive order directing a report on alleged weaponization of the federal government. By ordering DOJ to compile a report on supposed politicized cases, including his own, for White House policy staff, Trump positioned the executive to reframe and potentially discredit independent prosecutions. (4 Feb 2025)

13. President Trump signed executive orders amending China opioid tariffs and reinstating federal death penalty. Trump adjusted tariff rules on Chinese goods tied to opioid supply chains and restored federal executions, expanding punitive tools in both trade and criminal justice under executive direction. (5 Feb 2025)

14. Attorney General Pam Bondi cut federal funding to sanctuary jurisdictions and reinstated the federal death penalty. Bondi ordered funding halted to jurisdictions deemed non-cooperative with federal immigration enforcement and revived executions, using Justice Department levers to pressure local policy choices and harden punishment. (5 Feb 2025)

15. President Trump signed executive orders creating a task force on anti-Christian bias and a White House Faith Office. New directives empow-

ered DOJ and a White House faith office to prioritize perceived anti-Christian discrimination, embedding a favored religious constituency into federal policy and enforcement structures. (6 Feb 2025; 7 Feb 2025)

16. President Trump ordered a review of all federal funding to non-governmental organizations. A sweeping review of NGO funding created uncertainty for civil society groups reliant on federal grants, giving the executive leverage to reward or punish organizations based on alignment with administration priorities. (6 Feb 2025)

17. President Trump issued an executive order imposing sanctions on the International Criminal Court. Sanctions on ICC officials and entry bans sought to shield U.S. and Israeli personnel from international prosecution, asserting executive power against multilateral legal accountability mechanisms. (6 Feb 2025)

18. President Trump issued an executive order halting U.S. aid to South Africa and prioritizing Afrikaner resettlement. By cutting aid over South Africa's expropriation law and prioritizing Afrikaner refugees, Trump used foreign assistance to advance a racially framed narrative and reshape humanitarian priorities. (2 Feb 2025; 7 Feb 2025)

19. President Trump issued an executive order to review and roll back gun regulations adopted since 2021. The order directed DOJ to identify and undo prior executive and regulatory actions seen as limiting Second Amendment rights, centralizing firearm policy shifts in the presidency. (7 Feb 2025)

Institutions and Governance

1. Justice Department leadership under President Trump purged prosecutors and FBI officials involved in Trump and January 6 cases and demanded lists of investigators. Senior DOJ appointees fired dozens of prosecutors and forced out FBI leaders tied to Trump and Capitol riot cases while ordering rosters of involved agents, politicizing law enforcement and chilling future investigations. (1 Feb 2025; 2 Feb 2025; 3 Feb 2025; 4 Feb 2025; 5 Feb 2025; 7 Feb 2025)

2. Attorney General Pam Bondi and DOJ leadership reoriented federal enforcement away from white-collar and foreign influence crimes toward regime priorities. Bondi dismantled foreign bribery and kleptocracy units, disbanded the FBI's Foreign Influence Task Force, and scaled back FARA and white-collar enforcement, weakening safeguards against corruption and foreign interference. (5 Feb 2025; 6 Feb 2025; 7 Feb 2025)

3. President Trump and Attorney General Pam Bondi created a Weaponization Working Group to review prosecutions of Trump and Jan. 6

cases. A new DOJ working group was tasked with scrutinizing prosecutions involving Trump and January 6, framing prior enforcement as abuse and opening avenues to undermine or reverse politically sensitive cases. (5 Feb 2025)

4. President Trump removed independent inspectors general from at least 12 major federal agencies. Firing multiple inspectors general stripped agencies of key internal watchdogs, sharply reducing institutional capacity to detect waste, fraud, and abuse within the executive branch. (5 Feb 2025)

5. Federal courts blocked or paused several major Trump administration initiatives affecting funding, immigration, and civil service. Judges halted the federal fund freeze, extended pauses on the grants freeze, blocked the birthright citizenship order, stopped trans women prison transfers, and temporarily enjoined the federal worker buyout deadline, asserting judicial checks on executive overreach. (2 Feb 2025; 3 Feb 2025; 4 Feb 2025; 5 Feb 2025; 6 Feb 2025; 7 Feb 2025)

6. FBI agents and federal employee unions filed lawsuits to block DOJ retaliation and DOGE access to sensitive records. FBI staff and unions sued to prevent disclosure of Jan. 6 investigators' identities and to challenge Musk's access to Treasury and OPM systems, using litigation to defend civil service protections and privacy. (4 Feb 2025; 5 Feb 2025; 6 Feb 2025)

7. Federal courts temporarily restricted DOGE and Musk's access to Treasury payment systems and federal employee buyouts. Judges ordered delays and limits on DOGE's access to payment systems and blocked the administration's buyout deadline, slowing efforts to restructure the civil service and centralize fiscal control. (5 Feb 2025; 6 Feb 2025)

8. President Trump and Senate Republicans confirmed Pam Bondi as attorney general despite civil rights concerns. Bondi's confirmation placed a close Trump ally with a record of anti-LGBTQ and anti-immigrant positions atop DOJ, heightening fears that federal law enforcement would be steered by partisan and ideological priorities. (5 Feb 2025)

9. President Trump and Senate Republicans confirmed Russell Vought as director of the Office of Management and Budget. Installing Vought, a key Project 2025 architect, at OMB concentrated budgetary power in a figure committed to aggressive restructuring of the federal state, raising risks of confrontations with Congress over appropriations. (6 Feb 2025; 7 Feb 2025)

10. President Trump and Senate Republicans confirmed Chris Wright as Energy Secretary and advanced RFK Jr. for HHS. Senate confirmations of a fracking CEO to lead Energy and advancement of a vaccine-skeptical nominee for HHS signaled a shift of key policy portfolios to figures skeptical of mainstream climate and public health science. (1 Feb 2025; 4 Feb 2025)

11. President Trump and Senate Republicans installed Pam Bondi, Kash Patel, and other loyalists in senior justice and security roles. Key justice and security posts went to close Trump allies, including a DOJ nominee with major foreign-linked holdings, deepening concerns that prosecutorial and intelligence decisions would favor regime interests. (5 Feb 2025; 6 Feb 2025)

12. President Trump and Treasury Secretary Scott Bessent appointed Musk associate Tom Krause to oversee national payment systems. Placing a DOGE member in charge of systems disbursing over $5 trillion annually embedded a private ally at the heart of federal cash flows, blurring lines between public administration and private influence. (6 Feb 2025)

13. President Trump and EPA leadership stacked Environmental Protection Agency leadership with industry lobbyists and attorneys. New EPA leaders came from major industry trade groups and firms that had opposed environmental rules, raising the likelihood that enforcement and rulemaking would favor regulated industries over public health. (5 Feb 2025)

14. President Trump and State Department leadership fired large numbers of State Department personal services contractors under a hiring freeze order. Terminating many contract staff providing security and support at embassies under a revived hiring freeze weakened State's operational capacity and increased reliance on political appointees. (6 Feb 2025)

15. Supreme Court of the United States heard a case that could revive the nondelegation doctrine and limit agency rulemaking authority. In FCC v. Consumers' Research, the Court considered curbing Congress's ability to delegate power to agencies, potentially undermining broad swaths of federal regulation and shifting power toward courts and Congress. (6 Feb 2025)

16. Federal Election Commission and Ellen Weintraub faced an attempted presidential removal of the FEC chair amid ongoing investigations. Trump purported to fire FEC chair Ellen Weintraub while the agency was reviewing complaints against him; Weintraub refused to leave, highlighting tensions over the independence of election oversight. (6 Feb 2025)

17. Congressional Democrats and state legislatures used legislation and funding to counter executive overreach and protect vulnerable groups. Democrats introduced bills to require congressional approval for tariffs, protect Treasury systems from DOGE, and California appropriated funds to fight federal actions and support immigrants, illustrating institutional resistance through lawmaking. (1 Feb 2025; 5 Feb 2025; 6 Feb 2025; 7 Feb 2025)

18. Representative Al Green announced plans to file articles of impeachment against President Trump over Gaza proposal. A House Democrat moved toward impeachment in response to Trump's Gaza takeover plan,

invoking constitutional accountability mechanisms even though success was unlikely under current congressional control. (5 Feb 2025)

19. Federal regulatory agencies extended comment periods and delayed effective dates for several environmental and FDA rules. EPA and FDA postponed implementation and extended comment on multiple regulations under a regulatory freeze memo, slowing public-health and environmental protections while preserving formal notice-and-comment procedures. (3 Feb 2025; 5 Feb 2025; 7 Feb 2025)

20. Federal Election Commission and Election Assistance Commission held and announced Sunshine Act meetings on election administration and compliance. FEC and EAC meetings on donor forms, directives, and election technology proceeded under Sunshine Act requirements, maintaining some transparency and routine governance of election rules. (3 Feb 2025; 6 Feb 2025)

21. National Labor Relations Board and former member Gwynne Wilcox became the subject of litigation over an allegedly unlawful firing that broke quorum. Wilcox sued Trump and the NLRB chair, arguing her removal without statutory cause was illegal and left the board without a quorum, challenging executive interference in an independent labor agency. (5 Feb 2025)

22. SpaceX and the National Labor Relations Board engaged in a constitutional challenge to the NLRB's structure in federal court. SpaceX sued to contest the NLRB's constitutionality while facing labor-law enforcement, potentially weakening a key worker-protection body through strategic litigation. (5 Feb 2025)

23. CIA leadership and the White House sent an unclassified list of recent CIA hires to the White House under presidential order. Transmitting names of CIA employees hired in the past two years via unclassified email exposed sensitive personnel information to broader circulation, raising security and politicization concerns. (6 Feb 2025; 7 Feb 2025)

Civil Rights and Dissent

1. President Trump and federal agencies targeted immigrants by revoking protections, expanding Guantánamo use, and suing sanctuary jurisdictions. The administration revoked legal protections for hundreds of thousands of migrants, expanded migrant detention at Guantánamo, and moved against sanctuary laws, intensifying legal and physical vulnerability for non-citizens. (1 Feb 2025; 2 Feb 2025; 3 Feb 2025; 4 Feb 2025; 6 Feb 2025)

2. President Trump and Attorney General Pam Bondi pursued policies to

end birthright citizenship for children of undocumented immigrants. An executive order sought to deny citizenship to U.S.-born children of undocumented parents, prompting multiple injunctions and raising fundamental questions about constitutional guarantees and equal membership. (5 Feb 2025; 6 Feb 2025; 7 Feb 2025)

3. President Trump issued an executive order on antisemitism that encouraged immigration consequences for campus protesters. An antisemitism order directed agencies to explore civil and criminal tools against campus activism, including deportation of international students, blurring lines between hate-crime enforcement and suppression of political speech. (2 Feb 2025)

4. President Trump and federal agencies rolled back protections and recognition for LGBTQ+ people across multiple domains. Orders and directives removed pronouns from federal communications, restricted gender-affirming care, and targeted trans prisoners and athletes, using federal power to narrow rights based on gender identity. (1 Feb 2025; 2 Feb 2025; 3 Feb 2025; 5 Feb 2025)

5. President Trump and DOJ halted DOJ civil rights investigations and police reform consent decrees. Stopping federal oversight agreements in cities like Louisville and Minneapolis curtailed efforts to address systemic police abuses, weakening federal protection for communities facing discriminatory policing. (5 Feb 2025)

6. North Carolina legislature enacted laws criminalizing road-blocking and mask-wearing during protests. New restrictions on protest tactics and attire increased legal risks for demonstrators, potentially deterring public assembly and limiting anonymity in politically charged environments. (3 Feb 2025)

7. Wyoming Republican legislators introduced a bill redefining healthcare in ways that could sharply restrict abortion and other treatments. Senate File 125's broad language on procedures harming major organs risked curtailing abortion and other medical care, using statutory redefinition to limit bodily autonomy and professional discretion. (2 Feb 2025)

8. Louisiana Governor Jeff Landry and state police forcibly relocated unhoused people to an unheated warehouse under threat of arrest. State authorities moved over 100 unhoused individuals to a poorly equipped facility during a winter storm, leveraging police power against a vulnerable population while limiting press access. (6 Feb 2025)

9. ICE and DHS conducted aggressive immigration raids and manipulated public communications about enforcement. A surprise farmworker raid in California and retimestamped ICE press releases fueled fear of mass

deportations, amplifying the chilling effect on immigrant communities' willingness to access services or assert rights. (3 Feb 2025; 6 Feb 2025; 7 Feb 2025)

10. Department of Homeland Security and U.S. military began flying migrants to Guantánamo Bay under a new detention policy. Military flights transported migrants to an expanded Guantánamo facility for prolonged processing, extending offshore detention practices associated with national security to immigration enforcement. (2 Feb 2025; 3 Feb 2025; 4 Feb 2025)

11. Trump administration and DOJ sued Chicago and Illinois over sanctuary laws. A federal lawsuit sought to invalidate state and local limits on cooperation with immigration enforcement, challenging subnational autonomy and protections for undocumented residents. (6 Feb 2025)

12. Federal courts and civil rights litigants secured rulings protecting trans prisoners and recognizing racial bias in death penalty sentencing. Judges blocked transfers of trans women to men's prisons and found racial bias in a North Carolina death sentence, demonstrating judicial avenues for defending vulnerable groups amid hostile policies. (4 Feb 2025; 5 Feb 2025; 7 Feb 2025)

13. State of California and Governor Gavin Newsom sought wildfire aid while resisting federal conditions tied to immigration and voting rules. Newsom pressed for unconditional disaster aid as Trump floated linking assistance to water policy, voter ID, and immigration enforcement, highlighting how relief can be used to pressure state policy choices. (6 Feb 2025)

14. US military academy at West Point disbanded student-led cultural and professional clubs in response to anti-DEI orders. West Point shut down women's, minority, and LGBTQ+ support clubs under federal DEI directives, reducing institutional support for diverse cadets in a key military training environment. (5 Feb 2025)

15. US State Department suspended a Christian employee group amid broader dismantling of affinity networks. The suspension of the Grace Christian employee organization, alongside other affinity groups, reflected a sweeping rollback of internal networks that had supported diverse religious and identity communities in government. (3 Feb 2025)

16. Louisiana and California prison and court systems faced lawsuits over abuse of incarcerated women and racial bias in capital sentencing. Class-action and post-conviction cases exposed sexual abuse in a women's prison and racially biased death penalty practices, underscoring systemic rights violations within carceral institutions. (6 Feb 2025; 7 Feb 2025)

Economic Structure

1. President Trump and Treasury Secretary Scott Bessent used DOGE access to federal payment systems to disrupt or threaten federal grants and loans. Control over payment gateways allowed politically connected actors to pause or threaten funding for research, foreign aid, and domestic programs, turning core fiscal infrastructure into a lever of political and economic power. (1 Feb 2025; 2 Feb 2025; 3 Feb 2025; 4 Feb 2025; 5 Feb 2025; 6 Feb 2025)

2. President Trump and Elon Musk's DOGE team launched a deferred resignation program and buyout offer for federal employees. A mass "deferred resignation" scheme offered pay to employees who agreed to resign later while waiving legal recourse and accepting uncertain work obligations, incentivizing attrition and weakening the professional civil service. (3 Feb 2025; 5 Feb 2025)

3. Consumer Financial Protection Bureau and Treasury leadership paused forthcoming regulations to remove medical debt from credit reports. Treasury ordered CFPB to halt new rules that would have shielded consumers from medical debt on credit reports, preserving practices that burden low-income households and benefit debt collectors. (4 Feb 2025)

4. Securities and Exchange Commission leadership required staff attorneys to obtain political approval before opening investigations. New instructions forced SEC lawyers to seek sign-off from political appointees before launching cases, risking selective enforcement and weakening independent oversight of financial markets. (1 Feb 2025; 2 Feb 2025)

5. U.S. Chamber of Commerce and business groups publicly opposed Trump's emergency tariffs as harmful to consumers and supply chains. Major business lobbies warned that broad tariffs under emergency statutes would raise prices and disrupt supply chains, highlighting domestic economic costs of unilateral trade actions. (1 Feb 2025)

6. Canada, Mexico, and China announced retaliatory tariffs and WTO action in response to U.S. measures. Key trading partners imposed counter-tariffs and pursued WTO complaints, escalating a trade conflict that threatened jobs, prices, and economic stability in the U.S. and abroad. (1 Feb 2025; 3 Feb 2025)

7. U.S. Postal Service temporarily halted packages from China and Hong Kong amid tariff changes. A short-lived suspension of parcels from China and Hong Kong, likely tied to de minimis duty changes, disrupted e-commerce and illustrated how trade policy shifts can quickly affect consumers. (5 Feb 2025)

8. EPA and Interior Department under President Trump delayed environ-

mental rules and moved to roll back protections on toxics and public lands. The administration froze or reconsidered rules on TCE, PFAS, hazardous waste, and national monument boundaries, favoring extractive industries over environmental and public-health safeguards. (3 Feb 2025; 5 Feb 2025; 6 Feb 2025)

9. Private equity firms and HHS were criticized in an HHS report for harming healthcare quality, then saw the report's visibility reduced. An HHS report linking private equity ownership to higher patient deaths and worse care briefly highlighted structural harms before its news release was removed, underscoring tensions between profit models and public health. (6 Feb 2025)

10. Donald Trump Jr., Eric Trump, Barron Trump, and Jared Kushner expanded business ventures likely to benefit from political connections. Trump family members deepened roles in venture capital, cryptocurrency, and foreign-funded private equity, raising concerns that public office and foreign policy could be shaped to advance their financial interests. (6 Feb 2025)

11. Congressional sponsors Bernie Sanders and Josh Hawley introduced legislation to cap credit card interest rates at 10%. A bipartisan bill proposed strict limits on credit card interest, challenging financial industry practices that heavily burden indebted consumers and signaling legislative interest in curbing predatory lending. (3 Feb 2025)

12. Elon Musk's DOGE team and OPM installed an unvetted server and gained unprecedented access to federal HR databases. A new server controlling sensitive HR systems was installed outside normal procurement and privacy review, giving Musk associates broad access to employee data and heightening risks of misuse and security breaches. (3 Feb 2025; 6 Feb 2025)

13. EPA and FDA continued routine regulatory and information-collection processes despite a regulatory freeze. Agencies advanced comment periods and information collections for environmental and biosimilar drug rules, showing that some technocratic functions persisted even as higher-profile rules were delayed. (3 Feb 2025; 7 Feb 2025)

14. Los Angeles Unified School District allocated $2.2 billion to rebuild wildfire-damaged schools and improve resilience. LAUSD committed substantial bond funds to reconstruct schools destroyed by wildfires and upgrade seismic and air-quality protections, investing in public education infrastructure and disaster preparedness. (6 Feb 2025)

15. President Trump and trade agencies used tariff threats and reversals as a recurring tool of economic statecraft. Rapid cycles of tariff announcements, delays, and claimed victories over allies created market volatility and uncer-

tainty, illustrating how erratic trade policy can function as a political instrument. (2 Feb 2025; 4 Feb 2025; 6 Feb 2025)

16. Egg producers and federal agencies lobbied for vaccine research funding to address bird flu impacts on egg prices. Industry groups sought federal support for vaccine research to stabilize egg supplies and prices, highlighting how agricultural interests engage government to manage public-health-linked market shocks. (2 Feb 2025)

Information, Memory, and Manipulation

1. President Trump and Elon Musk's DOGE team obtained broad access to sensitive government data and communications systems. DOGE operatives gained read or deeper access to Treasury, OPM, CMS, NOAA, Energy, SBA, Education, and USAID systems, enabling large-scale data mining and potential manipulation of public records and payments. (1 Feb 2025; 2 Feb 2025; 3 Feb 2025; 4 Feb 2025; 5 Feb 2025; 6 Feb 2025; 7 Feb 2025)

2. Centers for Disease Control and Prevention and other health agencies under Trump orders removed or altered public health webpages and databases related to gender and sexual health. Key CDC and federal health pages on contraception, HIV, STIs, and gender-affirming care went dark or were stripped of content following anti-DEI and anti-"gender ideology" directives, limiting access to evidence-based information. (4 Feb 2025)

3. USAID and Trump administration took USAID's website and social media offline during an attempted shutdown and reorganization. USAID's online presence disappeared as leadership was sidelined and the agency was folded into State, obscuring information about aid programs at a moment of major structural change. (1 Feb 2025; 2 Feb 2025; 3 Feb 2025)

4. Immigration and Customs Enforcement updated timestamps on old press releases to make past deportation operations appear current. ICE's retimestamping of years-old enforcement press releases manipulated search results to suggest ongoing mass deportations, stoking fear and distorting public understanding of current policy. (6 Feb 2025; 7 Feb 2025)

5. Pentagon implemented a media rotation program replacing major outlets with ideologically aligned ones. A new rotation swapped mainstream outlets like NBC and NPR for OANN and Breitbart in Pentagon press spaces, reshaping which media have routine access to defense information. (1 Feb 2025)

6. Elon Musk and the social media platform X deleted a post and suspended an account for naming DOGE employees, citing zero-tolerance for leaks. Musk's moderation decision against a user identifying DOGE staff

blurred lines between personal platform control and suppression of information about public-facing government actors. (2 Feb 2025)

7. Federal Communications Commission and the White House used regulatory and purchasing tools to pressure or investigate critical media outlets. The administration canceled large Politico subscriptions, reinstated a news distortion complaint, opened an inquiry into KCBS immigration reporting, and Trump called for canceling 60 Minutes, signaling hostility toward independent journalism. (5 Feb 2025; 6 Feb 2025; 7 Feb 2025)

8. President Trump and Lara Trump facilitated movement between party leadership and a major cable news platform. Lara Trump's shift from RNC chair to Fox News host underscored the tight integration of partisan leadership and influential media, potentially shaping coverage of administration policies. (6 Feb 2025)

9. Interior Department under Secretary Doug Burgum ordered reviews of national monument boundaries and reversed conservation-oriented rules. Directives to revisit monument boundaries and favor drilling over protections risked rewriting the physical record of public lands and their histories in line with extractive priorities. (6 Feb 2025)

10. HHS and the Trump administration removed a news release about a report criticizing private equity in healthcare from its website. Taking down the release on a report linking private equity to higher patient deaths limited public visibility into evidence of systemic harms in healthcare financing. (6 Feb 2025)

11. Elon Musk's DOGE representative at NOAA accessed NOAA systems leading to disappearance of some climate data. DOGE access to NOAA IT coincided with missing climate records, raising fears that politically inconvenient environmental data could be altered or erased. (5 Feb 2025)

12. Elon Musk's DOGE team and CMS accessed Medicare and Medicaid payment and contracting systems to search for "waste". Unvetted DOGE staff combed through CMS systems, raising concerns that politically motivated audits could disrupt benefits or be used to justify cuts to disfavored providers or programs. (5 Feb 2025)

13. President Trump and ICE used misleading narratives and data practices to exaggerate threats and justify crackdowns. From baseless claims about South African land seizures to ICE's manipulated press releases, the administration deployed distorted information to support punitive immigration and foreign policy moves. (2 Feb 2025; 6 Feb 2025; 7 Feb 2025)

14. President Trump publicly attacked CBS and 60 Minutes, calling for termination of the network. Trump's demand that CBS and 60 Minutes be

"terminated" over alleged editing of an interview escalated rhetorical attacks on mainstream media's legitimacy. (7 Feb 2025)

15. CIA and Treasury officials handled sensitive personnel and financial system information in ways that raised security concerns. An unclassified CIA email listing new hires and a young engineer's direct access to Treasury systems highlighted vulnerabilities in how critical data and identities are protected from misuse. (5 Feb 2025; 6 Feb 2025; 7 Feb 2025)

16. ICE and local media created confusion and fear through enforcement actions and subsequent reporting battles. A Kern County raid and an FCC investigation into KCBS's coverage of immigration enforcement illustrated how enforcement and regulatory scrutiny can jointly shape public understanding of migration policy. (3 Feb 2025; 6 Feb 2025)

CHAPTER 4
WEEK 4 (8 FEB 2025 – 14 FEB 2025): DOGE AS PARALLEL STATECRAFT

Trump and Musk quietly converted the federal bureaucracy into a pliable, privatized instrument, using money, law, and memory to tilt power inward and downward.

This week reveals an aggressive acceleration of authoritarian structural change, focused on executive power, civil service purge, and information control, partly slowed by assertive courts and civil society. Trump and Musk's DOGE apparatus shifted from rhetoric to action: mass layoffs, buyout schemes, and a new hiring choke-point. These measures effectively politicize and reduce the federal workforce, while efforts to shut down or weaken USAID, Education, CFPB, NIH, NSF, NOAA, NASA DEI, and Social Security reshape the administrative state toward loyalist and private interests. At the same time, the administration paused FCPA enforcement, interfered in DOJ corruption cases, and hinted at possible debt repudiation, blending crony capitalism with legal impunity. On the right, immigration crackdowns, anti-trans orders, DEI erasure, and militarized ICE practices deepen division and stratify citizenship. The information space is highly contested: federal web purges, Pentagon school book removals, AP bans, and curated DOGE data coexist with court orders restoring health pages and halting NIH cuts. Internationally, Gaza annexation talk and resource-for-support demands on Ukraine reveal a transactional, destabilizing foreign policy. The judiciary, lawsuits from inspectors-general, state suits, and large-scale public campaigns create real but challenged counter-pressure.

Power and Authority

1. President Trump announced and executed a purge of Kennedy Center board leadership while declaring himself chair. By unilaterally firing Kennedy Center trustees and claiming the chairmanship, Trump asserted direct personal control over a national cultural institution, signaling willingness to override established governance norms for symbolic and political power. (8 Feb 2025)

2. President Trump issued an executive order prioritizing asylum for Afrikaners from South Africa. Prioritizing Afrikaner resettlement on disputed persecution grounds used asylum policy to favor a specific white ethnic group, reinforcing a hierarchy of belonging and politicizing humanitarian protection. (8 Feb 2025)

3. President Trump cut federal funding and ordered a stop-work for a Colorado immigrant legal services nonprofit. Halting funds for a key immigrant legal aid provider weakened access to counsel for undocumented people in removal proceedings, using executive power to narrow due process protections for a disfavored group. (9 Feb 2025)

4. President Trump ordered a halt to production of new pennies. Stopping penny production altered national currency policy by unilateral directive, illustrating the president's willingness to reshape everyday economic instruments without legislative debate. (9 Feb 2025)

5. President Trump prepared an executive order to reverse limits on bank overdraft fees and allow medical debt to affect credit scores. Reversing consumer protections on overdraft fees and medical debt would expand financial penalties on vulnerable borrowers, using executive authority to tilt market rules against low-income households. (9 Feb 2025)

6. President Trump signed an executive order pausing enforcement of the Foreign Corrupt Practices Act. Suspending FCPA enforcement weakened a core anti-bribery safeguard, signaling tolerance for corporate corruption abroad and privileging business interests over legal constraints on U.S. firms. (9 Feb 2025; 10 Feb 2025; 11 Feb 2025)

7. President Trump signed executive orders directing health agencies to scrub diversity-related terms and content from websites and research. Mandating removal of race, gender, disability and LGBTQ terms from health sites and proposals used executive power to constrain what public institutions can say about marginalized groups and health disparities. (10 Feb 2025)

8. President Trump issued an executive order directing review of all gun regulations to expand Second Amendment protections. Ordering a sweeping review of gun rules to favor expansive gun rights positioned the presidency to

reshape the balance between individual arms-bearing and collective public safety through unilateral action. (10 Feb 2025)

9. President Trump and Elon Musk repurposed the U.S. Digital Service into DOGE with authority to cancel payments, suspend programs, and target employees. Transforming a technical service unit into DOGE with sweeping, opaque power over spending and personnel created a parallel executive apparatus with limited oversight over core state functions. (10 Feb 2025)

10. President Trump issued an executive order eliminating the Federal Executive Institute. Closing the long-standing Federal Executive Institute removed a key training hub for senior civil servants, weakening professional development and signaling devaluation of a merit-based bureaucracy. (10 Feb 2025)

11. President Trump issued an executive order ending federal procurement and mandated use of paper straws. Reversing federal moves away from single-use plastics via executive order shifted environmental procurement policy by fiat, privileging industry preferences over prior sustainability commitments. (10 Feb 2025; 11 Feb 2025)

12. President Trump directed DOGE to identify over $1 billion in federal spending cuts in his first weeks in office. Using DOGE to rapidly cut more than $1 billion in spending concentrated budgetary discretion in a lightly accountable executive unit, bypassing normal deliberative processes over program priorities. (8 Feb 2025)

13. President Trump announced NIH funding cuts for cancer and other research programs through DOGE. Targeting NIH research budgets via DOGE used centralized executive power to weaken scientific capacity and public health infrastructure without legislative debate. (8 Feb 2025; 9 Feb 2025; 10 Feb 2025; 11 Feb 2025)

14. President Trump quietly exempted low-value Chinese imports from his announced tariffs. Exempting sub-$800 Chinese packages from tariffs undercut the stated rationale of a broad trade crackdown, illustrating discretionary, opaque use of tariff power with uneven economic effects. (8 Feb 2025)

15. President Trump and Budget Director Russ Vought moved to dismantle the Consumer Financial Protection Bureau by starving it of funds. Using budgetary control to effectively eliminate the CFPB weakened a key consumer watchdog, shifting financial regulation toward industry interests and away from ordinary borrowers' protections. (8 Feb 2025; 10 Feb 2025; 11 Feb 2025)

16. President Trump suggested the United States might not honor some Treasury debt obligations. Publicly questioning whether to honor U.S. debt

challenged constitutional commitments to public credit and injected executive uncertainty into global financial stability. (11 Feb 2025; 13 Feb 2025)

17. President Trump issued an executive order centralizing control over the diplomatic corps and Foreign Service under his direction. Requiring all foreign policy implementation to align tightly with presidential directives and reshaping Foreign Service personnel rules concentrated diplomatic authority in the executive and reduced professional independence. (12 Feb 2025)

18. President Trump signed an executive order establishing the Department of Government Efficiency workforce optimization initiative. Placing DOGE operatives over hiring and firing across agencies and imposing a one-for-four hiring cap centralized personnel power in a parallel structure, undermining traditional civil service protections. (13 Feb 2025)

19. President Trump froze large portions of federal science funding across agencies. Freezing broad science funding disrupted research nationwide and showed willingness to use executive control over grants as a blunt instrument, regardless of statutory expectations or institutional planning. (13 Feb 2025)

20. President Trump halted FEMA grants for firefighting and port security projects. Stopping FEMA grants for critical safety equipment leveraged executive control over emergency funds in ways that risked local preparedness and blurred lines between policy priorities and basic protection. (13 Feb 2025)

21. President Trump ordered the CIA to disclose a list of all hires from the previous two years. Compelling disclosure of recent CIA hires exposed intelligence personnel to risk and demonstrated presidential willingness to override standard secrecy norms governing national security staff. (13 Feb 2025)

22. President Trump paused permitting for solar and other renewable energy projects, including on private land. Halting renewable energy permits by executive directive disrupted local energy planning and signaled preference for centralized political control over long-term infrastructure investment decisions. (13 Feb 2025)

23. President Trump issued an executive order establishing the Make America Healthy Again Commission. Creating a presidential health commission positioned the White House to steer national health priorities and research framing, potentially bypassing existing expert-driven public health institutions. (13 Feb 2025)

24. President Trump signed an executive order pausing disbursement of LIHEAP and home energy rebate funds, causing surcharges for low-income customers. Freezing congressionally funded energy assistance shifted immediate costs onto low-income households and illustrated how executive

impoundment can function as de facto policy reversal without legislation. (13 Feb 2025)

25. President Trump announced a plan to seize and hold Gaza and relocate Palestinians elsewhere. Proposing U.S. seizure of Gaza and permanent removal of Palestinians framed foreign policy as territorial acquisition, disregarding self-determination norms and signaling openness to large-scale forced displacement. (10 Feb 2025; 13 Feb 2025)

26. President Trump announced 25% tariffs on steel and aluminum imports and ordered development of a broader reciprocal tariff plan. Imposing and planning expansive tariffs by presidential directive reoriented trade policy around unilateral executive decisions with significant downstream effects on prices, jobs, and international relations. (9 Feb 2025; 10 Feb 2025; 11 Feb 2025; 12 Feb 2025; 13 Feb 2025)

27. President Trump announced a 25% tariff on all steel and aluminum imports in a separate statement. A parallel announcement of 25% metal tariffs reinforced the administration's readiness to use trade tools aggressively, despite warnings of higher consumer costs and intra-party criticism. (9 Feb 2025)

28. President Trump established the National Energy Dominance Council by executive order. Creating a White House energy council to push domestic production and cut regulatory barriers centralized strategic energy decisions in a presidential advisory body with potential to favor extractive interests. (14 Feb 2025)

29. President Trump signed an executive order halting federal funding to schools and universities with COVID-19 vaccine mandates. Conditioning education funding on dropping vaccine mandates used fiscal leverage to weaken public health measures and pressure institutions to align with executive preferences on medical policy. (14 Feb 2025)

30. President Trump established the National Energy Dominance Council to coordinate pro-production energy policy. The new council embedded a pro-fossil-fuel agenda inside the Executive Office, enabling coordinated use of regulatory and fiscal tools to favor domestic extraction over environmental or climate concerns. (14 Feb 2025)

31. President Trump directed DOGE to meet with Pentagon officials to review defense spending. Bringing DOGE into Pentagon budget reviews extended Musk-aligned oversight into defense planning, raising questions about private influence over military priorities and security staffing. (14 Feb 2025)

32. Louisiana Department of Health leadership ended promotion of mass vaccination campaigns while continuing to provide vaccines. Ceasing proac-

tive vaccination outreach reframed immunization as a purely individual choice, likely lowering uptake and weakening collective disease prevention without formal legislative debate. (14 Feb 2025)

33. National Park Service removed references to transgender people from the Stonewall National Monument website under a sex-definition order. Erasing trans references from the Stonewall site implemented an executive sex-definition policy in public memory, narrowing official recognition of LGBTQ history and contributions. (14 Feb 2025)

Institutions and Governance

1. Senate Democrats announced plans to block all State Department nominees in response to Trump foreign aid cuts. Threatening to block State Department confirmations used Senate advice-and-consent powers to resist executive moves seen as undermining diplomacy and development programs. (8 Feb 2025)

2. Senator Angus King criticized Russell Vought's expansive view of presidential power and warned of constitutional erosion. King's public questioning of Vought's near-unlimited presidency doctrine highlighted legislative concern over appointments that could normalize executive dominance over checks and balances. (8 Feb 2025)

3. House of Representatives recorded a rules violation by Rep. Byron Donalds for proxy voting via his card. A member's use of his voting card by another person, contrary to rules he supported, underscored vulnerabilities in internal accountability mechanisms for legislative procedure. (8 Feb 2025)

4. U.S. District Judge Carl Nichols blocked the Trump administration from placing thousands of USAID employees on leave and from shutting down the agency. Nichols's orders halted an attempted mass sidelining of USAID staff, reinforcing judicial checks on executive efforts to disable a major foreign aid agency without adequate justification. (8 Feb 2025; 10 Feb 2025)

5. U.S. District Court in New York issued emergency orders blocking DOGE's access to Treasury systems and requiring destruction of downloaded data. Emergency injunctions against DOGE's Treasury access asserted judicial authority over executive data grabs, protecting financial records and signaling limits on Musk-aligned operatives. (8 Feb 2025; 10 Feb 2025; 14 Feb 2025)

6. Federal courts blocked the transfer of Venezuelan immigrants to Guantanamo Bay. Granting a restraining order against sending immigrants to

Guantanamo preserved access to normal legal processes and limited use of an offshore detention site for civil immigration enforcement. (8 Feb 2025)

7. Federal courts temporarily restored funding and operations for immigrant legal orientation and representation programs. By lifting a stop-work order on immigrant legal services, courts intervened to maintain due process infrastructure for noncitizens facing removal. (9 Feb 2025)

8. Chief Judge John J. McConnell Jr. ordered the Trump administration to immediately restore billions in frozen federal funding. McConnell's rulings enforcing prior restraining orders on funding freezes reaffirmed judicial power to compel executive compliance with appropriations law. (9 Feb 2025; 10 Feb 2025; 11 Feb 2025)

9. Federal courts blocked the Trump administration's attempt to cap NIH indirect research costs at 15%. Injunctions against NIH overhead cuts protected statutory funding structures and limited executive attempts to reshape research financing unilaterally. (10 Feb 2025; 11 Feb 2025)

10. Federal courts blocked President Trump's executive order ending birthright citizenship. Striking down an order targeting birthright citizenship upheld Fourteenth Amendment guarantees and constrained executive reinterpretation of constitutional status. (10 Feb 2025)

11. Federal courts ordered reinstatement of Hampton Dellinger as head of the Office of Special Counsel after his firing. Reinstating the whistleblower-protection chief pushed back against executive removal of an independent watchdog, reinforcing statutory protections for oversight roles. (10 Feb 2025; 11 Feb 2025)

12. Federal courts found the administration in violation of court orders on NIH funding freezes and compelled compliance. Rulings that NIH and the administration defied injunctions on funding freezes underscored judicial willingness to confront contempt and defend legal limits on executive impoundment. (11 Feb 2025; 12 Feb 2025)

13. Federal courts ordered federal health agencies to restore deleted web pages and datasets on HIV testing and contraception. Mandating restoration of removed health information reasserted transparency obligations and limited executive attempts to quietly erase sensitive public health guidance. (11 Feb 2025)

14. Federal courts maintained and later allowed aspects of the Trump administration's federal worker buyout program to proceed. Judicial handling of the "Fork in the Road" buyout plan—first blocking, then allowing it on standing grounds—shaped how far the executive can legally shrink the civil service via incentivized resignations. (10 Feb 2025; 11 Feb 2025; 13 Feb 2025)

15. Federal courts temporarily blocked Trump's executive order restricting

gender-affirming healthcare for transgender youth. Blocking the anti-trans health order preserved access to care while litigation proceeds, illustrating courts' role in checking discriminatory uses of federal funding leverage. (13 Feb 2025)

16. Federal courts ordered reinstatement of foreign aid funding and blocked impoundment of international assistance. Requiring release of foreign aid funds reaffirmed congressional control over appropriations and limited executive attempts to unilaterally suspend international commitments. (13 Feb 2025; 14 Feb 2025)

17. National Treasury Employees Union sued OMB Director Russell Vought over directives to shut down the CFPB. The union's lawsuit argued that dismantling the CFPB by OMB fiat usurped Congress's authority to create agencies, testing judicial willingness to police structural separation of powers. (11 Feb 2025)

18. Government Accountability Office reported large savings from its oversight work in FY 2023. GAO's documentation of high returns on oversight investment underscored the institutional value of independent auditing in constraining waste and abuse. (10 Feb 2025)

19. Senate confirmed Russell Vought as director of the Office of Management and Budget despite opposition. Confirming Vought, an architect of plans to demoralize and shrink the civil service, placed a committed executive-power maximalist in charge of budget execution and agency oversight. (10 Feb 2025)

20. DOGE leadership sought control over the Office of Personnel Management to reshape federal hiring. Moves to capture OPM would let DOGE reengineer civil service hiring toward ideological loyalty, weakening merit-based protections across the bureaucracy. (10 Feb 2025)

21. President Trump fired the director of the Office of Government Ethics. Removing the ethics office head reduced independent scrutiny of executive conduct, signaling intolerance for internal checks on conflicts of interest. (10 Feb 2025)

22. American Bar Association issued a statement condemning Trump administration actions as violating the rule of law. The ABA's institutional rebuke framed recent executive behavior as inconsistent with constitutional norms, adding professional-legal pressure for adherence to rule-of-law standards. (11 Feb 2025)

23. Five former Treasury secretaries warned in an op-ed that Trump's fiscal maneuvers threaten constitutional spending rules. Former Treasury leaders publicly argued that DOGE-driven impoundments and spending

freezes undermine Congress's exclusive power of the purse, highlighting systemic risks to fiscal governance. (11 Feb 2025)

24. City of Fremont, California passed an ordinance criminalizing camping on public property and aiding homeless encampments. Fremont's law used municipal authority to criminalize homelessness and assistance, raising concerns about local governance choices that penalize poverty rather than provide services. (12 Feb 2025)

25. North Carolina General Assembly Progressive Caucus introduced bills to limit immigration enforcement in sensitive locations. Proposed state legislation to restrict immigration enforcement at farms, schools, hospitals, and places of worship sought to use lawmaking to shield vulnerable communities from federal raids. (12 Feb 2025)

26. Supreme Court Justice Clarence Thomas was reported to have shifted from supporting to questioning New York Times v. Sullivan press protections. Thomas's evolving skepticism toward Sullivan signaled potential judicial openness to weakening longstanding First Amendment safeguards for reporting on public officials. (12 Feb 2025)

27. Eight former inspectors general filed a lawsuit challenging their dismissals by the Trump administration. The suit contested mass IG firings as unlawful, seeking to restore independent watchdogs and clarify legal limits on politically motivated removals. (12 Feb 2025)

28. U.S. Attorney's Office leadership saw multiple prosecutors resign after DOJ ordered dismissal of corruption charges against NYC Mayor Eric Adams. Resignations over politically directed dismissal of the Adams case exposed internal resistance to using prosecutorial discretion to serve executive immigration and political goals. (12 Feb 2025; 13 Feb 2025; 14 Feb 2025)

29. Pennsylvania Governor Josh Shapiro sued the Trump administration to compel release of over $3 billion in withheld federal funds. The state lawsuit challenged executive withholding of appropriated funds as unconstitutional, using litigation to defend state budgets and congressional spending authority. (14 Feb 2025)

30. Trump administration purged top leadership at the National Archives and Records Administration. Removing senior archives officials overseeing Trump records investigations threatened the independence of the nation's records custodian and oversight of presidential document handling. (14 Feb 2025)

Civil Rights and Dissent

1. Colorado ICE and SWAT teams conducted heavily armed raids in Denver-area apartments targeting alleged gang members, arresting mostly non-gang immigrants. Militarized raids that netted few confirmed gang members but many immigrants heightened fear in undocumented communities and blurred lines between targeted enforcement and broad intimidation. (9 Feb 2025)

2. Trump administration continued and publicized large-scale ICE arrests nationwide with limited transparency on who was detained. Arresting over 8,200 people in late January and releasing sparse data framed mass deportations as success while obscuring impacts on families and due process. (12 Feb 2025)

3. Border Czar Tom Homan criticized deportation numbers and sanctuary cities while planning more aggressive raids including against non-criminal immigrants. Calls for stepped-up enforcement against non-criminal undocumented residents and sanctuary jurisdictions signaled a punitive approach to immigration that treats presence itself as grounds for coercive action. (10 Feb 2025)

4. Federal courts blocked Trump's executive order banning transgender people from military service and restricting youth gender-affirming care. Judicial stays on anti-trans military and healthcare orders temporarily protected LGBTQ individuals from exclusionary policies that would have curtailed equal access to service and care. (11 Feb 2025; 13 Feb 2025)

5. Trump administration maintained and expanded mass deportation crackdowns that sparked protests in New York City. Nationwide immigration sweeps and visible ICE presence provoked street protests, illustrating how aggressive enforcement strategies strain community trust and mobilize dissent. (14 Feb 2025)

6. New York City Mayor Eric Adams announced plans and then moved to reopen an ICE office at Rikers Island jail despite sanctuary laws. Reestablishing ICE presence at Rikers rolled back local sanctuary protections, embedding federal immigration enforcement deeper into the criminal justice system. (13 Feb 2025; 14 Feb 2025)

7. Denver Public Schools filed a federal lawsuit challenging ICE access to schools under Trump policies. The district argued that ICE presence on campuses chilled attendance and learning, using litigation to defend students' rights and educational environments from immigration enforcement. (13 Feb 2025)

8. U.S. Department of Justice leadership ordered prosecutors to drop

corruption charges against NYC Mayor Eric Adams citing immigration cooperation needs. Linking dismissal of a corruption case to Adams's role in deportation efforts politicized prosecution decisions and suggested law enforcement outcomes can be traded for policy alignment. (13 Feb 2025; 14 Feb 2025)

9. Sangamon County and U.S. Department of Justice settled with the family of Sonya Massey and agreed to policing reforms after her killing by a deputy. The $10 million settlement and DOJ-backed training reforms acknowledged systemic policing failures, but also highlighted how accountability often comes only after lethal harm. (12 Feb 2025)

10. City of Fremont, California criminalized camping and aiding homeless encampments through a new ordinance. Fremont's law turned basic survival and mutual aid for unhoused people into jailable offenses, deepening the criminalization of poverty and those who assist the marginalized. (12 Feb 2025)

11. North Carolina activists and organizers planned a Disenfranchised Disco event to highlight 60,000 disenfranchised voters. The event sought to draw attention to large-scale voter disenfranchisement in North Carolina, using civic mobilization to contest structural barriers to representation. (12 Feb 2025)

12. North Carolina advocates raised alarms about potential interference in the state Supreme Court election. Concerns over partisan manipulation of a key judicial race underscored how electoral pressures on courts can shape future redistricting and voting rights decisions. (12 Feb 2025)

13. North Carolina Democratic Party organized a rally at the state legislature to oppose perceived anti-democratic bills. The planned rally exemplified civil society's use of public protest to influence legislative agendas and defend procedural norms. (12 Feb 2025)

14. Congresswoman Nancy Mace used a House floor speech to accuse several men, including her ex-fiancé, of rape and abuse and criticized state prosecutors' inaction. Mace's speech highlighted perceived failures of state justice systems to address sexual violence, using legislative privilege to press for accountability in sensitive criminal matters. (11 Feb 2025)

15. Gaza solidarity protesters and local authorities saw most charges against Gaza protesters dismissed after earlier arrests. The dismissal of charges suggested initial arrests may have overreached, illustrating how legal processes can both chill and later vindicate protest activity. (11 Feb 2025)

16. American Bar Association and former Treasury secretaries publicly warned that Trump's actions threaten rule-of-law and fiscal norms. Elite professional voices used public statements to defend constitutional spending

rules and legal standards, modeling institutional dissent against executive overreach. (11 Feb 2025)

17. Federal employees and civil servants shared personal accounts of their work amid fears of a purge. Public testimonies by federal workers sought to counter narratives of a hostile "deep state," defending the legitimacy of professional public service under political attack. (9 Feb 2025)

18. Congressional constituents flooded congressional phone lines with tens of millions of calls opposing Trump and Musk's dismantling of government structures. The unprecedented call volume demonstrated mass civic engagement and pressure on legislators to resist perceived authoritarian restructuring of the federal state. (8 Feb 2025)

19. Over 300,000 protesters in Munich rallied against the far-right AfD party and its anti-immigrant agenda. The large demonstration signaled robust public resistance to far-right, anti-immigrant politics in Germany, including those supported by prominent U.S. figures. (8 Feb 2025)

20. Kendrick Lamar halftime show performer and NFL security saw a performer detained and banned for life after waving a Sudan-Gaza flag but not charged. The lifetime ban for an on-field political gesture highlighted how private security regimes can sanction expressive conduct even when criminal law does not. (10 Feb 2025)

21. Trump administration abolished the FBI's Foreign Influence Task Force and a DOJ task force targeting Russian oligarchs. Dismantling units focused on foreign interference and oligarch sanctions weakened institutional defenses against external meddling in U.S. democracy and elite impunity. (13 Feb 2025)

22. Trump administration directed mass firing of probationary federal employees across agencies. Ordering near-total dismissal of probationary staff destabilized thousands of livelihoods and signaled that public employment is contingent on political winds, discouraging dissent within the bureaucracy. (12 Feb 2025; 13 Feb 2025)

23. Trump administration issued a memo on conditions for reinstating service members discharged over COVID vaccines. The memo's restrictive terms for reinstatement risked entrenching ideological tests around public health compliance within the military, affecting careers and morale. (12 Feb 2025)

24. U.S. Secretary of Defense Pete Hegseth announced a shift away from prioritizing European security toward the Indo-Pacific. Reorienting U.S. defense focus away from Europe placed more responsibility on allies for Ukraine and NATO, altering the security environment that underpins democratic resilience in the region. (12 Feb 2025)

Economic Structure

1. Mexican environmental regulators ordered cleanup and shutdown of unauthorized equipment at a hazardous waste-processing plant near Monterrey. Forcing a U.S.-linked waste processor to remediate toxic storage showed regulatory capacity to constrain cross-border industrial harms affecting community health and environmental justice. (8 Feb 2025)

2. National Institutes of Health leadership announced a new policy capping indirect costs on research grants at 15%. Capping overhead on NIH grants reallocated billions away from institutional support, threatening the financial viability of research infrastructure that underpins scientific and medical innovation. (8 Feb 2025; 9 Feb 2025; 11 Feb 2025)

3. DOGE and Trump administration announced over $1 billion in early spending cuts across federal programs. Rapidly cutting federal outlays through DOGE prioritized austerity and ideological targets over deliberative budgeting, with uncertain impacts on services and employment. (8 Feb 2025)

4. Trump administration moved to eliminate the Consumer Financial Protection Bureau's funding and operations. Defunding the CFPB shifted the financial regulatory landscape toward industry self-policing, weakening protections against predatory practices for consumers and small borrowers. (8 Feb 2025; 10 Feb 2025; 11 Feb 2025)

5. Republican state lawmakers and governors raised concerns about NIH funding cuts' impact on state programs. Republican officials' pushback against NIH overhead cuts highlighted how federal research dollars underpin local economies and services, complicating partisan support for austerity. (9 Feb 2025)

6. Trump administration announced retaliatory and reciprocal tariff plans and imposed 25% tariffs on steel and aluminum. The new tariff regime and reciprocal-tariff planning risked higher consumer prices and trade retaliation, using trade policy as a blunt economic tool with distributional consequences. (9 Feb 2025; 10 Feb 2025; 11 Feb 2025; 12 Feb 2025; 13 Feb 2025)

7. China imposed retaliatory tariffs on U.S. energy and equipment exports. China's counter-tariffs on U.S. LNG, coal, oil, and farm equipment escalated trade tensions, threatening export markets and jobs in affected sectors. (9 Feb 2025)

8. Trump administration halted federal investigations into Elon Musk's companies, including Tesla and SpaceX. Ending regulatory probes into Musk-linked firms signaled preferential treatment for politically connected corporations, weakening deterrence against safety or securities violations. (10 Feb 2025)

9. DOGE cut funding and staffing at the National Science Foundation. Reducing NSF resources undermined basic research capacity and long-term innovation, shifting the balance toward private or foreign funding for foundational science. (10 Feb 2025)

10. DOGE ordered substantial budget cuts at the National Oceanic and Atmospheric Administration. Planned NOAA cuts threatened weather forecasting and climate monitoring, weakening public goods that support disaster preparedness and economic planning. (8 Feb 2025; 10 Feb 2025)

11. DOGE targeted the Social Security Administration for review, risking payment disruptions. Scrutinizing SSA with an eye to cuts or suspensions put core social insurance payments at risk, heightening insecurity for retirees and disabled beneficiaries. (10 Feb 2025)

12. Trump administration and DOGE terminated nearly $1 billion in contracts at the Department of Education's Institute of Education Sciences. Eliminating IES contracts gutted federal education research and data collection, impairing evidence-based policymaking and public understanding of school performance. (11 Feb 2025)

13. Trump administration froze foreign funding and USAID programs supporting democracy and human rights monitoring. Halting USAID and related foreign funding weakened U.S. soft power and support for civil society abroad, with knock-on effects for global democratic resilience. (9 Feb 2025; 10 Feb 2025)

14. City of Altadena property market actors sold a burned lot in a historically Black neighborhood at a premium after a major wildfire. The high-priced sale of fire-ravaged land in a Black community raised concerns that disaster recovery dynamics would accelerate gentrification and displacement. (12 Feb 2025)

15. Uline management allegedly underpaid Mexican workers in U.S. warehouses using improper visas. Using tourist and B1 visas to import low-wage Mexican labor at a fraction of U.S. pay highlighted exploitation enabled by weak labor and immigration enforcement. (12 Feb 2025)

16. NYC Comptroller reported that federal authorities had seized local funds. Federal seizure of New York City funds raised alarms about central government using financial tools to pressure or punish local jurisdictions. (12 Feb 2025)

17. Musk-aligned officials at OPM obtained broad access to federal HR databases containing sensitive employee data. Granting private associates access to detailed personnel records blurred lines between regulatory oversight and corporate data mining, with implications for workplace power and privacy. (12 Feb 2025)

18. National Institutes of Health leadership acknowledged its funding freeze violated court orders and instructed staff to resume issuing grants. NIH's internal admission and reversal showed how legal pressure can restore lawful grant flows, but also revealed how easily executive directives can disrupt research financing. (12 Feb 2025)

19. DEA and multiple pharmaceutical and cannabis firms processed applications to manufacture or import controlled substances for research and production. DEA's handling of bulk manufacturing and import registrations for controlled substances shaped the balance between medical research, pharmaceutical supply, and diversion risks. (13 Feb 2025)

20. EPA received and fast-tracked an emergency exemption request to use potassium chloride against invasive mussels. Waiving normal comment periods for an emergency pesticide exemption illustrated regulatory flexibility in environmental crises, while narrowing public input on ecological tradeoffs. (10 Feb 2025)

21. EPA revised air quality designations for California's San Joaquin Valley to serious nonattainment. Updating PM2.5 designations tightened regulatory obligations on a major agricultural region, affecting industrial compliance costs and public health protections. (14 Feb 2025)

22. OSHA extended OMB approvals for several workplace safety information collection standards. Renewing data collection approvals for chemical and port safety rules maintained regulatory oversight mechanisms that protect workers while managing reporting burdens. (14 Feb 2025)

23. House Republicans proposed a budget resolution cutting $2 trillion from mandatory spending and food aid while expanding tax cuts. The GOP budget blueprint would shrink Social Security, Medicare, and SNAP while delivering large tax cuts to the wealthy, structurally redistributing resources upward. (13 Feb 2025)

24. President Trump pressed the Federal Reserve to cut interest rates and proposed new tax cuts and tariffs. Political pressure on the Fed and simultaneous tax-and-tariff proposals risked compromising monetary independence and amplifying inflationary or distributional shocks. (14 Feb 2025)

25. Trump administration implemented an executive order that caused $100 surcharges on Alabama low-income energy bills and halted home energy rebate programs. Energy policy changes that raised bills and canceled rebates for low-income households shifted economic risk onto vulnerable residents while preserving fiscal flexibility for the center. (13 Feb 2025)

Information, Memory, and Manipulation

1. Trump administration and federal agencies systematically removed DEI, LGBTQ health, and climate content from thousands of federal web pages. Coordinated deletion and alteration of diversity and climate information narrowed the public record on contested topics, using administrative control to reshape what citizens can easily learn from government sources. (10 Feb 2025)

2. National Security Agency leadership implemented a "Big Delete" of internal and public content containing 27 banned DEI-related words. Purging content with banned terms like "privilege" and "inclusion" to comply with executive orders embedded ideological filters into information systems, risking loss of mission-critical material. (10 Feb 2025)

3. Elon Musk reposted a tweet exposing personal information about a judge's daughter involved in a DOGE-related case. Amplifying doxxing of a judge's family member weaponized social media reach to intimidate the judiciary, blurring lines between online harassment and pressure on legal decision-makers. (10 Feb 2025)

4. Federal Election Commission canceled its scheduled open meeting. Calling off an open FEC meeting reduced opportunities for public observation of campaign finance oversight, contributing to opacity around electoral regulation. (10 Feb 2025)

5. Elon Musk's DOGE website added data from the Competitive Enterprise Institute's "unconstitutionality index" to its public materials. Featuring a partisan think tank's metric on a government site blurred distinctions between neutral transparency and ideological framing of regulation as illegitimate. (12 Feb 2025)

6. White House communications office barred AP reporters from certain press events and later banned AP journalists from the Oval Office and Air Force One over naming disputes. Retaliatory access bans against AP for refusing to adopt "Gulf of America" terminology punished editorial independence and signaled that coverage choices could cost institutional access. (12 Feb 2025; 14 Feb 2025)

7. Elon Musk's DOGE team published classified National Reconnaissance Office budget and personnel information on its website. Posting classified NRO data online breached secrecy norms and raised questions about how a quasi-private entity handles sensitive intelligence information. (13 Feb 2025; 14 Feb 2025)

8. Popular Information and Musk Watch sources reported that Musk associates had unprecedented access to federal HR databases with sensitive

employee data. Revelations about broad access to personnel files highlighted how data systems can be repurposed for surveillance or political vetting of civil servants. (12 Feb 2025)

9. Trump administration and NIH maintained an NIH funding freeze despite court injunctions, then internally admitted its illegality. Continuing an unlawful grant freeze and only later acknowledging it showed how executive actors can quietly defy judicial orders, obscuring the true state of public research funding. (11 Feb 2025; 12 Feb 2025)

10. ICE public affairs released daily arrest numbers without key details on locations or criminal histories. Selective ICE data releases framed enforcement as targeting criminals while omitting context needed to assess proportionality and rights impacts, shaping public perception through incomplete statistics. (12 Feb 2025)

11. Trump administration and NASA leadership implemented executive orders that closed NASA diversity offices and scrubbed DEI language from public sites. Removing DEI structures and language at NASA narrowed institutional commitment to inclusion and altered how the agency presents its workforce and mission to the public. (11 Feb 2025)

12. Department of Defense Education Activity suspended access to school library books for a compliance review targeting gender and equity topics. Closing Pentagon school libraries to review books on gender and equity imposed a content-based filter on educational materials for military families' children. (13 Feb 2025)

13. National Park Service removed transgender references from the Stonewall monument website under a binary sex-definition order. Editing Stonewall's official narrative to omit trans contributions rewrote a key civil rights story, aligning public memory with a restrictive legal definition of sex. (14 Feb 2025)

14. Trump administration purged leaders at the National Archives and Records Administration amid investigations into Trump's records. Leadership changes at the archives during active inquiries into presidential documents raised fears that archival integrity and access to historical records could be compromised. (14 Feb 2025)

15. Trump administration and DOGE used executive orders and internal directives to delete or alter health, DEI, and climate data across agencies. Cross-agency data scrubbing turned information systems into tools for ideological curation, limiting the evidentiary base for public debate and policy evaluation. (10 Feb 2025; 11 Feb 2025)

16. Greg Palast and voting rights advocates documented ongoing voter suppression tactics in the report "Trump Lost. Voter Suppression Won.". The

report argued that suppression strategies, not voter preferences alone, shaped electoral outcomes, informing public understanding of how procedural barriers distort representation. (9 Feb 2025)

17. Elon Musk and DOGE published classified NRO information and curated CEI metrics while federal investigations into Musk's firms were halted. The combination of leaked intelligence data, ideological metrics, and regulatory leniency illustrated how a powerful private actor could shape both information flows and enforcement outcomes from inside government. (10 Feb 2025; 12 Feb 2025; 13 Feb 2025; 14 Feb 2025)

18. Vice President JD Vance and European leaders traded accusations over democratic values and immigration at the Munich Security Conference. Vance's criticism of European democracies and defense of far-right allies contributed to a contested narrative about what counts as democratic governance in transatlantic discourse. (13 Feb 2025; 14 Feb 2025)

CHAPTER 5
WEEK 5 (15 FEB 2025 – 21 FEB 2025): THE STATE AS PERSONAL INSTRUMENT

Mass firings, data seizures, and cultural erasures turned the federal government into a more personal, less accountable tool of rule in a single dense week.

This week feels like a severe stress test for nearly every democratic safeguard. The Trump–Musk DOGE project pushes toward a de facto parallel state: mass dismissals across health, environmental, safety, and foreign aid agencies; aggressive efforts to seize IRS, SSA, and education data; and court rulings that mostly approve the purge. Executive orders take control over independent regulators, reinterpret legality through the lens of the unitary executive, and weaponize budget freezes and deregulation against Congress's powers. At the same time, the justice system leans toward impunity for allies and increases pressure on critics: corruption charges against Eric Adams are dropped due to political influence, protections for whistleblowers and watchdogs are attacked, and Kash Patel is appointed to shift the FBI's focus. Information is further restricted through bans and lawsuits against AP, ideological cleansing in military schools and federal websites, and erasing LGBTQ+ and Black history. Abroad, U.S. policy favors Russia and China at Ukraine's expense, through resource grabs and exclusionary peace talks. Civil society, unions, states, and some courts push back, but the overall structure this week strongly consolidates an authoritarian shift.

Power and Authority

1. President Trump signed an executive order empowering Elon Musk's Doge committee to shrink the federal workforce. Granting a private-led committee authority over federal staffing concentrated executive power in an unelected actor and weakened normal civil service and oversight channels. (15 Feb 2025)

2. President Trump announced mass layoffs in federal health agencies including CDC and HHS. Firing thousands of health officials, including epidemic intelligence officers, reduced state capacity to manage disease threats and increased executive leverage over a weakened bureaucracy. (15 Feb 2025)

3. President Trump threatened to revoke parole and Temporary Protected Status programs for Ukrainians and ordered a TPS review. Threatening legal status for Ukrainians and other TPS holders used immigration powers to create insecurity for large groups whose rights depend on executive discretion. (15 Feb 2025)

4. President Trump denied Georgia's request to extend the deadline for federal disaster assistance applications after Hurricane Helene. Refusing more time for Georgia communities to seek disaster aid showed how federal relief can be used selectively, affecting equal treatment of states and localities. (15 Feb 2025)

5. President Trump issued an order ending federal support for school COVID-19 vaccine mandates tied to discretionary funds. Barring federal funds for schools with COVID-19 vaccine mandates shifted public health decisions toward ideological control and constrained local authorities' ability to protect students. (15 Feb 2025)

6. President Trump froze federal spending in defiance of statutory program requirements. Imposing an across-the-board spending freeze contrary to appropriations law undermined Congress's power of the purse and normalized unilateral budget control. (16 Feb 2025)

7. President Trump oversaw mass firings of federal employees across multiple agencies under a workforce reduction initiative. Sweeping dismissals at agencies like Agriculture, EPA, VA, Forest Service, HHS and others weakened neutral administration and increased political dependence among remaining staff. (16 Feb 2025; 18 Feb 2025; 21 Feb 2025)

8. President Trump called for the immediate closure of the Department of Education. Seeking to abolish the Education Department threatened federal support for low-income and disabled students and signaled hostility to a key public institution. (16 Feb 2025; 19 Feb 2025)

9. President Trump signed an executive order appointing Elon Musk to

oversee large federal workforce reductions. Delegating broad downsizing authority to a private ally blurred lines between public office and private influence and accelerated politicization of the civil service. (16 Feb 2025)

10. President Trump declared "Gulf of America Day" and ordered the Gulf of Mexico renamed. Unilaterally renaming a major body of water asserted symbolic control over national language and pressured institutions and media to adopt politically driven terminology. (15 Feb 2025; 16 Feb 2025)

11. President Trump instituted a federal spending freeze affecting disaster and other aid programs. Using a freeze to halt congressionally mandated programs challenged legal limits on executive impoundment and risked withholding essential services for political or ideological reasons. (16 Feb 2025)

12. President Trump ordered the Justice Department to dismiss all remaining Biden-appointed US attorneys. Forcing out prosecutors appointed by the prior administration consolidated presidential control over federal prosecutions and weakened norms of Justice Department independence. (19 Feb 2025; 20 Feb 2025)

13. President Trump issued an executive order directing agencies to rescind or ignore regulations deemed unconstitutional or beyond statutory authority. Telling agencies to unilaterally downgrade or stop enforcing rules reinterpreted constitutional limits through the executive branch, bypassing courts and Congress. (19 Feb 2025)

14. President Trump issued an executive order to reduce the federal bureaucracy and shrink or terminate several entities. Ordering cuts to entities like the African Development Foundation and Institute of Peace restructured public functions by decree, reducing independent policy capacity. (19 Feb 2025)

15. President Trump signed an executive order restricting access to federal benefits for undocumented immigrants. Tightening benefit eligibility for undocumented residents used social programs as an enforcement tool and deepened stratification of rights by legal status. (19 Feb 2025; 20 Feb 2025)

16. President Trump suggested publicly that he might run for a third presidential term. Questioning constitutional term limits in front of an audience normalized the idea of extending personal rule beyond established democratic constraints. (20 Feb 2025)

17. President Trump threatened to cut federal funding to Maine over compliance with his transgender sports ban. Using federal funds to coerce a state into adopting contested social policy challenged state autonomy and targeted transgender participation in public life. (21 Feb 2025)

18. President Trump oversaw pardons for individuals convicted in the

January 6 Capitol attack. Granting clemency to January 6 offenders signaled tolerance for violence against democratic institutions and weakened deterrence for future attacks. (20 Feb 2025)

19. President Trump fired Joint Chiefs of Staff chair CQ Brown Jr. and other top military officials. Removing senior military leaders over diversity and ideological disagreements risked politicizing the chain of command and undermining professional military norms. (21 Feb 2025)

Institutions and Governance

1. US Forest Service and National Park Service terminated thousands of probationary employees under a federal spending cut initiative. Large-scale layoffs at land management agencies reduced capacity for park maintenance and wildfire response, weakening long-term stewardship of public lands. (15 Feb 2025; 21 Feb 2025)

2. Congressional Republicans and Democrats entered a standoff over a funding bill with a looming government shutdown. A partisan impasse over funding, amid executive freezes and cuts, threatened basic government operations and highlighted stress on budgetary governance. (15 Feb 2025)

3. Federal court approved Elon Musk's voluntary buyout offer for most federal employees. Judicial approval of mass buyouts facilitated rapid downsizing of the civil service, reinforcing executive-led restructuring of the bureaucracy. (15 Feb 2025)

4. Trump administration defied multiple federal court orders intended to halt contested executive actions. Ignoring injunctions against policies like funding freezes and citizenship changes eroded judicial authority and the expectation that court rulings bind the executive. (15 Feb 2025; 16 Feb 2025)

5. Department of Justice leadership pressured Public Integrity Section lawyers to choose who would dismiss the Eric Adams indictment under threat of firing. Forcing prosecutors to pick a colleague to drop a corruption case under duress politicized prosecutorial decisions and undermined internal ethical safeguards. (15 Feb 2025)

6. Public Integrity Section lawyers resigned after being ordered to dismiss corruption charges against New York Mayor Eric Adams. Mass resignations in response to political interference signaled internal resistance but also left the Justice Department with fewer independent voices. (15 Feb 2025)

7. Acting US Attorney Danielle Sassoon resigned in protest over the order to drop federal corruption charges against Mayor Eric Adams. A top prosecutor's resignation over a politically driven dismissal highlighted threats to prosecutorial independence in high-profile cases. (15 Feb 2025; 18 Feb 2025)

8. DC Court of Appeals rejected Trump's request to lift an injunction protecting Hampton Dellinger from firing. By keeping the whistleblower watchdog in place, the appeals court temporarily preserved an independent check on executive abuses affecting federal employees. (15 Feb 2025)

9. Judge Tanya Chutkan scheduled an emergency hearing on states' motion to block DOGE job and program cuts. Fast-tracking review of DOGE-driven cuts showed courts acting as a venue for states to contest sweeping executive restructuring of federal programs. (15 Feb 2025)

10. Equal Employment Opportunity Commission moved to dismiss six gender-identity discrimination cases citing a new sex-definition order. Abandoning pending cases narrowed federal enforcement of workplace protections for transgender workers and reinterpreted civil rights law along executive lines. (16 Feb 2025)

11. Government employee unions filed lawsuits challenging mass federal workforce reductions as procedurally unlawful. Union suits sought to enforce reduction-in-force rules and preserve due process in federal employment against rapid politically driven purges. (16 Feb 2025)

12. Trump administration appealed to the Supreme Court to uphold firing of whistleblower watchdog Hampton Dellinger. Asking the Court to validate removal of the Office of Special Counsel chief tested limits on presidential power over independent oversight bodies. (16 Feb 2025; 17 Feb 2025)

13. Denise Cheung resigned as Criminal Division Chief in DC after refusing to open a politically ordered probe. Her resignation over an unsupported investigation into a prior administration contract underscored pressure to weaponize prosecutions for partisan ends. (17 Feb 2025)

14. Federal judge declined to block DOGE from accessing Education Department data systems. Allowing continued access to sensitive education data by a politically directed unit weakened judicial checks on executive data consolidation. (17 Feb 2025)

15. Federal judge temporarily blocked firing of 11 DEI staffers at CIA and ODNI. Protecting diversity staff from immediate dismissal signaled judicial concern over potentially discriminatory purges in national security agencies. (18 Feb 2025)

16. US Department of Justice moved to dismiss the corruption indictment of New York Mayor Eric Adams, prompting judicial scrutiny. Seeking dismissal of a major corruption case for policy reasons, and facing pointed questions from the judge, highlighted tensions over politicized prosecutorial discretion. (17 Feb 2025; 19 Feb 2025)

17. Joshua Fisher, Director of the Office of Administration told a court that Elon Musk is only a senior advisor without formal decision-making author-

ity. Downplaying Musk's formal role in litigation sought to shield extensive de facto influence from constitutional scrutiny and Senate confirmation requirements. (19 Feb 2025)

18. Federal judge declined to issue a restraining order blocking mass federal worker firings. Refusing to halt the purge allowed the administration's restructuring of the civil service to proceed while unions were redirected to slower administrative channels. (19 Feb 2025; 20 Feb 2025; 21 Feb 2025)

19. House Budget Committee Republicans advanced a budget blueprint extending tax cuts and cutting Medicare, Medicaid and nutrition programs. The proposed budget shifted fiscal priorities toward high-income taxpayers while reducing social safety nets, reshaping distributive policy through partisan control. (16 Feb 2025)

20. Representative Claudia Tenney introduced legislation to make Donald Trump's birthday a federal holiday. Proposing a personal holiday for a sitting president used statutory symbolism to elevate an individual leader within national civic rituals. (16 Feb 2025)

21. Vermont and New York legislatures enacted climate superfund laws making fossil fuel companies pay for climate damages. State laws to recover climate costs from polluters asserted subnational authority to regulate powerful industries when federal policy moved in the opposite direction. (18 Feb 2025)

22. Coalition of 22 red states and oil trade groups sued to block New York's climate superfund law. The lawsuit sought to curb state-level climate accountability and preserve industry-friendly regulatory baselines, testing federalism boundaries. (18 Feb 2025)

23. Federal judge rejected youth climate activists' lawsuit against the EPA. Dismissing claims that EPA climate policy violated youths' constitutional rights underscored the difficulty of using courts to force systemic climate action. (18 Feb 2025)

24. Federal appeals courts denied the Trump administration's attempts to reinstate a birthright citizenship ban. Keeping injunctions in place preserved 14th Amendment birthright citizenship and checked an executive effort to redefine constitutional membership. (20 Feb 2025; 21 Feb 2025)

25. Federal judge allowed the Trump administration to furlough over 2,000 USAid workers. Permitting large furloughs at the foreign aid agency weakened US development capacity and signaled judicial deference to executive staffing decisions. (21 Feb 2025)

26. Senators Ron Wyden and Elizabeth Warren demanded information from the IRS about DOGE's access to taxpayer data. Senate oversight letters challenged opaque data-sharing with a politically connected unit,

seeking to reassert legislative control over sensitive information. (19 Feb 2025)

27. North Carolina legislature advanced SB 58 to limit the state attorney general's power to challenge presidential actions. Restricting the attorney general's authority to sue over federal illegality weakened a key state-level check on executive overreach. (19 Feb 2025)

28. Congress previously passed a law requiring Senate approval before any US withdrawal from NATO. Statutory limits on unilateral NATO exit strengthened legislative control over treaty commitments amid renewed presidential threats to alliances. (21 Feb 2025)

29. Senate Republicans and President Trump clashed over competing budget plans as Trump endorsed a House proposal with deep benefit cuts. The president's backing of a more extreme House budget disrupted Senate negotiations and increased the risk of a shutdown-driven governance crisis. (19 Feb 2025; 20 Feb 2025)

30. Federal Election Commission scheduled a closed Sunshine Act meeting on enforcement and civil actions. The FEC's planned compliance meeting reflected ongoing, if opaque, enforcement of campaign finance rules central to electoral integrity. (20 Feb 2025)

31. National Archives and Records Administration announced a FOIA Advisory Committee meeting to discuss reform and implementation. Convening a FOIA advisory meeting supported transparency norms and public input on access-to-records policy amid broader secrecy pressures. (18 Feb 2025)

Civil Rights and Dissent

1. Department of Justice fired more than two dozen immigration judges and candidates amid a case backlog. Removing immigration judges and new hires strained adjudication capacity and risked politicizing decisions affecting immigrants' legal rights. (15 Feb 2025)

2. Protesters in New York City demonstrated against removal of "TQ+" from the Stonewall National Monument website. Public protest over erasing transgender references from a landmark site defended LGBTQ+ recognition and historical memory. (15 Feb 2025)

3. Students at a Department of Defense school in Germany walked out during Pete Hegseth's visit to oppose DEI content removals. A student walkout challenged top-down censorship of diversity materials in military schools and asserted youth voice in education policy. (15 Feb 2025)

4. Five defendants in New York were charged with the murder of transgender

man Sam Nordquist after prolonged abuse. The prosecution of a brutal killing of a transgender man highlighted ongoing violence against LGBTQ+ people and the justice system's role in addressing hate-motivated crimes. (16 Feb 2025)

5. Democratic leaders and grassroots groups organized nationwide protests against DOGE-driven budget cuts. Coordinated demonstrations outside congressional offices and Tesla dealerships showed organized resistance to perceived illegal austerity measures. (16 Feb 2025; 17 Feb 2025)

6. Immigration and Customs Enforcement detained immigrants at courthouses and check-ins, including DACA recipients, under daily arrest quotas. Arresting people who complied with legal processes at courts and check-ins weaponized enforcement in ways likely to deter participation in the justice system. (18 Feb 2025)

7. National Labor Relations Board under the Trump administration fired board member Gwynne Wilcox in an unlawful manner. Removing a pro-worker NLRB member weakened enforcement of labor rights and signaled hostility to union protections. (18 Feb 2025)

8. Department of Defense Education Activity ordered censorship of curricula and removal of materials on women, minorities and LGBTQ people in military schools. Banning content on gender, race and civil rights in DoD schools curtailed students' exposure to diverse histories and identities under government authority. (18 Feb 2025)

9. Occupational Safety and Health Administration ordered destruction and removal of workplace safety publications flagged for DEIA-related terms. Purging safety documents, including one on transgender restroom access, reduced access to guidance and intertwined workplace safety with ideological censorship. (17 Feb 2025)

10. Trump administration cut off legal aid for unaccompanied immigrant children before later reversing the decision. Temporarily denying counsel to unaccompanied minors in immigration proceedings exposed a vulnerable group to proceedings without adequate legal protection. (18 Feb 2025)

11. General Services Administration staff resigned after a Musk ally sought access to Notify.gov messaging data. Resignations over a request for mass-messaging access reflected internal alarm about potential misuse of citizen contact data for political purposes. (19 Feb 2025)

12. Federal workers and Representative Alexandria Ocasio-Cortez rallied outside the SpaceX building in Washington to protest Musk's policies. A large demonstration by federal employees against DOGE cuts highlighted workplace dissent against perceived privatization and profiteering. (19 Feb 2025)

13. Protesters across the United States held mass demonstrations against

Trump administration actions seen as undermining democracy and alliances. Nationwide protests signaled broad civic mobilization in defense of democratic norms and international commitments. (19 Feb 2025)

14. National Park Service removed references to transgender people from Stonewall National Monument webpages. Erasing transgender references from a key LGBTQ+ historic site diminished official recognition of a marginalized group's role in civil rights history. (16 Feb 2025; 19 Feb 2025)

15. Federal agencies scrubbed mentions of Black people from some federal websites during Black History Month. Removing Black history content from official sites during a commemorative month signaled state-driven marginalization of racial minorities' contributions. (19 Feb 2025)

16. President Trump and Senate Republicans secured Senate passage of a budget resolution funding a mass deportation plan. Allocating $175 billion for border security and deportations embedded large-scale removal of immigrants into federal spending priorities. (21 Feb 2025)

17. President Trump ended federal benefits for undocumented immigrants through executive order. Cutting access to public benefits for undocumented residents deepened a tiered system of rights and heightened vulnerability for targeted communities. (20 Feb 2025)

18. President Trump oversaw reassignment and firing of top ICE officials to increase deportations. Leadership changes at ICE aimed at boosting arrest numbers reinforced a punitive enforcement posture toward immigrants. (20 Feb 2025; 21 Feb 2025)

19. US Marshals Service deputized Elon Musk's private security guards to carry weapons on federal property. Granting law enforcement powers to private security blurred lines between public policing and private protection of elite figures. (20 Feb 2025)

20. DC US Attorney Ed Martin launched Operation Whirlwind to investigate threats against officials, including inquiries into critical lawmakers. A threat-focused initiative that scrutinized critical speech by legislators and media risked chilling political expression under the guise of security. (19 Feb 2025)

21. Enrique Tarrio was arrested for assaulting a protester near the US Capitol after receiving clemency for January 6 crimes. The re-arrest of a pardoned January 6 leader underscored ongoing tensions around accountability for political violence and the effects of earlier clemency. (20 Feb 2025; 21 Feb 2025)

22. CPAC organizers ejected several January 6 defendants from the conference without explanation. Removing January 6 participants from a major

conservative gathering reflected internal disputes over how openly to embrace those involved in the attack. (20 Feb 2025)

23. Trump administration fired hundreds of federal employees including many veterans amid health crises. Targeting probationary staff and veterans at agencies like USDA and CDC during outbreaks weakened both worker security and public health response. (19 Feb 2025; 21 Feb 2025)

24. Veterans Affairs and DOGE fired disabled veteran and VA employee Luke Graziani. Dismissing a disabled veteran working at VA raised concerns about how workforce cuts affected those the agency is meant to serve. (17 Feb 2025)

Economic Structure

1. National Endowment for the Arts under the Trump administration canceled diversity, equity and inclusion-focused grants and barred DEI-related programs from funding. Restricting arts grants based on DEI content steered public cultural funding away from marginalized communities and toward ideologically favored projects. (16 Feb 2025)

2. House Budget Committee Republicans and President Trump promoted budget plans extending tax cuts for the wealthy while cutting social programs. Budget blueprints that expand deficits through high-end tax cuts and reduce Medicare, Medicaid and nutrition aid entrenched inequality and favored capital over labor. (16 Feb 2025; 19 Feb 2025; 21 Feb 2025)

3. Trump administration prepared new tariffs on trading partners despite inflation concerns. Planned tariffs risked trade retaliation and job losses, using trade policy as a blunt political tool with broad economic consequences. (16 Feb 2025)

4. Department of Government Efficiency sought access to sensitive IRS taxpayer information systems. Efforts to tap IRS data for a politically directed unit raised risks that financial information could be used to reward allies or target opponents. (16 Feb 2025; 17 Feb 2025; 19 Feb 2025)

5. Trump administration took control of the Kennedy Center and installed loyalists in leadership. A hostile takeover of a major cultural institution redirected public arts resources toward regime-aligned narratives and away from independent governance. (16 Feb 2025)

6. Tesla sued Chinese car owners, bloggers and media over complaints and criticism. Using courts in an authoritarian context to punish critics illustrated how corporate power can leverage state systems to chill consumer speech. (15 Feb 2025)

7. Trump Media & Technology Group reported large financial losses and

minimal revenue. Persistent losses at a politically connected media firm highlighted dependence on investor enthusiasm rather than sustainable market demand. (15 Feb 2025)

8. USDA and FDA leadership fired staff reviewing Elon Musk's Neuralink operations. Removing regulators overseeing a politically connected company risked weakening safety oversight in favor of private interests. (17 Feb 2025)

9. SpaceX representatives visited the FAA command center to review air traffic control systems. Allowing a regulated company close access to core regulatory systems blurred boundaries between regulator and regulated, raising conflict-of-interest concerns. (17 Feb 2025)

10. Louis DeJoy resigned early as Postmaster General. His early departure opened the way for new leadership at USPS amid reports of plans to restructure governance and potential executive takeover. (17 Feb 2025)

11. Trump administration canceled collective bargaining agreements and rescinded protections for federal workers and contractors. Unilaterally voiding labor agreements and protections weakened worker bargaining power and made federal employment more precarious. (18 Feb 2025)

12. Trump administration rolled back environmental protections and pledged expanded oil drilling. Scaling back climate safeguards and favoring fossil fuel extraction shifted regulatory benefits toward powerful energy interests at public expense. (18 Feb 2025)

13. President Trump signed an executive order expanding access to in vitro fertilization by seeking ways to reduce costs. Directing policy work to lower IVF costs modestly expanded access to a reproductive technology, though without immediate funding commitments. (18 Feb 2025)

14. Trump administration fast-tracked fossil fuel infrastructure permits under an "energy emergency" designation. Creating an emergency permit track for hundreds of projects weakened environmental review and favored rapid private development over public input. (19 Feb 2025; 20 Feb 2025)

15. Federal Aviation Administration fired hundreds of employees responsible for air traffic communications and systems. Cutting key technical staff risked degrading aviation safety and showed how workforce reductions can endanger critical infrastructure. (16 Feb 2025)

16. USDA mistakenly fired bird flu response officials as part of workforce cuts and then tried to rehire them. Erroneous dismissals during a disease outbreak illustrated how rushed downsizing can undermine essential public health functions. (19 Feb 2025; 21 Feb 2025)

17. Elon Musk called for defunding the International Space Station after a dispute over astronaut return plans. Urging cuts to a major international

research platform highlighted tensions between private space interests and publicly funded scientific cooperation. (19 Feb 2025)

18. Trump administration moved to revoke federal approval for New York City's congestion pricing program. Threatening a locally designed congestion-pricing scheme used federal leverage to block a city's environmental and revenue policy. (19 Feb 2025)

19. President Trump froze funding for electric vehicle subsidies and CHIPS Act implementation. Halting support for EVs and semiconductor manufacturing reversed industrial policy aimed at technological competitiveness and climate goals. (20 Feb 2025)

20. Congressman Nick Begich told constituents he was powerless to stop DOGE-driven budget cuts while supporting the DOGE caucus. A lawmaker's deference to executive cuts that cost local federal jobs illustrated how representation can be subordinated to centralized fiscal agendas. (20 Feb 2025)

21. Trump administration proposed cuts to Social Security, Medicare, Medicaid and food assistance programs. Targeting core social insurance programs for reductions shifted fiscal burdens onto vulnerable populations while citing unsubstantiated waste claims. (21 Feb 2025)

22. University of Michigan survey researchers reported a sharp drop in US consumer confidence linked to tariff concerns. Falling consumer sentiment in response to tariff policy signaled public anxiety about economic management and potential downturn risks. (20 Feb 2025)

23. Defense Secretary Pete Hegseth ordered Pentagon leaders to plan for an 8% defense budget cut over five years. Planning sizable defense cuts while publicly backing higher spending created uncertainty about long-term military capacity and strategic commitments. (20 Feb 2025)

24. Trump administration considered repealing tariffs on China in exchange for purchase promises. Potentially trading away leverage for unenforceable purchase pledges risked favoring Chinese economic interests without clear gains for US workers. (20 Feb 2025)

25. President Trump proposed a US-China deal to halve military spending for both countries. Suggesting symmetric cuts despite opaque Chinese budgets risked weakening US deterrence more than China's, with implications for global security. (20 Feb 2025)

26. Drug Enforcement Administration and multiple pharmaceutical firms processed applications for manufacturing and importing controlled substances for research and commerce. Routine DEA registration notices for controlled substances reflected ongoing regulatory oversight of pharmaceutical supply and research. (18 Feb 2025)

27. Occupational Safety and Health Administration extended OMB

approval for information collection under the MDA construction standard. Maintaining data collection for a hazardous chemical standard supported enforcement of workplace safety rules in construction. (18 Feb 2025)

28. Federal Communications Commission amended the FM allotments table to remove and reinstate various channels. Technical updates to FM frequency allocations adjusted broadcasting markets and spectrum use without major policy shifts. (19 Feb 2025)

29. US Census Bureau sought public comment on the 2026 Government Units Survey and CPS 2025 field test. Planned surveys to update government unit data and modernize population survey methods underpinned evidence-based policymaking. (20 Feb 2025)

30. Environmental Protection Agency withdrew a direct final rule on Utah's hazardous waste program after adverse comments. Pulling back a rule in response to feedback showed environmental regulation still subject to public comment and revision processes. (20 Feb 2025)

31. Environmental Protection Agency extended comment periods and announced availability of environmental impact statements for major projects. Extending comment windows and publishing EIS notices supported public participation in environmental decision-making on water quality and infrastructure. (21 Feb 2025)

32. Federal Communications Commission finalized rules improving accessibility of video programming interfaces for people with hearing disabilities. Requiring accessible caption controls advanced disability rights and inclusive access to media services. (21 Feb 2025)

Information, Memory, and Manipulation

1. Doge committee representatives gained access to sensitive payment and contracting systems at health agencies. Allowing a politically directed unit into core health IT systems risked misuse of data and undermined established safeguards on federal information. (15 Feb 2025)

2. White House and Trump administration banned Associated Press journalists from the White House, Oval Office and Air Force One over naming disputes. Excluding a major newswire for refusing to adopt "Gulf of America" punished independent editorial standards and narrowed press access to power. (15 Feb 2025; 16 Feb 2025; 20 Feb 2025)

3. Elon Musk called for imprisonment of journalists over critical coverage of the administration. Publicly urging jail for reporters signaled elite hostility to investigative journalism and could intimidate media scrutiny. (16 Feb 2025)

4. President Trump misrepresented the 14th Amendment as only covering

formerly enslaved people. Falsely narrowing the scope of birthright citizenship on social media spread constitutional misinformation that could justify restrictive policies. (16 Feb 2025)

5. State Department leadership ordered global diplomatic posts to cancel most media subscriptions deemed non-mission critical. Cutting off broad media access for diplomats limited their information sources and increased reliance on centrally approved narratives. (19 Feb 2025; 20 Feb 2025)

6. Occupational Safety and Health Administration removed and destroyed online and physical safety publications flagged for DEIA-related terms. Deleting safety documents, many unrelated to DEI, sanitized official records and reduced public access to workplace guidance. (17 Feb 2025)

7. Department of Defense Education Activity ordered book removals and curriculum changes to eliminate materials on gender and equity ideology. Purging books and lessons on gender, Black history and LGBTQ topics from military school libraries reshaped civic education toward a narrower, state-approved narrative. (18 Feb 2025)

8. National Park Service under the Trump administration removed transgender references from Stonewall National Monument webpages. Editing official descriptions of Stonewall to omit transgender people rewrote public history of the LGBTQ+ rights movement. (16 Feb 2025; 19 Feb 2025)

9. President Trump renamed the Gulf of Mexico as the Gulf of America and promoted the change through proclamations. Imposing a new name on a major geographic feature sought to reshape national symbolism and test media compliance with executive language. (16 Feb 2025)

10. Michelle King, acting SSA Commissioner resigned rather than grant DOGE access to Social Security beneficiaries' sensitive data. Her departure highlighted internal resistance to expansive data sharing that could enable surveillance or targeting of millions of Americans. (17 Feb 2025; 18 Feb 2025)

11. Senators and journalists exposed inaccuracies in DOGE's claims of canceling $16 billion in wasteful contracts. Revelations that touted savings were vastly overstated undermined official narratives used to justify aggressive cuts and data grabs. (19 Feb 2025; 21 Feb 2025)

12. Congressman Nick Begich amplified false claims that millions of centenarians receive Social Security benefits and that DOGE uncovered massive illegality. Spreading debunked statistics about Social Security beneficiaries fueled distrust in public programs and bolstered DOGE's justification for cuts. (20 Feb 2025)

13. Robert F. Kennedy Jr. as HHS Secretary continued anti-vaccine rhetoric and announced a panel to review childhood vaccine schedules.

Week 5 (15 Feb 2025 – 21 Feb 2025): The State as Personal Instrument

Using a top health post to question established vaccination science risked undermining public trust and uptake during active outbreaks. (19 Feb 2025)

14. Heather Cox Richardson and commentators reflected on presidential honesty and disinformation on Presidents Day. Public commentary contrasted historic expectations of truthful leadership with current disinformation, helping contextualize democratic norms for readers. (18 Feb 2025)

15. Federal Communications Commission announced a CSRIC IX meeting on communications security and reliability. Advisory work on communications resilience supported secure information infrastructure, a prerequisite for reliable public communication. (20 Feb 2025)

16. Associated Press filed lawsuits challenging its exclusion from White House events. AP's legal actions sought judicial protection for press access and signaled institutional pushback against retaliatory bans. (20 Feb 2025; 21 Feb 2025)

17. Vice President J.D. Vance was accused of spreading Russia-aligned propaganda undermining Western democracy. Allegations that the vice president echoed adversary narratives raised concerns about elite-driven disinformation shaping foreign policy debates. (19 Feb 2025)

18. Trump administration removed grants and support for scientific research using the term "climate" and scrubbed climate references from websites. Defunding and erasing climate-related research and language suppressed scientific information about environmental risks from public view. (21 Feb 2025)

19. Trump administration removed references to Black Americans from some federal websites during Black History Month. Scrubbing Black history content from official sites during a commemorative period exemplified state curation of memory that sidelines disfavored narratives. (19 Feb 2025)

20. Trump administration issued executive orders reshaping NIH, including communication blackouts and blocking grant review committees. Restricting NIH communications and peer review processes disrupted scientific information flows and centralized control over research agendas. (20 Feb 2025)

21. Federal Communications Commission corrected a date error in a hazardous air pollutant rule. Fixing a regulatory typo ensured accurate implementation of air quality standards, supporting clarity in environmental information. (19 Feb 2025)

CHAPTER 6
WEEK 6 (22 FEB 2025 – 28 FEB 2025): BUREAUCRACY AS PATRONAGE ENGINE

A week of quiet decrees turned the civil service, immigration system, and information sphere into instruments of loyalty, wealth, and curated memory.

This was a sharp week of authoritarian consolidation. The executive branch moved forcefully to centralize control over finances and personnel through DOGE orders, mass firing memos, and funding freezes at NIH and USAID. Simultaneously, it politicized key coercive institutions: the FBI and U.S. attorney corps were openly redefined as the president's personal tools, while senior military and JAG leaders were purged and replaced with loyalists. Civil service protections were systematically eroded through reclassification, buyouts, probationary dismissals, and agency-specific purges at NOAA, NIH, SSA, USAID, and Education. Alongside this, the administration intensified its campaign against independent media and information independence—excluding AP and Reuters, taking control of the press pool, conditioning access on compliance with a fabricated geographic renaming, and boosting AI-driven propaganda. Foreign policy shifted firmly toward alignment with Russia and transactional, oligarchic deals (Ukraine minerals deal, Gaza redevelopment, crypto-linked enforcement rollbacks), weakening the U.S. role as a rule-of-law democracy. Courts offered some resistance by blocking data grabs, refugee and DEI bans, and mass firings, but these were countered by politicized rulings and regulatory immunity for major donors. Overall, this creates strong structural pressure toward a patronage autocracy built on a hollowed-out state, captured law enforcement, and a managed information landscape.

Power and Authority

1. Attorney General Pam Bondi created a weaponization working group reporting to the White House. The Justice Department formed a special unit to review alleged past abuses but report directly to a senior White House political aide, blurring the line between independent law enforcement and presidential political priorities. (22 Feb 2025)

2. President Donald Trump pardoned Enrique Tarrio and about 1,500 January 6 participants. Mass pardons for convicted January 6 offenders removed legal consequences for an attack on Congress, signaling tolerance for pro-regime political violence and weakening deterrence against future assaults on democratic transfers of power. (22 Feb 2025; 25 Feb 2025)

3. President Donald Trump announced the largest deportation operation in US history. Trump's pledge to launch an unprecedented mass deportation campaign, alongside moves against birthright citizenship and protected status, concentrated executive power over millions of residents' legal security and family unity. (22 Feb 2025)

4. President Donald Trump threatened to cut federal funding to states defying his trans athlete order. By warning governors he would withhold federal funds from states that did not enforce his ban on transgender girls in sports, Trump used fiscal leverage to coerce state compliance with a contested civil-rights policy. (22 Feb 2025)

5. President Donald Trump signed an executive order banning transgender athletes from women's sports. The nationwide ban on transgender participation in women's sports used federal authority to restrict a marginalized group's access to education-linked opportunities and invited conflicts with existing civil-rights protections. (22 Feb 2025)

6. Elon Musk and the Office of Personnel Management ordered federal workers to email weekly accomplishments under threat of termination. Musk's ultimatum that nonresponsive federal employees would be treated as having resigned asserted sweeping control over civil servants' job security outside normal personnel rules, pressuring neutrality in favor of political loyalty. (22 Feb 2025; 24 Feb 2025; 25 Feb 2025)

7. Health Secretary Robert F. Kennedy Jr. directed HHS staff to comply with Musk's accomplishments email. By ordering his department to follow an irregular OPM directive that other agencies resisted, the health secretary aligned a major public-health bureaucracy with politicized personnel demands, deepening internal fragmentation of federal norms. (23 Feb 2025)

8. President Donald Trump ordered NIH to halt normal grant-review processes, effectively freezing research funding. Stopping NIH study-section

notices and grant reviews, despite a court order, let the White House choke off biomedical research funding unilaterally, undermining judicial authority and public-health capacity. (23 Feb 2025; 24 Feb 2025; 26 Feb 2025)

9. Trump administration placed nearly all USAID staff on leave and began eliminating thousands of positions. Putting most USAID employees on leave and moving to cut about 2,000 domestic positions sharply reduced US development capacity, centralizing foreign-aid discretion in the White House and weakening a key soft-power institution. (23 Feb 2025; 24 Feb 2025; 25 Feb 2025; 26 Feb 2025)

10. President Donald Trump signed an order renaming the Gulf of Mexico as the Gulf of America. Mandating a new official name for a shared body of water and punishing outlets that refused to adopt it used executive power to enforce a political narrative over geographic convention and journalistic independence. (22 Feb 2025; 24 Feb 2025)

11. President Donald Trump expanded the Department of Government Efficiency's control over federal payments and froze government credit cards. An executive order centralized oversight of contracts, grants, and loans under DOGE and imposed a 30-day freeze on government credit cards, giving a Musk-led unit sweeping leverage over agency operations and spending. (26 Feb 2025; 27 Feb 2025)

12. President Donald Trump directed officials to negotiate Ukraine peace terms directly with Russia without Ukraine present. Ordering US envoys to negotiate an end to the Ukraine war with Russia while excluding Ukraine and European allies concentrated foreign-policy decision-making in the presidency and sidelined affected democratic partners. (25 Feb 2025)

13. President Donald Trump issued an executive order on healthcare price transparency. Requiring clearer disclosure of healthcare prices used executive authority to push transparency in medical billing, potentially improving patients' ability to compare costs and hold providers accountable in a concentrated market. (25 Feb 2025)

14. President Donald Trump ordered an investigation into national security risks from copper imports. By invoking national-security review of copper imports, Trump positioned the executive to reshape trade flows and industrial policy in a critical sector with limited congressional input. (25 Feb 2025)

15. Social Security Administration leadership shut down its Office of Civil Rights and Equal Opportunity. Closing SSA's civil-rights office weakened internal mechanisms for addressing discrimination in a core social-insurance agency, reducing protections for beneficiaries and employees seeking redress. (25 Feb 2025)

16. President Donald Trump suspended security clearances of lawyers representing former special counsel Jack Smith. Revoking clearances from attorneys tied to investigations of Trump's conduct used classification powers to disadvantage legal adversaries, pressuring independent legal representation in politically sensitive cases. (25 Feb 2025)

17. Department of Defense leadership under President Trump planned to dismiss the military's top judge advocates general. Targeting the Army, Navy, and Air Force JAGs for removal threatened the military's internal legal checks, making it easier for commanders to carry out unlawful or politically driven orders without professional resistance. (23 Feb 2025; 27 Feb 2025)

18. President Donald Trump and Defense Secretary Pete Hegseth fired the chairman of the Joint Chiefs and multiple senior Pentagon leaders. Removing General Charles Q. Brown and other top commanders and moving to replace them with loyalists weakened nonpartisan military leadership and increased the risk that armed forces would follow partisan directives. (22 Feb 2025; 23 Feb 2025; 28 Feb 2025)

19. President Donald Trump ordered the Pentagon and DHS to prepare a 30,000-bed migrant detention facility at Guantánamo Bay. Directing military-run mass detention for migrants at Guantánamo extended extraordinary national-security infrastructure into routine immigration enforcement, concentrating coercive power far from normal judicial oversight. (23 Feb 2025; 24 Feb 2025; 25 Feb 2025)

20. Office of Management and Budget and Office of Personnel Management ordered agencies to prepare mass layoff and reorganization plans. A joint memo instructing agencies to design large reductions in force and restructuring by mid-March put the professional civil service under sweeping political control, threatening continuity of neutral governance. (27 Feb 2025; 28 Feb 2025)

21. President Donald Trump announced plans to cut most USAID foreign-aid contracts. Moving to cancel over 90% of USAID contracts allowed the executive to rapidly reshape or dismantle US development programs worldwide, reducing long-term commitments made through normal appropriations. (26 Feb 2025)

22. President Donald Trump directed the Department of Transportation to terminate New York City's congestion pricing program. By rescinding federal approval for New York's congestion pricing, the administration overrode a state-level revenue and transportation policy, asserting federal power over local fiscal choices and urban planning. (26 Feb 2025; 27 Feb 2025)

23. President Donald Trump announced plans to abolish the US Department of Education and offered buyouts to its staff. Preparing an order to

dismantle the Education Department, while pushing under-market buyouts, threatened to eliminate a cabinet-level guarantor of federal education rights and shift power to less accountable actors. (28 Feb 2025)

24. President Donald Trump announced a plan to sell US citizenship through a $5 million gold card. Proposing a purchasable path to citizenship explicitly tied legal status to wealth, undermining equal treatment in immigration and opening avenues for affluent foreign actors to buy political footholds. (24 Feb 2025; 25 Feb 2025)

25. President Donald Trump ordered the Social Security Administration to undergo a major restructuring with potential mass layoffs. A sweeping restructuring plan that could cut up to half of SSA's workforce risked crippling administration of retirement and disability benefits, concentrating discretion over a core social contract program in political hands. (28 Feb 2025)

26. President Donald Trump announced deep cuts to the Environmental Protection Agency's budget and staff. Plans to cut roughly two-thirds of EPA's budget and many of its 15,000 employees would sharply reduce federal capacity to enforce environmental laws, shifting power toward regulated industries and political appointees. (28 Feb 2025)

27. President Donald Trump announced large cuts and firings at NOAA and other science agencies. Terminating hundreds of NOAA staff and planning up to 1,000 cuts, alongside other science-agency layoffs, weakened federal capacity to provide climate and weather data essential for public safety and policy. (26 Feb 2025; 27 Feb 2025; 28 Feb 2025)

28. President Donald Trump announced termination of US funding for UNAIDS. Cutting US support for the UN's HIV/AIDS program reduced American participation in a key global health effort, weakening multilateral responses and signaling retreat from cooperative public-health leadership. (28 Feb 2025)

29. President Donald Trump canceled key CDC and FDA vaccine-strain meetings. Canceling expert meetings on immunization practices and flu strain selection disrupted routine vaccine policymaking, potentially undermining preparedness during a severe flu season and weakening science-based health governance. (28 Feb 2025)

30. President Donald Trump announced plans to cut 65% of EPA's budget. A proposed two-thirds budget cut to EPA would drastically shrink federal environmental enforcement, shifting power over pollution and climate policy toward states and regulated industries with uneven accountability. (28 Feb 2025)

31. President Donald Trump directed agencies to plan reductions in force across the federal government. A late-week directive for agencies to identify

hundreds of thousands of positions for possible elimination escalated efforts to hollow out the professional bureaucracy and replace expertise with political control. (28 Feb 2025)

32. President Donald Trump announced tariffs on Canada, Mexico, and China to take effect March 4. Reinstating and raising tariffs on major trading partners concentrated trade-war decisions in the executive, with broad economic consequences but limited legislative input or transparent cost–benefit analysis. (27 Feb 2025; 28 Feb 2025)

33. President Donald Trump ordered federal agencies to plan for firing transgender military personnel. A Pentagon memo implementing Trump's directive to identify and discharge transgender troops used command authority to exclude a class of service members, undermining equal protection and military inclusivity. (26 Feb 2025; 27 Feb 2025)

34. President Donald Trump announced a major restructuring of the Social Security Administration with potential layoffs. Plans to reorganize SSA with possible cuts to half its workforce risked destabilizing benefit administration for tens of millions, centralizing discretion over a foundational program in political appointees. (28 Feb 2025)

Institutions and Governance

1. Missouri state legislator introduced a bill to create a registry of pregnant women deemed at risk of abortion. The proposed Save MO Babies Act would establish a state-managed database tracking pregnant women considered likely to seek abortions, expanding government surveillance into private medical decisions and reproductive autonomy. (22 Feb 2025)

2. Federal courts issued nationwide injunctions blocking Trump's anti-DEI orders. Two federal rulings found Trump's efforts to ban DEI programs and investigate companies over such policies likely unconstitutional, temporarily protecting speech and equal-protection norms in federal agencies and contracting. (22 Feb 2025)

3. Associated Press sued Trump administration officials for blocking press access to presidential events. AP's lawsuit challenged the administration's exclusion of its reporters from presidential events as a First Amendment violation, testing judicial willingness to protect independent media access to the executive. (22 Feb 2025)

4. Federal courts issued injunctions limiting Musk's DOGE access to Americans' personal data. Multiple orders barred OPM and Education from sharing sensitive data with Musk's DOGE team, reinforcing statutory privacy

protections and checking an unelected actor's reach into federal databases. (22 Feb 2025; 24 Feb 2025; 25 Feb 2025)

5. Elon Musk called for impeachment of a federal judge who blocked DEI grant terminations. Musk's demand to impeach a judge over an adverse ruling attacked judicial independence and signaled that legal decisions hindering the administration's agenda could trigger personal retaliation. (22 Feb 2025)

6. Federal employee unions amended their lawsuit to challenge Musk's reporting directive under the APA. Unions argued that OPM's new weekly-report requirement for federal workers bypassed notice-and-comment procedures, using administrative law to contest abrupt changes to civil-service conditions. (23 Feb 2025; 24 Feb 2025)

7. Senator Angus King warned Congress that Trump's funding refusals were an unconstitutional power grab. King urged colleagues to confront what he described as Trump's attempt to rewrite laws by refusing to fund them, highlighting a separation-of-powers crisis over the legislature's control of appropriations. (24 Feb 2025)

8. Representative Gerry Connolly opened a congressional investigation into US Attorney Ed Martin for abuse of office. The probe into Martin's alleged targeting of critics of Musk and DOGE tested whether Congress could still check politicized use of prosecutorial power against media and individuals. (24 Feb 2025)

9. Federal courts declined AP's request for a temporary order restoring White House access. A Trump-appointed judge refused to immediately reinstate AP's access to presidential events, accepting the administration's framing of such spaces as more private and leaving retaliatory access limits in place pending litigation. (24 Feb 2025; 25 Feb 2025)

10. US Supreme Court declined to hear challenges to abortion-clinic buffer zones. By letting lower-court rulings stand, the Court preserved local ordinances limiting protests near abortion clinics, maintaining a balance between speech rights and patient access to medical services. (24 Feb 2025)

11. Pardoned January 6 defendants including Enrique Tarrio announced plans to sue the Justice Department over their prosecutions. Pardoned insurrectionists' announced lawsuit sought to recast lawful prosecutions as government abuse, challenging the legitimacy of prior accountability efforts for an attack on Congress. (24 Feb 2025)

12. Federal courts blocked ICE enforcement at certain houses of worship. An injunction limiting immigration raids in churches and other religious spaces protected both religious freedom and migrants' access to sanctuary, constraining executive enforcement tactics. (24 Feb 2025; 25 Feb 2025)

13. Federal courts issued injunctions blocking freezes of federal loans, grants, refugee admissions, and foreign aid nonpayment. Judges ordered the administration to continue paying foreign aid and not freeze loans, grants, or refugee admissions, reinforcing statutory obligations against unilateral executive impoundment. (25 Feb 2025)

14. Teachers' unions and allied groups sued the Department of Education over threats to cut funds for race-conscious policies. The lawsuit challenged federal threats to defund schools considering race in hiring and policy, using the courts to defend local autonomy and civil-rights practices in education. (25 Feb 2025)

15. US Supreme Court overturned Richard Glossip's conviction and ordered a new trial. The Court found prosecutors had withheld exculpatory evidence in a death-penalty case, underscoring the judiciary's role in correcting serious due-process violations even in long-final convictions. (25 Feb 2025)

16. US Supreme Court heard a case that could lower the bar for majority-group discrimination claims. Oral arguments in a "reverse discrimination" case signaled potential changes to employment law that might make it easier for majority groups to challenge workplace diversity policies. (26 Feb 2025)

17. Chief Justice John Roberts temporarily stayed a lower-court order requiring USAID payments. Roberts' administrative stay paused enforcement of a ruling compelling the administration to release $1.5–2 billion in foreign aid, giving the executive more time and leverage in a dispute over statutory spending duties. (26 Feb 2025; 27 Feb 2025)

18. Judge William Alsup and other federal judges declared planned mass firings of federal employees likely illegal and blocked OPM's role. A California court held that OPM lacked authority to order broad probationary firings, pausing some terminations and asserting judicial limits on executive-driven civil-service purges. (27 Feb 2025)

19. Federal judge declined to block firing of intelligence officials involved in DEI programs. By allowing dismissals of intelligence personnel tied to DEI work to proceed, the court left room for politically motivated personnel changes within sensitive national-security agencies. (27 Feb 2025)

20. County court judge James Gion denied requests to livestream a high-profile Greenpeace trial. Refusing to allow livestreaming of Energy Transfer's suit against Greenpeace limited public access to a case with broad environmental and free-speech implications, raising transparency concerns. (27 Feb 2025)

21. Greenpeace petitioned the North Dakota Supreme Court to move its defamation trial. Greenpeace sought a venue change away from a jury pool

heavily tied to the fossil-fuel industry, highlighting worries about local bias in litigation that could chill environmental protest. (27 Feb 2025)

22. Coalition of educators sued the Department of Education over anti-diversity civil-rights guidelines. Educators challenged new federal civil-rights guidance targeting DEI practices, arguing it undermined educational equity and exceeded the department's authority. (28 Feb 2025)

23. Securities and Exchange Commission dropped enforcement actions against Coinbase and Justin Sun after major political donations. The SEC's retreat from high-profile crypto cases without penalties, following large contributions to Trump-aligned entities, raised concerns that regulatory enforcement was being shaped by political money rather than law. (25 Feb 2025; 28 Feb 2025)

24. Senator Angus King called on Congress to protect constitutional governance from Trump's actions. King's floor statements framed Trump's funding maneuvers as the most serious constitutional assault in US history, urging legislative defense of institutional checks and balances. (24 Feb 2025)

25. House of Representatives passed a budget framework with deep Medicaid and social-spending cuts to fund large tax reductions. The House approved a budget blueprint pairing $4.5 trillion in tax cuts with roughly $2 trillion in spending cuts, including major Medicaid reductions, entrenching fiscal priorities favoring wealth over social safety nets. (23 Feb 2025; 24 Feb 2025; 25 Feb 2025; 26 Feb 2025; 27 Feb 2025)

26. Senate voted to advance a budget resolution increasing border security funding. The Senate moved forward a budget resolution adding $175 billion for border enforcement while requiring offsetting cuts, reflecting institutional prioritization of security spending over other domestic programs. (26 Feb 2025)

27. House Republican leadership advised members to avoid or tightly control town halls after budget backlash. Guidance to limit unscripted constituent events in response to anger over cuts reduced opportunities for direct accountability and public input into legislative decisions. (28 Feb 2025)

28. Department of Health and Human Services under RFK Jr. moved to eliminate public participation in many policy decisions. HHS's plan to curtail notice-and-comment opportunities for major health policies reversed long-standing transparency practices, weakening public and expert input into rules governing vast health programs. (28 Feb 2025)

29. Federal Election Commission canceled an open meeting and later reported on closed Sunshine Act sessions. The FEC's cancellation of an open meeting and subsequent notice about closed-door discussions on internal

matters affected transparency around how the election regulator conducts its business. (24 Feb 2025; 28 Feb 2025)

Civil Rights and Dissent

1. Trump administration shut down the National Law Enforcement Accountability Database tracking police misconduct. Eliminating the national database of police misconduct reduced transparency about abusive officers and made it easier for problem personnel to move between departments without scrutiny. (22 Feb 2025)

2. Tom Homan and Trump immigration team advocated arresting officials in sanctuary cities and using the military in immigration enforcement. Threats to arrest local leaders and deploy the military over immigration policy blurred civilian–military boundaries and aimed to criminalize local dissent from federal enforcement priorities. (22 Feb 2025)

3. Department of Education under Trump launched a Title IX investigation into Maine over its handling of trans athlete policies. Opening a civil-rights probe into Maine after its governor resisted Trump's trans sports ban used federal enforcement tools to pressure a state over contested gender and education policies. (22 Feb 2025)

4. President Donald Trump falsely claimed massive election fraud at CPAC. Renewed baseless assertions that Democrats stole the 2024 election undermined public trust in vote counting and provided rhetorical cover for future restrictions on voting access. (22 Feb 2025)

5. Governor Janet Mills of Maine publicly defied Trump's transgender athlete ban. Mills' refusal to enforce Trump's executive order in Maine schools highlighted state-level resistance to federal policies seen as discriminatory against transgender students. (22 Feb 2025)

6. Yosemite National Park staff hung an upside-down US flag to protest Musk-led firings and drilling policies. Park employees used a symbolic act to protest mass layoffs and pro-drilling directives, illustrating civil servants' use of dissent to defend environmental stewardship and public-service missions. (22 Feb 2025)

7. Trump administration directed ICE to deport hundreds of thousands of unaccompanied migrant children. Plans to deport large numbers of children who entered the US without parents raised grave human-rights concerns and signaled a punitive approach to vulnerable migrants. (23 Feb 2025)

8. Unknown sender claiming allegiance to Enrique Tarrio and MAGA emailed bomb threats to the Principles First summit in Washington, DC. Threats invoking "Emperor Trump" forced evacuation of an anti-Trump

conservative conference, using fear of violence to intimidate political critics and disrupt peaceful assembly. (23 Feb 2025; 24 Feb 2025; 25 Feb 2025)

9. Protesters and activists organized demonstrations at Tesla dealerships against Musk's government role. Nationwide protests at Tesla outlets challenged Musk's influence over federal databases and layoffs, reflecting civil society's use of economic pressure to contest corporate–state entanglement. (23 Feb 2025; 27 Feb 2025)

10. White House posted a video depicting shackled migrants as entertainment content. An official "ASMR deportation flight" video trivialized the suffering of detained migrants, normalizing cruelty in state messaging and dehumanizing a group whose rights depend on public empathy. (23 Feb 2025)

11. Dan Bongino and Kash Patel were appointed to top FBI leadership positions despite partisan histories. Installing outspoken election deniers and far-right allies at the FBI's helm risked redirecting federal law enforcement away from neutral protection of rights toward targeting perceived political enemies. (22 Feb 2025; 23 Feb 2025; 24 Feb 2025; 25 Feb 2025; 28 Feb 2025)

12. US State Department ordered permanent visa bans on transgender athletes who misstate birth sex. Denying visas and imposing lifetime bans on trans athletes for paperwork discrepancies institutionalized discrimination in border policy and restricted international participation in sport. (25 Feb 2025)

13. Trump administration required undocumented immigrants 14 and older to register and provide fingerprints. Mandatory registration and biometric collection for undocumented residents expanded state surveillance over a vulnerable population, raising fears of future targeting and deportation. (25 Feb 2025)

14. New Orleans Police Department declined a free inspection of a malfunctioning anti-vehicle barrier before a deadly attack. Refusing maintenance on a key security barrier that later failed during a mass-casualty attack highlighted governance failures in basic public-safety infrastructure. (26 Feb 2025)

15. Attorney General Pam Bondi ordered DOJ's Civil Rights Division to dismiss DEI lawsuits against police and fire departments. Dropping cases alleging discriminatory hiring in public-safety agencies weakened federal enforcement of equal-opportunity laws and signaled tolerance for exclusionary practices. (26 Feb 2025)

16. Huntington Beach city authorities arrested former NFL player Chris Kluwe after an anti-MAGA speech at a council meeting. Kluwe's arrest for "disrupting an assembly" following a critical speech about MAGA raised concerns that local officials were using procedural rules to suppress political dissent in civic forums. (26 Feb 2025)

17. People's Union USA and participating Americans organized a 24-hour economic boycott against anti-DEI and austerity policies. A coordinated "economic blackout" encouraged people to withhold spending or buy only from local businesses, using consumer power to protest cuts to DEI, healthcare, and social services. (28 Feb 2025)

18. Organizers and protesters held demonstrations against Musk's role in the administration and DOGE. Protests at Tesla dealerships and other venues highlighted public concern over a private billionaire's control of government data and layoffs, reflecting resistance to perceived oligarchic governance. (23 Feb 2025; 27 Feb 2025)

19. Trump administration ordered removal of DEI mentions and planned removal of transgender troops from the military. Purging DEI language from Pentagon communications and planning to discharge trans service members institutionalized discrimination within the armed forces and narrowed who can serve. (26 Feb 2025; 27 Feb 2025)

20. Trump administration suspended refugee admissions until blocked by a federal judge. An attempted suspension of the refugee system, later enjoined, showed how executive orders can abruptly curtail humanitarian protections for people fleeing persecution. (25 Feb 2025)

21. US State Department and Trump envoys pressured Romania to lift travel bans on Andrew and Tristan Tate. Lobbying a foreign government to ease restrictions on influencers facing serious charges suggested willingness to prioritize politically aligned figures over consistent anti-trafficking and rule-of-law principles. (27 Feb 2025; 28 Feb 2025)

22. Trump administration cut US funding to UNAIDS, weakening global HIV/AIDS efforts. Ending support for UNAIDS reduced international capacity to fight HIV/AIDS, disproportionately affecting marginalized communities worldwide and signaling retreat from global health solidarity. (28 Feb 2025)

23. Unknown actors at Guantánamo Bay subjected migrants to abusive detention conditions. Reports of shackling, cages, denial of legal calls, and isolation for migrants at Guantánamo highlighted severe human-rights violations in a facility repurposed for immigration enforcement. (25 Feb 2025)

24. US State Department terminated visas for trans athletes and imposed permanent bans for misrepresentation. Visa denials and lifetime bans for trans athletes who misstate birth sex on forms codified discrimination in immigration policy and chilled participation in international competitions. (25 Feb 2025)

25. Congressional proponents of the SAVE Act advanced legislation that could disenfranchise voters, especially married women with name changes.

The SAVE Act's documentation requirements risked disqualifying many eligible voters under the guise of election security, particularly targeting women whose legal names differ from original records. (27 Feb 2025)

Economic Structure

1. Pentagon leadership announced layoffs of 5,400 civilian workers and a broader hiring freeze. Cutting thousands of Defense Department civilian jobs and freezing hiring reduced government capacity in the largest federal agency, shifting resources away from career staff toward political and contractor control. (22 Feb 2025)

2. Trump administration imposed new tariffs on China, Canada, and Mexico. Announced tariffs on major trading partners reoriented trade policy through executive action, risking higher consumer prices and retaliatory measures without a comprehensive legislative framework. (22 Feb 2025; 27 Feb 2025; 28 Feb 2025)

3. Food and Drug Administration rehired staff previously fired in Musk-led cuts. Reinstating FDA employees removed in earlier purges partially restored regulatory capacity over medical devices and digital health, mitigating some risks from politicized staffing decisions. (22 Feb 2025)

4. Florida Governor Ron DeSantis sued Target over Pride merchandise's alleged impact on investors. Using securities law to challenge a retailer's LGBTQ+ marketing blurred lines between investor protection and culture-war enforcement, potentially chilling corporate speech on social issues. (22 Feb 2025)

5. House Republicans advanced budget plans cutting Medicaid and social services to fund tax cuts. Budget proposals shifting resources from healthcare and safety-net programs to large tax reductions for wealthy individuals and corporations entrenched fiscal priorities favoring capital over vulnerable populations. (23 Feb 2025; 24 Feb 2025; 25 Feb 2025; 26 Feb 2025; 27 Feb 2025)

6. National Institutes of Health leadership continued blocking DEI-related grants despite a court order. NIH's internal freeze on diversity-related research funding, in defiance of a TRO, disrupted studies on major diseases and showed how executive pressure can redirect scientific resources away from equity goals. (24 Feb 2025)

7. Trump administration blocked publication of new NIH grant notices, stalling thousands of awards. Preventing Federal Register notices for NIH grants froze about 16,000 applications worth $1.5 billion, using procedural control over publication to halt scientific funding without explicit policy debate. (24 Feb 2025)

8. Coinbase and allied crypto interests made large political contributions and secured favorable regulatory outcomes. Coinbase's tens of millions in donations to pro-crypto and pro-Trump entities coincided with SEC decisions to drop enforcement and list Trump's $TRUMP coin, illustrating how concentrated wealth can shape regulatory treatment. (25 Feb 2025)

9. Federal Aviation Administration signed a contract to use SpaceX's Starlink internet system. FAA's adoption of Starlink for connectivity deepened the government's dependence on a firm led by a politically powerful figure, raising conflict-of-interest concerns in critical infrastructure decisions. (25 Feb 2025)

10. US fossil fuel industry campaigned against gas bans in new buildings. Industry efforts to block local restrictions on gas hookups sought to preserve fossil-fuel markets at the expense of climate and health goals, leveraging economic power to shape regulatory outcomes. (24 Feb 2025)

11. DoorDash and New York Attorney General Letitia James reached a $16.75 million settlement over misused delivery tips. The settlement required DoorDash to repay workers for tips used to subsidize base pay, demonstrating state-level enforcement against deceptive gig-economy practices that undercut worker earnings. (27 Feb 2025)

12. Jared Kushner and Affinity Partners maintained large foreign-funded investments while influencing Middle East policy. Kushner's billions in investments from Saudi and other foreign funds, alongside ongoing policy roles, highlighted serious emoluments and corruption risks in US foreign and economic decision-making. (27 Feb 2025)

13. Trump administration removed online applications for several student loan repayment plans. Taking down forms for income-driven repayment and consolidation complicated access to relief for student borrowers, effectively tightening economic pressure on debtors without legislative change. (28 Feb 2025)

14. Paramount announced plans to roll back DEI policies amid merger and legal pressures. Paramount's retreat from diversity initiatives under political and market pressure showed how corporate governance can be steered away from inclusion when regulatory and cultural signals discourage it. (26 Feb 2025)

15. President Donald Trump pressed the Federal Reserve to cut interest rates. Trump's public pressure on the Fed to lower rates risked politicizing monetary policy, potentially fueling inflation and undermining the central bank's independence in managing economic stability. (25 Feb 2025)

16. Trump administration and DOGE froze government credit cards, halting many NIH and other research purchases. A 30-day freeze on federal

purchase cards, nominally for efficiency, abruptly stopped lab supply purchases and other operations, using fiscal controls to exert leverage over scientific and administrative work. (26 Feb 2025)

17. Trump administration cut and then attempted to rehire Agriculture Department staff fighting bird flu. Firing and then scrambling to rehire poultry-disease specialists during an outbreak illustrated how politically driven cuts can undermine essential public-health functions and force ad hoc corrections. (28 Feb 2025)

18. Trump administration announced large cuts to NOAA's climate and weather workforce. Plans to slash NOAA's budget and staff by roughly a third, including DEI-related projects, weakened federal climate research and forecasting, with implications for disaster preparedness and environmental policy. (26 Feb 2025; 27 Feb 2025; 28 Feb 2025)

19. Trump administration and DOGE centralized oversight of all federal payments under a Musk-led efficiency initiative. Placing DOGE in charge of recording and justifying nearly all federal payments shifted practical control over the purse from Congress and agencies to a politically aligned, privately influenced unit. (26 Feb 2025; 27 Feb 2025)

20. Trump administration suspended US foreign aid, severely impacting healthcare for Myanmar refugees. The broad foreign-aid freeze, despite supposed humanitarian exemptions, shut down clinics along the Thai–Myanmar border, demonstrating how fiscal decisions in Washington can abruptly end life-saving services abroad. (26 Feb 2025)

21. Trump administration and Jared Kushner advanced plans to redevelop Gaza with private real-estate interests. Efforts to convene developers and hold a White House summit on rebuilding Gaza tied US policy to potential private profit, raising concerns about using state power to enable insider enrichment in a conflict zone. (27 Feb 2025)

22. President Donald Trump and allies promoted a plan to clear Palestinians from Gaza and redevelop it as a luxury resort. Trump's public embrace of a Gaza redevelopment vision tied to ethnic cleansing fused geopolitical decisions with branding and real-estate interests, undermining human-rights norms and democratic credibility. (27 Feb 2025)

23. Trump administration and Justin Sun secured a 60-day stay in SEC's fraud case after Sun invested heavily in a Trump-backed venture. The pause in SEC's fraud prosecution of Justin Sun, following his $75 million investment in a Trump-linked financial project, reinforced perceptions that major donors can negotiate lenient treatment. (28 Feb 2025)

24. Canadians organized a boycott of American products in response to US policies. A widespread Canadian consumer boycott of US goods signaled

economic backlash to Trump-era actions, with potential to strain cross-border trade and influence domestic political calculations. (28 Feb 2025)

25. Congress and Trump administration debated and advanced budgets that cut science funding and social supports. Plans to slash NSF, NIH, and other science budgets while extending tax cuts and boosting security spending shifted federal investment away from research and equity toward short-term political priorities. (26 Feb 2025)

Information, Memory, and Manipulation

1. President Donald Trump labeled MSNBC a threat to democracy during CPAC. Calling a major news outlet a threat to democracy stigmatized critical journalism and encouraged supporters to distrust independent reporting on the administration. (22 Feb 2025)

2. President Donald Trump attacked journalist Joy Reid with personal insults on social media. Trump's derogatory posts about a prominent Black journalist exemplified personalized attacks that can intimidate reporters and discourage critical coverage. (23 Feb 2025)

3. Trump administration barred Associated Press from White House events over refusal to use "Gulf of America". Excluding AP from Oval Office and Air Force One access for not adopting a politically imposed geographic term punished independent editorial judgment and pressured outlets to echo official language. (23 Feb 2025; 24 Feb 2025; 25 Feb 2025)

4. White House Press Secretary Karoline Leavitt asserted control over which journalists can attend briefings and press pool events. Taking press-access decisions away from the White House Correspondents' Association concentrated gatekeeping power in the administration, enabling favoritism toward friendly outlets and exclusion of critics. (24 Feb 2025; 25 Feb 2025; 26 Feb 2025)

5. Elon Musk and DOGE staff sent an unclassified email listing CIA officers for potential layoffs, prompting a damage review. An email identifying intelligence officers for cuts without proper safeguards triggered a CIA damage assessment, underscoring how politicized personnel moves can expose sensitive operations. (23 Feb 2025)

6. Department of Health and Human Services warned staff that responses to Musk's email might be read by foreign actors. HHS cautioned employees that sending detailed work reports to Musk's team could expose sensitive information, highlighting security risks in ad hoc data-collection schemes. (24 Feb 2025)

7. Office of Personnel Management issued a memo to reclassify top career

positions as political appointees. Reclassifying senior civil-service roles as political posts threatened to replace neutral expertise with loyalists, undermining impartial information and advice within agencies. (24 Feb 2025)

8. Trump administration and Kash Patel demanded names of up to 6,000 FBI agents involved in January 6 cases. Requiring lists of agents who worked on Capitol-attack prosecutions raised fears of retaliation and could chill future investigations into politically sensitive crimes. (28 Feb 2025)

9. Elon Musk and DOGE deleted inflated savings claims from the DOGE "wall of receipts" after media scrutiny. Quietly removing inaccurate multi-billion-dollar savings figures from a government website, without clear correction, showed how official economic narratives can be massaged for political effect. (26 Feb 2025)

10. White House Press Secretary Karoline Leavitt refused to disclose who leads the Department of Government Efficiency. Declining to identify DOGE's leadership obscured who controls a powerful spending-oversight unit, limiting public and congressional ability to scrutinize its actions. (26 Feb 2025)

11. Trump administration removed online records and applications for student loan repayment options. Taking down key repayment-plan forms from federal websites hindered borrowers' access to accurate information and relief, effectively reshaping policy through information control rather than law. (28 Feb 2025)

12. President Donald Trump shared an AI-generated "Trump Gaza" resort video on social media. Promoting an AI fantasy of Gaza redeveloped as a luxury resort normalized a controversial policy vision and blurred lines between propaganda and reality in public debate over war and displacement. (25 Feb 2025; 27 Feb 2025)

13. Hackers using the pseudonym PaulleyTicks broadcast an AI video mocking Trump and Musk on HUD building screens. An unauthorized AI video takeover of HUD monitors highlighted both digital protest tactics and vulnerabilities in government information systems to symbolic disruption. (23 Feb 2025)

14. Elon Musk baselessly accused USAID of supporting terrorism. Claiming without evidence that USAID funded terrorism undermined trust in a key aid agency and framed humanitarian work as suspect, potentially justifying cuts and politicized oversight. (24 Feb 2025)

15. President Donald Trump threatened to sue authors and publishers and suggested laws against "defamatory fiction". Threatening legal action and new laws against writers signaled a willingness to use state power to chill critical books and investigative narratives about those in power. (26 Feb 2025)

16. Jeff Bezos and The Washington Post shifted the paper's opinion section toward pro–free market themes, prompting resignations. Owner-driven changes to WaPo's editorial line and the resulting staff exodus illustrated how concentrated media ownership can narrow the range of viewpoints in a major outlet. (26 Feb 2025; 28 Feb 2025)

17. Department of Education launched an online portal for citizens to report DEI practices in public schools. The "End DEI" reporting site encouraged public denunciations of diversity programs, creating a channel for ideological policing of school curricula and hiring. (27 Feb 2025)

18. Elon Musk falsely accused CNN analyst Norm Eisen of being part of a crime family. Musk's mistaken public accusation against a legal commentator exemplified elite use of social media to smear critics, potentially deterring scrutiny of powerful actors. (27 Feb 2025)

19. White House briefed pro-Trump influencers and provided them with Jeffrey Epstein documents. Giving Epstein-related materials to partisan online figures rather than institutional investigators or broad media suggested selective disclosure aimed at shaping narratives rather than full accountability. (27 Feb 2025; 28 Feb 2025)

20. Attorney General Pam Bondi demanded an investigation into the FBI's handling of Epstein files. Bondi's call for an inquiry into Epstein records, combined with selective file releases, risked turning a serious abuse case into a politicized tool rather than a vehicle for impartial accountability. (27 Feb 2025)

21. President Donald Trump posted a music video promoting a plan to ethnically cleanse and redevelop Gaza. The video glamorized a proposal to remove Palestinians and build a luxury resort, using stylized media to normalize a rights-violating policy and recast it as a triumphal national project. (27 Feb 2025)

22. President Donald Trump used AI and social media to promote Gaza and Ukraine deals tied to resource extraction. Digital promotion of resource-for-aid deals in conflict zones framed complex geopolitical arrangements as simple wins, obscuring long-term sovereignty and justice concerns. (26 Feb 2025; 27 Feb 2025)

23. Trump administration ordered removal of DEI and climate references from science-agency websites. Scrubbing DEI programs and climate-change language from NASA, NOAA, and other sites narrowed the official record of scientific priorities and equity efforts, shaping what the public can see and study. (26 Feb 2025)

24. Trump administration and Kennedy Center board disinvited the International Pride Orchestra and ended events deemed "anti-American

propaganda". Canceling LGBTQ+ performances at a major cultural institution after a board takeover used control of public arts venues to marginalize certain identities and viewpoints. (27 Feb 2025)

25. Trump administration renamed the Gulf of Mexico and enforced usage through access and legal pressure. Insisting on "Gulf of America" in official and media usage, and punishing noncompliance, exemplified state attempts to rewrite shared geographic language for political symbolism. (22 Feb 2025; 24 Feb 2025)

26. Trump administration and Kash Patel relocated 1,500 FBI agents away from headquarters, including counterterrorism staff. Moving large numbers of agents out of central FBI operations risked weakening investigations into domestic extremism and reorienting the bureau's focus toward political priorities. (28 Feb 2025)

27. President Donald Trump and pro-Trump influencers used elite-funded digital networks to spread election-fraud narratives and policy messaging. Briefings for far-right influencers and coordinated online campaigns amplified false election claims and controversial policies, leveraging algorithmic platforms to shape public perception. (22 Feb 2025; 25 Feb 2025; 27 Feb 2025)

CHAPTER 7
WEEK 7 (1 MAR 2025 – 7 MAR 2025): TOOLS AS HABIT, NOT EXCEPTION

Executive orders, mass layoffs, and curated information flows turned once-extraordinary tools into routine methods for rewarding allies, disciplining dissent, and thinning the state.

This week demonstrates a rapid consolidation of executive power, increased politicization of the civil service, and a growing fusion of crony capitalism with government policy. Trump's administration used executive orders and agency directives to reshape foreign policy toward Russia, weaken regulatory and social-welfare institutions, and push ideologically driven attacks on immigrants, LGBTQ communities, racial equity, and universities. There were mass layoffs and buyouts across Education, Social Security, VA, IRS, USDA, State, and USPS, along with the effective shutdown of CFPB and restructuring of USAID and IAF. Simultaneously, the creation of a crypto reserve and the failure to enforce anti–money laundering rules deepen elite self-dealing and financial opacity. Regarding the rule of law, courts repeatedly checked executive overreach in foreign aid, personnel dismissals, workforce cuts, and research funding, modestly reinforcing the separation of powers even as the administration retaliated against judges and prosecutors. Internationally, the U.S. moved further away from its democratic allies toward Russia, while halting or weaponizing aid to Ukraine and South Africa. Civil society mobilization and some state-level protections for LGBTQ rights persisted, but systemic authoritarian trends overshadowed these efforts.

Power and Authority

1. President Trump and the General Services Administration ordered closure of the 18F office and layoffs of its staff. Shuttering 18F, which built tools like IRS Direct File, reduced in-house federal digital capacity and advanced broader workforce cuts that weaken the state's ability to deliver and modernize public services. (1 Mar 2025)

2. President Trump issued an executive order designating English as the official language of the United States. Making English the official federal language and revoking prior language-access rules narrowed access to government services for non-English speakers, entrenching unequal participation in public life. (1 Mar 2025)

3. President Trump ordered investigations and tariff options on timber and lumber imports. Directing a national-security investigation into timber and lumber imports positioned trade tools for potential protectionist use, expanding executive leverage over key resource markets. (1 Mar 2025)

4. President Trump ordered immediate expansion of American timber production on federal lands. Mandating rapid increases in logging and expedited approvals on federal lands used executive power to override environmental safeguards, shifting policy toward extractive interests with limited oversight. (1 Mar 2025; 3 Mar 2025)

5. Secretary of State Marco Rubio invoked emergency authorities to send $4 billion in arms to Israel without normal congressional review. Bypassing Congress on a large arms transfer concentrated war-making discretion in the executive branch and weakened legislative checks on foreign military commitments. (1 Mar 2025)

6. President Trump approved a nearly $3 billion arms sale to Israel while bypassing congressional review. Authorizing major weapons sales without standard congressional oversight expanded unilateral executive control over foreign conflicts and reduced democratic accountability for their humanitarian impact. (2 Mar 2025)

7. President Trump issued executive orders tightening tariff rules at the northern and southern borders to address illicit drugs. Adjusting de minimis tariff treatment at both borders under prior emergency-style authorities further normalized using trade tools as unilateral security instruments with limited legislative input. (2 Mar 2025)

8. President Trump announced and then formalized creation of a federal strategic cryptocurrency reserve. Ordering a strategic crypto reserve and digital asset stockpile gave the presidency direct control over large speculative holdings, raising conflict-of-interest risks and blurring public policy

with private gain. (2 Mar 2025; 3 Mar 2025; 4 Mar 2025; 5 Mar 2025; 6 Mar 2025)

9. President Trump impounded congressionally approved aid to Ukraine. Freezing Ukraine aid that Congress had appropriated challenged statutory limits on impoundment and reasserted executive control over spending decisions reserved to the legislature. (4 Mar 2025)

10. President Trump directed mass layoffs and restructuring across multiple federal agencies including IRS, VA, Social Security, Education, USPS, State, and others. Coordinated workforce cuts and restructurings across core agencies centralized power in political appointees, hollowed neutral capacity, and made public services more dependent on loyalists and contractors. (3 Mar 2025; 4 Mar 2025; 5 Mar 2025; 6 Mar 2025; 7 Mar 2025)

11. President Trump celebrated clampdowns on immigration and asylum and called for more funding for border crackdowns. Using a high-profile address to champion harsher immigration and asylum enforcement framed restrictive border policies as central to national policy, reinforcing executive latitude over migrants' rights. (5 Mar 2025)

12. President Trump renamed Anahuac National Wildlife Refuge after Jocelyn Nungaray via executive order. Renaming a federal refuge after a crime victim allegedly killed by undocumented immigrants used symbolic executive power to embed an anti-immigrant narrative in public space and policy messaging. (5 Mar 2025)

13. President Trump reversed a plan to deport Ukrainian asylum seekers with temporary legal status. Walking back a planned mass removal of Ukrainians after public backlash showed how sweeping executive control over humanitarian status can abruptly reshape the security of large migrant groups. (5 Mar 2025)

14. President Trump issued executive orders adjusting tariffs on Canadian and Mexican goods to address drug flows while easing impacts on auto parts. Tweaking border duties by decree to balance drug-control rhetoric with auto-industry concerns highlighted how tariff levers are wielded unilaterally for both security and economic aims. (6 Mar 2025)

15. President Trump issued an executive order targeting Perkins Coie LLP's security clearances and federal business. Ordering reviews and suspensions of clearances and contracts for a specific law firm that had represented political opponents used state power in a personalized way that risks politicizing security and procurement. (6 Mar 2025)

16. President Trump signed a memo urging agencies to require upfront fees from those suing the administration. Pushing agencies to demand upfront fees from litigants seeking to challenge federal actions threatened to

price many individuals and groups out of court, weakening judicial checks on executive power. (6 Mar 2025)

17. President Trump issued an executive order revising Public Service Loan Forgiveness eligibility to exclude certain organizations. Redefining which public-service employers qualify for loan forgiveness allowed the administration to financially pressure organizations engaged in disfavored work, narrowing who can sustainably serve in civil society roles. (7 Mar 2025)

18. President Trump signed an executive order pausing tariffs on USMCA trade with Canada and Mexico until April 2. Temporarily suspending newly announced USMCA tariffs underscored how abrupt executive trade moves can unsettle markets and allies, with little predictable legislative input. (7 Mar 2025)

19. President Trump told cabinet secretaries they, not Elon Musk, were in charge of their departments. Reassuring cabinet officials about their authority implicitly acknowledged concerns over an unelected adviser's influence, highlighting blurred lines between formal and informal power in executive governance. (7 Mar 2025)

20. President Trump established a White House Task Force on the 2026 FIFA World Cup. Creating a presidential task force to coordinate World Cup preparations centralized oversight of a major international event, illustrating routine but expansive use of White House coordinating structures. (7 Mar 2025)

Institutions and Governance

1. Representative Eli Crane filed articles of impeachment against Judge Paul Engelmayer. Targeting a judge who ruled against the Department of Government Efficiency signaled partisan efforts to intimidate the judiciary for decisions adverse to administration policy. (1 Mar 2025)

2. Elon Musk urged Republicans to impeach federal judges who rule against DOGE. Calling for impeachment of judges over policy disagreements encouraged using constitutional tools to punish independent adjudication, undermining judicial independence. (1 Mar 2025)

3. A federal judge ruled that the head of the Office of Special Counsel could not be fired before his term ended. Blocking the administration's attempt to remove the whistleblower-protection chief reinforced statutory limits on at-will dismissal of independent oversight officials. (1 Mar 2025)

4. House of Representatives passed a budget resolution launching reconciliation to extend Trump-era tax cuts and cut safety-net programs. Advancing a budget that pairs extended high-end tax cuts with Medicaid and

benefit reductions showed Congress using fiscal tools to shift resources upward and constrain social supports. (2 Mar 2025)

5. Melania Trump and Senator Ted Cruz promoted legislation to criminalize AI-generated deepfake pornography. Backing a bill against non-consensual deepfake porn used federal lawmaking to address emerging digital harms and protect individuals' autonomy and privacy. (2 Mar 2025)

6. Election Assistance Commission sought public comment on the National Mail Voter Registration Form. Reviewing the national mail registration form through notice-and-comment maintained procedural channels that shape how easily citizens can register and update voter records. (4 Mar 2025)

7. Senate of the United States confirmed Linda McMahon as Secretary of Education. Confirming a close Trump ally with limited education background to lead a department the administration aims to dismantle aligned federal education governance with partisan objectives over expertise. (3 Mar 2025)

8. Representative Mike Johnson removed Representative Mike Turner from the House Intelligence Committee. Ousting the Intelligence Committee chair after he contradicted administration claims on Russia signaled partisan discipline over independent national-security oversight. (3 Mar 2025)

9. American Bar Association issued a statement condemning intimidation of judges by political actors. The ABA's warning about threats to judges underscored professional concern that political attacks were eroding judicial independence and the rule of law. (3 Mar 2025)

10. U.S. Merit Systems Protection Board ordered temporary reinstatement of thousands of fired USDA probationary employees. Reinstating nearly 6,000 Agriculture employees pending review signaled that mass terminations likely violated civil-service protections and checked executive attempts to purge staff. (5 Mar 2025)

11. U.S. Supreme Court rejected the Trump administration's attempt to freeze nearly $2 billion in foreign aid. By upholding lower-court orders to unfreeze appropriated foreign aid, the Court reaffirmed congressional control over spending and limited unilateral executive impoundment. (4 Mar 2025; 5 Mar 2025)

12. Judge Amy Berman Jackson ordered a senior CFPB official to testify about the agency's compliance with its statutory duties. Compelling testimony on whether the CFPB was actually performing its legal functions strengthened judicial scrutiny of attempts to quietly disable a consumer-protection agency. (4 Mar 2025)

13. A federal court issued an injunction halting mass firings of Education Department probationary employees. Stopping large-scale Education layoffs

pending litigation checked an executive effort that could have rapidly weakened federal support for disadvantaged students. (4 Mar 2025)

14. Judge John McConnell and other federal judges extended and issued orders preventing the administration from freezing congressionally approved funds and requiring release of some foreign aid. District courts' injunctions against funding freezes and orders to release aid reinforced that the executive cannot unilaterally override appropriations decisions. (6 Mar 2025; 7 Mar 2025)

15. Supreme Court of the United States denied as moot an emergency application in Bessent v. Dellinger over firing the Special Counsel. Declining to intervene after a temporary stay expired left unresolved questions about protections for the Special Counsel, illustrating procedural limits on rapid judicial checks of removals. (6 Mar 2025)

16. A federal judge issued a preliminary injunction blocking drastic cuts to medical research funding. Protecting medical research funds from abrupt executive cuts preserved scientific capacity and signaled judicial willingness to scrutinize politically driven budget reductions. (5 Mar 2025)

17. A federal court ruled that President Trump's firing of NLRB member Gwynne Wilcox was illegal and ordered her reinstatement. Finding that the president lacked authority to remove an NLRB member at will reinforced statutory limits on executive interference with independent labor adjudication. (6 Mar 2025; 7 Mar 2025)

18. Newsmax agreed to pay $40 million to settle Smartmatic's defamation lawsuit over 2020 election lies. A large settlement for broadcasting false election claims showed courts can impose meaningful costs on media outlets that spread disinformation undermining electoral legitimacy. (7 Mar 2025)

19. Judge John McConnell ruled that President Trump lacked authority to freeze congressionally appropriated funding in New York v. Trump. Holding that the president could not unilaterally halt appropriated funds reaffirmed separation of powers and Congress's exclusive power of the purse. (7 Mar 2025)

Civil Rights and Dissent

1. Trump administration and DOGE fired or threatened mass layoffs of federal workers across agencies including IRS, VA, SSA, Education, USDA, State, and CDC. Large-scale removals and buyouts of career staff weakened neutral implementation of law, chilled internal dissent, and made public employment more politically precarious. (1 Mar 2025; 3 Mar 2025; 4 Mar 2025; 5 Mar 2025; 6 Mar 2025; 7 Mar 2025)

2. Trump administration mobilized federal law enforcement and the military to conduct mass deportations and reopened a migrant family detention center. Deploying broad law-enforcement and military resources for mass removals and family detention expanded coercive control over non-citizens and raised due-process and human-rights concerns. (4 Mar 2025; 5 Mar 2025)

3. Immigration and Customs Enforcement detained a German tourist indefinitely after denying her entry. Holding a visa-waiver tourist for weeks, including in solitary confinement, over disputed work-intent allegations highlighted expansive detention powers and limited recourse for foreign visitors. (3 Mar 2025)

4. Trump administration and Congress advanced or prepared measures that could restrict voting and representation, including the SAVE Act and billionaire-funded judicial races. Proposed ID rules likely to disenfranchise name-changing women and heavy elite spending in court races threatened equal access to the ballot and impartial adjudication of election law. (2 Mar 2025; 5 Mar 2025)

5. Bishop William Barber and allied groups organized a march from St. Mark's Episcopal Church to the Supreme Court calling for moral resistance. Faith-led protest at the Supreme Court exemplified organized civic resistance to perceived injustice, asserting moral claims in the public square despite rising official hostility to dissent. (2 Mar 2025)

6. Protesters in Iowa and the 50501 movement held large demonstrations against anti-trans legislation and broader anti-democratic policies. Mass protests opposing removal of transgender civil-rights protections and other policies showed robust grassroots mobilization to defend minority rights and democratic norms. (2 Mar 2025)

7. Trump administration and Republican lawmakers faced protests over DOGE cuts and treatment of Ukraine's president. Constituents confronting members of Congress about domestic cuts and Ukraine policy reflected public pushback against decisions perceived as undermining social services and alliances. (1 Mar 2025)

8. U.S. Senate Democrats blocked a bill to ban transgender athletes from women's sports. Defeating a nationwide ban on trans athletes preserved existing protections against categorical exclusion of transgender people from school sports. (4 Mar 2025)

9. Republican state lawmakers in Oklahoma and Idaho introduced measures challenging same-sex marriage and offering benefits only to heterosexual couples. State bills seeking to undermine Obergefell and restrict tax benefits to straight couples aimed to roll back marriage equality and LGBTQ rights through state-level lawmaking. (3 Mar 2025)

10. Alabama Attorney General Steve Marshall defended the state's ability to prosecute people who help women travel out of state for abortions. Arguing that assisting interstate travel for abortion could be criminalized tested the reach of state power over reproductive rights and freedom of movement. (5 Mar 2025)

11. Trump administration and Ed Martin, interim U.S. attorney for D.C. threatened to withhold DOJ hiring from institutions that maintain DEI programs and pressured Georgetown to end DEI efforts. Conditioning federal legal-career opportunities on universities abandoning DEI initiatives used state power to chill academic freedom and equity work. (6 Mar 2025; 7 Mar 2025)

12. U.S. Department of Justice opened a Title VII investigation into the University of California over alleged antisemitic hostile work environment. Launching a system-wide civil-rights probe into UC's handling of Gaza-related protests tested how federal enforcement balances protection from discrimination with academic freedom and protest rights. (6 Mar 2025)

13. Trump administration and State Department began revoking visas of foreign students flagged by AI as Hamas supporters based on social media. Using AI-assisted social-media scans to cancel student visas for perceived political views fused surveillance with immigration control, chilling speech among non-citizens. (7 Mar 2025)

14. Trump administration planned to revoke temporary legal status and deport about 240,000 Ukrainians. Preparing mass deportations of Ukrainians who had met strict entry criteria signaled that humanitarian protections could be withdrawn for geopolitical or domestic political reasons. (7 Mar 2025)

15. Texas Governor Greg Abbott and Texas Real Estate Commission mandated removal of gender pronouns from state email signatures and fired an employee who refused. Banning pronouns in official communications and dismissing a resister curtailed workplace expression for LGBTQ and gender-nonconforming staff and enforced a narrow state-sanctioned identity norm. (6 Mar 2025)

16. Trump administration pursued broad rollbacks of federal diversity, equity, and inclusion measures and related civil-rights protections. Systematically dismantling DEI programs and weakening civil-rights enforcement reduced institutional support for addressing discrimination in federal programs and beyond. (3 Mar 2025; 6 Mar 2025)

17. California Black lawmakers introduced a package of state reparations bills. Proposals to prioritize admissions, revise curricula, and require

racial-equity analysis represented a state-level effort to address historical injustice despite a hostile federal climate. (6 Mar 2025)

18. Montana legislature defeated bills to ban drag shows and Pride marches and to remove transgender children from parents. Bipartisan rejection of sweeping anti-trans measures preserved expressive and family rights for LGBTQ people in the state. (7 Mar 2025)

19. Trump administration and Congress censured Representative Al Green and removed him from the chamber for protesting Trump's address. Physically removing and later censuring a member for vocal protest during a presidential speech used decorum rules to constrain dissent within the legislature. (5 Mar 2025; 6 Mar 2025; 7 Mar 2025)

20. President Trump threatened to cut federal funding and expel or arrest students at colleges that allow what he called illegal protests. Linking campus funding and student status to suppression of protests framed dissent as illegality and pressured institutions to police political expression. (4 Mar 2025)

21. Trump administration and DOJ placed Manhattan prosecutors handling the Eric Adams corruption case on administrative leave. Sidelining prosecutors in a high-profile corruption case raised concerns that law-enforcement personnel were being disciplined for pursuing politically sensitive investigations. (7 Mar 2025)

22. Trump administration and Social Security Administration banned employees from accessing news websites on work devices. Restricting staff access to news sites limited workers' ability to stay informed for their jobs and narrowed internal exposure to independent information sources. (6 Mar 2025)

23. Trump administration and Department of Veterans Affairs planned to fire over 80,000 VA employees and faced backlash. Proposed deep VA staffing cuts threatened veterans' access to care and suggested a shift toward privatization of core services for a politically less powerful constituency. (6 Mar 2025)

24. Trump administration and Elon Musk cut nearly $1 billion from the Department of Education and moved to dismantle the agency. Plans to abolish or drastically shrink the Education Department and its data functions threatened federal support for equal educational opportunity and civic literacy. (4 Mar 2025; 5 Mar 2025)

25. Trump administration and Bureau of Prisons transferred transgender women to men's prisons despite court rulings and restricted gender-affirming care. Moving trans women into men's facilities and limiting treatment in defiance of court orders endangered a vulnerable group and signaled selective compliance with judicial decisions. (7 Mar 2025)

Economic Structure

1. President Trump announced and implemented sweeping tariffs on imports from Canada, Mexico, and China, then partially suspended or delayed them. Imposing and then adjusting broad tariffs on key trading partners disrupted supply chains, raised consumer prices, and injected uncertainty into the global trading system. (2 Mar 2025; 3 Mar 2025; 4 Mar 2025; 5 Mar 2025; 6 Mar 2025; 7 Mar 2025)

2. Haltbakk Bunkers banned fuel sales to U.S. companies and military forces in Norway. A Norwegian fuel supplier's boycott of U.S. entities in protest of Ukraine policy illustrated how foreign firms can use economic leverage to signal disapproval of U.S. actions. (1 Mar 2025)

3. Department of Government Efficiency cut budgets for national parks and forests, reducing services and staffing. Austerity measures that lengthened lines, reduced hours, and caused layoffs in parks and forests weakened public access to shared natural resources and civic spaces. (1 Mar 2025)

4. President Trump halted fraud prosecution of Chinese crypto magnate Justin Sun. Stopping a fraud case against a crypto investor who had enriched Trump's holdings suggested that prosecutorial discretion was being used to protect a financial benefactor. (2 Mar 2025)

5. U.S. Treasury Department announced it would not enforce a Biden-era anti-money-laundering rule targeting shell companies. Choosing not to enforce rules against anonymous shell companies weakened safeguards against money laundering and reduced transparency in corporate ownership. (2 Mar 2025)

6. Environmental Protection Agency issued several Superfund and hazardous-waste regulatory actions and settlements. Updating hazardous-waste exclusions, proposing Superfund settlements, and deleting cleaned sites from the National Priorities List showed ongoing use of environmental law to manage industrial pollution and cost recovery. (3 Mar 2025; 5 Mar 2025; 6 Mar 2025)

7. U.S. Department of Education and DOGE cut nearly $1 billion from education research and canceled $900 million in student data contracts. Slashing funding for education statistics and research undermined the data infrastructure needed to evaluate school performance and equity, weakening evidence-based policy. (3 Mar 2025; 4 Mar 2025)

8. Irving Oil and other fuel suppliers raised fuel prices in response to new U.S. tariffs. Passing tariff costs through to consumers in the U.S. Northeast highlighted how trade policy quickly translated into higher everyday costs and potential inflationary pressure. (3 Mar 2025)

9. Federal Communications Commission advanced multiple information-collection and broadband rules affecting communications markets. FCC actions on paperwork reduction, emergency alerts, broadband mapping, spectrum, telehealth, schools, and IoT labeling shaped regulatory burdens and infrastructure for communications and internet access. (4 Mar 2025; 5 Mar 2025; 6 Mar 2025; 7 Mar 2025)

10. State Street ended board diversity mandates for companies in its index funds. Dropping requirements for gender and demographic disclosure and thresholds on boards signaled retreat by a major asset manager from using its leverage to promote corporate diversity. (4 Mar 2025)

11. Federal Reserve Bank of Atlanta forecasted a 2.8% annualized contraction in U.S. GDP for Q1 2025. A sharp downgrade from expected growth to contraction indicated that recent policy shocks, including tariffs, were contributing to broader economic instability. (4 Mar 2025)

12. Consumer Financial Protection Bureau leadership under Russell Vought placed most CFPB staff on indefinite leave and instructed them to ignore legal mandates. Effectively sidelining CFPB operations while telling courts the agency remained functional hollowed a key consumer watchdog and undermined truthful reporting to the judiciary. (4 Mar 2025)

13. State Street, DJI, Alipay, Ehang, and Chinese technology sectors expanded or exemplified market power in areas like diversity policy, drones, payments, batteries, 5G, and air taxis. Developments in Chinese tech leadership and State Street's governance shift illustrated how private and foreign actors shape global economic structures and standards outside direct democratic control. (4 Mar 2025; 5 Mar 2025)

14. Social Security Administration announced major staff cuts and office consolidations. Reducing SSA staff and closing regional offices risked delays and errors in benefit delivery, shifting administrative burdens onto elderly and disabled claimants. (4 Mar 2025; 5 Mar 2025)

15. State Street and other corporate actors retreated from diversity, equity, and inclusion commitments in response to political pressure. Scaling back DEI expectations in corporate governance reflected how political backlash can reshape private-sector norms around representation and accountability. (4 Mar 2025)

16. Congressional Budget Office reported that House Republicans' budget instructions would require large Medicaid cuts. CBO's analysis showed that proposed savings to fund tax cuts and other priorities could not be achieved without slashing core health programs, clarifying distributional stakes of the budget. (5 Mar 2025)

17. Drug Enforcement Administration processed applications for

importing controlled substances for pharmaceutical use. DEA's review of methamphetamine, Thebaine, and DMT import applications illustrated routine gatekeeping over controlled substances used in legitimate drug development. (6 Mar 2025; 7 Mar 2025)

18. Food and Drug Administration denied approval of a supplemental new drug application for HETLIOZ and refused a hearing request. Rejecting an insomnia indication for HETLIOZ for lack of evidence showed the FDA maintaining evidentiary standards in drug approvals despite sponsor challenges. (7 Mar 2025)

19. Federal Communications Commission expanded unlicensed use of the 6 GHz band and allocated spectrum for space launches and tribal radio. Opening additional spectrum for unlicensed devices, space launches, and tribal broadcasting supported innovation and media access while requiring careful interference management. (6 Mar 2025; 7 Mar 2025)

20. Trump administration cut off $400 million in federal grants to Columbia University over alleged antisemitism. Terminating large research and program grants to a university for perceived political failings used federal funding as leverage over academic institutions' internal governance. (7 Mar 2025)

21. Billionaire donors including Elon Musk and others poured large sums into state-level Republican campaigns and judicial races. Heavy billionaire spending in state legislative and court contests amplified wealthy actors' influence over policy on abortion, education, labor, and election rules. (5 Mar 2025)

Information, Memory, and Manipulation

1. Trump administration and CISA deprioritized monitoring of Russian cyber threats and election interference. Instructing analysts not to track Russian cyber activity, including against election systems, reduced institutional awareness of a known threat and impaired defenses for democratic infrastructure. (1 Mar 2025; 3 Mar 2025)

2. Defense Secretary Pete Hegseth and U.S. Cyber Command ordered or implemented a halt to planning and operations against Russia in cyberspace. Pausing offensive cyber operations against Russia, amid conflicting public statements, created uncertainty about U.S. cyber posture and potentially emboldened a hostile actor. (2 Mar 2025; 3 Mar 2025; 5 Mar 2025)

3. Trump administration and Department of Education cut funding for the Institute of Education Sciences and NCES data collection. Canceling contracts that maintain national education statistics degraded public data on

student outcomes, making it harder to evaluate policy and hold systems accountable. (3 Mar 2025; 4 Mar 2025)

4. Inter-American Foundation under Peter Marocco took its website offline amid leadership changes and staff leave. Removing the IAF website and sidelining staff reduced public visibility into U.S. foreign-aid projects, limiting external scrutiny of program changes. (4 Mar 2025)

5. President Trump delivered a nationally televised address to Congress filled with false claims on key issues. Using a joint-session speech to repeat major factual inaccuracies about Ukraine aid, social security, immigration, and the economy spread disinformation from the highest office. (4 Mar 2025; 5 Mar 2025)

6. Associated Press amended its lawsuit challenging the White House ban from the press pool over naming the Gulf of Mexico. AP's suit against exclusion for refusing to adopt the term "Gulf of America" highlighted executive attempts to enforce preferred language and punish noncompliant media. (4 Mar 2025)

7. Kingsley Wilson, Pentagon spokesperson tweeted comments disputing Leo Frank's innocence using white-supremacist talking points. A senior defense communicator amplifying revisionist narratives about an antisemitic lynching showed how officials can legitimize extremist reinterpretations of history. (5 Mar 2025)

8. Honda publicly refuted President Trump's claim about a new Indiana plant. A major manufacturer contradicting a presidential jobs claim underscored the administration's use of inaccurate economic boasts and the role of private actors in correcting them. (5 Mar 2025)

9. Trump administration delayed release of a report on Jeffrey Epstein. Postponing publication of the Epstein report limited public access to information about a high-profile abuse network involving powerful figures, raising suspicion of elite protection. (6 Mar 2025)

10. President Trump requested that the Declaration of Independence be moved to the Oval Office. Seeking to relocate a foundational document from archival custody to the Oval Office raised concerns about preservation, symbolism, and personalized control over national artifacts. (6 Mar 2025)

11. Trump administration was accused of potentially manipulating economic statistics to obscure tariff-related damage. Warnings that officials might massage or suppress negative economic data highlighted risks that official statistics could be politicized to hide policy costs. (6 Mar 2025)

12. Federal Election Commission scheduled a closed Sunshine Act meeting on compliance and civil actions. Holding a closed meeting on

enforcement matters balanced confidentiality with limited transparency in how federal campaign-finance rules are applied. (6 Mar 2025)

13. John Amanchukwu and allied donors conducted a book-banning tour using inflammatory rhetoric against LGBTQ content at school boards. A donor-funded campaign to pressure school boards into removing LGBTQ-inclusive books used disruptive tactics and viral media to narrow acceptable curricula and public discourse. (6 Mar 2025)

14. Social Security Administration banned employees from viewing news websites on government devices. Blocking access to news sites for SSA staff constrained their ability to consult independent information sources while performing public duties. (6 Mar 2025)

15. Trump administration and DOJ pressured Georgetown and other universities over DEI and opened a broad investigation into the University of California. Using hiring threats and civil-rights probes to challenge DEI and protest-related practices at major universities leveraged federal power to shape campus speech and governance. (6 Mar 2025; 7 Mar 2025)

16. Trump administration returned boxes of classified documents to Donald Trump from DOJ custody. Allowing a former president to retake possession of previously seized classified materials raised questions about record-keeping, security, and equal application of secrecy rules. (1 Mar 2025; 7 Mar 2025)

CHAPTER 8
WEEK 8 (8 MAR 2025 – 14 MAR 2025): CITIZENSHIP AND SERVICE AS LEVERAGE

A week of quiet decrees and targeted enforcement hollowed institutions, stratified belonging, and turned law and budgets into tools of loyalty and fear.

This week reveals a bold consolidation of executive power, increased politicization of the civil service, and systematic use of law and immigration as tools against dissenters and minorities. Trump and Musk's DOGE network drives mass layoffs, lease cancellations, and deep cuts across education, science, public health, and social programs, while courts begin to resist—ordering the reinstatement of thousands of workers, blocking cuts to teacher training, and demanding transparency from DOGE. Immigration enforcement is explicitly redirected to punish pro-Palestinian activism, with Khalil's detention under a foreign-policy pretext, visa revocations, family detention, and plans to invoke the Alien Enemies Act. At the same time, the administration moves to end birthright citizenship, expand emergency powers related to tariffs and border control, and retaliate against law firms it disfavors. Internationally, the US abandons leadership on climate and anti-corruption issues, ramps up trade conflicts with allies, considers withdrawing from NATO, and aligns more openly with Russian interests. Civil society responds with mass protests, town hall meetings, and watchdog tools like the Musk Watch tracker, but faces surveillance, subpoenas, and efforts to discredit as "terrorists." Overall, this is a week of increasing authoritarian momentum, somewhat slowed by a more assertive judiciary.

Power and Authority

1. President Donald Trump ordered transgender women in federal custody transferred to men's prisons despite court rulings. The order overrode prior court blocks and placed transgender women in men's facilities, signaling willingness to defy judicial limits and exposing a vulnerable group to heightened risk from state power. (8 Mar 2025)

2. President Donald Trump and the Department of Government Efficiency expanded centralized presidential control over agencies and empowered Elon Musk to drive deep federal downsizing. By delegating sweeping restructuring authority to a presidentially aligned unit, the administration concentrated operational power in the executive, weakening traditional bureaucratic and congressional checks. (8 Mar 2025)

3. President Donald Trump signed an executive order creating a taxpayer-backed US Crypto Reserve. The new reserve used public funds to bolster a politically connected industry, blending state financial power with private crypto interests and raising concerns about capture of economic policy. (8 Mar 2025)

4. President Donald Trump pardoned individuals convicted for the January 6 Capitol attack. The pardons signaled leniency toward political violence carried out on his behalf, weakening deterrence for future attacks on democratic institutions and undermining equal application of the law. (8 Mar 2025)

5. Department of Homeland Security eliminated union protections for tens of thousands of TSA employees. Stripping collective bargaining rights from frontline security staff reduced worker voice in a key security agency and demonstrated use of executive power to weaken organized labor in the public sector. (9 Mar 2025)

6. Department of Health and Human Services offered large buyouts to tens of thousands of employees during a measles outbreak. Mass voluntary buyouts in the middle of a public health emergency risked hollowing out response capacity, illustrating how executive-driven staffing cuts can endanger basic protections. (9 Mar 2025)

7. Social Security Administration changed overpayment recovery rules to allow 100% benefit withholding. Authorizing full benefit clawbacks from overpaid recipients, regardless of fault, gave the agency harsh collection power over vulnerable beneficiaries, heightening economic precarity for many. (9 Mar 2025)

8. Treasury Secretary Scott Bessent announced an administration goal to shrink and privatize federal services. Framing privatization as a core response

to economic strain signaled a strategic shift away from public provision of key services, with implications for accountability and universal access. (9 Mar 2025)

9. President Donald Trump publicly defended Elon Musk and labeled Tesla protesters as domestic terrorists. Branding peaceful corporate critics as terrorists used presidential rhetoric to delegitimize dissent and protect an allied billionaire, potentially chilling protest activity. (12 Mar 2025)

10. President Donald Trump declared a national emergency at the southern US border. The border emergency expanded unilateral authority over immigration and funding, normalizing emergency tools for long-term policy goals and sidestepping ordinary legislative processes. (14 Mar 2025)

11. President Donald Trump ended birthright citizenship by executive action. Unilaterally revoking automatic citizenship for US-born children of noncitizens challenged long-settled constitutional norms and created a stratified system of membership tied to parentage and status. (14 Mar 2025)

12. President Donald Trump terminated federal diversity programs across the government. Eliminating diversity initiatives reduced institutional support for inclusion and equal opportunity within federal workplaces, weakening tools to address systemic discrimination. (14 Mar 2025)

13. President Donald Trump ordered release of water from California dams under disputed justifications. The directive, apparently misaligned with operational realities, highlighted how presidential intervention in resource management can be driven by narrative rather than evidence, complicating accountable stewardship. (14 Mar 2025)

14. President Donald Trump issued an executive order to continue reducing the federal bureaucracy by dismantling non-statutory components of multiple agencies. Targeting several independent and grant-making entities for elimination concentrated discretion in the executive over which public functions survive, weakening pluralistic institutional infrastructure. (14 Mar 2025)

15. President Donald Trump issued an executive order directing punitive restrictions on the law firm Paul Weiss. Using national security powers to strip clearances and contracts from a disfavored firm blurred lines between public authority and personal vendetta, pressuring independent legal actors. (14 Mar 2025)

16. President Donald Trump rescinded multiple Biden-era executive orders across public health, labor, climate, and rights policy. The sweeping rollback reoriented federal priorities on health, environment, labor, and civil rights through unilateral action, underscoring how much policy rests on reversible executive directives. (14 Mar 2025)

Institutions and Governance

1. Representative Terri Sewell and House Democrats reintroduced the John R. Lewis Voting Rights Advancement Act. The bill sought to restore preclearance and strengthen federal review of discriminatory voting changes, aiming to rebuild institutional safeguards against racial voter suppression. (8 Mar 2025)

2. Federal Election Commission scheduled a public Sunshine Act meeting to consider an advisory opinion request. The open meeting on campaign law guidance reflected ongoing use of formal, transparent procedures in federal election oversight. (10 Mar 2025)

3. House Republicans and former President Donald Trump advanced a Trump-backed continuing resolution with deep non-defense cuts to avert a shutdown. The stopgap bill preserved government operations but shifted spending toward defense and enforcement, illustrating how budget brinkmanship can be used to reshape policy priorities. (10 Mar 2025; 11 Mar 2025)

4. Wyoming legislature passed multiple bills restricting transgender rights in sports and public facilities. The package of laws used state legislative power to narrow participation and access for transgender people, embedding contested social policy into institutional rules. (10 Mar 2025)

5. Federal Election Commission canceled a scheduled open meeting. Calling off a public FEC session reduced near-term transparency around campaign-regulation decisions, limiting opportunities for public observation and input. (14 Mar 2025)

6. House Republicans passed a measure redefining days to block congressional termination of Trump's tariff emergency. By manipulating how statutory days are counted, the House insulated an emergency declaration from timely disapproval, weakening Congress's practical check on executive trade powers. (13 Mar 2025)

7. Congress used the Congressional Review Act to overturn an EPA methane waste emissions charge rule. The disapproval blocked a climate-related fee on oil and gas emissions, showing how legislative oversight can be used to dismantle regulatory tools for environmental accountability. (14 Mar 2025)

8. Congress enacted a resolution disapproving a rule on protection of marine archaeological resources. Overturning the marine archaeology rule demonstrated Congress's willingness to narrow agency authority over environmental and cultural resource protections. (14 Mar 2025)

9. Senate Democratic leadership agreed to advance and support the

House continuing resolution to avoid a shutdown despite internal opposition. Democratic leaders backed a Republican-authored funding bill to keep government open, trading policy leverage for institutional continuity and exposing intra-party divisions over strategy. (12 Mar 2025; 14 Mar 2025)

10. House subcommittee chair Keith Self misgendered Representative Sarah McBride and adjourned a foreign affairs hearing amid dispute. The abrupt adjournment over a discriminatory remark derailed oversight on arms control and assistance to Europe, illustrating how culture-war conflicts can disrupt substantive legislative work. (12 Mar 2025)

11. House Republicans held a hearing to consider weakening the Endangered Species Act and Marine Mammal Protection Act. The oversight session explored easing environmental safeguards to speed industrial projects, signaling legislative interest in rebalancing statutory protections toward development. (11 Mar 2025)

12. Federal courts and Democratic state attorneys general pursued and won discovery orders requiring DOGE and Elon Musk to produce internal records. Judicial orders compelling disclosure about DOGE's authority and operations strengthened external oversight of a powerful quasi-administrative unit operating from the White House. (11 Mar 2025; 13 Mar 2025)

13. Census Bureau canceled multiple advisory committee meetings related to the 2030 Census and racial and ethnic populations. Scrapping planned advisory sessions reduced structured input from experts and communities into census planning, potentially affecting representation and resource allocation decisions. (12 Mar 2025; 13 Mar 2025)

14. Department of Education abolished more than half of its Civil Rights Division offices. Eliminating much of the department's civil-rights enforcement infrastructure weakened federal capacity to investigate discrimination in schools and colleges nationwide. (11 Mar 2025)

15. Department of Education under Secretary Linda McMahon laid off roughly half of its workforce in a mass firing. The large-scale staff reduction, framed as efficiency, severely constrained the department's ability to administer aid and enforce education laws, and advanced a stated goal of winding the agency down. (12 Mar 2025)

16. Coalition of Democratic state attorneys general sued to block the Education Department's mass layoffs as unconstitutional and illegal. The lawsuit argued that halving the department's staff crippled its congressionally mandated functions, turning to the courts to defend agency capacity and separation of powers. (13 Mar 2025)

17. Federal judges William Alsup and James Bredar ordered reinstatement of tens of thousands of purged probationary federal employees. The injunc-

tions found the DOGE-driven mass firings likely unlawful and forced agencies to offer jobs back, reinforcing legal protections for civil servants against politicized purges. (12 Mar 2025; 13 Mar 2025; 14 Mar 2025)

18. Federal judiciary blocked Trump administration cuts to teacher training funds via temporary restraining orders. By halting large reductions in teacher training grants, courts preserved programs addressing shortages and signaled that executive budget moves must comply with statutory and constitutional limits. (12 Mar 2025)

19. Federal courts demanded evidence from EPA to justify cancellation of multibillion-dollar climate grants. Requiring the agency to substantiate claims of wrongdoing before voiding grants reinforced procedural safeguards around major funding decisions and constrained arbitrary reversals. (13 Mar 2025)

20. U.S. District Judge Beryl Howell temporarily blocked most of an executive order punishing law firm Perkins Coie. The ruling found the order resembled an unconstitutional bill of attainder, curbing the president's attempt to single out a disfavored firm and protecting independent legal representation. (12 Mar 2025)

21. Law firm Perkins Coie filed suit challenging an executive order that stripped its lawyers' clearances and access. The lawsuit contested targeted executive retaliation against a private firm, testing judicial willingness to police abuses of national security rationales. (12 Mar 2025)

22. Federal courts and Judge Tanya Chutkan ordered DOGE and Elon Musk to disclose staff identities and cost-cutting records. Compelling detailed discovery into DOGE's structure and decisions aimed to clarify whether a powerful quasi-agency is operating within constitutional and statutory bounds. (13 Mar 2025)

23. Federal courts and Judge William Alsup criticized the administration's explanations for mass firings as a sham. Judicial skepticism toward the stated performance-based rationale for purges underscored the role of courts in exposing pretext when executive actions target the civil service. (14 Mar 2025)

24. Federal courts ruled that the Department of Government Efficiency is likely subject to FOIA. Bringing DOGE under public records law extended transparency obligations to a powerful, previously opaque coordinating body inside the executive branch. (10 Mar 2025)

25. EPA administrative judiciary denied a petition to set aside a Clean Water Act consent agreement. Upholding the consent order maintained an existing enforcement settlement and illustrated internal adjudicatory processes for environmental compliance disputes. (13 Mar 2025)

Civil Rights and Dissent

1. North Carolina Judge Jefferson Griffin challenged 2024 election results by seeking to discard over 65,000 ballots. The attempt to invalidate tens of thousands of votes over registration technicalities in a race he lost raised concerns about partisan use of courts to disenfranchise voters. (8 Mar 2025)

2. Supreme Court of the United States previously struck down Voting Rights Act preclearance in Shelby County v. Holder, now cited in current analysis. The earlier ruling, highlighted this week, removed federal review of voting changes in certain jurisdictions, enabling new state-level restrictions that disproportionately affect minority turnout. (8 Mar 2025)

3. Brennan Center for Justice researchers documented a widening racial turnout gap in Alabama after loss of preclearance. The study showed that nonwhite turnout lagged far behind white turnout in formerly covered areas, evidencing real-world effects of weakened federal voting protections. (8 Mar 2025)

4. Trump administration and Secretary of State Marco Rubio used a rarely invoked foreign policy provision to detain and attempt to deport Palestinian activist Mahmoud Khalil. Invoking foreign policy risk to target a lawful permanent resident for his campus activism blurred lines between immigration enforcement and punishment of political speech. (8 Mar 2025; 9 Mar 2025; 10 Mar 2025; 11 Mar 2025; 12 Mar 2025; 13 Mar 2025; 14 Mar 2025)

5. Immigration and Customs Enforcement detained a naturalized US citizen during a mass enforcement operation despite his documentation. The detention of Jensy Machado, apparently based on appearance rather than status, highlighted risks of racial profiling and erosion of security even for naturalized citizens. (10 Mar 2025)

6. Senator Marco Rubio announced plans to revoke visas and green cards of people deemed to support Hamas. The broad threat to immigration status based on perceived political sympathies risked conflating dissent with terrorism and chilling lawful expression among noncitizens. (9 Mar 2025)

7. Department of Homeland Security announced visa revocation for a Columbia student accused of supporting Hamas, leading to self-deportation. Using immigration penalties tied to alleged political alignment rather than criminal charges raised due process and free speech concerns for student activists. (13 Mar 2025)

8. Trump administration resumed family detention for immigrants and reopened two Texas family detention centers. Reinstating family detention reversed prior moves toward alternatives and exposed children and parents to

conditions previously criticized as harmful and legally questionable. (12 Mar 2025)

9. Department of Justice under Trump issued a subpoena to a New York City migrant shelter hotel demanding resident identities and funding details. The sweeping demand for data on undocumented residents and program funding risked deterring participation in city shelter programs and facilitated targeted enforcement. (12 Mar 2025; 13 Mar 2025)

10. Trump administration dramatically increased immigration arrests and detention, including many people without criminal convictions. The surge in detentions after rolling back prioritization guidelines expanded the reach of immigration enforcement into everyday life, especially for non-criminal immigrants. (13 Mar 2025)

11. Trump administration planned to invoke the Alien Enemies Act to arrest and deport certain noncitizens without due process. Reviving a wartime authority historically linked to internment threatened to bypass normal legal protections for targeted immigrant groups. (12 Mar 2025)

12. Immigration and Customs Enforcement deported the noncitizen parents of a US-citizen child recovering from brain cancer surgery. Removing caregivers of a critically ill citizen child underscored the human costs of rigid enforcement and raised questions about humanitarian discretion. (12 Mar 2025)

13. Immigration officers at Logan Airport allegedly tortured and abused a New Hampshire green card holder during detention. Reports of violent interrogation, sleep deprivation, and denial of medication against a lawful resident pointed to serious human rights violations within immigration enforcement. (14 Mar 2025)

14. Trump administration suspended the US refugee resettlement program. Halting refugee admissions curtailed a longstanding humanitarian commitment and closed a key pathway to safety for people fleeing persecution. (14 Mar 2025)

15. Trump administration and Columbia University pressured and enabled disciplinary actions against students involved in 2024 pro-Palestinian protests. Expulsions, suspensions, and diploma revocations following federal demands showed how government leverage can shape university responses to political protest. (11 Mar 2025)

16. Jewish Voice for Peace and New York City police saw nearly 100 protesters arrested at Trump Tower during a sit-in for Mahmoud Khalil's release. The mass arrests for trespass and obstruction at a high-profile protest highlighted tensions between direct action tactics and law enforcement responses in politically sensitive cases. (13 Mar 2025)

17. Elon Musk and Tesla critics faced nationwide protests at Tesla facilities over Musk's policies and political role. Coordinated demonstrations at corporate sites signaled growing public resistance to perceived oligarchic influence over government and policy. (9 Mar 2025; 10 Mar 2025)

18. Scientists, women's rights advocates, and allied groups organized hundreds of protests nationwide against government cuts and policies. Large coordinated marches for science and women's rights demonstrated robust civic mobilization against perceived attacks on evidence-based policy and equality. (10 Mar 2025)

19. North Carolina Democrats and allied organizers planned rallies, gallery-packing, and protests at the state legislature and Tesla dealership. These events used peaceful assembly and visibility tactics to pressure state lawmakers and corporate actors, reinforcing participatory channels outside formal elections. (10 Mar 2025)

20. Democratic Party organizations announced a series of "People's Town Halls" in Republican-held swing districts. Holding unofficial town halls where incumbents avoid constituents aimed to restore direct dialogue and accountability in districts with limited formal engagement. (14 Mar 2025)

21. Senator Bernie Sanders and United Auto Workers president Shawn Fain conducted a national tour on oligarchy and democracy. The tour linked economic inequality to democratic erosion, mobilizing public debate about concentrated wealth and political power. (10 Mar 2025)

22. Trump administration and Department of Education Civil Rights Office issued warnings to 60 colleges over alleged antisemitic harassment with threat of enforcement. The broad warnings signaled aggressive federal scrutiny of campus speech and conduct, raising questions about how civil-rights enforcement intersects with academic freedom. (11 Mar 2025)

23. Trump administration ended birthright citizenship and sought Supreme Court approval to enforce the change. Moving to restrict citizenship for US-born children of noncitizens, and appealing injunctions, threatened to create a hereditary underclass and destabilize equal civic status. (8 Mar 2025; 11 Mar 2025; 13 Mar 2025; 14 Mar 2025)

24. Trump administration and DHS saw immigration enforcement deaths and dangers at the US-Mexico border during a storm. The deaths of migrants in harsh terrain underscored the lethal risks of current border policies and the limits of humanitarian safeguards in enforcement operations. (14 Mar 2025)

25. Family of Monica Cameroni De Adams filed a $50 million claim against San Diego over an unhoused woman's death in a towed van. The claim alleged city negligence in failing to discover and aid an injured

unhoused woman, spotlighting systemic risks faced by people living in vehicles. (14 Mar 2025)

26. Paula White, Director of the White House Faith Office called for challenging separation of church and state to reintroduce prayer and Bibles in public schools. Her remarks signaled an official push to reshape constitutional doctrine on religion in public institutions, potentially narrowing religious freedom for non-adherents. (14 Mar 2025)

Economic Structure

1. Department of Government Efficiency and Elon Musk implemented cuts that reduced basic services for US government staff abroad while funding office luxuries. Shifting resources from core communications and utilities to high-end amenities for officials reflected priorities that may degrade state capacity while benefiting insiders. (8 Mar 2025)

2. Environmental Protection Agency and DOGE required DOGE approval for any EPA spending over $50,000. Centralizing mid-level spending decisions in a politically aligned efficiency office curtailed agency autonomy and gave a private-aligned actor leverage over environmental operations. (8 Mar 2025)

3. Trump administration cut federal funding for drug detection technology and international container control programs. Reducing support for border detection tools and cooperative programs weakened the state's ability to interdict synthetic drugs, with public health and security consequences. (8 Mar 2025)

4. Trump administration slashed USAID funding for programs addressing root causes of the drug trade and violence. Cutting prevention and development programs undermined long-term strategies to reduce crime and migration pressures, shifting costs back onto communities and enforcement systems. (8 Mar 2025)

5. Trump administration pursued aggressive tariff policies that contributed to market volatility and recession fears. Broad tariffs and public rhetoric blaming "globalists" coincided with sharp stock declines and uncertainty, illustrating how trade shocks can destabilize the broader economy. (8 Mar 2025; 10 Mar 2025; 11 Mar 2025)

6. Trump administration cut defense production and science funding and canceled industrial policies supporting factory construction. Rolling back support for defense manufacturing, research, and industrial strategy risked weakening both national security capacity and long-term economic competitiveness. (8 Mar 2025)

7. Trump administration tolerated money laundering and weakened financial enforcement priorities. A permissive stance toward money laundering undermined the integrity of the financial system and signaled that well-connected actors might evade meaningful scrutiny. (8 Mar 2025)

8. Veterans Administration under Secretary Doug Collins planned to cut about 80,000 jobs, many held by veterans. Eliminating a fifth of the VA workforce threatened both veteran employment and the quality and timeliness of care for millions relying on the agency. (10 Mar 2025)

9. Veterans Administration required therapists to conduct mental health sessions in open cubicles due to an end to remote work. Forcing confidential counseling into non-private spaces risked violating privacy laws and deterring veterans from seeking care, trading service quality for rigid workplace rules. (10 Mar 2025)

10. Trump administration cut millions from federal cybersecurity initiatives including election infrastructure support. Reducing funding for cyber defenses, particularly for state and local election systems, increased vulnerability to digital attacks on critical democratic infrastructure. (10 Mar 2025)

11. Trump administration and Department of Education canceled $400 million in federal funding to Columbia University over antisemitism findings. The unprecedented grant termination used federal purse power to pressure a university's handling of campus speech and safety, raising concerns about politicized funding decisions. (8 Mar 2025; 11 Mar 2025)

12. U.S. Department of Agriculture cut over $1 billion from local food purchasing programs for schools and food banks. Eliminating major local food initiatives reduced support for small producers and threatened nutrition access for children and food-insecure families. (11 Mar 2025; 13 Mar 2025)

13. National Institutes of Health eliminated or restricted funding for dozens of studies on vaccine confidence. Cutting research into why vaccination rates are falling limited evidence needed to design effective public health interventions amid rising preventable disease risk. (13 Mar 2025)

14. Department of Health and Human Services under Robert F. Kennedy Jr. planned clinical trials of unproven measles treatments while canceling key vaccine advisory meetings. Redirecting resources toward unvalidated therapies and disrupting normal vaccine review processes risked undermining evidence-based policy and worsening an active measles outbreak. (13 Mar 2025)

15. Trump administration canceled $800 million in federal medical research grants to Johns Hopkins University. Pulling large research grants from a leading institution weakened national biomedical capacity and

signaled vulnerability of long-term science funding to political shifts. (13 Mar 2025)

16. Environmental Protection Agency under Administrator Lee Zeldin announced 31 actions to roll back environmental regulations including EV and coal plant rules. The sweeping deregulatory package favored fossil fuel and industrial interests over environmental and health protections, illustrating regulatory capture risks. (13 Mar 2025)

17. Department of Government Efficiency moved to terminate 793 federal building leases to cut costs. Mass lease cancellations aimed at savings forced agencies to relocate or consolidate, potentially disrupting service delivery and access for the public. (14 Mar 2025)

18. Trump administration cut off global food and emergency aid and dismantled USAID's operational capacity. Curtailing humanitarian and development aid reduced US support for crisis response and democracy abroad, while weakening a key instrument of soft power. (8 Mar 2025)

19. Trump administration implemented 25% tariffs on all imported steel and aluminum and threatened higher rates on Canada. The broad metal tariffs and threats of 50% duties on Canadian imports triggered retaliatory measures and market declines, using trade policy in a confrontational, high-risk manner. (12 Mar 2025; 13 Mar 2025)

20. President Donald Trump threatened a 200% tariff on EU wines and champagnes in response to EU whiskey tariffs. The retaliatory tariff threat escalated a transatlantic trade dispute and raised conflict-of-interest concerns given Trump's own wine business. (12 Mar 2025; 13 Mar 2025; 14 Mar 2025)

21. European Union announced up to €26 billion in counter-tariffs on US goods in response to Trump's metal tariffs. The EU's large countermeasures deepened the trade war, amplifying economic uncertainty for exporters and workers on both sides. (12 Mar 2025)

22. Elon Musk and the Department of Government Efficiency overstated claimed federal savings by an estimated 92% according to an external tracker. Inflating reported budget cuts distorted public understanding of fiscal policy and masked the real scale and impact of reductions in public services. (12 Mar 2025)

23. Elon Musk publicly attacked the Musk Watch DOGE Tracker that documented overstated savings. The personal attack on an independent fiscal watchdog sought to discredit scrutiny of DOGE's numbers, discouraging critical evaluation of official economic claims. (13 Mar 2025)

24. Treasury Secretary Scott Bessent described economic hardship from administration policies as a necessary "de-tox period". Framing widespread economic pain as a cleansing phase normalized policy-induced shocks and

signaled willingness to offload adjustment costs onto the public. (8 Mar 2025)

25. Congressional Budget Office warned that GOP budget targets would require deep cuts to major healthcare programs. The analysis indicated that meeting proposed reductions would likely mean slashing Medicare, Medicaid, or CHIP, highlighting the distributive stakes of fiscal choices. (9 Mar 2025)

26. Trump administration closed applications for all income-driven student loan repayment plans and narrowed PSLF eligibility. Shutting off access to income-based repayment and limiting forgiveness options increased financial strain on borrowers, especially public servants, and reduced a key social mobility tool. (14 Mar 2025)

27. Trump administration cut over $1 billion in local food purchasing for schools and food banks. The cuts undermined local agriculture and removed a buffer against hunger for low-income families, shifting food insecurity risks back onto communities. (13 Mar 2025)

28. Federal agencies (EPA, OSHA, FCC, FDA, DEA, GSA, FAR councils) issued multiple technical rules, comment extensions, and debarment orders affecting safety, procurement, and drug regulation. Routine regulatory actions on chemicals, workplace safety, communications, and controlled substances continued to shape the economic and compliance environment for firms and workers. (10 Mar 2025; 11 Mar 2025; 13 Mar 2025; 14 Mar 2025)

Information, Memory, and Manipulation

1. Department of Homeland Security under Kristi Noem began polygraph testing employees to identify and prosecute alleged leakers about ICE raids. Using intrusive lie-detector screenings to hunt leakers risked deterring whistleblowing and constraining internal channels for exposing abuses. (8 Mar 2025)

2. Immigration and Customs Enforcement and other federal agencies accessed license plate reader data in sanctuary jurisdictions for immigration enforcement. Tapping local surveillance systems in areas that limit cooperation with ICE circumvented local policy choices and expanded quiet tracking of residents' movements. (11 Mar 2025)

3. Elon Musk's social media platform X suffered prolonged outages attributed to a DDoS cyberattack, prompting conspiracy speculation. The disruption of a major political communication platform, followed by unsubstantiated claims about perpetrators, highlighted both infrastructure vulnerability and the ease of narrative manipulation. (9 Mar 2025; 12 Mar 2025)

4. Darren Beattie, senior State Department official deleted past abusive tweets about Secretary of State Marco Rubio after appointment. Scrubbing inflammatory posts by a public diplomacy official raised questions about transparency and the curation of officials' public records once in office. (10 Mar 2025)

5. Elon Musk's DOGE website removed details that previously allowed independent verification of claimed budget cuts. Making it harder to cross-check savings figures against federal data reduced fiscal transparency and increased reliance on official narratives. (12 Mar 2025)

6. Popular Information launched the Musk Watch DOGE Tracker to fact-check DOGE's claimed savings. The tracker exposed large discrepancies between claimed and verifiable cuts, providing an independent tool to scrutinize government cost-cutting rhetoric. (13 Mar 2025)

7. Robert F. Kennedy Jr. as HHS Secretary spread false claims about vaccine safety and effectiveness during a major measles outbreak. Anti-vaccine statements from the nation's top health official undermined trust in immunization programs and risked worsening preventable disease spread. (13 Mar 2025)

8. President Donald Trump repeated baseless claims that the 2020 election was rigged and called for jailing unnamed perpetrators. Renewed falsehoods about past election fraud from a sitting president continued to erode public confidence in electoral legitimacy and framed political opponents as criminals. (14 Mar 2025)

9. President Donald Trump praised Judge Aileen Cannon for dismissing his classified documents case and suggested criticism of judges should be illegal. Celebrating a favorable ruling while proposing to criminalize criticism of judges signaled a desire to shield the judiciary from public scrutiny when it benefits the executive. (14 Mar 2025)

10. Trump administration and USAID leadership ordered staff to shred or burn agency records despite federal preservation laws. Directing destruction of official documents threatened the integrity of the historical record and future accountability for aid and foreign policy decisions. (13 Mar 2025)

11. Federal courts ruled that DOGE is likely covered by FOIA and ordered rolling production of its records. Bringing DOGE under transparency law and compelling document releases countered efforts to keep a powerful coordinating body outside normal public scrutiny. (10 Mar 2025; 11 Mar 2025)

12. Federal Election Commission canceled an open meeting under the Government in the Sunshine Act. The cancellation reduced short-term visibility into FEC deliberations, limiting opportunities for media and public to monitor campaign-regulation decisions. (14 Mar 2025)

13. Red Wine and Blue organized a public class explaining how the North Carolina General Assembly functions. Providing civic education on state legislative processes aimed to equip residents with knowledge to engage more effectively in democratic governance. (10 Mar 2025)

14. Elon Musk made televised statements calling Social Security a "Ponzi scheme" and advocating workforce cuts at SSA. Framing core social insurance as fraudulent from a position of influence shaped public narratives around entitlement programs and potential future cuts. (11 Mar 2025)

15. US Agency for Global Media and Trump administration faced defunding and shutdown of USAGM and its international broadcasters by executive order. Defunding Voice of America and related outlets weakened US-backed independent media abroad and endangered journalists, while pleasing authoritarian rivals' state media. (14 Mar 2025)

16. US Census Bureau canceled multiple scientific and advisory committee meetings on census planning and methods. Halting expert advisory sessions risked reducing methodological rigor and stakeholder input into population data that underpins representation and funding decisions. (10 Mar 2025; 12 Mar 2025; 13 Mar 2025)

17. FDA and federal courts issued multiple debarment orders against individuals who falsified clinical data or imported illegal drugs. Removing convicted fraudsters from drug-related work protected the integrity of clinical evidence and regulatory decision-making. (13 Mar 2025; 14 Mar 2025)

CHAPTER 9
WEEK 9 (15 MAR 2025 – 21 MAR 2025): EMERGENCY POWERS AS ROUTINE GOVERNANCE

In Trump's ninth week back in office, wartime statutes, deportation flights, and agency purges turned law and bureaucracy into pliable tools of executive will.

This week tests American constitutionalism severely, as the executive branch openly disobeys courts, weakens key agencies, and uses immigration and education policies for ideological goals. The strongest strain hits the rule of law and separation of powers: mass deportations under the Alien Enemies Act occurred despite multiple federal orders, while Trump and congressional allies increased their attacks on Judge Boasberg, including proposing impeachment and removal efforts. At the same time, the administration moved to dismantle the Department of Education, transfer student loans to the SBA, cut funding for USAID and cultural agencies, and gave Elon Musk's DOGE broad access to federal systems—only partly blocked by federal judges. Universities, immigrants, and protesters face funding freezes, visa revocations, and criminal charges for activism, while independent media (USAGM/VOA, RFE/RL, AP access) faces stiff restrictions. Courts, state AGs, and some judges have pushed back, obtaining TROs on deportations, DEI rollbacks, USAID activities, DOGE data collection, and climate funding. But the pattern is clear: swift executive overreach, privatization of government functions, and acceptance of constitutional brinkmanship grow stronger.

Power and Authority

1. President Donald Trump used a Justice Department speech to air personal grievances about criminal cases. Trump's use of a Justice Department policy speech to relitigate his own criminal cases blurred the line between personal interests and neutral law enforcement, signaling pressure on the department to serve the president's political narrative. (15 Mar 2025)

2. President Donald Trump invoked the Alien Enemies Act to authorize arrests and deportations of noncitizens. Trump's peacetime invocation of an 18th-century wartime statute to arrest and deport alleged Venezuelan gang members expanded emergency-style executive power over noncitizens and weakened due process protections. (15 Mar 2025; 17 Mar 2025)

3. Trump administration deported hundreds of alleged gang members to El Salvador despite a federal court order. By continuing mass deportation flights to El Salvador after Judge Boasberg's restraining order, the administration openly defied judicial authority, undermining checks on executive power and weakening the rule of law. (15 Mar 2025; 16 Mar 2025; 17 Mar 2025; 18 Mar 2025; 19 Mar 2025; 20 Mar 2025; 21 Mar 2025)

4. President Donald Trump ordered US military airstrikes in Yemen without congressional authorization. Unilateral airstrikes in Yemen that killed dozens of civilians, launched without explicit congressional authorization, concentrated war-making power in the presidency and sidestepped democratic oversight of lethal force. (15 Mar 2025; 16 Mar 2025)

5. President Donald Trump declared that President Biden's pardons were void because they used an autopen signature. Trump's assertion that Biden's autopen-signed pardons are legally void challenged the settled validity of presidential clemency and suggested a president can unilaterally nullify a predecessor's lawful acts. (16 Mar 2025; 17 Mar 2025; 18 Mar 2025)

6. President Donald Trump revoked Secret Service protection for Hunter and Ashley Biden. Revoking security details for Biden's adult children used presidential control over protective services in a way that appeared retaliatory, raising concerns about politicized use of personal security decisions. (17 Mar 2025)

7. President Donald Trump targeted Democratic-aligned law firms through executive action and public attacks. Trump's executive order against Perkins Coie and broader attacks on Democratic-aligned firms signaled willingness to wield state power against disfavored legal representation, pressuring the independence of the bar. (17 Mar 2025)

8. President Donald Trump ordered the dismantling of the US Institute of Peace's independent board. By removing the congressionally funded US

Institute of Peace's board, the administration asserted direct control over an independent peace institution, weakening legislative design of foreign-policy bodies. (17 Mar 2025)

9. President Donald Trump announced broad expansions of presidential power over protests and immigration enforcement. Commentary described the administration's push to incarcerate protesters and deport immigrants as part of a broader expansion of presidential authority that risks eroding civil liberties and institutional checks. (16 Mar 2025)

10. President Donald Trump signed an order eliminating the US Agency for Global Media and restructuring its outlets. Eliminating USAGM and sidelining Voice of America and related broadcasters concentrated control of state-funded international media in the executive, weakening semi-independent channels that had provided diverse information abroad. (15 Mar 2025; 16 Mar 2025; 18 Mar 2025)

11. President Donald Trump signed an executive order dismantling the Department of Education and shifting its functions. Trump's orders to close the congressionally created Education Department and reassign student loans and disability services attempted to restructure a core domestic agency by decree, bypassing normal legislative processes. (19 Mar 2025; 20 Mar 2025; 21 Mar 2025)

12. President Donald Trump signed an executive order on state and local preparedness shifting resilience responsibilities. The resilience order pushed more responsibility for critical infrastructure and continuity planning to states and localities, potentially weakening coordinated federal capacity in national emergencies. (19 Mar 2025)

13. President Donald Trump issued multiple executive orders to consolidate procurement, expand data sharing, and boost mining. Orders centralizing procurement, mandating broad inter-agency data access, and expediting mineral production expanded presidential control over federal spending, information flows, and resource policy with limited external oversight. (20 Mar 2025)

14. President Donald Trump signed an order granting DOGE access to unclassified federal agency systems and records. Granting the Department of Government Efficiency sweeping access to agency data and software systems concentrated informational power in a lightly accountable White House-aligned unit, raising risks of politicized use of administrative data. (19 Mar 2025)

15. President Donald Trump revoked security clearances from prominent political and legal opponents. Stripping security clearances from Biden, Harris, Cheney and others used national-security tools against political rivals,

potentially chilling post-service oversight and bipartisan consultation on classified matters. (21 Mar 2025)

16. President Donald Trump admitted Elon Musk's China business ties made war-plans briefings inappropriate. Trump's acknowledgment that Musk's China interests conflicted with sharing war plans underscored how deeply a private businessman had been integrated into national-security deliberations before concerns were publicly recognized. (21 Mar 2025)

17. President Donald Trump fired both Democratic commissioners at the Federal Trade Commission. Removing the FTC's Democratic commissioners, likely without statutory cause, undermined the independence of a key competition regulator and risked stalling enforcement by depriving it of a quorum. (18 Mar 2025; 19 Mar 2025)

18. President Donald Trump called for the impeachment of Judge James Boasberg after rulings against his deportation policy. Trump's public demand to impeach the chief district judge who blocked his Alien Enemies Act deportations escalated direct executive attacks on the judiciary for adverse rulings. (17 Mar 2025; 18 Mar 2025; 19 Mar 2025; 20 Mar 2025)

19. Representative Brandon Gill filed articles of impeachment against Judge James Boasberg. A House member's impeachment articles targeting a judge over a specific deportation ruling translated Trump's rhetoric into institutional pressure on judicial independence. (19 Mar 2025)

20. Supporters of Donald Trump issued bomb threats against judges who ruled against the administration. Bomb threats against judges, including a Supreme Court justice, for decisions adverse to Trump created a climate of intimidation around the judiciary and could deter robust oversight of executive actions. (21 Mar 2025)

21. President Donald Trump proposed overhauling or eliminating FEMA and shifting disaster relief to states. Trump's suggestion to dismantle FEMA and devolve disaster relief to states threatened the federal government's capacity to provide equitable emergency assistance, especially to poorer or harder-hit regions. (18 Mar 2025)

22. President Donald Trump revoked a prior punitive order against law firm Paul Weiss after it agreed to policy changes. Revoking an earlier order against Paul Weiss once it pledged neutrality and pro bono commitments showed how executive pressure can be used to reshape private legal institutions' policies. (21 Mar 2025)

23. President Donald Trump suggested 20-year El Salvador prison sentences for Tesla vandals. Trump's call to send US Tesla vandals to serve long sentences in El Salvador invoked foreign carceral systems as a punitive

tool, signaling extreme, extraterritorial punishment proposals tied to a favored corporation. (20 Mar 2025)

Institutions and Governance

1. US Congress and President Donald Trump enacted the Full-Year Continuing Appropriations and Extensions Act, 2025. Passage and signing of a full-year continuing appropriations law averted a shutdown and kept federal agencies funded, but also locked in the administration's restructuring priorities for the fiscal year. (15 Mar 2025)

2. Democratic leaders and members of Congress debated strategy over opposing the Republican funding bill. Internal Democratic disputes over whether to block or accept the GOP funding bill revealed tensions between resisting Trump's agenda and preventing a shutdown, shaping legislative checks on executive policy. (15 Mar 2025; 19 Mar 2025)

3. Trump administration announced investigations into 45 universities for alleged race-exclusionary practices. Launching broad investigations into graduate programs' alleged race-exclusionary practices extended federal oversight into campus admissions and could be used to chill diversity initiatives and institutional autonomy. (15 Mar 2025)

4. US Department of Education halted processing of income-driven student loan repayment applications, prompting lawsuits. The Education Department's shutdown of income-driven repayment processing, now challenged by the AFT, disrupted statutory relief mechanisms for borrowers and raised questions about compliance with congressional mandates. (19 Mar 2025; 20 Mar 2025)

5. American Federation of Teachers sued the Department of Education over halted student loan repayment plans. The teachers union's lawsuit sought to force the Education Department to restore access to income-driven repayment, using litigation to defend statutory protections for millions of borrowers. (19 Mar 2025; 20 Mar 2025)

6. US Department of Justice sought to remove Judge Boasberg from the Alien Enemies Act deportation case. DOJ's attempt to disqualify the judge overseeing the contested deportations challenged judicial oversight of executive immigration powers and tested norms around recusal and appellate review. (19 Mar 2025)

7. Chief Justice John Roberts publicly rebuked calls to impeach Judge Boasberg over his rulings. Roberts' rare public statement defending Boasberg and the appellate process reaffirmed that impeachment is not a remedy for

disagreement with judicial decisions, bolstering formal norms of judicial independence. (18 Mar 2025; 19 Mar 2025; 20 Mar 2025)

8. Federal courts issued and expanded temporary restraining orders limiting deportations under the Alien Enemies Act. Judge Boasberg's TROs restricting use of the Alien Enemies Act to deport Venezuelans asserted that wartime powers cannot be stretched to peacetime mass removals, reinforcing legal limits on executive immigration authority. (15 Mar 2025; 16 Mar 2025; 17 Mar 2025; 20 Mar 2025)

9. Federal courts held hearings on possible Trump administration violations of deportation orders. Boasberg's hearings into whether officials intentionally violated his deportation halt orders highlighted the judiciary's limited but active tools to investigate executive noncompliance. (16 Mar 2025; 17 Mar 2025; 19 Mar 2025; 21 Mar 2025)

10. Federal courts blocked or limited Trump administration efforts to dismantle USAID and access Social Security data. Judges Chuang and Hollander ruled that shutting down USAID and letting DOGE mine Social Security data likely violated constitutional and privacy protections, ordering restoration of agency functions and deletion of improperly accessed data. (18 Mar 2025; 19 Mar 2025; 20 Mar 2025; 21 Mar 2025)

11. Federal courts blocked Trump administration attempts to claw back EPA climate grants and ban transgender military service. Judges temporarily halted efforts to rescind $20 billion in climate grants and to bar transgender people from military service, preserving existing environmental and equal-service policies pending further review. (18 Mar 2025)

12. Federal courts lifted prior blocks on executive orders terminating federal DEI programs. Appeals court decisions allowing Trump's anti-DEI orders to proceed cleared the way for dismantling diversity and inclusion programs across federal agencies, reshaping civil-service norms and protections. (16 Mar 2025; 18 Mar 2025)

13. Federal courts blocked DOGE from accessing Social Security systems as a fishing expedition. By characterizing DOGE's Social Security data demands as a fishing expedition and ordering destruction of collected personal data, a district judge reinforced judicial oversight of executive data-mining initiatives. (20 Mar 2025; 21 Mar 2025)

14. Federal courts blocked the Trump administration from dismantling USAID as unconstitutional. Judge Chuang's ruling that USAID's shutdown likely violated Congress's constitutional role in creating agencies forced partial restoration of the aid agency and checked executive attempts to unilaterally abolish it. (18 Mar 2025; 19 Mar 2025)

15. Federal courts blocked EPA from clawing back climate grants and

DOGE from Social Security data access. Judicial blocks on climate grant clawbacks and DOGE's SSA access preserved existing environmental funding and data privacy while broader legal challenges proceed. (18 Mar 2025; 20 Mar 2025)

16. Federal courts demanded explanations from the White House for continuing deportation flights to El Salvador. Boasberg's order requiring the administration to justify its deportation flights underscored judicial insistence on accountability when executive agencies appear to ignore court directives. (21 Mar 2025)

17. Democratic state attorneys general filed multiple lawsuits and secured restraining orders against Trump administration directives. State AGs used coordinated litigation and community hearings to block or pause several Trump policies, including grant freezes and agency shutdowns, demonstrating subnational checks on federal overreach. (21 Mar 2025)

18. Demand Justice warned that Trump could appoint over 300 federal judges in coming years. An advocacy analysis projected that Trump could fill hundreds of judicial vacancies, highlighting how future appointments could entrench a judiciary more aligned with his policy agenda. (18 Mar 2025)

19. Federal courts blocked DOGE from accessing Social Security data and ordered deletion of collected PII. A district judge's order to destroy personally identifiable information DOGE had obtained from SSA limited executive fishing expeditions into sensitive citizen data and reinforced privacy safeguards. (20 Mar 2025; 21 Mar 2025)

20. Federal courts ruled that Elon Musk's USAID shutdown likely violated the Constitution. By finding the USAID shutdown likely unconstitutional and ordering restoration steps, the court reasserted that executive-branch contractors cannot unilaterally dismantle congressionally created agencies. (18 Mar 2025; 19 Mar 2025)

21. Federal courts blocked the Trump administration from clawing back EPA climate grants. A judge's injunction against reclaiming $20 billion in climate grants preserved long-term environmental investments and limited the administration's ability to reverse appropriated funds unilaterally. (18 Mar 2025)

22. Federal courts blocked the Trump administration's ban on transgender military service. A ruling calling the transgender service ban demeaning and animus-driven temporarily protected LGBTQ+ individuals' right to serve, checking discriminatory use of military policy. (18 Mar 2025)

23. Federal courts blocked DOGE from accessing Social Security systems as unconstitutional overreach. The Social Security data ruling underscored that even executive-created efficiency units must respect statutory limits

and privacy rights when probing for fraud or waste. (20 Mar 2025; 21 Mar 2025)

24. Federal courts ordered the Trump administration to explain noncompliance with deportation orders. Boasberg's demand for a detailed explanation of deportation flights signaled that courts may escalate scrutiny and potential sanctions when executive agencies evade clear judicial instructions. (21 Mar 2025)

25. Federal courts blocked DOGE from accessing Social Security data and called efforts a fishing expedition. Labeling DOGE's SSA data push a fishing expedition, the court limited broad, suspicion-less data trawls that could be used to justify politicized purges or benefit cuts. (20 Mar 2025; 21 Mar 2025)

26. Federal courts blocked DOGE from accessing Social Security data and ordered deletion of personal data. Ordering deletion of any personal data DOGE had already accessed from SSA reinforced judicial power to remediate overbroad executive data collection after the fact. (20 Mar 2025; 21 Mar 2025)

27. Federal courts blocked DOGE from accessing Social Security data and criticized lack of fraud evidence. The court's skepticism about DOGE's fraud claims highlighted the need for concrete evidence before granting sweeping access to sensitive administrative records. (20 Mar 2025; 21 Mar 2025)

28. Federal courts blocked DOGE from accessing Social Security data and ordered destruction of collected PII. Mandating destruction of personally identifiable information obtained by DOGE from SSA set a precedent for rolling back unauthorized executive data grabs. (20 Mar 2025; 21 Mar 2025)

29. Federal courts blocked DOGE from accessing Social Security data and criticized fishing expedition. The repeated characterization of DOGE's SSA efforts as a fishing expedition underscored judicial concern about politicized use of fraud narratives to justify intrusive data access. (20 Mar 2025; 21 Mar 2025)

30. Federal courts blocked DOGE from accessing Social Security data and ordered deletion of any collected data. The Social Security data ruling reinforced that executive efficiency drives cannot override statutory privacy protections or judicially enforced limits on data use. (20 Mar 2025; 21 Mar 2025)

31. Federal courts blocked DOGE from accessing Social Security data and ordered destruction of personal data. By ordering destruction of personal data DOGE had accessed, the court provided a concrete remedy against overbroad executive data collection, reinforcing judicial oversight of administrative surveillance. (20 Mar 2025; 21 Mar 2025)

32. Federal courts blocked DOGE from accessing Social Security data and criticized fishing expedition. The repeated judicial description of DOGE's

SSA access as a fishing expedition highlighted skepticism toward broad, poorly justified data grabs framed as anti-fraud efforts. (20 Mar 2025; 21 Mar 2025)

33. Federal courts blocked DOGE from accessing Social Security data and ordered deletion of collected PII. The Social Security data decision underscored that courts can not only halt but also unwind executive overreach into citizen records, protecting privacy and limiting politicized data use. (20 Mar 2025; 21 Mar 2025)

34. Federal courts blocked DOGE from accessing Social Security data and criticized lack of fraud evidence. Judicial skepticism about DOGE's fraud rationale for SSA access emphasized that efficiency rhetoric cannot substitute for evidence when seeking intrusive data powers. (20 Mar 2025; 21 Mar 2025)

35. Federal courts blocked DOGE from accessing Social Security data and ordered destruction of personal data. The order to destroy personal data obtained by DOGE from SSA reinforced judicial capacity to remediate privacy violations after executive overreach has occurred. (20 Mar 2025; 21 Mar 2025)

36. Federal courts blocked DOGE from accessing Social Security data and criticized fishing expedition. The Social Security ruling's repeated references to a fishing expedition signaled judicial concern that anti-fraud narratives were being used to justify broad, unspecific data access. (20 Mar 2025; 21 Mar 2025)

37. Federal courts blocked DOGE from accessing Social Security data and ordered deletion of collected PII. By requiring deletion of personally identifiable information DOGE had accessed, the court underscored that executive data overreach can be rolled back, not just halted prospectively. (20 Mar 2025; 21 Mar 2025)

38. Federal courts blocked DOGE from accessing Social Security data and criticized fishing expedition. The Social Security decision's repeated criticism of DOGE's fishing expedition highlighted judicial resistance to vague, wide-ranging data demands lacking clear legal basis. (20 Mar 2025; 21 Mar 2025)

39. Federal courts blocked DOGE from accessing Social Security data and ordered destruction of personal data. The Social Security ruling's destruction order demonstrated that courts can require executive agencies to unwind unauthorized data collection, not just stop future access. (20 Mar 2025; 21 Mar 2025)

40. Federal courts blocked DOGE from accessing Social Security data and criticized fishing expedition. The Social Security decision's repeated fish-

ing-expedition language signaled judicial skepticism toward broad, poorly justified data grabs framed as efficiency or anti-fraud measures. (20 Mar 2025; 21 Mar 2025)

41. Federal courts blocked DOGE from accessing Social Security data and ordered deletion of collected PII. The Social Security ruling's deletion requirement underscored that courts can compel executive agencies to erase improperly obtained citizen data, reinforcing privacy protections. (20 Mar 2025; 21 Mar 2025)

42. Federal courts blocked DOGE from accessing Social Security data and criticized fishing expedition. The Social Security decision's repeated criticism of DOGE's fishing expedition highlighted judicial concern about politicized use of fraud narratives to justify intrusive data access. (20 Mar 2025; 21 Mar 2025)

43. Federal courts blocked DOGE from accessing Social Security data and ordered destruction of personal data. The Social Security ruling's destruction order demonstrated that courts can require executive agencies to unwind unauthorized data collection, not just stop future access. (20 Mar 2025; 21 Mar 2025)

44. Federal courts blocked DOGE from accessing Social Security data and criticized fishing expedition. The Social Security decision's repeated fishing-expedition language signaled judicial skepticism toward broad, poorly justified data grabs framed as efficiency or anti-fraud measures. (20 Mar 2025; 21 Mar 2025)

Civil Rights and Dissent

1. Trump administration used the Alien Enemies Act to deport migrants without normal due process protections. Invoking a wartime law to deport Venezuelan and Salvadoran migrants without standard hearings eroded due process for noncitizens and normalized emergency powers in routine immigration enforcement. (15 Mar 2025; 16 Mar 2025; 17 Mar 2025; 19 Mar 2025)

2. Trump administration and ICE deported Andry José Hernández Romero and other migrants based on tattoos and alleged gang ties. Deporting migrants, including LGBTQ+ individuals, to harsh Salvadoran prisons based largely on tattoos and tenuous gang allegations highlighted arbitrary criteria and severe consequences in immigration enforcement. (15 Mar 2025; 16 Mar 2025; 17 Mar 2025; 18 Mar 2025; 19 Mar 2025)

3. ICE and DHS detained and sought to deport pro-Palestinian activists and academics. Arrests and visa revocations targeting Mahmoud Khalil, Badar Khan Suri, and other pro-Palestinian scholars suggested immigration

powers were being used to punish political speech and campus activism. (15 Mar 2025; 17 Mar 2025; 19 Mar 2025; 20 Mar 2025)

4. ICE and DHS detained foreign residents and workers with valid status under harsh conditions. Cases involving a German green-card holder and a Canadian worker detained and mistreated at the border highlighted aggressive enforcement practices that jeopardize lawful residents' rights and international trust. (18 Mar 2025; 19 Mar 2025)

5. ICE intensified arrests and deportations of Chinese immigrants, including in sanctuary cities. Expanded ICE raids and deportations targeting Chinese nationals, even in sanctuary jurisdictions, deepened fears in immigrant communities and underscored selective, nationality-based enforcement. (18 Mar 2025)

6. ICE detained prominent immigration advocate Jeanette Vizguerra in Colorado. The arrest of a long-time immigrant rights leader suggested that outspoken advocacy can increase vulnerability to enforcement, potentially chilling organizing and protest. (19 Mar 2025)

7. CBP and DHS allegedly abused a mixed-status family and denied urgent medical care to a child with brain cancer. A complaint alleging CBP denied medical care and mistreated a family with a recovering child underscored how border enforcement practices can violate basic rights and dignity. (18 Mar 2025)

8. Texas authorities arrested a midwife under the state's near-total abortion ban. Charging a Texas midwife with illegal abortion and unlicensed practice marked an aggressive use of criminal law to enforce abortion bans, heightening risks for reproductive health providers. (17 Mar 2025)

9. Trump administration and DOJ sought delays in mifepristone lawsuits and signaled reviews that could restrict access. Requests to delay abortion-pill litigation and new safety reviews by HHS and FDA leadership raised the prospect of regulatory pathways being used to curtail medication abortion access. (18 Mar 2025)

10. Republican-controlled state legislatures advanced bills to reclassify mifepristone as a controlled substance and restrict its use. State efforts to treat mifepristone like opioids and enable lawsuits against providers would sharply limit medication abortion, using criminal and civil law to narrow reproductive rights. (18 Mar 2025)

11. Trump administration revoked temporary legal status for over 530,000 immigrants from four countries. Ending parole protections for hundreds of thousands of Cubans, Haitians, Nicaraguans, and Venezuelans exposed them to deportation and destabilized communities built under prior legal assurances. (21 Mar 2025)

12. Trump administration planned a militarized buffer zone along the New Mexico border staffed by active-duty troops. Proposals to station active-duty troops with detention powers in a border buffer zone blurred lines between military and civilian law enforcement, raising serious civil-liberties concerns. (20 Mar 2025)

13. Trump administration and DHS used an obscure foreign-policy deportation provision to arrest Mahmoud Khalil. Invoking a rarely used authority to deport a student activist for alleged adverse foreign-policy consequences expanded executive discretion to remove critics under vague national-interest claims. (20 Mar 2025)

14. US Attorney General Pam Bondi charged Tesla vandals with domestic terrorism and sought severe penalties. Labeling property damage at Tesla sites as domestic terrorism and pursuing long sentences broadened terrorism frameworks into protest-adjacent conduct, potentially chilling direct action. (20 Mar 2025; 21 Mar 2025)

15. Steve Bannon publicly dismissed concerns about innocent people caught in mass deportations. Bannon's comments that innocent deportees were a "tough break" reflected an elite discourse that normalizes collateral harm in enforcement, undermining norms of individualized justice. (20 Mar 2025)

16. Trump administration and DHS revoked temporary legal status for over 530,000 immigrants from four countries. Ending parole protections for hundreds of thousands of Cubans, Haitians, Nicaraguans, and Venezuelans exposed them to deportation and destabilized communities built under prior legal assurances. (21 Mar 2025)

17. Trump administration and DHS used an obscure foreign-policy deportation provision to arrest Mahmoud Khalil. Invoking a rarely used authority to deport a student activist for alleged adverse foreign-policy consequences expanded executive discretion to remove critics under vague national-interest claims. (20 Mar 2025)

18. US Attorney General Pam Bondi charged Tesla vandals with domestic terrorism and sought severe penalties. Labeling property damage at Tesla sites as domestic terrorism and pursuing long sentences broadened terrorism frameworks into protest-adjacent conduct, potentially chilling direct action. (20 Mar 2025; 21 Mar 2025)

19. Steve Bannon publicly dismissed concerns about innocent people caught in mass deportations. Bannon's comments that innocent deportees were a "tough break" reflected an elite discourse that normalizes collateral harm in enforcement, undermining norms of individualized justice. (20 Mar 2025)

20. Supporters of Donald Trump issued bomb threats against judges who ruled against the administration. Bomb threats against judges, including a Supreme Court justice, for decisions adverse to Trump created a climate of intimidation around the judiciary and could deter robust oversight of executive actions. (21 Mar 2025)

Economic Structure

1. EPA Administrator Lee Zeldin announced plans to roll back 31 environmental regulations on air, water, and climate. Rolling back dozens of pollution rules weakened regulatory protections for public health and climate, shifting costs from regulated industries to communities and future taxpayers. (15 Mar 2025; 19 Mar 2025)

2. Trump administration withdrew $400 million in federal funding from Columbia University and threatened similar actions. Cutting Columbia's federal funding and warning dozens of other schools used economic leverage to pressure universities over campus dissent and alleged antisemitism, risking politicized allocation of public funds. (15 Mar 2025; 19 Mar 2025; 20 Mar 2025)

3. Department of Government Efficiency and IRS leadership implemented deep IRS staffing cuts and closures that disrupted tax administration. Mass firings and office closures at the IRS, justified as anti-waste measures, impaired tax collection and enforcement capacity, undermining revenue needed for public services. (15 Mar 2025; 20 Mar 2025)

4. Trump administration froze $175 million in federal funding to the University of Pennsylvania over trans athlete policies. Freezing Penn's federal funds in response to its trans athlete policies used economic pressure to influence campus inclusion rules, intertwining civil-rights disputes with institutional financing. (19 Mar 2025; 20 Mar 2025)

5. Trump administration froze and redirected key Pentagon support packages to Ukraine. Halting intelligence and weapons packages for Ukraine signaled a shift in US security commitments that could weaken a partner's defense and alter the geopolitical balance with Russia. (15 Mar 2025)

6. Trump administration terminated a contract tracking Russian abductions of Ukrainian children. Ending support for a project documenting Russian child abductions undercut international accountability efforts and reduced US backing for evidence-based human-rights enforcement. (15 Mar 2025)

7. Trump administration cut USDA inspection teams for plant and food imports. Reductions in USDA inspection staff increased risks from invasive

pests and delayed food inspections, weakening federal safeguards for food safety and agricultural resilience. (18 Mar 2025)

8. Trump administration advanced plans to open protected federal lands for housing and mining. Proposals to develop protected federal lands for housing and resource extraction prioritized short-term economic gains over conservation, shifting public goods toward private use. (17 Mar 2025)

9. President Donald Trump announced a clean coal initiative and criticized prior environmental policies. Restarting "clean coal" plants and attacking environmental rules favored fossil-fuel interests and risked locking in higher emissions, despite public-health and climate costs. (17 Mar 2025)

10. Social Security Administration leadership proposed and began implementing stricter in-person ID verification for benefit claims. SSA's new ID rules and internal memo warning of service disruptions signaled a shift toward more burdensome access to benefits, especially for elderly and disabled claimants, risking de facto benefit denial. (17 Mar 2025; 18 Mar 2025; 20 Mar 2025)

11. Social Security Administration froze the Enumeration Beyond Entry program that auto-issues Social Security numbers to new workers. Suspending automatic SSN issuance for newly authorized workers and citizens forced tens of thousands into field offices weekly, straining SSA capacity and delaying access to work and benefits. (20 Mar 2025)

12. Trump administration planned large tax cuts likely to increase the national debt amid rising interest rates. Plans for major tax cuts without offsetting spending reductions risked worsening debt sustainability, potentially constraining future fiscal space for social programs and public investment. (16 Mar 2025)

13. Trump administration implemented tariffs that increased costs of living and harmed the job market. Tariff policies that raised consumer prices and threatened jobs illustrated how trade tools can be used in ways that burden households while serving protectionist or political aims. (20 Mar 2025)

14. Department of Government Efficiency and agency allies moved to dismantle USAID and the Institute of Museum and Library Services. DOGE's role in shutting down USAID and canceling museum and library grants reflected a broader project to shrink or eliminate public-goods institutions via executive action. (18 Mar 2025; 19 Mar 2025; 21 Mar 2025)

15. Trump administration froze $175 million in funding to the University of Pennsylvania over trans policies. The Penn funding freeze used federal dollars to pressure a private university's inclusion policies, intertwining

civil-rights disputes with economic leverage over higher education. (19 Mar 2025; 20 Mar 2025)

16. Trump administration moved the federal student loan program from the Education Department to the SBA. Transferring student loan management to the Small Business Administration raised concerns about administrative competence and continuity in servicing obligations affecting millions of borrowers. (21 Mar 2025)

17. Trump administration considered relinquishing the US role as NATO's Supreme Allied Commander Europe. Exploring withdrawal from NATO's top command role signaled potential retrenchment from longstanding alliance leadership, with implications for defense spending and global security architecture. (21 Mar 2025)

18. Federal regulatory agencies (EPA, FCC, TSA, FDA, OSHA) issued multiple routine rules and information-collection notices affecting environment, safety, and communications. A series of technical rules on air quality, emergency alerts, pesticides, medical devices, and workplace safety showed ongoing regulatory activity that shapes economic incentives and public protections. (17 Mar 2025; 18 Mar 2025; 19 Mar 2025; 20 Mar 2025; 21 Mar 2025)

19. Trump administration and Elon Musk's companies benefited from FAA contract shifts and Starlink installations in government facilities. Replacing a Verizon FAA contract with Starlink and installing Starlink across the White House deepened reliance on a politically connected contractor for critical infrastructure, raising cronyism and conflict-of-interest concerns. (18 Mar 2025)

20. Trump administration pursued broad deregulation and privatization through DOGE and executive orders. DOGE's expanding role, procurement consolidation, and mining orders collectively advanced a deregulatory, privatizing agenda that shifts public functions and assets toward favored private actors. (19 Mar 2025; 20 Mar 2025; 21 Mar 2025)

21. Trump administration froze and redirected key support to Ukraine while courting Russia diplomatically. Freezing Ukraine support and pursuing ceasefire talks aligned with Russian demands signaled a reorientation of US economic and security commitments away from European allies. (15 Mar 2025; 16 Mar 2025; 17 Mar 2025; 19 Mar 2025)

22. Trump administration used tariffs and other economic tools in ways that harmed domestic consumers and jobs. Tariffs that raised living costs and threatened employment illustrated how trade policy can be wielded for political effect despite broad economic harm, affecting public perceptions of governance. (20 Mar 2025)

23. Trump administration implemented policies that increased national

debt through tax cuts and spending choices. Plans to expand the national debt via large tax cuts without structural reforms risked constraining future democratic choices over social spending and investment. (16 Mar 2025)

24. Trump administration pursued deregulation and privatization through DOGE and executive orders. DOGE's expanding role, procurement consolidation, and mining orders collectively advanced a deregulatory, privatizing agenda that shifts public functions and assets toward favored private actors. (19 Mar 2025; 20 Mar 2025; 21 Mar 2025)

Information, Memory, and Manipulation

1. White House restricted Associated Press access to the Oval Office and Air Force One over naming dispute. Barring AP from key presidential venues after it refused to adopt "Gulf of America" signaled retaliatory use of access to pressure media outlets on editorial choices. (15 Mar 2025)

2. Trump administration eliminated the US Agency for Global Media and sidelined Voice of America and sister outlets. Shutting down USAGM structures and placing VOA staff on leave dismantled long-standing semi-independent international broadcasters, weakening US-funded sources of pluralistic news. (15 Mar 2025; 16 Mar 2025; 18 Mar 2025)

3. Radio Free Europe/Radio Liberty sued the Trump administration over termination of federal funding. RFE/RL's lawsuit argued that cutting its funding violated constitutional and statutory protections, using the courts to defend the independence of US-funded international journalism. (18 Mar 2025)

4. Department of Justice removed ADA disability guidance and COVID-related materials from its website. Taking down ADA compliance and COVID guidance reduced accessible information for disabled people and businesses, weakening transparency around civil-rights obligations. (19 Mar 2025)

5. Trump administration removed a Surgeon General advisory framing gun violence as a public health issue. Deleting federal health content that treated gun violence as a public-health problem narrowed the evidence base available to the public and policymakers on firearm harms. (17 Mar 2025)

6. US military and Defense Department removed and then partially restored online content about minority veterans and DEI-linked history. Deleting pages on Code Talkers, Black veterans, and women pilots—later restoring some under pressure—showed how DEI rollbacks can erase or marginalize histories of minority service. (15 Mar 2025; 18 Mar 2025)

7. Trump administration used the song "Closing Time" without permission in a deportation video. Repurposing a popular song in a deportation

video without consent illustrated how cultural works can be co-opted into state messaging that normalizes harsh enforcement. (18 Mar 2025)

8. President Donald Trump and allies claimed Biden's pardons were invalid due to autopen signatures despite archival clarification. Trump's repeated assertions that autopen-signed pardons are void, countered by the National Archives, injected disinformation into public understanding of constitutional processes. (16 Mar 2025; 17 Mar 2025; 18 Mar 2025)

9. Trump administration removed online application forms for income-driven student loan plans from federal websites. Taking down digital applications for key repayment plans made it harder for borrowers to access statutory relief, using information design to constrain practical rights. (20 Mar 2025)

10. White House Press Secretary Karoline Leavitt attacked Judge Boasberg and his family in public statements. Smearing a sitting judge as a partisan and targeting his spouse's donations aimed to delegitimize judicial oversight and frame legal rulings as partisan warfare. (21 Mar 2025)

11. Trump administration falsely claimed thousands of IRS employees were fired for poor performance. Misrepresenting mass IRS firings as performance-based, despite internal warnings this was false, distorted public understanding of civil-service cuts and undermined trust in official explanations. (20 Mar 2025)

12. Trump administration released thousands of JFK assassination files as part of a transparency initiative. Releasing long-sealed JFK records expanded public access to historical documents, though experts doubted the new material would significantly change established accounts. (19 Mar 2025)

13. Elon Musk threatened legal action and prosecution over leaks about a planned Pentagon briefing. Musk's calls to prosecute alleged Pentagon leakers over his China war-plans briefing highlighted tensions between leak investigations and the public's interest in transparency about private influence on security policy. (20 Mar 2025)

14. Trump administration and DOGE sought broad access to unclassified federal records and Social Security data. Orders expanding DOGE's access to agency records and SSA systems concentrated informational power in a politically aligned unit, raising risks of data being used to justify purges or policy shifts. (19 Mar 2025; 20 Mar 2025; 21 Mar 2025)

15. Trump administration removed disability and gun-violence guidance and DEI-linked content from federal sites. Deleting ADA, gun-violence, and DEI-related materials from official websites narrowed the informational record on marginalized groups' experiences and public-health harms. (15 Mar 2025; 17 Mar 2025; 18 Mar 2025; 19 Mar 2025)

16. Trump administration used deportation footage of shackled migrants as public messaging. Sharing images of shackled, shaved migrants in Salvadoran prisons as political content framed harsh treatment as a spectacle, shaping public perceptions of enforcement and dehumanizing deportees. (16 Mar 2025)

17. Trump administration removed online application forms for income-driven student loan plans from federal websites. Taking down digital applications for key repayment plans made it harder for borrowers to access statutory relief, using information design to constrain practical rights. (20 Mar 2025)

18. Elon Musk threatened legal action and prosecution over leaks about a planned Pentagon briefing. Musk's calls to prosecute alleged Pentagon leakers over his China war-plans briefing highlighted tensions between leak investigations and the public's interest in transparency about private influence on security policy. (20 Mar 2025)

CHAPTER 10
WEEK 10 (22 MAR 2025 – 28 MAR 2025): VOTER ROLLS AS LEVERAGE

A quiet executive blitz rewired elections, immigration, law, and information systems to make the state more tool than commons, with courts mostly reacting at the edges.

This week was heavily focused on democratic erosion, with multiple issues advancing at once. The biggest concerns involved voting access and federalism: the executive order requiring proof of citizenship and giving DOGE access to voter lists marks a major, possibly lasting shift toward voter suppression and centralized election control. Immigration and citizenship policies were weaponized through data-sharing between IRS and ICE, social media screening, tough deportation tactics, and threats to offshore detainees, which deepens division in citizenship status. The executive also extended control over the civil service, law enforcement, and independent agencies, while using tariffs, budget cuts, and specific executive orders to reward allies and punish opponents, mixing crony capitalism with governance. Civil liberties faced both rhetorical and real attacks—protesters being called "domestic terrorists," chilling political speech, and expanding surveillance. Courts offered some resistance—blocking parts of the trans military ban, DOGE data access, use of the Alien Enemies Act, and maintaining funding for Sullivan and Radio Free Europe—but these victories only slightly offset a week largely marked by executive overreach, structural voter suppression, and the normalization of law as a weapon rather than a check.

Power and Authority

1. President Donald Trump issued and then withdrew an executive order punishing law firm Paul, Weiss after extracting concessions. Trump used an executive order to suspend Paul, Weiss's clearances and contracts, then rescinded it after the firm agreed to pro-bono work and anti-DEI audits, showing presidential power leveraged to coerce private legal actors. (22 Mar 2025)

2. President Donald Trump ordered the attorney general to flag partisan lawsuits and recommend punitive actions against involved law firms. By directing the attorney general to route disfavored lawsuits to the White House for potential sanctions, Trump blurred the line between neutral law enforcement and political retaliation against legal challengers. (22 Mar 2025)

3. President Donald Trump signed executive orders abolishing federal diversity, equity, and inclusion programs. Eliminating DEI programs across the federal government centralized cultural policy in the executive branch and reduced institutional support for equal treatment within public employment and services. (22 Mar 2025)

4. Trump administration cut funding for legal aid programs serving unaccompanied migrant children. Terminating major grants for lawyers representing unaccompanied children in immigration court used executive control over contracts to weaken access to counsel for a highly vulnerable group. (22 Mar 2025)

5. Acting Social Security Commissioner Leland Dudek threatened to shut down the Social Security Administration in response to a court order limiting data sharing. Threatening to halt Social Security operations over a privacy-related restraining order showed willingness to use essential services as leverage against judicial constraints. (22 Mar 2025)

6. President Donald Trump revoked security clearances of several political opponents. Stripping former officials and rivals of security clearances for political reasons politicized access to national security information and signaled that loyalty, not risk, governs clearance decisions. (22 Mar 2025)

7. President Donald Trump signed executive orders dismantling the Department of Education and ordering its functions wound down. Ordering the de facto closure of a cabinet department by executive fiat, without new legislation, expanded unilateral presidential control over the federal role in education and public services. (23 Mar 2025)

8. President Donald Trump issued executive orders penalizing multiple law firms that had opposed his interests. Targeting Covington & Burling, Perkins Coie, Paul Weiss, Jenner & Block, and WilmerHale with clearance

revocations and contract bans used executive power to intimidate legal adversaries and chill representation against the government. (24 Mar 2025)

9. President Donald Trump issued an executive order imposing tariffs on imports from countries that buy Venezuelan oil. Linking broad tariffs to other countries' purchases of Venezuelan oil used trade sanctions as a unilateral foreign-policy tool with significant economic and diplomatic consequences. (24 Mar 2025)

10. President Donald Trump signed executive orders to modernize and tighten controls over federal payments. Mandating electronic payments and stricter Treasury oversight centralized control over federal disbursements, potentially improving accountability while concentrating financial levers in the executive branch. (25 Mar 2025)

11. President Donald Trump issued an executive order restructuring federal labor-management relations and excluding security agencies from bargaining. Removing many intelligence and security-related agencies from federal labor-relations statutes curtailed collective bargaining rights and strengthened executive control over key parts of the civil service. (27 Mar 2025)

12. President Donald Trump issued an executive order directing federal institutions to reshape American history presentations and remove "improper" ideologies. Ordering the Smithsonian and related sites to purge narratives deemed divisive asserted presidential control over historical interpretation in public institutions, with implications for pluralistic memory and civic education. (27 Mar 2025)

13. President Donald Trump created the DC Safe and Beautiful Task Force to coordinate immigration enforcement and policing in Washington, DC. Establishing a White House–led task force to intensify immigration enforcement and policing in the capital expanded federal security presence in a local jurisdiction and linked urban management to immigration crackdowns. (28 Mar 2025)

14. President Donald Trump signed an executive order eliminating collective bargaining rights for large numbers of federal workers. Directing agencies to terminate union contracts and stop dues collection sharply reduced organized labor's role inside the federal workforce and increased unilateral managerial power over public employees. (28 Mar 2025)

15. Trump administration planned deep workforce cuts across multiple federal agencies. Seeking to cut between 8% and 50% of staff at key agencies would shrink state capacity and make core regulatory and service functions more dependent on political appointees and contractors. (28 Mar 2025)

16. Trump administration withheld hundreds of millions in federal grants

from Columbia University to force policy changes. Using federal grant funding as leverage over a university's internal policies showed how executive control of appropriations can pressure academic institutions and chill campus expression. (28 Mar 2025)

17. Trump administration announced plans to eliminate FEMA following an earlier order to shutter the Department of Education. Moving to abolish FEMA, the federal disaster-response agency, extended the administration's effort to dismantle major executive departments, reshaping the state's capacity to respond to emergencies. (28 Mar 2025)

18. President Donald Trump refused to dismiss senior officials involved in the Signal war-plans leak. Keeping national security leaders in place after an acknowledged operational-security breach signaled limited accountability for mishandling sensitive military information at the top of the executive branch. (27 Mar 2025)

19. President Donald Trump publicly threatened Maine's governor over noncompliance with his transgender athlete order. Demanding an apology from a governor for following state and federal civil-rights law rather than his executive order highlighted pressure on states to subordinate their own legal obligations to presidential directives. (22 Mar 2025)

20. President Donald Trump denied personally signing a proclamation used to deport Venezuelan migrants under the Alien Enemies Act. Disputing authorship of a proclamation that triggered mass deportations obscured responsibility for a major rights-affecting policy and complicated accountability for its legality. (22 Mar 2025)

21. President Donald Trump promoted his personal $TRUMP cryptocurrency to the public while holding a dominant stake. Using the presidency's megaphone to tout a meme coin he largely owns blurred public office and private enrichment, inviting conflicts between personal gain and impartial economic governance. (24 Mar 2025)

22. President Donald Trump pardoned Nikola founder Trevor Milton after fraud convictions, followed by large donations from Milton to Republican causes. Granting clemency to a convicted fraudster who then donated millions to Trump-aligned entities raised concerns that the pardon power was being used in a pay-to-play fashion. (27 Mar 2025)

Institutions and Governance

1. Washington state lawmakers and advocates advanced legislation to ban police deception during interrogations and require recording of interactions. Proposed limits on deceptive interrogation tactics and mandatory recording

aimed to reduce coerced confessions and strengthen procedural fairness in the criminal justice system. (22 Mar 2025)

2. Judge Ellen Lipton Hollander clarified that her restraining order on SSA data sharing did not affect benefit payments. By specifying that Social Security benefits must continue despite limits on data transfers to DOGE, the court reinforced judicial oversight while protecting service continuity. (22 Mar 2025)

3. House Republicans introduced resolutions to impeach federal judges who ruled against Trump administration policies. Targeting judges for adverse rulings used impeachment threats to pressure the judiciary, challenging separation of powers and judicial independence. (23 Mar 2025)

4. Chief Justice John Roberts publicly rebuked calls to impeach judges over their rulings. Roberts's statement that impeachment is not a remedy for disagreement with decisions defended the judiciary's role as an independent check on the political branches. (23 Mar 2025)

5. Minnesota legislature considered a bill labeling "Trump derangement syndrome" as a mental illness. Proposing to medicalize intense criticism of Trump risked using statutory definitions of mental illness to stigmatize political opposition and chill free expression. (26 Mar 2025)

6. House Speaker Mike Johnson suggested Congress could defund, restructure, or eliminate federal courts in response to rulings. Floating the idea of abolishing or defunding courts over policy disagreements highlighted legislative pressure on the judiciary's institutional existence and independence. (26 Mar 2025)

7. California attorney general and city attorneys negotiated a large wage-theft settlement with Uber and Lyft over driver misclassification. Pursuing massive claims for misclassified gig workers used state legal tools to enforce labor standards against powerful platforms and clarify employment rights. (26 Mar 2025)

8. US courts blocked or limited Trump administration deportations under the Alien Enemies Act. District and appellate rulings requiring hearings and halting removals to El Salvador asserted judicial authority over wartime statutes and protected due process for migrants. (27 Mar 2025)

9. US Court of Appeals for the Ninth Circuit refused to pause reinstatement of over 17,000 fired probationary federal employees. Upholding an order to restore thousands of improperly terminated civil servants limited executive attempts to reshape the federal workforce outside established procedures. (27 Mar 2025)

10. US district court in Washington, DC blocked enforcement of Trump's executive order against Perkins Coie. Granting a temporary restraining

order against a punitive executive order protected a targeted law firm and underscored judicial checks on retaliatory use of presidential power. (26 Mar 2025)

11. Law firms Jenner & Block and WilmerHale filed lawsuits challenging Trump executive orders that restricted their federal work and clearances. By suing to block orders that cut off contracts and clearances, major firms sought judicial protection against executive retaliation for representing political adversaries. (28 Mar 2025)

12. Judge James Boasberg ordered preservation of Signal chat messages and oversaw a records lawsuit against Trump officials. Requiring officials to retain auto-deleting Signal messages about Yemen strikes enforced federal records laws and preserved evidence for oversight of national-security decision-making. (27 Mar 2025)

13. American Oversight sued Trump administration officials over alleged Federal Records Act violations in Signal war-plans chats. The watchdog's lawsuit sought to enforce transparency rules on encrypted messaging by senior officials, testing whether off-platform communications can evade archival obligations. (27 Mar 2025)

14. Senate Armed Services Committee leaders requested an inspector general investigation into the Signal chat leak. A bipartisan call for a Pentagon IG probe into the Yemen war-plans chat reflected congressional concern over security practices and record-keeping by the national security team. (27 Mar 2025)

15. House Intelligence Committee questioned intelligence chiefs about their use of Signal and testimony on the Yemen leak. Lawmakers pressed Tulsi Gabbard and John Ratcliffe on whether they mishandled classified information and misled Congress, illustrating legislative oversight of intelligence practices. (26 Mar 2025)

16. Senate Armed Services Committee sought a Defense Department investigation into the Signal chat leak in a bipartisan letter. The committee's formal request for an IG review of Signal's use for war planning underscored institutional concern about secure communications and compliance with records law. (27 Mar 2025)

17. National Labor Relations Board created a new FOIA records system and rescinded two older systems. Consolidating FOIA tracking into a new system aimed to modernize public-records processing while maintaining privacy protections, affecting how labor-related information is accessed. (26 Mar 2025)

18. National Labor Relations Board announced a new Privacy Act system for FOIA records. Establishing a dedicated Privacy Act system for FOIA mate-

rials clarified how request data are stored and accessed, with implications for transparency and personal-data safeguards. (26 Mar 2025)

19. Social Security Administration appointed former DOGE operative Scott Coulter as chief information officer despite a court order limiting DOGE access. Installing a DOGE affiliate in a key SSA role appeared to circumvent a restraining order on DOGE's access to sensitive data, raising questions about compliance with judicial limits. (26 Mar 2025)

20. President Donald Trump withdrew Elise Stefanik's nomination for UN ambassador to preserve a House seat. Pulling back a high-profile diplomatic nomination to avoid risking a House majority showed how legislative arithmetic can override merit or policy considerations in appointments. (26 Mar 2025)

21. President Donald Trump appointed personal attorney Alina Habba as interim U.S. Attorney for New Jersey. Naming a close personal lawyer with questioned qualifications to a top prosecutorial post blurred the line between independent law enforcement and presidential loyalty. (23 Mar 2025)

22. Wisconsin Department of Justice announced plans to sue Elon Musk over alleged vote-buying in a state supreme court race. State prosecutors' move to challenge Musk's million-dollar prize offers to voters sought to enforce election-law limits on inducements and protect ballot integrity. (27 Mar 2025)

23. Congressional subcommittee chaired by Marjorie Taylor Greene held a hearing attacking NPR and PBS and exploring defunding public media. Questioning public broadcasters over alleged bias and threatening their funding put political pressure on independent media institutions that provide noncommercial news and education. (26 Mar 2025)

24. Texas Senate advanced bills to criminalize certain educational materials and mandate religious content in schools. Legislation exposing educators to prison for providing some books and requiring school prayer and Ten Commandments displays reoriented public education toward specific ideological and religious norms. (25 Mar 2025)

25. North Carolina General Assembly considered a bill targeting DEI initiatives in state agencies. NC HB 171's effort to roll back DEI programs in government would narrow institutional commitments to inclusion and representation in public administration. (23 Mar 2025)

26. National Labor Relations Board updated FOIA systems by consolidating and rescinding older record systems. Streamlining FOIA record systems aimed to improve efficiency and clarity in responding to public information requests about labor disputes and decisions. (26 Mar 2025)

27. US Supreme Court heard arguments in a Louisiana redistricting case

that could narrow Voting Rights Act protections. The Court's review of Louisiana's second majority-Black district put at risk legal standards that safeguard minority representation in congressional maps. (24 Mar 2025)

28. US Congress saw internal Democratic conflict over supporting a Republican-led funding bill to avert a shutdown. Schumer's backing of a GOP funding bill to avoid a shutdown highlighted tradeoffs between institutional stability and partisan strategy in budget governance. (23 Mar 2025)

29. National Labor Relations Board announced a new FOIA records system under the Privacy Act. Creating NLRB-37 for FOIA records formalized how labor-related information is stored and accessed, affecting transparency in labor-rights enforcement. (26 Mar 2025)

Civil Rights and Dissent

1. President Donald Trump signed an executive order imposing strict proof-of-citizenship and ballot-deadline rules for federal elections. Requiring documentary citizenship proof and banning late-arriving mail ballots threatened to disenfranchise many eligible voters and encroached on state control of election administration. (25 Mar 2025)

2. Immigration and Customs Enforcement detained Cuban immigrants at scheduled appointments after ending their special status. Arresting 18 Cubans who appeared for immigration appointments signaled a shift toward more punitive enforcement that may deter cooperation and heighten fear among migrants. (22 Mar 2025)

3. Immigration and Customs Enforcement and DOJ allegedly ignored a court order halting a deportation flight to El Salvador. An affidavit claiming ICE proceeded with a deportation flight despite a judge's order raised serious concerns about executive agencies disregarding judicial protections for migrants. (23 Mar 2025)

4. Trump administration used the Alien Enemies Act to deport hundreds of Venezuelan men to El Salvador based on suspected gang ties. Mass deportations of TPS holders and others under a wartime statute, often on thin evidence like tattoos, bypassed normal due process and exposed deportees to harsh conditions. (26 Mar 2025)

5. Federal courts in New York blocked the deportation and detention of Columbia student Yunseo Chung. Temporary restraining orders protecting a pro-Palestinian student from deportation underscored judicial willingness to check immigration enforcement used against political protesters. (25 Mar 2025)

6. American Association of University Professors and Middle East Studies

Association sued the Trump administration to stop deportations of pro-Palestinian students and scholars. Academic groups' lawsuit alleged that immigration tools were being used to create a climate of repression on campuses, defending free speech and academic freedom for noncitizens. (25 Mar 2025)

7. Immigration and Customs Enforcement detained multiple international students and academics, including Rumeysa Ozturk and Alireza Doroudi, amid pro-Palestinian activism. ICE's arrests and transfers of student activists, sometimes in defiance of court orders, used immigration enforcement in ways that threatened free expression and academic exchange. (27 Mar 2025)

8. Immigration and Customs Enforcement detained Russian scientist Kseniia Petrova upon arrival in Boston and moved her to Louisiana. Holding a Russian antiwar scientist in immigration detention highlighted how visa revocations and asylum processes can intersect with political risk and academic work. (28 Mar 2025)

9. Trump administration expanded social-media–based screening and denial criteria for student visas. New State Department guidance requiring intensive social media reviews for student visas risked penalizing political speech and chilled expression among international students. (28 Mar 2025)

10. Trump administration withheld federal funding from Columbia University over alleged antisemitism until it made demanded changes. Conditioning $400 million in grants on institutional changes allowed the executive to pressure a university's governance and potentially its handling of campus speech. (28 Mar 2025)

11. Trump administration targeted at least five immigrant students and academics of color for pro-Palestine protests. Visa revocations and detentions of pro-Palestinian students used immigration status as leverage against political activism, disproportionately affecting minorities. (26 Mar 2025)

12. US district court in Washington, DC blocked the Trump administration's transgender military ban from taking effect. Keeping an injunction in place against a trans service ban preserved equal access to military service and rejected intrusive self-reporting requirements. (27 Mar 2025)

13. Phoenix Police Department suspended officers involved in the violent arrest of a deaf Black man with cerebral palsy. Disciplining officers after a brutal arrest of a disabled Black resident highlighted ongoing struggles over police accountability and treatment of marginalized communities. (26 Mar 2025)

14. North Bergen Police Chief Robert Farley was accused by officers of harassment, retaliation, and creating a hostile work environment. Allegations that a police chief abused subordinates and retaliated against civil-rights

investigators pointed to internal cultures that can undermine lawful, rights-respecting policing. (27 Mar 2025)

15. Attorney General Pam Bondi and federal law enforcement formed a task force and brought domestic-terrorism charges over Tesla vandalism. Creating a large FBI task force and using terrorism rhetoric to protect Tesla facilities elevated corporate property damage into a national security priority. (25 Mar 2025)

16. President Donald Trump compared Tesla vandalism to being worse than the January 6 Capitol attack and called for harsh prison terms. Equating property damage against Tesla with an attack on Congress minimized political violence against democratic institutions while demanding extreme punishment for corporate-targeted vandalism. (22 Mar 2025)

17. Grassroots activists organized TeslaTakedown protests at Tesla dealerships against Musk's role in government cuts. Peaceful protests at Tesla sites expressed public opposition to perceived corporate capture of government, illustrating civil society's role in contesting policy choices. (22 Mar 2025)

18. Senator Bernie Sanders and Representative Alexandria Ocasio-Cortez held rallies in Republican districts criticizing oligarchic influence. The "Fighting Oligarchy" tour mobilized constituents in opposition strongholds, demonstrating robust rights to organize and contest concentrated economic power. (22 Mar 2025)

19. Republican lawmakers and constituents clashed at town halls marked by heckling and avoidance of in-person events. Rowdy town halls and some members' refusal to hold them showed fraying channels for direct democratic accountability between representatives and voters. (22 Mar 2025)

20. Democratic Association of Secretaries of State announced a $40 million plan to contest key 2026 election-oversight races. Heavy investment in secretary-of-state races reflected recognition that control over election administration offices is central to protecting or reshaping voting rules. (27 Mar 2025)

21. Democratic candidates James Malone and others won or contested races in traditionally pro-Trump districts. Upset and competitive races in Trump-leaning areas suggested shifting voter preferences and the continued openness of electoral competition. (26 Mar 2025)

22. Elon Musk and allied PACs poured tens of millions into Wisconsin Supreme Court races and offered financial incentives to voters. Massive spending and controversial prize offers in a state judicial election highlighted how moneyed actors can shape courts that interpret election and rights law. (22 Mar 2025)

23. Joe Molloy announced a mayoral campaign in Seattle while living

unhoused. An unhoused candidate's run for mayor foregrounded homelessness and economic precarity in local politics, expanding who can visibly contest for power. (26 Mar 2025)

24. Blue-state governments faced severe homelessness crises linked to housing scarcity and restrictive development policies. High housing costs and limited building in some states contributed to homelessness and out-migration, affecting social stability and representation. (25 Mar 2025)

25. Arizona prosecutors charged a woman with criminal negligence and animal cruelty after her mother was killed by dogs. The case underscored enforcement of laws protecting vulnerable elders and animals, though it did not directly alter broader civil-rights structures. (24 Mar 2025)

26. Police in Las Cruces, New Mexico arrested suspects in a mass shooting at a car show. Law enforcement's response to a deadly shooting highlighted ongoing public-safety challenges and the criminal-justice system's role in addressing gun violence. (23 Mar 2025)

27. American courts and advocates pressed the Trump administration to justify detention of Tufts student Rumeysa Ozturk. A judge's demand for an explanation of Ozturk's detention, after ICE moved her despite a notice order, spotlighted judicial efforts to enforce civil-liberties protections. (27 Mar 2025)

Economic Structure

1. Internal Revenue Service allowed Immigration and Customs Enforcement to access confidential tax data on migrants. Permitting ICE to mine tax records for immigration enforcement broke longstanding confidentiality norms, risking tax compliance and deepening surveillance of undocumented workers. (22 Mar 2025)

2. Internal Revenue Service reduced staff sharply, leading to an estimated $500 billion revenue shortfall. Staff cuts that forced the IRS to drop high-value audits weakened enforcement against wealthy taxpayers and corporations, shifting the tax burden and undermining fiscal capacity. (22 Mar 2025)

3. White House solicited corporate sponsorships and naming rights for the Easter Egg Roll. Opening a historic public event to paid branding opportunities blurred the boundary between civic traditions and corporate marketing on government grounds. (22 Mar 2025)

4. President Donald Trump announced 25% tariffs on imported cars and parts, including from allies. New auto tariffs threatened to raise consumer prices and disrupt supply chains, using trade policy as a blunt instrument with broad economic and geopolitical effects. (27 Mar 2025)

5. Department of Veterans Affairs leadership planned layoffs of more than

80,000 VA employees nationwide. Proposed mass layoffs at VA hospitals risked degrading veterans' healthcare and shifting services toward privatization, altering how a core public obligation is delivered. (27 Mar 2025)

6. Department of Energy under Secretary Chris Wright compiled a "hit list" of clean energy projects and major funding cuts for cancellation. Targeting long-duration storage and other clean-energy programs for defunding would slow the energy transition and redirect federal investment away from climate-related infrastructure. (27 Mar 2025)

7. Department of Health and Human Services canceled over $12 billion in state health grants and announced 10,000 job cuts. Eliminating large grants for mental health, addiction treatment, and disease tracking, alongside workforce cuts, weakened public health infrastructure and state-level safety nets. (28 Mar 2025)

8. Coinbase and other trading platforms listed and promoted the $TRUMP meme coin soon after SEC dropped its lawsuit. Rapidly listing a politically branded coin after regulators abandoned a case against Coinbase raised questions about crypto oversight and the entanglement of markets with partisan branding. (24 Mar 2025)

9. Large $TRUMP coin investors reaped huge profits from well-timed trades following Trump's promotion of the coin. Tens of millions in gains by a few wallets after Trump's endorsement suggested possible insider knowledge, undermining perceptions of fair and transparent markets. (24 Mar 2025)

10. Environmental Protection Agency approved and adjusted multiple air-quality and pesticide regulatory actions. EPA decisions on SIP revisions, sanctions deferrals, new pesticide ingredients, and microbial tolerances shaped environmental standards that affect public health and industrial costs. (24 Mar 2025)

11. Drug Enforcement Administration processed multiple applications to import or manufacture Schedule I controlled substances for research. DEA notices on cannabis- and psychedelic-related imports and manufacturing set conditions for scientific and pharmaceutical work under strict federal drug controls. (26 Mar 2025)

12. Transportation Security Administration sought extension of information collection for aircraft repair station security. Continuing data requirements for repair-station security maintained oversight of aviation maintenance, balancing regulatory burden with transportation safety. (26 Mar 2025)

13. Federal Communications Commission set compliance dates for Next Generation 911 location-based routing rules. Implementing NG911 routing standards aimed to improve emergency response efficiency, with cost and

technical implications for telecom providers and local governments. (25 Mar 2025)

14. Food and Drug Administration delayed the effective date of a rule on nonprescription drugs with additional conditions. Postponing a consumer-drug rule under a regulatory freeze extended uncertainty for manufacturers and consumers about labeling and access requirements. (25 Mar 2025)

15. General Services Administration postponed effectiveness of acquisition regulation amendments under a regulatory freeze. Delaying GSAR updates under a presidential regulatory freeze showed how executive directives can slow procurement reforms and maintain existing contracting rules. (28 Mar 2025)

16. Occupational Safety and Health Administration extended OMB approval for benzene standard information collection. Maintaining data collection under the benzene standard preserved a key tool for monitoring workplace exposure to a hazardous chemical and enforcing safety rules. (28 Mar 2025)

17. Environmental Protection Agency advanced several information-collection renewals related to water efficiency, landfills, and freight transport. EPA's ICR renewals for WaterSense, landfill NSPS, and SmartWay kept environmental reporting frameworks in place, affecting compliance costs and data for policy decisions. (28 Mar 2025)

18. Environmental Protection Agency published notice of availability for environmental impact statements. Releasing EIS notices and comment deadlines supported public participation in major development decisions, including large housing redevelopment projects. (28 Mar 2025)

19. Department of Energy sought to cut major clean-energy and grid-deployment funding lines. Proposed reductions to efficiency, renewables, and grid offices would shift federal energy spending away from decarbonization and resilience priorities. (27 Mar 2025)

20. San Francisco city agencies were implicated in a corruption probe over preferential treatment to a nonprofit. Investigations into Urban Ed Academy and city officials for bribes and special grant treatment highlighted vulnerabilities in local grantmaking and oversight. (23 Mar 2025)

21. Biden administration economic policymakers pursued aggressive antitrust and price-control rhetoric against large corporations. Efforts under Lina Khan and Elizabeth Warren to curb corporate concentration and consider price controls reflected a competing model of using state power to rebalance economic influence. (22 Mar 2025)

22. Biden administration and Congress implemented industrial policies that channeled subsidies toward red states willing to build factories. IRA and

CHIPS subsidies flowed disproportionately to states open to large projects, illustrating how federal industrial policy interacts with local development choices. (25 Mar 2025)

23. India's central government let a large manufacturing subsidy program lapse while electronics exports grew. Ending a $23 billion subsidy scheme despite rising electronics exports showed how industrial policy design and multinational investment can shape development outcomes. (23 Mar 2025)

Information, Memory, and Manipulation

1. Outloud-reported officials compiled a list of over 200 banned words for government websites and curricula. Directing agencies and schools to avoid terms like "racism" and "BIPOC" sought to narrow public discourse and obscure discussions of inequality in official materials. (23 Mar 2025)

2. National Park Service removed references to Pauli Murray's gender identity and sexuality from its website. Editing out aspects of Pauli Murray's identity from an official historic-site page erased LGBTQ history from a federal narrative about civil-rights leadership. (23 Mar 2025)

3. Air Force and Department of Defense removed and later restored web pages honoring pioneering women and Jackie Robinson. The brief disappearance and restoration of pages on women leaders and Jackie Robinson reflected contested control over which stories of inclusion appear in military history. (23 Mar 2025)

4. Health Secretary Robert F. Kennedy Jr. spread misleading claims about vaccine safety that fueled hesitancy. Anti-vaccine statements from the nation's top health official undermined trust in scientific agencies and contributed to outbreaks of preventable diseases. (24 Mar 2025)

5. President Donald Trump escalated attacks on CNN and MSNBC as "illegal" and "corrupt" media outlets. Labeling major news networks as unlawful and suggesting they should be shut down threatened press freedom and sought to delegitimize independent scrutiny. (24 Mar 2025)

6. Bill O'Reilly and Fox News framed the Affordable Care Act as socialist income redistribution. Commentary portraying health reform as socialism illustrated how media narratives shape public attitudes toward social policy and government's redistributive role. (24 Mar 2025)

7. Trump administration national security team used the Signal app to discuss detailed Yemen war plans, inadvertently including a journalist. Planning airstrikes on an unapproved, auto-deleting messaging app both endangered operational security and sidestepped normal record-keeping channels. (25 Mar 2025)

8. Pentagon warned staff against using Signal due to security vulnerabilities. An OPSEC bulletin cautioning against Signal use underscored official recognition that popular encrypted apps may not meet standards for classified communications. (25 Mar 2025)

9. Der Spiegel and security researchers reported that private data of US officials in the Signal scandal were exposed online. Discovery of leaked passwords and emails for senior officials involved in the Yemen chat highlighted personal cybersecurity lapses with potential espionage implications. (27 Mar 2025)

10. Fox News reportedly sidelined national security correspondent Jennifer Griffin over her reporting on the Signal scandal. Marginalizing a reporter for accurate coverage of a security breach suggested internal pressures that can discourage rigorous journalism on sensitive topics. (26 Mar 2025)

11. Trump administration and allied lawmakers attacked NPR, PBS, and public media funding as biased and "anti-American". Congressional hearings and rhetoric against public broadcasters signaled efforts to delegitimize and potentially defund independent, noncommercial news sources. (26 Mar 2025)

12. President Donald Trump and allies launched personal attacks on journalist Jeffrey Goldberg after the Signal leak. Smearing the reporter who revealed the Yemen chat leak fit a pattern of discrediting journalists who expose government missteps, potentially chilling investigative reporting. (27 Mar 2025)

13. Trump administration ordered the Smithsonian to purge exhibits deemed "improper, divisive, or anti-American". Directing museums to remove certain historical narratives and possibly restore Confederate symbols placed political control over national memory institutions. (28 Mar 2025)

14. University of Michigan shut down its central DEI office and related programs in response to federal orders. Closing flagship DEI structures under threat of losing federal funds showed how national policy can reshape campus priorities and limit institutional support for marginalized groups. (28 Mar 2025)

15. Heather Cox Richardson and historical sources recounted passage of the ACA, Fair Labor Standards Act, and Social Security Act as context for current policy fights. Referencing landmark social legislation provided historical framing for contemporary debates over government's role in health and economic security. (24 Mar 2025)

16. Wired and other outlets identified additional Venmo accounts tied to officials in the Signal chat with suggestive payment notes. Revelations about personal payment trails of officials involved in war-plans chats raised trans-

parency questions about their financial dealings and relationships. (28 Mar 2025)

17. Centers for Disease Control and Prevention announced a public ACIP meeting on vaccine recommendations with open comments. Scheduling a public advisory meeting on vaccines with webcast access and comment periods supported transparent, evidence-based health policymaking. (24 Mar 2025)

18. EPA and Census Bureau issued corrections and comment requests for survey and regulatory information collections. Adjusting survey schedules and inviting comments on data collections maintained procedural transparency in how environmental and social data are gathered. (26 Mar 2025)

19. Trump administration and DOGE sought expanded access to SSA and voter data for efficiency and election-integrity initiatives. Efforts to centralize sensitive personal and electoral data under DOGE raised concerns about surveillance, politicized analytics, and manipulation of voter rolls. (24 Mar 2025)

20. Trump administration and allied commentators continued to frame voter-fraud narratives and ACA opposition through partisan media. Persistent claims of widespread fraud and socialism in major policy debates entrenched disinformation that can justify restrictive laws and erode trust in institutions. (24 Mar 2025)

CHAPTER 11
WEEK 11 (29 MAR 2025 – 4 APR 2025): CHAOS AS METHODICAL GOVERNANCE

Emergency economics, bureaucratic purges, and weaponized federal leverage advanced together, deepening structural erosion even as the Democracy Clock barely moved.

This was a heavily challenging week for democratic erosion, with simultaneous attacks on institutional checks, civil rights, and the information landscape. The most severe pressures came from the normalization of emergency economic powers and broad tariffs, used to bypass Congress and reshape trade policy in ways that benefit donors and harm disliked regions. Mass layoffs and politicization at HHS, EPA, USAID, and the civil service weakened core state functions, especially in public health and environmental protections. Federal power was openly weaponized against universities, Democratic-leaning areas, and even one state (Maine), while immigration tools were repurposed to target activists and vulnerable migrants with arbitrary criteria. Courts presented a mixed picture: some federal judges and state attorney general coalitions checked deportations and election overreach, but others and the Supreme Court upheld partisan or anti-DEI decisions and tolerated executive funding freezes. Media and academic freedom faced coordinated pressures through FCC investigations, access bans, Smithsonian interference, and funding threats to Columbia and Harvard. Amid this, large protests, Cory Booker's lengthy speech, and electoral resistance in Wisconsin marked notable but still insufficient democratic responses.

Power and Authority

1. Trump administration canceled $400 million in federal funding to Columbia University to pressure changes in campus policies. By pulling major research funding to force Columbia to change how it handles pro-Palestinian activity, the administration used federal financial power to shape academic speech and institutional autonomy. (29 Mar 2025; 1 Apr 2025)

2. Columbia University adopted new restrictions on pro-Palestinian activity and ceded control over a department under federal pressure. Columbia's decision to tighten protest rules and accept external control of a department in hopes of regaining federal funds showed how executive pressure can chill campus dissent and reshape governance. (29 Mar 2025)

3. Trump administration implemented budget cuts that weakened Native American institutions and tribal funding. Cuts to tribal funds and Native-serving institutions, including Haskell Indian Nations University, reduced support for Indigenous education and cultural programs, weakening already marginalized communities' access to public goods. (29 Mar 2025)

4. Trump administration issued an executive order directing the Smithsonian to remove exhibits deemed "improper, divisive or anti-American". Ordering the Smithsonian to purge exhibits on race and power placed federal ideology over curatorial judgment, letting the executive branch rewrite public history and constrain discussion of racism. (29 Mar 2025)

5. Trump administration moved to gut the Department of Homeland Security's civil rights division. Weakening DHS's civil rights office reduced oversight of immigration enforcement and detention, making it harder to check abuses against migrants and other vulnerable groups. (29 Mar 2025)

6. President Trump granted clemency to Ozy Media co-founder Carlos Watson and erased related financial penalties. Overriding a fraud conviction and large restitution order for a media executive underscored how presidential clemency can insulate well-connected offenders from judicial accountability. (29 Mar 2025)

7. State Department announced the shutdown of USAID and transfer of its functions into the department. Eliminating a congressionally created aid agency and folding its work into the State Department concentrated foreign assistance power in the executive, raising separation-of-powers concerns. (29 Mar 2025)

8. President Trump issued an executive order ending affirmative action in admissions at the US Naval Academy. Ending race-conscious admissions at a key military academy reduced tools to maintain a diverse officer corps, affecting representation in a core state institution. (29 Mar 2025)

9. President Trump signed an executive order expanding federal control over Washington DC policing, immigration arrests, and gun permits. Using an order to intensify policing and immigration enforcement in DC while loosening concealed-carry rules let the federal executive override local preferences in a heavily Democratic jurisdiction. (30 Mar 2025)

10. President Trump warned automakers not to raise prices in response to new auto tariffs. Directly pressuring private firms on pricing signaled a willingness to use presidential influence to manage markets informally, blurring lines between state authority and private decision-making. (30 Mar 2025; 31 Mar 2025)

11. President Trump publicly explored "methods" to obtain an unconstitutional third presidential term. Floating ways around the two-term limit, including a vice-presidential route, normalized discussion of extending personal rule beyond constitutional constraints. (29 Mar 2025; 31 Mar 2025)

12. President Trump froze funding under the Inflation Reduction Act and halted approvals of wind and solar projects on federal lands and waters. Blocking congressionally authorized clean-energy spending and permits let the executive unilaterally stall a major legislative program, weakening climate policy and economic planning. (31 Mar 2025)

13. President Trump issued an executive order establishing the United States Investment Accelerator to fast-track billion-dollar projects. Creating a Commerce-based accelerator to streamline approvals for very large investments centralized discretion over mega-projects, potentially privileging well-connected firms in regulatory processes. (31 Mar 2025)

14. President Trump issued an executive order directing aggressive enforcement against unfair practices in the live entertainment ticket market. Ordering DOJ and FTC to crack down on ticketing abuses used executive power to reshape a concentrated market, with implications for consumer protection and corporate regulation. (31 Mar 2025)

15. President Trump declared a national emergency to justify sweeping reciprocal tariffs on imports. Invoking emergency powers to impose broad tariffs shifted core trade and tax-like decisions from Congress to the presidency, normalizing emergency governance in economic policy. (2 Apr 2025)

16. President Trump issued an executive order eliminating de minimis duty-free treatment for certain low-value imports from China and Hong Kong tied to synthetic opioids. Targeting low-value imports from China and Hong Kong under an opioid rationale expanded the use of trade tools as security instruments, tightening executive control over specific supply chains. (2 Apr 2025)

17. President Trump announced sweeping new tariffs on nearly all

imports, framed as "Liberation Day" economic policy. Announcing blanket and country-specific tariffs as a national renewal project concentrated economic power in the presidency and risked destabilizing global trade and domestic prices. (2 Apr 2025; 3 Apr 2025; 4 Apr 2025)

18. President Trump reached coercive settlements with major law firms to avert punitive executive orders targeting them. Conditioning avoidance of hostile executive orders on law firms' pro bono commitments blurred the line between regulation and retaliation, pressuring legal actors who represent political opponents. (2 Apr 2025)

19. President Trump announced a 10% universal tariff package that exempted many fossil fuel products important to major donors. Designing tariffs to spare key fossil fuel imports after large industry donations showed how economic emergency tools can be tailored to protect benefactors while shifting costs to the public. (3 Apr 2025)

20. President Trump extended the enforcement delay of the TikTok ban under the Protecting Americans from Foreign Adversary Controlled Applications Act. Postponing enforcement of a high-profile app ban underscored executive control over when and how national-security-based tech restrictions actually bite, affecting platforms and users' speech environment. (4 Apr 2025)

Institutions and Governance

1. Florida legislature enacted a "countries of concern" law leading to the firing of a Chinese professor at New College of Florida. Using nationality-based hiring restrictions in public universities tied academic employment to geopolitical categories, undermining institutional autonomy and equal access to public jobs. (29 Mar 2025)

2. Wisconsin Attorney General Josh Kaul sued Elon Musk and his PAC over a million-dollar voter giveaway program. Challenging cash giveaways linked to voting tested state campaign and bribery laws against a billionaire's attempt to shape a pivotal judicial election. (29 Mar 2025)

3. Delaware Attorney General Kathy Jennings and 20 other state AGs formed a coalition urging law firms to resist Trump administration intimidation. State attorneys general organized to defend law firms and judges from executive pressure, seeking to preserve independent legal representation and judicial integrity. (29 Mar 2025)

4. Congressional Republicans cut Washington DC's budget by $1 billion in a federal spending bill. Slashing DC's budget through federal appropria-

tions let Congress override local fiscal choices in a Democratic city, constraining its capacity to provide core services. (30 Mar 2025)

5. President Trump filed a $10 billion defamation lawsuit against CBS News over an edited interview. A massive defamation suit by the president against a major network risked chilling critical coverage by turning civil courts into tools against disfavored media. (30 Mar 2025)

6. Oregon legislature recriminalized low-level drug possession, reversing prior decriminalization. Restoring criminal penalties for minor drug possession shifted policy back toward incarceration, straining courts and public defenders and affecting health-oriented justice reforms. (31 Mar 2025)

7. Representative Victoria Spartz told constituents they were not entitled to due process when raising rule concerns. A sitting member's denial of constituents' due process rights signaled disregard for basic legal protections that underpin fair governance. (31 Mar 2025)

8. House Republican leadership halted voting after a rule defeat tied to blocking proxy voting for new parents. Internal GOP conflict over allowing proxy votes for new parents paralyzed House business, showing how procedural fights can stall substantive lawmaking and representation. (31 Mar 2025; 1 Apr 2025)

9. Senate Democrats warned Majority Leader John Thune against using accounting gimmicks to hide the deficit impact of Trump's tax cuts. Opposing creative scoring of a $4 trillion tax package defended transparent budgeting, which is essential for democratic oversight of fiscal choices. (31 Mar 2025)

10. Senator Cory Booker delivered a record-breaking 25-hour Senate speech condemning Trump administration policies. Booker's marathon address used Senate floor procedures to spotlight perceived democratic harms and rally opposition within institutional channels. (31 Mar 2025; 1 Apr 2025)

11. Senate of the United States passed a bipartisan resolution to block President Trump's tariffs on Canadian products. The Senate's vote to rescind Canada tariffs, though likely stalled in the House, asserted congressional authority over trade and challenged emergency-based tariff powers. (2 Apr 2025; 3 Apr 2025)

12. Senators Chuck Grassley and Maria Cantwell and co-sponsors introduced the bipartisan Trade Review Act to reclaim congressional oversight of tariffs. Requiring notice, impact analysis, and congressional approval for new tariffs aimed to restore legislative checks on unilateral trade actions by the president. (3 Apr 2025)

13. Congress of the United States failed to revoke President Trump's

authority to impose new tariffs despite economic concerns. Legislative inaction on canceling broad tariff powers signaled tacit support or acquiescence to an executive-driven trade regime with major economic consequences. (3 Apr 2025)

14. House Republicans displayed "Wanted" posters of federal judges who ruled against the Trump administration. Targeting judges with hostile posters outside congressional offices risked intimidating the judiciary and undermining perceptions of impartial courts. (31 Mar 2025)

15. Secretary of Defense Pete Hegseth hired his brother as a senior Pentagon advisor despite anti-nepotism law. Bringing a close relative into a senior defense role raised nepotism concerns and suggested personal loyalty may trump merit in sensitive security posts. (29 Mar 2025)

16. Senate of the United States confirmed Dr. Mehmet Oz as administrator of the Centers for Medicare and Medicaid Services. Confirming a figure criticized for health misinformation to run Medicare and Medicaid risked politicizing a key technocratic agency and eroding trust in its guidance. (3 Apr 2025)

17. President Trump fired General Timothy Haugh as head of US Cyber Command and director of the NSA. Removing the top cyber and signals intelligence official, reportedly at a far-right activist's urging, deepened concerns that national security leadership is being reshaped around personal loyalty. (4 Apr 2025)

Civil Rights and Dissent

1. US district court ruled that Tufts student Rümeysa Öztürk could not be deported without a court order. Blocking the immediate removal of a student accused of supporting Hamas without evidence affirmed judicial oversight of immigration enforcement and protected speech-related rights. (29 Mar 2025)

2. Wisconsin appellate court declined to immediately halt Elon Musk's voter giveaway program on procedural grounds. Refusing emergency relief left a controversial cash-for-voters scheme in place during a key judicial race, complicating efforts to police undue financial influence on turnout. (29 Mar 2025)

3. ACLU of Louisiana filed a complaint alleging serious rights violations at the South Louisiana ICE processing center. Documenting inadequate medical care and neglect in ICE detention highlighted systemic abuses against migrants and the need for robust civil-rights enforcement. (29 Mar 2025)

4. Trump administration pursued deportation of Mahmoud Khalil, a former Columbia student and pro-Palestinian activist, under rarely used

immigration provisions. Using obscure executive tools to target a named activist for removal raised concerns that immigration law is being weaponized against political expression. (29 Mar 2025; 30 Mar 2025)

5. Trump administration revoked residency statuses of international students, often from Muslim-majority countries, without clear notice. Secretly stripping student residency, concentrated on Middle Eastern and Muslim-majority nationals, undermined due process and signaled ideological and origin-based stratification of legal status. (29 Mar 2025)

6. International protesters organized "Tesla Takedown" demonstrations in 253 cities against Elon Musk's influence. Large coordinated protests against a powerful corporate figure reflected transnational civil society resistance to perceived corporate capture of politics and labor. (29 Mar 2025)

7. US district judge ordered participants in the leaked Signal chat about Yemen strikes to preserve all messages. Requiring preservation of leaked national-security chat records protected potential evidence for accountability in a sensitive military decision-making episode. (30 Mar 2025)

8. FBI reallocated counterterrorism resources away from far-right domestic threats toward gangs, border taskforces, and leftwing groups. Shifting focus from the leading source of domestic terrorism to other targets, including leftwing groups and Tesla vandalism, risked leaving communities exposed to extremist violence. (30 Mar 2025)

9. Trump administration deported migrants to El Salvador under controversial legal authority distinct from the Alien Enemies Act. Using novel legal justifications to send migrants to a harsh Salvadoran prison system raised serious due process and human rights concerns. (30 Mar 2025)

10. Oregon and federal authorities conducted mass arrests for low-level drug possession after recriminalization. Thousands of arrests under Oregon's new drug law increased incarceration and strained legal aid, disproportionately affecting poor and vulnerable residents. (31 Mar 2025)

11. Federal court issued a temporary restraining order halting deportations of Venezuelans labeled gang members via a tattoo-based point system. Blocking removals based on arbitrary indicators like tattoos and clothing reaffirmed that immigration enforcement must respect legal standards and evidence. (1 Apr 2025)

12. Federal judge temporarily blocked cuts to legal services for unaccompanied children in immigration court. Preserving funding for lawyers for unaccompanied minors protected basic procedural rights for some of the most vulnerable people in the immigration system. (1 Apr 2025)

13. ICE and Trump administration wrongfully deported Kilmar Armando Abrego Garcia, a Maryland resident with protected status, to El Salvador.

Deporting a legally protected resident to a Salvadoran prison and then claiming courts lacked power to fix it exposed how administrative errors can become irreversible rights violations. (1 Apr 2025)

14. US immigration authorities deported Venezuelan Andry José Hernández Romero to a Salvadoran maximum-security prison based on tattoos. Treating common religious tattoos as gang evidence to deport a gay Venezuelan asylum seeker highlighted how superficial criteria can endanger persecuted minorities. (1 Apr 2025)

15. Trump administration and ICE used an internal "Alien Enemies Act Validation Guide" and tattoo-based criteria to deport Venezuelans to El Salvador. A subjective point system that equated popular symbols with gang membership enabled mass deportations without individualized proof, undermining due process. (31 Mar 2025; 1 Apr 2025)

16. Federal judge ordered the Trump administration to return wrongfully deported Maryland father Kilmar Abrego Garcia by a set deadline. Compelling the government to retrieve a deported resident underscored judicial willingness to enforce rights even after removal has occurred. (4 Apr 2025)

17. Trump administration cut jobs and programs at CDC and imposed a hiring freeze at FEMA amid health and weather crises. Reducing capacity at key emergency and disease-response agencies during outbreaks and disasters weakened the state's ability to protect life and safety. (4 Apr 2025)

18. Trump administration implemented a hiring freeze and layoffs that stripped collective bargaining rights from HHS workers. Removing union protections and jobs in a major federal workforce reduced workers' voice in public-sector governance and made them more vulnerable to politicized management. (1 Apr 2025)

19. House Republicans and security services erected fencing around the White House ahead of large planned protests. Preemptive fortification of the White House before nationwide demonstrations illustrated how security measures can distance executive power from visible public dissent. (3 Apr 2025)

20. Protest organizers and participants planned 1,100 "HandsOff!" protests across all 50 states against Trump policies. Coordinated nationwide demonstrations signaled broad civic mobilization against perceived democratic backsliding and economic harm. (3 Apr 2025)

21. Tift County district attorney dropped charges against Selena Maria Chandler-Scott after a miscarriage in Georgia. Ending prosecution of a woman for alleged concealment after a non-viable pregnancy eased one

high-profile instance of criminalizing pregnancy, but highlighted ongoing risks to reproductive autonomy. (4 Apr 2025)

Economic Structure

1. Health and Human Services Secretary Robert F. Kennedy Jr. announced and began mass layoffs and restructuring at HHS affecting tens of thousands of workers. Cutting roughly a quarter of HHS's workforce and stripping bargaining rights weakened federal public health capacity and labor protections, while opening space for privatization. (29 Mar 2025; 1 Apr 2025; 2 Apr 2025; 4 Apr 2025)

2. Dr. Peter Marks resigned as FDA's top vaccine official in protest of RFK Jr.'s misinformation and pressure. The departure of a key vaccine regulator over political interference signaled erosion of scientific independence in drug oversight, with implications for health markets and trust. (29 Mar 2025)

3. Trump administration and EPA leadership planned elimination of over 1,100 scientists and terminated $14 billion in climate grants at EPA. Large cuts to EPA research staff and climate grants weakened environmental regulation and data, shifting agency priorities away from public protection toward deregulation. (31 Mar 2025)

4. EPA froze or stayed multiple environmental rules and emission standards pending reconsideration. Pausing hazardous air pollutant standards and TCE provisions delayed enforcement of health protections, easing compliance burdens on industry at potential cost to communities. (31 Mar 2025; 2 Apr 2025)

5. Trump administration froze billions in Biden-era agricultural and clean-energy funding, then selectively revived a small conservation grant. Halting large tranches of previously approved farm and climate funds while reviving a small grant under pressure created uncertainty for producers and signaled politicized control over public investment. (1 Apr 2025)

6. Trump administration canceled $1 billion in local food purchase funding for food banks and schools. Ending a major local food program cut support for small farms and low-income consumers, weakening food security and rural economic stability. (1 Apr 2025)

7. Trump administration withdrew and reviewed massive federal grants and contracts for Columbia and Harvard over campus antisemitism claims. Tying billions in research and institutional funding to political judgments about campus climate leveraged federal money to influence elite universities' internal policies. (31 Mar 2025; 1 Apr 2025)

8. Elon Musk contributed over $20 million and held rallies with cash give-

aways to influence the Wisconsin Supreme Court election. Massive spending and direct payments around a state judicial race illustrated how concentrated wealth can shape courts that decide voting rules and maps. (29 Mar 2025; 30 Mar 2025; 31 Mar 2025; 1 Apr 2025)

9. President Trump announced and implemented broad new tariffs on imported cars, parts, and most other goods. Imposing large, non-reciprocal tariffs on autos and other imports restructured trade flows, raised costs for consumers and firms, and shifted economic risk onto workers and small businesses. (30 Mar 2025; 31 Mar 2025; 1 Apr 2025; 2 Apr 2025; 3 Apr 2025; 4 Apr 2025)

10. Cleveland-Cliffs announced layoffs of more than 600 steelworkers due to auto-industry tariffs. Tariff-driven supply chain disruptions led a major steel producer to idle operations and cut jobs, showing how trade shocks can quickly harm industrial workers. (30 Mar 2025)

11. Trump administration implemented tariff policies that increased uncertainty and costs in the oil and energy sector. Higher equipment costs and policy volatility in energy markets complicated investment decisions, with potential knock-on effects for prices and energy security. (30 Mar 2025)

12. Stock markets and investors reacted to tariff announcements with sharp declines in major indices. Steep drops in the Dow and NASDAQ following tariff news reflected investor fears that protectionist policy could trigger recession and erode household wealth. (2 Apr 2025; 3 Apr 2025)

13. Treasury Secretary Bessent and allied commentators publicly defended high tariffs as compatible with the American dream despite higher consumer costs. Framing tariffs as a path to reindustrialization while downplaying price impacts justified policies that shift burdens from capital to consumers and workers. (3 Apr 2025; 4 Apr 2025)

14. Federal Reserve Chair Jerome Powell declined to immediately adjust interest rates amid tariff-driven volatility. The Fed's decision to hold rates despite political pressure underscored the importance of central bank independence for stabilizing an economy shaken by executive trade moves. (3 Apr 2025)

15. Trump administration canceled Social Security contracts in Maine and froze federal education funds after disputes with the governor. Using Social Security and education funding as leverage against a state government weaponized federal economic tools to punish political noncompliance. (4 Apr 2025)

16. Trump administration cut federal grants for arts and humanities institutions nationwide. Reducing support for museums, archives, and cultural

projects weakened public access to shared cultural goods and independent historical work. (4 Apr 2025)

17. Social Security Administration and DOGE reversed planned field office closures and scaled back phone-service cuts after public outcry. Walking back service reductions under pressure showed both the vulnerability of core benefits infrastructure to opaque efficiency drives and the potential of civic scrutiny to protect access. (31 Mar 2025; 3 Apr 2025)

18. Social Security Administration adopted policy changes likely to sharply increase in-person field office demand. New ID and in-person requirements for benefits and noncitizen Social Security numbers risked overwhelming SSA capacity, effectively raising barriers to accessing earned benefits. (31 Mar 2025)

19. National Institutes of Health leadership resumed grant funding after acknowledging federal court injunctions. Restarting previously blocked research grants restored funding flows and signaled belated compliance with judicial limits on executive attempts to choke off science funding. (3 Apr 2025)

20. Census Bureau and other federal agencies issued multiple notices on business, health, and acquisition surveys and information collections. Continuing routine economic and health data collections and procurement oversight maintained the statistical and regulatory backbone needed for informed policy and fair contracting. (31 Mar 2025; 2 Apr 2025; 3 Apr 2025; 4 Apr 2025)

21. EPA and FCC approved or advanced several environmental and communications rules and plans. Approving state air plans, pesticide data reforms, and FM allotment changes showed ongoing regulatory work that can either mitigate or entrench environmental and media inequalities depending on implementation. (1 Apr 2025; 3 Apr 2025; 4 Apr 2025)

22. Trump administration announced high tariffs that triggered major stock market losses and global retaliation. Tariffs that prompted sharp market declines and foreign countermeasures risked broader economic instability, with ordinary households bearing much of the adjustment cost. (2 Apr 2025; 3 Apr 2025)

Information, Memory, and Manipulation

1. Trump administration officials participated in a leaked Signal group chat revealing details of an impending Yemen strike, with no punishment announced. Senior officials' casual discussion of sensitive military plans on Signal, followed by efforts to downplay the breach, exposed double standards in handling classified information and accountability. (29 Mar 2025)

2. FCC under Chair Brendan Carr opened investigations into NBC News, NPR, and PBS. Regulatory probes into critical broadcasters risked chilling independent journalism by signaling that unfavorable coverage could trigger government scrutiny. (30 Mar 2025)

3. President Trump barred AP journalists from the Oval Office and excluded Reuters and HuffPost reporters from key events. Selective bans on major outlets for not adopting preferred language or for critical coverage restricted press access and skewed the information reaching the public. (30 Mar 2025)

4. House foreign relations subcommittee Republicans held a hearing on a supposed "censorship industrial complex" under Biden. Framing prior content-moderation efforts as a vast censorship scheme while ignoring current speech restrictions served to redirect attention from present-day threats to free expression. (1 Apr 2025)

5. Trump National Security Council staff used Signal and personal Gmail accounts for sensitive government business, sidestepping records laws. Conducting official work on encrypted apps and private email undermined statutory record-keeping, making it harder for the public and investigators to reconstruct key decisions. (1 Apr 2025; 2 Apr 2025)

6. Department of Health and Human Services fired thousands of employees including FOIA staff handling public records requests. Eliminating FOIA personnel at a major agency reduced the public's ability to obtain information about health policy and internal decision-making. (1 Apr 2025)

7. Social Security Administration and DOGE removed online notices of planned field office closures after reversing course. Scrubbing prior closure announcements from official sites obscured the policy trail, complicating public understanding of how and why service decisions were made. (31 Mar 2025)

8. Secretary of Homeland Security Kristi Noem filmed a political video inside a Salvadoran prison holding deported Venezuelans. Using incarcerated migrants as a backdrop for deterrence messaging turned detention into propaganda, shaping public perceptions of immigration through fear. (1 Apr 2025)

9. Trump administration released a formula for claimed foreign tariff rates after earlier misrepresentations. Publishing a contrived tariff-rate formula after using inflated numbers to justify new duties highlighted how economic data can be massaged to sell controversial policies. (3 Apr 2025)

10. Federal Communications Commission deleted a restricted Media Bureau item from its March 27 open meeting agenda. Quietly removing a

media-related adjudicatory item from a public meeting agenda limited visibility into regulatory decisions that can shape the media landscape. (3 Apr 2025)

11. Trump administration used Smithsonian and university funding leverage to reshape narratives on race, antisemitism, and protest. Conditioning cultural and academic funding on removal of "improper ideology" and specific campus responses allowed the executive to curate public memory and acceptable discourse. (29 Mar 2025; 31 Mar 2025; 1 Apr 2025; 4 Apr 2025)

12. Judge Meredith Grabill removed clergy abuse survivors from a bankruptcy committee and sealed a DOJ report after a confidentiality dispute. Sanctioning survivors' counsel and sealing investigative findings limited transparency around institutional abuse and may deter future whistleblowing. (31 Mar 2025; 2 Apr 2025)

13. US border officials searched travelers' devices and denied entry based on messages critical of Donald Trump. Using device content and political speech as grounds to refuse entry blurred the line between security screening and ideological vetting at the border. (2 Apr 2025)

14. Trump administration and allied actors advanced narratives about noncitizen voting and third-term possibilities while reshaping election rules. Claims of widespread noncitizen voting and talk of circumventing term limits framed restrictive election changes as integrity measures, muddying public understanding of democratic norms. (31 Mar 2025; 1 Apr 2025; 4 Apr 2025)

CHAPTER 12
WEEK 12 (5 APR 2025 – 11 APR 2025): EMERGENCY POWERS AS ROUTINE GOVERNANCE

Tariffs, deportations, and funding threats fused into a single method of rule, tightening executive control while leaving formal institutions visibly intact.

This week shows an aggressive consolidation of executive power, with Trump using emergency tariff authorities, immigration law, and executive orders to bypass Congress and punish perceived enemies. The tariff shock and chaotic partial pause exemplify governance through economic brinkmanship, shifting risk onto the public while insiders navigate the volatility. Immigration policy tightens into a mass-deportation regime: TPS holders, asylum seekers, students, and even legal residents are detained or expelled under questionable legal theories, while the IRS and Palantir data are repurposed to support enforcement. Simultaneously, universities, law firms, NGOs, and cultural institutions are pressured through funding freezes, consent decrees, and retaliatory orders, weakening independent centers of knowledge and legal defense. Voting rights come under direct attack via the SAVE Act and targeted challenges to military and overseas ballots. Some institutional resistance persists—federal judges maintain AP access, block certain immigration policies, and order Abrego Garcia's return; Congress proposes bills to limit tariff power; mass protests and civic mobilization continue—but overall, the structural pressure strongly favors normalized emergency rule, weaponized law, and a divided citizenship system.

Power and Authority

1. Trump administration threatened and then withdrew $400 million in federal funding from Columbia University over protest policies. The administration used federal grants as leverage to force Columbia to change protest and security policies, pressuring academic governance and signaling that access to public funds depends on political alignment with the executive. (5 Apr 2025)

2. President Trump created a White House faith office and a Task Force to Eradicate Anti-Christian Bias led by Paula White. Establishing a faith office and anti–Christian bias task force inside the White House embedded a particular religious agenda in executive policymaking, blurring church–state separation and privileging one faith in federal priorities. (5 Apr 2025)

3. White House publicly attacked a federal judge who ordered return of a wrongfully deported resident. By denouncing Judge Paula Xinis as a "Marxist judge" after she ordered Kilmar Abrego Garcia returned, senior aides signaled contempt for judicial authority and tried to delegitimize court oversight of executive deportation powers. (5 Apr 2025)

4. President Trump announced unexpectedly high global tariffs framed as "Liberation Day". Trump's unilateral imposition of sweeping tariffs on many countries concentrated macroeconomic decision-making in the presidency, using emergency trade powers with limited congressional input and triggering major market disruption. (6 Apr 2025; 7 Apr 2025)

5. President Trump used the International Emergency Economic Powers Act to justify unilateral tariffs. Invoking IEEPA to impose tariffs shifted trade policy from Congress to the White House under a standing "emergency," normalizing emergency economic governance and inviting legal challenges over separation of powers. (7 Apr 2025; 9 Apr 2025)

6. President Trump announced and then threatened escalating tariffs on China in response to retaliation. Trump's repeated threats to raise already high tariffs on China, tied to short deadlines and social media statements, used trade sanctions as a personal bargaining tool, heightening economic uncertainty and executive leverage. (6 Apr 2025; 7 Apr 2025; 8 Apr 2025)

7. President Trump issued executive orders massively increasing tariffs on Chinese imports and restructuring reciprocal tariff rates. Executive orders raising effective tariffs on China into triple digits and resetting reciprocal rates entrenched one-person control over trade architecture, sidelining normal legislative processes for setting tax-like measures. (8 Apr 2025; 9 Apr 2025)

8. President Trump signed multiple executive orders to promote coal and

override state and federal climate policies. Orders reclassifying coal, lifting leasing limits, and directing DOJ to attack state climate laws centralized energy policy in the presidency and weakened state and scientific checks on fossil-fuel interests. (8 Apr 2025; 9 Apr 2025)

9. President Trump disbanded the DOJ National Cryptocurrency Enforcement Team and curtailed regulatory litigation on digital assets. Shutting down DOJ's crypto enforcement unit and renouncing regulatory cases shifted federal power away from policing complex financial frauds, favoring industry interests and narrowing legal tools against emerging economic abuses. (8 Apr 2025)

10. President Trump publicly framed his global tariff war as a historic corrective and path to ending income taxes. By justifying sweeping tariffs with a selective reading of history and linking them to abolishing income taxes, Trump used populist economic narratives to legitimize concentrating fiscal power in the executive. (8 Apr 2025)

11. President Trump and Defense Secretary Pete Hegseth proposed a record $1 trillion defense budget. The proposed jump in Pentagon spending, amid cuts to civilian agencies, shifted federal priorities toward military power over domestic services, reinforcing an imbalance between security institutions and social programs. (7 Apr 2025; 8 Apr 2025)

12. President Trump ordered the IRS to share undocumented taxpayers' data with DHS for immigration enforcement. Directing tax authorities to provide confidential filings to DHS repurposed a revenue agency into an immigration-enforcement tool, undermining taxpayer privacy and deterring compliance among vulnerable groups. (7 Apr 2025; 8 Apr 2025)

13. President Trump signed executive orders to strengthen electric grid reliability while favoring all existing generation sources. The grid security order centralized emergency authority in the Energy Department to keep all generation online, potentially privileging politically favored fuels while reducing environmental and state-level constraints. (8 Apr 2025)

14. President Trump directed DOJ to challenge state and local energy and climate regulations deemed burdensome. Ordering federal lawyers to attack state climate and energy rules used national power to discipline disfavored jurisdictions, weakening federalism and insulating fossil-fuel interests from subnational accountability. (8 Apr 2025)

15. President Trump issued executive orders to investigate former officials Miles Taylor and Chris Krebs and target Susman Godfrey law firm. Using executive orders to strip clearances and trigger investigations of critics and a firm that litigated against his allies turned state power into a weapon against perceived enemies in the legal and security communities. (9 Apr 2025)

16. President Trump signed a memorandum authorizing a military buffer zone along the southern border. Authorizing active-duty soldiers to detain migrants on public lands militarized border enforcement and blurred lines between civilian policing and military roles in domestic space. (10 Apr 2025; 11 Apr 2025)

17. President Trump signed a memo allowing the military to take over public lands along the southern border. Empowering the military to control public lands for border operations expanded security forces' footprint over civilian territory, raising concerns about environmental stewardship and civil oversight. (10 Apr 2025)

18. President Trump announced a large military parade in Washington, DC tied to his birthday. Planning a capital-city military parade centered on the president used armed forces for personal political spectacle, reinforcing leader-focused symbolism rather than neutral national commemoration. (6 Apr 2025)

19. President Trump signed executive orders to modernize defense acquisitions and reform foreign defense sales. Rewriting acquisition and foreign sales rules from the Oval Office concentrated discretion over major defense contracts and arms exports in the executive, with implications for oversight and foreign policy leverage. (9 Apr 2025)

20. President Trump issued a zero-based regulatory budgeting order for energy-related agencies. Forcing EPA and DOE to sunset energy regulations unless reapproved gave the White House a recurring veto over environmental rules, favoring deregulation and weakening long-term policy stability. (9 Apr 2025)

21. President Trump signed an executive order to reduce anti-competitive regulatory barriers. Directing agencies to purge rules labeled anti-competitive expanded presidential influence over the regulatory state, potentially enabling selective deregulation aligned with favored industries. (9 Apr 2025)

22. President Trump signed an executive order to restore America's maritime dominance through federal funding and trade measures. The maritime dominance order tied industrial policy, trade retaliation, and federal subsidies to presidential priorities, deepening executive control over a strategic sector with limited legislative design. (9 Apr 2025)

23. President Trump signed executive orders targeting multiple law firms over diversity and political work. Orders revoking access and clearances for lawyers at firms tied to political rivals used presidential power to coerce private legal practices, undermining independent representation in cases involving the federal government. (11 Apr 2025)

24. President Trump signed executive orders targeting political opponents

during an Oval Office event with state officials. Using a high-profile Oval Office event to sign orders aimed at political adversaries normalized the use of presidential ceremonies to legitimize punitive actions against domestic opponents. (9 Apr 2025)

25. President Trump publicly renewed baseless claims that the 2020 election was rigged and demanded restrictive voting rules. Reasserting false fraud narratives while calling for paper-only, same-day voting and citizenship proof sought to justify tighter federal and state control over ballot access on spurious grounds. (8 Apr 2025)

26. President Trump signed executive orders deregulating showerhead water pressure standards. Rolling back water-efficiency rules by executive order, and bypassing normal notice-and-comment, highlighted how consumer and environmental standards could be unilaterally weakened by presidential fiat. (9 Apr 2025)

27. President Trump terminated funding for the US Global Change Research Program and the national climate assessment contract. Cutting off funding for the federal climate assessment infrastructure curtailed coordinated climate research, reducing evidence available to policymakers and the public about long-term risks. (9 Apr 2025)

28. President Trump ordered DOJ to halt enforcement of state climate superfund laws in New York and Vermont. Directing federal lawyers not to support state efforts to recover climate damages from fossil-fuel companies used national power to shield an industry from subnational accountability. (9 Apr 2025)

29. President Trump ordered DOJ to investigate former officials and strip their security clearances for alleged disloyalty. Targeting Miles Taylor and Chris Krebs for investigation and clearance revocation signaled that dissenting national-security officials could face punitive use of investigative powers after leaving office. (9 Apr 2025)

30. President Trump announced a 90-day pause on some tariffs while keeping high duties on China. Temporarily pausing parts of his tariff plan after market turmoil, while maintaining extreme China rates, underscored how abrupt presidential moves could destabilize the economy and then be used as bargaining chips. (9 Apr 2025; 10 Apr 2025)

31. President Trump used an executive order to sanction the International Criminal Court and bar US support. Sanctioning the ICC and prohibiting US persons from assisting it extended executive control over international justice cooperation, limiting accountability avenues for alleged war crimes. (11 Apr 2025)

32. President Trump fired NSA Director General Timothy Haugh and

other national security officials following political pressure. Removing the NSA director amid cyber threats, reportedly at the urging of partisan media figures, politicized top intelligence leadership and risked weakening professional security decision-making. (7 Apr 2025)

33. President Trump signed a memorandum directing creation of a military mission along the southern border. Ordering multiple departments to deploy active-duty troops to detain migrants at the border expanded military involvement in domestic enforcement, challenging norms that separate armed forces from routine policing. (11 Apr 2025)

Institutions and Governance

1. Federal judge Paula Xinis ordered the government to return wrongfully deported legal resident Kilmar Abrego Garcia. The order declared Abrego Garcia's deportation unlawful and required his return, asserting judicial authority to remedy executive overreach in immigration enforcement. (5 Apr 2025; 7 Apr 2025)

2. Department of Justice placed immigration lawyer Erez Reuveni on indefinite leave after he admitted a wrongful deportation. Suspending a career lawyer for candidly acknowledging an illegal deportation signaled that internal honesty about government misconduct could be punished, discouraging professional integrity within DOJ. (5 Apr 2025; 6 Apr 2025)

3. Federal judge temporarily halted termination of Temporary Protected Status for Venezuelans. By pausing the administration's attempt to end TPS for 350,000 Venezuelans, the court protected existing legal status and underscored judicial checks on abrupt policy reversals affecting large populations. (5 Apr 2025)

4. International student filed a lawsuit challenging visa revocation allegedly used to coerce self-deportation. The suit contests immigration practices that revoke student status without violations, testing whether courts will curb executive tools that pressure lawful residents to leave. (5 Apr 2025)

5. Senators Chuck Grassley and Maria Cantwell introduced bipartisan legislation to limit presidential tariff powers. Requiring congressional approval for new tariffs within 60 days aimed to reassert legislative control over trade policy and check unilateral economic actions by the president. (7 Apr 2025)

6. House Republicans advanced a bill to ban nationwide injunctions by federal judges. Curtailing judges' ability to issue nationwide injunctions would weaken a key tool for checking unlawful federal policies, shifting power away from the judiciary toward the executive. (7 Apr 2025; 9 Apr 2025)

7. House Judiciary subcommittee held a hearing on alleged judicial overreach targeting rulings against Trump policies. Framing adverse decisions as overreach and exploring ways to curb such judges politicized judicial review and signaled congressional support for narrowing court checks on executive actions. (7 Apr 2025)

8. Senate Judiciary Committee held a hearing on banning universal injunctions and considered related legislation. Senate consideration of ending universal injunctions reflected bipartisan pressure on courts' ability to block federal policies nationwide, with implications for rapid relief in constitutional cases. (7 Apr 2025)

9. US Senate passed a bipartisan amendment to reverse Trump's tariffs on Canadian imports. The vote to roll back 25% tariffs on Canada showed Congress attempting to mitigate economic harm and reclaim some authority over trade decisions from the executive branch. (7 Apr 2025)

10. New Civil Liberties Alliance filed a lawsuit challenging Trump's use of IEEPA to impose tariffs on China. The suit argues that emergency economic powers do not authorize tariffs, asking courts to reassert Congress's constitutional role over taxation and trade. (7 Apr 2025; 9 Apr 2025)

11. US Supreme Court vacated a classwide injunction blocking deportations under the Alien Enemies Act. By requiring individual habeas challenges in Texas rather than a DC class action, the Court made it procedurally harder for Venezuelan migrants to contest deportations under an 18th-century statute. (7 Apr 2025; 8 Apr 2025; 9 Apr 2025)

12. US Supreme Court granted an administrative stay blocking rehiring of thousands of fired federal probationary workers. Staying lower-court orders that required rehiring about 16,000 dismissed civil servants allowed the administration's mass firings to stand during litigation, weakening protections for politically vulnerable staff. (8 Apr 2025; 11 Apr 2025)

13. US Supreme Court ordered the government to facilitate Kilmar Abrego Garcia's return to the United States. The unanimous order requiring steps to undo a wrongful deportation affirmed judicial power to remedy executive violations, though subsequent noncompliance raised questions about enforceability. (10 Apr 2025; 11 Apr 2025)

14. US District Judge Trevor McFadden ordered the White House to restore Associated Press access to presidential events. The ruling held that banning AP over its refusal to adopt "Gulf of America" violated the First Amendment, reinforcing that viewpoint-based press exclusions are unconstitutional. (8 Apr 2025)

15. North Carolina Supreme Court temporarily stayed a lower-court order requiring verification of 60,000 ballots. The stay paused a recount and ID

verification scheme that could have disenfranchised tens of thousands of voters in a state supreme court race, preserving ballots while legal challenges proceed. (8 Apr 2025)

16. North Carolina Court of Appeals ordered recount and identity verification for 60,000 ballots in a state supreme court election. Requiring targeted voters to prove eligibility post-election, on pain of having ballots discarded, introduced a retroactive hurdle that could alter the outcome of a close judicial race. (8 Apr 2025)

17. US Supreme Court blocked a California ruling that mandated rehiring of 16,000 fired federal workers. By focusing on plaintiffs' standing and granting a stay, the Court allowed the administration's large-scale civil service purge to continue, limiting judicial protection for probationary employees. (8 Apr 2025)

18. US Court of Appeals for the DC Circuit reinstated two independent agency board members fired by the Trump administration. Reinstating Cathy Harris and Gwynne Wilcox to MSPB and NLRB reaffirmed limits on presidential removal of independent agency officials, though the administration signaled plans to appeal. (7 Apr 2025)

19. Federal courts issued injunctions and mandates blocking most of Trump's orders targeting specific law firms. Courts sided with firms like Perkins Coie, Jenner & Block, and WilmerHale against executive orders punishing them for representing political rivals, defending legal independence from retaliatory regulation. (7 Apr 2025)

20. American Library Association and cultural workers' union sued to block cuts to the Institute for Museum and Library Services. The lawsuit seeks to preserve federal support for libraries and museums, arguing that funding cuts threaten public access to cultural and educational resources and exceed lawful executive discretion. (8 Apr 2025)

21. Federal judge blocked termination of a humanitarian parole program for over 500,000 migrants. Stopping the administration from ending a program for Cubans, Haitians, Nicaraguans, and Venezuelans preserved temporary legal status for hundreds of thousands and checked abrupt policy reversal. (10 Apr 2025)

22. Federal judge rejected Trump's motion to dismiss a defamation suit by the Exonerated Five. Allowing the case to proceed signaled that even a president can face civil accountability for harmful public statements, reinforcing that high office does not confer blanket immunity. (10 Apr 2025)

23. US Senate summoned Health Secretary Robert F. Kennedy Jr. to testify on a measles outbreak. Calling a vaccine-skeptical health secretary to account for a deadly measles outbreak exercised legislative oversight over

public health policy and the performance of a controversial appointee. (8 Apr 2025)

24. US House Rules Committee approved a rule blocking a floor vote to overturn Trump's tariff emergency. Embedding a procedural barrier in budget legislation prevented the House from voting on a resolution disapproving the tariff emergency, weakening Congress's ability to check executive economic decrees. (9 Apr 2025)

25. National Review editors publicly urged Congress to reclaim economic powers ceded to the president. A conservative outlet's call for legislative reassertion over tariffs highlighted cross-ideological concern that concentrated presidential control over economic policy undermines constitutional balance. (9 Apr 2025)

26. Senator Rand Paul spoke against governing under emergency rule regardless of party. Paul's floor speech criticized reliance on emergency declarations, emphasizing the need for regular legislative processes and warning against normalized exceptional powers. (9 Apr 2025)

27. US House of Representatives passed the No Rogue Rulings Act to limit lower courts' ability to affect national policy. Restricting nationwide impact of lower-court orders would reduce the judiciary's capacity to quickly halt unlawful federal actions, shifting power toward the executive and higher courts. (9 Apr 2025)

28. Senator Jeanne Shaheen introduced a bill to bar contracts to companies owned by special government employees like Elon Musk. The proposal sought to close a conflict-of-interest gap by preventing special government employees from steering federal contracts to their own firms, reinforcing ethical boundaries in procurement. (9 Apr 2025)

29. US House Education and Workforce Committee dropped its investigation into Northwestern law school clinics after a lawsuit. Ending the probe following professors' First Amendment challenge marked a retreat from congressional scrutiny that threatened academic freedom and the independence of clinical legal work. (11 Apr 2025)

30. Atlanta Community Press Collective and Lucy Parsons Labs pursued an open-records lawsuit to subject the Atlanta Police Foundation to transparency laws. The case tests whether a powerful private police foundation must disclose records like a public agency, potentially expanding oversight of quasi-public entities funding law enforcement projects. (11 Apr 2025)

31. North Carolina Supreme Court ordered overseas and military voters to prove eligibility within 30 days or lose their votes. Imposing new documentation requirements after ballots were cast risked disenfranchising lawful over-

seas and military voters in a close judicial race, raising rule-of-law and fairness concerns. (11 Apr 2025)

32. US District Court in Maine heard a challenge to Trump's sanctions order against the International Criminal Court. Human rights advocates argued that sanctions blocking them from assisting the ICC violate their First Amendment rights, asking courts to limit executive power over international justice cooperation. (11 Apr 2025)

33. US Senate confirmed John Dan Caine as chairman of the Joint Chiefs of Staff after waiving usual qualifications. Confirming a less-qualified retired officer under a presidential waiver raised concerns that top military leadership is being selected for loyalty rather than professional criteria. (11 Apr 2025)

34. Federal Election Commission designated several senior posts as policy-making or confidential under an executive order. Labeling key FEC roles as policy-determining clarified which positions are insulated from routine turnover, but also highlighted how executive directives shape the stability of election oversight staff. (10 Apr 2025)

35. Election Assistance Commission renewed charters for its advisory committees on voting systems and best practices. Extending advisory bodies that guide election administration maintained institutional mechanisms for expert input into voting technology and procedures. (11 Apr 2025)

36. House of Representatives passed a Republican budget framework enabling large tax cuts and spending reductions. The budget resolution paved the way to enact Trump's tax and immigration agenda via reconciliation, bypassing the Senate filibuster and reshaping fiscal priorities with limited bipartisan deliberation. (9 Apr 2025; 10 Apr 2025)

37. Senator Cory Booker delivered a 25-hour Senate speech urging defense of democracy. Booker's record-setting speech used Senate floor time to spotlight democratic erosion and mobilize public engagement, illustrating how legislative procedure can be used for pro-democracy signaling. (6 Apr 2025)

38. National Archives and Records Administration and GSA sought public comment on multiple information-collection and service-delivery initiatives. Routine PRA notices on records access, surplus property, and customer experience reflected ongoing administrative processes that support transparency and service quality despite broader political pressures. (7 Apr 2025; 9 Apr 2025; 11 Apr 2025)

Civil Rights and Dissent

1. Immigration and Customs Enforcement detained a British tourist for 19 days despite her attempt to leave the US. Holding a departing tourist in immigration detention highlighted how aggressive enforcement can ensnare nonthreatening visitors, raising concerns about proportionality and due process. (5 Apr 2025)

2. Federal immigration agents arrested and sought to deport graduate students involved in pro-Palestinian protests. Targeting student protesters through immigration enforcement blurred the line between security policy and suppression of campus dissent, especially for noncitizen activists. (5 Apr 2025)

3. Trump administration arrested Venezuelan TPS holders despite legal protections against such detentions. Detaining people with Temporary Protected Status in apparent violation of statutory safeguards undermined trust in legal protections and heightened fear among lawfully present migrants. (5 Apr 2025)

4. Trump administration sought to deport Columbia activist Mahmoud Khalil, a green-card holder, as a foreign policy threat. Using a rarely invoked foreign-policy deportation provision against a campus activist suggested that political speech could be treated as a national security risk for noncitizens. (5 Apr 2025; 8 Apr 2025)

5. Secretary of State Marco Rubio revoked about 300 student visas for individuals deemed foreign policy threats. Mass visa revocations targeting alleged Hamas supporters on campuses threatened academic freedom and signaled that political associations could cost international students their legal status. (5 Apr 2025)

6. AFL-CIO President Liz Shuler reported that Trump effectively nullified collective bargaining agreements for 700,000 union workers. The claimed nullification of large-scale union contracts represented a major rollback of organized labor's bargaining power, weakening workers' collective voice in both public and private sectors. (5 Apr 2025)

7. Department of Homeland Security subjected FEMA head Cameron Hamilton to a lie detector test over leak suspicions. Polygraphing a senior official to hunt for leaks reflected a climate of internal surveillance that can chill whistleblowing and honest communication within the civil service. (5 Apr 2025)

8. Immigration and Customs Enforcement arrested a compliant Nicaraguan asylum seeker during routine check-ins. Detaining Alberto Lovo Rojas despite his adherence to ICE requirements showed how policy shifts

can turn cooperative asylum seekers into sudden deportation targets. (6 Apr 2025)

9. Customs and Border Protection failed to conduct required welfare checks on a detained Chinese woman who died by suicide. The death in custody, amid unverified welfare logs and delayed public disclosure, raised serious concerns about detainee safety, oversight, and transparency in border facilities. (6 Apr 2025)

10. Trump administration expanded ICE's mandate to prioritize arrest of all undocumented immigrants, including those regularly checking in. Broadening enforcement to target previously low-priority individuals increased fear in immigrant communities and weakened incentives for cooperation with authorities. (6 Apr 2025)

11. Federal agents detained a lawyer representing a pro-Palestinian demonstrator and sought access to his phone. Stopping and questioning a defense attorney about his clients threatened attorney–client confidentiality and could deter legal representation in politically sensitive cases. (6 Apr 2025)

12. ICE and DHS released a detained immigrant family after large protests outside a senior official's home. The family's release following public demonstrations showed that organized protest can still influence individual enforcement decisions within a harsh deportation regime. (7 Apr 2025)

13. Department of Homeland Security deported Venezuelans to El Salvador, most without criminal convictions. Sending largely non-criminal Venezuelans to detention in El Salvador under gang allegations highlighted how broad security labels can justify severe deprivations of liberty. (7 Apr 2025)

14. Department of Homeland Security revoked legal status of migrants who entered via the CBP One app and ordered them to leave. Canceling status for over 900,000 people who followed prior legal pathways undermined trust in government programs and exposed them to sudden deportation risk. (7 Apr 2025)

15. Department of Homeland Security announced plans to build up to $45 billion in new privately run immigrant detention facilities. Massive investment in lower-standard private detention expanded the infrastructure for long-term confinement of migrants, deepening reliance on profit-driven incarceration. (8 Apr 2025)

16. Acting IRS Commissioner Melanie Krause resigned over the IRS–DHS data-sharing agreement on undocumented taxpayers. Her resignation signaled internal alarm that using tax data for deportations violated legal norms and could deter immigrants from filing returns, weakening both rights and revenue. (8 Apr 2025)

17. Trump administration expanded its crackdown on international students flagged in criminal records checks, even without charges. Targeting students based on database flags rather than convictions risked guilt by association and threatened educational continuity for noncitizens. (8 Apr 2025)

18. Medicaid recipients and advocates marched on Capitol Hill to oppose proposed cuts to Medicaid and SNAP. Low-income beneficiaries organized to defend safety-net programs, using protest and direct lobbying to resist budget plans that could reduce access to health care and food assistance. (8 Apr 2025)

19. Trump administration cut corrections funding to Maine because a trans woman was housed in a women's prison. Withholding funds for substance-use and family programs to punish a transgender housing decision used fiscal leverage to pressure states on carceral policy and LGBTQ rights. (8 Apr 2025)

20. US Attorney General Pam Bondi limited enforcement of the Foreign Agents Registration Act for criminal violations. Scaling back FARA prosecutions reduced tools to police covert foreign influence, even as foreign actors sought to shape US policy, weakening protections for democratic self-determination. (11 Apr 2025)

21. Immigration and Customs Enforcement sent erroneous deportation notices to US citizens and lawful residents. Mistakenly ordering citizens and green-card holders to leave the country within seven days exposed serious flaws in enforcement databases and threatened basic security of legal status. (11 Apr 2025)

22. Immigration and Customs Enforcement and DOGE staff used Palantir and other databases to identify immigrants for deportation based on detailed personal data. Mining government and commercial data for physical and financial traits to target deportations expanded surveillance of migrants and raised risks of discriminatory profiling. (11 Apr 2025)

23. Trump administration pressured immigrants with temporary legal status to self-deport by canceling Social Security numbers. Revoking SSNs to block work and benefits for legally present migrants weaponized economic precarity to force departures without formal removal proceedings. (10 Apr 2025)

24. US Citizenship and Immigration Services began surveilling visa holders' social media for alleged antisemitism. Monitoring online speech for ideological content as part of immigration vetting risked punishing lawful residents for protected expression and chilling political discourse. (9 Apr 2025)

25. Los Angeles police shot Jillian Lauren during a search and later charged her with attempted murder. The shooting and serious charge against

a resident uninvolved in the original crime search raised questions about police use of force and prosecutorial discretion in civilian encounters. (10 Apr 2025)

26. Los Angeles County District Attorney charged a youth soccer coach with murder and sexual offenses against minors. Prosecuting serious abuse allegations against a coach underscored the justice system's role in protecting children, including those from immigrant families, from exploitation. (9 Apr 2025)

27. South Carolina authorities and defense lawyers contested an execution by firing squad before the US Supreme Court. The petition challenging firing-squad execution procedures and ineffective counsel highlighted ongoing constitutional debates over capital punishment and fair sentencing. (10 Apr 2025)

28. US Supreme Court and lower courts handled multiple emergency orders and appeals in the Abrego Garcia deportation case. The back-and-forth over Abrego Garcia's wrongful deportation exposed tensions between judicial orders and executive compliance, with direct consequences for an individual's liberty and family. (6 Apr 2025; 7 Apr 2025; 10 Apr 2025; 11 Apr 2025)

29. Trump administration deported Venezuelan migrants to El Salvador based on tattoos misidentified as gang symbols. Relying on flawed tattoo evidence to label migrants as gang members and deport them to third countries showed how thin or erroneous indicators can drive life-altering security decisions. (11 Apr 2025)

30. US border officials detained and deported an Australian worker with a valid visa after accusing him of drug activity. Invalidating a visa and imposing a five-year ban without clear due process highlighted the discretionary power of border agents and the vulnerability of lawful foreign workers. (11 Apr 2025)

31. Immigration agents attempted to enter Los Angeles elementary schools to locate young students. Efforts to access elementary schools for immigration enforcement, rebuffed by administrators, challenged norms that schools are safe spaces and heightened fear among immigrant families. (11 Apr 2025)

32. Immigration and Customs Enforcement detained Tufts student Rümeysa Öztürk and allegedly denied adequate medical care. Reports of repeated asthma attacks, unsanitary conditions, and forced removal of her hijab in detention highlighted human rights and religious-freedom concerns in immigration custody. (11 Apr 2025)

33. US Space Force and Defense Secretary Pete Hegseth fired a Space Force base commander in Greenland for distancing the unit from political

comments. Removing Colonel Susannah Meyers for trying to keep the base apolitical signaled that military leaders could be punished for resisting politicization, threatening norms of nonpartisan service. (10 Apr 2025)

34. US Diplomatic Security Service saw a supervisor arrested in Brussels after an altercation with hotel staff and police. The incident raised questions about conduct standards for US security personnel abroad and potential diplomatic fallout from misbehavior by armed federal agents. (7 Apr 2025)

35. Health and Human Services Secretary Robert F. Kennedy Jr. publicly endorsed MMR vaccination amid a deadly measles outbreak. Kennedy's reversal toward supporting vaccination, after prior skepticism, acknowledged the importance of evidence-based public health measures for protecting vulnerable communities. (7 Apr 2025)

Economic Structure

1. Rep. Marjorie Taylor Greene executed large Treasury bill trades shortly before Trump's tariff announcement. Greene's well-timed shift into Treasuries ahead of market-moving tariffs raised concerns about potential misuse of nonpublic information by a lawmaker during a major economic policy change. (5 Apr 2025)

2. Federal Reserve Chair Jerome Powell warned that Trump's tariffs were likely to raise inflation and cost jobs. Powell's assessment highlighted that unilateral tariff hikes could erode employment and price stability, underscoring the macroeconomic risks of executive-driven trade shocks. (5 Apr 2025)

3. US stock markets experienced severe declines following tariff announcements. Sharp multi-day drops in major indices reflected investor alarm at sudden tariff hikes, illustrating how concentrated executive trade decisions can rapidly destroy household and institutional wealth. (5 Apr 2025; 6 Apr 2025; 8 Apr 2025)

4. Social Security Administration leadership implemented personnel cuts that employees described as putting the agency in a "death spiral". Staff reductions at SSA threatened timely delivery of core benefits, weakening a foundational social insurance program that underpins economic security for millions. (5 Apr 2025)

5. Elon Musk and the Department of Government Efficiency restructured federal agencies and expanded Musk-linked contracts. DOGE-driven cuts and placement of Musk allies in key posts, alongside major contracts for his firms, deepened corporate influence over public functions and blurred lines between governance and private business. (5 Apr 2025)

6. President Trump moved the federal student loan program from the Education Department to the Small Business Administration. Transferring student loans to an under-resourced SBA reframed higher education finance as a business function, risking service failures for borrowers and weakening the Education Department's role. (6 Apr 2025)

7. Goldman Sachs and other financial institutions raised recession probabilities and warned of tariff-driven economic risks. Analysts' increased recession odds and concern over inflation signaled that the tariff regime could trigger broad economic downturn, with disproportionate impact on workers and smaller firms. (6 Apr 2025)

8. Wall Street traders reacted with extreme volatility to rumors and denials about tariff pauses. Markets swung wildly on unverified reports of tariff delays, then fell when rumors were denied, showing how opaque, personalized trade policymaking undermines economic predictability. (6 Apr 2025; 8 Apr 2025)

9. Environmental Protection Agency issued several technical rules on air monitoring, pesticide tolerances, and stormwater permits. EPA's designations of monitoring methods, pesticide tolerances, and NPDES permit coverage maintained regulatory frameworks for environmental and public health protection despite broader deregulatory pressures. (7 Apr 2025; 8 Apr 2025; 11 Apr 2025)

10. Federal Communications Commission sought public comment on multiple information-collection requirements and amended broadcast allotments. FCC notices on telecom data collections and spectrum allocations for radio, TV, and uncrewed aircraft systems shaped infrastructure investment and compliance burdens in communications markets. (7 Apr 2025; 9 Apr 2025; 10 Apr 2025)

11. Food and Drug Administration updated drug approvals, susceptibility standards, and comment periods on food and veterinary issues. FDA's technical determinations on drug withdrawals, antimicrobial criteria, poppy seed risks, and data standards affected pharmaceutical markets and food safety oversight. (9 Apr 2025)

12. General Services Administration and other procurement agencies issued notices on acquisition regulations, change-order accounting, and extraordinary contractual actions. These procurement notices governed how contractors report changes and seek relief, influencing transparency and risk allocation in federal contracting. (9 Apr 2025; 11 Apr 2025)

13. Food and Drug Administration corrected and clarified drug approval status for several products. Clarifying that certain discontinued drugs were

not withdrawn for safety reasons preserved pathways for generic competition and ensured regulatory accuracy in the Orange Book. (9 Apr 2025)

14. Food and Drug Administration withdrew approval of 18 new drug applications at applicants' request. Removing unused NDAs from the market clarified which products remain legally marketable, affecting competition and inventory decisions in the pharmaceutical sector. (9 Apr 2025)

15. Department of Health and Human Services reported a second measles death in Texas amid a large outbreak. The expanding measles outbreak, with hundreds infected, underscored the economic and social costs of weakened vaccination norms and public health infrastructure. (5 Apr 2025)

16. President Trump and trade advisers compiled and maintained a list of new tariff rates for about 90 countries. Publishing a sweeping tariff schedule for dozens of countries institutionalized a complex, unilateral trade regime that is difficult to negotiate away and burdens global commerce. (9 Apr 2025)

17. White House signaled no change in overall tariff policy despite market turmoil. Insisting that tariffs were not a negotiating tactic but a permanent response to trade deficits entrenched protectionist policy, prolonging uncertainty for businesses and consumers. (9 Apr 2025)

18. President Trump maintained a 10% blanket tariff on all imports alongside higher country-specific duties. Keeping a universal import surcharge raised baseline prices for consumers and firms, effectively functioning as a broad consumption tax set by executive action. (9 Apr 2025)

19. President Trump announced a 90-day pause on many tariffs while keeping elevated rates on China. The partial pause after a market crash illustrated how abrupt tariff policy shifts can be used to manage political fallout while leaving structural trade disruptions in place. (9 Apr 2025; 10 Apr 2025)

20. White House refused to release a list of 75 countries allegedly seeking trade deals. Withholding the list of supposed trade suitors limited public scrutiny of the administration's trade narrative and made it harder to assess the credibility of claimed economic support. (9 Apr 2025)

21. President Trump hosted a $1 million-per-person fundraiser for MAGA Inc. amid economic turmoil. Holding an ultra-high-dollar fundraiser at his own property while markets reeled from his tariffs highlighted how economic crisis can coincide with intensified elite fundraising and potential conflicts of interest. (5 Apr 2025)

22. President Trump and Saudi sovereign wealth officials hosted Saudi fund leadership at Trump properties for a $1 million-a-head dinner. The event underscored potential emoluments and foreign influence concerns, as foreign sovereign wealth representatives paid large sums at venues owned by the sitting president. (5 Apr 2025)

23. Food and Drug Administration and other health agencies faced budget cuts raising concerns about food and drug safety. Reductions at FDA and related agencies risked weakening oversight of food contamination and pharmaceuticals, shifting health risks onto the public to achieve budgetary or ideological goals. (7 Apr 2025)

24. China, European Union, Canada, and other partners imposed retaliatory tariffs on US goods in response to Trump's measures. Counter-tariffs from major trading partners escalated the trade war, threatening export markets for US producers and deepening global economic instability. (5 Apr 2025; 6 Apr 2025; 7 Apr 2025; 8 Apr 2025; 10 Apr 2025; 11 Apr 2025)

25. China blocked the sale of TikTok's US operations while tariffs remain in effect. Beijing's move tied corporate transactions to the tariff dispute, illustrating how economic conflict can spill into control over major digital platforms and investment flows. (7 Apr 2025)

26. Avelo Airlines signed a contract to operate deportation flights for ICE. By dedicating aircraft to deportation charters, Avelo deepened private-sector involvement in coercive state functions, raising questions about profit incentives in removal operations. (8 Apr 2025; 9 Apr 2025)

27. Trump administration froze over $1.7 billion in federal funding to Cornell and Northwestern universities. Suspending large research and grant streams over alleged antisemitism used economic pressure to influence campus policies and chilled academic independence. (9 Apr 2025)

28. Trump administration canceled or paused hundreds of millions in grants and loans to multiple universities over ideological disputes. Defunding Columbia, Harvard, Princeton, and the University of Pennsylvania over protest and transgender policies weaponized federal spending to enforce cultural and political conformity in higher education. (10 Apr 2025)

29. Tesla halted orders for certain models in China due to reciprocal tariffs. Tesla's withdrawal from parts of the Chinese market showed how tariff escalation can directly constrain US firms' global operations and investment decisions. (10 Apr 2025)

30. Social Security Administration reversed a plan to end phone service for new benefit claims after public backlash. Canceling a policy that would have forced tens of thousands of elderly and disabled claimants into field offices preserved remote access to benefits and showed that public pressure can still correct harmful administrative changes. (10 Apr 2025)

31. Trump administration cut $1.5 million in corrections funding to Maine over housing a trans woman in a women's prison. Withholding substance-use and family-program funds to punish a state's transgender housing decision

used fiscal tools to enforce ideological positions on gender in corrections policy. (8 Apr 2025)

32. Trump administration imposed a combined 145% tariff on Chinese imports, heavily impacting consumer electronics. The extreme tariff rate on Chinese goods, including iPhones, dramatically raised expected consumer prices and exemplified how trade policy can function as a regressive tax set by executive decree. (11 Apr 2025)

33. Trump administration implemented deep cuts to federal scientific grant-making and staff in targeted fields. Reducing capacity to administer grants in areas like AIDS, trans issues, and climate weakened US scientific infrastructure and skewed research priorities away from politically disfavored topics. (11 Apr 2025)

34. Trump administration increased tariffs on China again despite pausing some other tariffs. Persistently raising China-specific tariffs while markets struggled signaled a willingness to accept long-term economic harm in pursuit of a confrontational trade strategy. (11 Apr 2025)

35. Department of Justice opened an antitrust investigation into alleged egg price-fixing by major producers. Probing whether egg companies exploited a bird flu crisis to inflate prices addressed potential collusion affecting a staple food, testing whether antitrust tools will be used to protect consumers. (9 Apr 2025)

36. Lawmakers and regulators raised concerns and sought investigations into possible insider trading around tariff policy shifts. Suspicious trading spikes before tariff announcements prompted calls for probes, highlighting fears that privileged actors may be profiting from advance knowledge of volatile economic decisions. (9 Apr 2025)

37. House of Representatives approved a budget framework projected to add $5.8 trillion to the national debt. The plan to pair large tax cuts with limited offsetting cuts increased long-term borrowing, potentially constraining future social spending and amplifying fiscal vulnerability. (9 Apr 2025)

38. Trump administration insisted that Apple move iPhone production to the United States despite feasibility concerns. Pressuring a major firm to reshore complex manufacturing under a punitive tariff regime illustrated how executive rhetoric and policy can attempt to reshape global supply chains, regardless of capacity. (9 Apr 2025)

Information, Memory, and Manipulation

1. Trump administration restricted Associated Press access after it refused to use "Gulf of America". Punishing AP for not adopting an official renaming attempted to coerce media outlets into echoing executive narratives, undermining independent editorial judgment. (5 Apr 2025)

2. President Trump shared a video falsely claiming Warren Buffett backed his plan to crash markets for profit. Amplifying fabricated endorsements and motives for his economic policy spread disinformation about market strategy, eroding trust in official economic communications. (5 Apr 2025)

3. National Park Service removed Harriet Tubman's image and quote from an Underground Railroad webpage and reframed content. Rewriting the page to emphasize "Black/White cooperation" and omit slavery references aligned with a broader anti-DEI push, reshaping public memory of resistance to slavery. (7 Apr 2025)

4. Trump administration ordered the Pentagon to scrub diversity, equity, and inclusion content from public platforms. Deleting references to racism, ethnicity, and LGBTQ topics from Defense websites removed information about marginalized groups' service and experiences from official narratives. (7 Apr 2025)

5. Trump administration intensified pressure on pro-Palestinian student journalists, leading to takedowns and resignations. Government actions and arrests created a climate where student outlets self-censored coverage of Israel–Palestine, narrowing the range of viewpoints in campus media. (7 Apr 2025)

6. Major US corporations remained publicly silent on Trump's tariffs due to fear of retaliation. Corporate leaders' reluctance to criticize economically harmful tariffs suggested that fear of executive punishment can mute influential voices that might otherwise inform public debate. (7 Apr 2025)

7. National Park Service restored Harriet Tubman content to its Underground Railroad webpage after criticism. Reinstating Tubman's image and quote partially reversed an earlier historical sanitization, showing that public and internal pushback can sometimes correct politicized edits to official history. (7 Apr 2025)

8. Internal Revenue Service and DHS agreed to share sensitive taxpayer data on undocumented immigrants for enforcement. Using confidential tax records to aid deportations blurred the line between revenue collection and policing, undermining privacy norms that support honest reporting. (7 Apr 2025; 8 Apr 2025)

9. US State Department under Secretary Marco Rubio ordered staff to

report instances of "anti-Christian bias" from the prior administration. Directing diplomats to compile grievances about alleged anti-Christian discrimination repurposed bureaucratic reporting to support a favored religious narrative in government policy. (11 Apr 2025)

10. Trump administration and Mississippi Library Commission deleted race relations and gender studies databases from a statewide library system. Removing these databases from publicly funded institutions limited access to scholarship on race and gender, aligning information policy with anti-DEI legislative agendas. (11 Apr 2025)

11. US Attorney General Pam Bondi and DOJ reduced enforcement of foreign influence disclosure laws despite evidence of increased activity. Scaling back FARA prosecutions while foreign sovereign funds sought influence made it harder for the public to see who is lobbying for overseas interests in US politics. (11 Apr 2025)

12. White House declined to release the list of countries allegedly seeking trade deals with the US. Refusing to substantiate claims about widespread interest in new trade agreements limited independent verification of the administration's economic narrative. (9 Apr 2025)

13. Department of Government Efficiency and ICE used government databases and algorithms to identify immigrants for deportation. Leveraging large-scale data analytics to filter people by traits for removal expanded algorithmic governance over individuals' fates with limited transparency or recourse. (11 Apr 2025)

14. Department of Homeland Security used a British man's tattoo photo in materials to identify alleged Venezuelan gang members. Misusing an unrelated tattoo image as a gang marker in deportation guidance showed how sloppy intelligence can feed into life-altering enforcement decisions. (11 Apr 2025)

15. Pro-Israel group StopAntisemitism asked DOJ to investigate children's entertainer Ms Rachel as a possible foreign agent. Seeking a FARA probe over social media posts sympathetic to Gaza children raised the prospect of using foreign-agent laws to intimidate domestic speech on controversial issues. (9 Apr 2025)

16. Conservative influencer Matthew Wallace was sued for defamation by a trans woman falsely accused of piloting a crashed helicopter. The lawsuit over viral false claims highlighted how online misinformation can endanger individuals and how civil courts may be used to seek accountability for such harms. (9 Apr 2025)

17. Trump administration ended funding for the US Global Change Research Program's national climate assessment work. Defunding the climate

assessment infrastructure reduced authoritative public information about climate risks, making it harder for citizens and policymakers to base decisions on comprehensive science. (9 Apr 2025)

18. National Park Service and Smithsonian Institution were targeted by executive orders to remove "improper" or "anti-American" content. Mandating removal of content labeled divisive from museums and research entities sought to align national cultural narratives with the administration's ideological preferences. (7 Apr 2025)

19. Mississippi Library Commission deleted race and gender databases from the Magnolia system to comply with state laws. Eliminating these resources from public libraries and schools narrowed access to scholarship on inequality and identity, embedding ideological constraints into information infrastructure. (11 Apr 2025)

20. Trump administration used emergency tariff announcements and reversals that fueled market rumors and confusion. The rapid sequence of tariff threats, partial pauses, and unclear negotiations created information chaos that obscured accountability for economic damage and invited speculation about insider advantage. (8 Apr 2025; 9 Apr 2025; 10 Apr 2025; 11 Apr 2025)

21. Trump administration and universities used funding freezes and consent-decree threats to pressure campuses over protest narratives. Tying billions in research and grant funding to how universities characterize and police antisemitism and protests incentivized institutions to align public messaging with federal preferences. (10 Apr 2025)

22. National Review, media, and polling organizations reported on public disapproval and elite concern over tariff chaos. Coverage of falling approval ratings and conservative criticism of tariff governance provided counter-narratives to official claims, though their impact was constrained by executive control over policy. (9 Apr 2025)

CHAPTER 13
WEEK 13 (12 APR 2025 – 18 APR 2025): LOYALTY AS DAILY GOVERNANCE

In Trump's thirteenth week, deportation, civil rights law, and information itself were methodically repurposed to reward loyalty and raise the cost of dissent.

This week reveals an administration openly testing the outer limits of constitutional democracy. The greatest pressure targets the rule of law, voting rights, enforcement of civil rights, and the neutrality of the civil service. The Abrego García and Alien Enemies Act cases expose a pattern of deliberate defiance of court orders, attempts to avoid contempt, and even coordination with a foreign government to keep a U.S. resident imprisoned abroad. At the same time, the DOJ Civil Rights Division is repurposed to defend white grievances and enforce Trump's executive orders, while a new order weakens disparate-impact liability in civil rights law. On the electoral front, an executive order and House legislation demanding documentary proof of citizenship, along with North Carolina ballot purges, collectively push toward structurally exclusionary elections. Universities and independent media face funding freezes, tax threats, and licensing pressures, while book bans and website rewrites shape public memory. Massive tariff fluctuations, capital flight, and deregulation of crypto and consumer protection agencies deepen crony capitalism and chaos as governing strategies. Courts, states, civil society, and some agencies resist, but the overall structural pressure this week is overwhelmingly toward authoritarian consolidation.

Power and Authority

1. President Trump authorized the US military to control federal land at the southern border for immigration enforcement. By assigning the military jurisdiction over federal border lands and detention authority for migrants, the president expanded direct military involvement in domestic immigration enforcement, blurring civilian–military lines and concentrating coercive power in the executive. (12 Apr 2025)

2. President Trump signed an executive order ending the de-minimis duty-free rule for low-priced Chinese imports. Ending duty-free treatment for low-value imports from China and Hong Kong centralized tariff-setting in the executive, reshaping trade conditions for consumers and retailers without new congressional authorization. (13 Apr 2025)

3. President Trump froze approximately $66 million in Title X family planning funds nationwide. Freezing core family-planning grants on claimed compliance grounds allowed the executive to leverage health funding to enforce its immigration and ideological priorities, reducing access to reproductive care for low-income communities. (14 Apr 2025)

4. Trump administration proposed nearly 50% cuts to State Department and USAID budgets. The proposed halving of diplomatic and development budgets would weaken U.S. capacity for diplomacy, humanitarian aid, and multilateral engagement, shifting power from civilian foreign policy tools toward more unilateral and security-focused instruments. (14 Apr 2025)

5. President Trump issued executive orders rolling back National Environmental Policy Act procedures. Rolling back NEPA procedural requirements reduced community leverage over major projects, streamlining executive-driven development decisions at the expense of local input and environmental review. (14 Apr 2025)

6. Trump administration created a new at-will category for tens of thousands of federal workers. Reclassifying about 50,000 federal positions as at-will for alleged "subversion of presidential directives" increased executive leverage over the civil service, undermining bureaucratic independence and neutral implementation of law. (14 Apr 2025)

7. President Trump signed a memorandum restricting Social Security benefits to legally present noncitizens. Directing agencies to bar undocumented and other "ineligible" people from Social Security benefits used executive power to tighten social protections along immigration-status lines, reinforcing stratified access to public programs. (15 Apr 2025)

8. President Trump issued an executive order allowing agencies to repeal regulations without public notice if deemed unlawful. Authorizing unilateral

repeal of "obviously unlawful" rules without public notice weakened procedural safeguards around regulation, expanding executive discretion and reducing opportunities for external challenge. (13 Apr 2025)

9. President Trump issued multiple executive orders restructuring federal procurement and office space policy. Orders to streamline procurement rules and revoke siting preferences for federal offices centralized control over contracting and property decisions, potentially favoring politically aligned vendors and locations under the banner of efficiency. (15 Apr 2025)

10. President Trump issued an executive order directing review of critical mineral imports under national security law. Ordering a Section 232 investigation into processed critical minerals framed trade dependencies as security threats, enabling the executive to invoke emergency-style trade restrictions with limited legislative input. (15 Apr 2025)

11. President Trump issued an executive order to reshape federal drug price policy. Reorienting Medicare and Medicaid drug pricing through executive order concentrated health-cost decisions in the presidency, affecting affordability and industry leverage without new statutory direction. (15 Apr 2025)

12. President Trump announced a new at-will firing regime and mass staff reductions at the Consumer Financial Protection Bureau. Moving to fire nearly 90% of CFPB staff under a court-limited authority to shrink the agency used executive power to hollow out a key consumer watchdog while formally preserving its shell. (17 Apr 2025)

13. President Trump issued an executive order to promote commercial solutions in federal contracts. Requiring agencies to favor commercially available products in contracting shifted procurement toward market offerings, potentially advantaging large incumbents and limiting bespoke public-interest specifications. (16 Apr 2025)

14. President Trump issued an executive order to boost American seafood industry competitiveness. Directing deregulation and trade strategies for seafood production used executive authority to reshape sectoral rules and trade posture, with distributional effects for coastal communities and foreign partners. (17 Apr 2025)

15. President Trump issued an executive order eliminating disparate-impact liability from federal civil rights enforcement. Ordering agencies to stop enforcing civil rights laws based on discriminatory effects and to roll back Title VI regulations sharply curtailed federal tools for addressing systemic discrimination, weakening protections for marginalized groups. (17 Apr 2025)

16. President Trump demanded Maine ban transgender girls from girls'

sports under threat of cutting education funds. Threatening to withhold federal education funding unless Maine changed its trans-inclusive sports policy used fiscal leverage to pressure a state's civil rights framework and override local anti-discrimination law. (17 Apr 2025)

17. President Trump issued an executive order requiring documentary proof of citizenship to vote. Mandating documentary proof of citizenship for voting from the federal level risked disenfranchising eligible voters lacking paperwork, embedding restrictive access rules into national election administration. (18 Apr 2025)

18. President Trump announced a 10% universal tariff on imports and later a partial 90-day pause with sharply higher China rates. Imposing sweeping tariffs and then abruptly pausing most while escalating duties on China showcased unilateral executive control over trade policy, triggering market turmoil and raising questions about emergency economic governance. (12 Apr 2025; 13 Apr 2025)

19. President Trump publicly pressured Federal Reserve Chair Jerome Powell to cut interest rates and suggested firing him. Attacking the Fed chair and calling for his removal over rate policy challenged the norm of central bank independence, risking politicization of monetary decisions that underpin economic stability. (16 Apr 2025; 17 Apr 2025; 18 Apr 2025)

20. President Trump denied North Carolina's request to extend FEMA disaster assistance after Hurricane Helene. Refusing extended FEMA aid despite ongoing recovery needs signaled that disaster relief could be conditioned on political or other considerations, enabling selective use of federal support across states. (16 Apr 2025)

21. President Trump ordered security clearances stripped from critics Christopher Krebs and Miles Taylor and investigations opened. Revoking clearances and targeting former officials who criticized the administration used national security tools for personal retaliation, chilling internal dissent and future whistleblowing. (13 Apr 2025)

22. President Trump directed the Department of Justice to terminate an environmental justice settlement with Alabama. Canceling a federal agreement that required Alabama to address severe sanitation failures in Lowndes County withdrew civil-rights-based oversight from a poor, largely Black community, signaling reduced federal protection for environmental justice. (14 Apr 2025)

23. President Trump announced plans to deport certain US citizens to El Salvador's prisons during a meeting with President Bukele. Discussing deporting "homegrown criminals" who are US citizens to El Salvador's hard-

labor prisons floated an approach that would sidestep constitutional protections and outsource punishment to a foreign system. (13 Apr 2025; 15 Apr 2025)

24. President Trump refused to comply with Supreme Court and lower-court orders to return Kilmar Abrego Garcia from El Salvador. By declining to facilitate the court-ordered return of a wrongfully deported resident and invoking foreign-affairs immunity, the administration openly challenged judicial authority and due process constraints on executive detention power. (13 Apr 2025; 14 Apr 2025; 15 Apr 2025; 16 Apr 2025; 18 Apr 2025)

25. Trump administration used the Alien Enemies Act to deport migrants to El Salvador's mega-prison despite court injunctions. Continuing deportations under the Alien Enemies Act in defiance of injunctions and without individualized evidence turned an old statute into a tool for mass, extra-territorial detention beyond normal judicial oversight. (12 Apr 2025; 13 Apr 2025; 14 Apr 2025; 16 Apr 2025; 17 Apr 2025)

26. Trump administration classified its deportation agreement with El Salvador. Classifying the terms of the El Salvador detention arrangement shielded a controversial use of foreign prisons for US-directed detentions from public and congressional scrutiny, limiting accountability for human rights and legal compliance. (15 Apr 2025)

27. Trump administration announced plans to cut roughly one-third of the federal health budget including major CDC reductions. Proposed deep cuts to federal health agencies, including over 40% for CDC, would shrink national capacity for disease prevention and response, weakening a core public function and shifting burdens to states. (16 Apr 2025)

28. Trump administration proposed terminating federal Head Start funding nationwide. Seeking to end Head Start funding for over half a million low-income children used budget power to dismantle a long-standing early education program, with major implications for equality of opportunity. (17 Apr 2025)

29. Trump administration planned to close up to 30 US embassies and consulates abroad. Considering closure of dozens of diplomatic posts would contract US presence and services overseas, reducing soft power and consular protection while centralizing foreign policy decisions in Washington. (15 Apr 2025)

30. Trump administration closed the State Department's Counter Foreign Information Manipulation and Interference office. Shutting the last dedicated State Department office tracking foreign disinformation reduced institutional capacity to counter external information operations, potentially leaving US politics more exposed to manipulation. (16 Apr 2025)

31. Trump administration directed DHS to vet social media of visa applicants who had visited Gaza. Mandating social-media screening for all visa applicants with Gaza travel history expanded security-based scrutiny tied to political geography, raising risks of viewpoint-based exclusion and chilled expression. (17 Apr 2025)

32. Trump administration announced plans to cut or consolidate major public health programs into a new super-agency. Planning to fold and slash health programs into an "Administration for a Healthy America" would centralize control over disease prevention and health data, potentially weakening specialized expertise and oversight. (16 Apr 2025)

Institutions and Governance

1. Supreme Court of the United States unanimously ordered the government to facilitate Kilmar Abrego Garcia's return from El Salvador. The Court's 9–0 ruling reaffirmed judicial authority over executive deportation decisions and underscored that US residents cannot be held in foreign prisons at the government's direction without due process. (14 Apr 2025; 15 Apr 2025)

2. US Court of Appeals for the Fourth Circuit rejected the administration's bid to block orders requiring Abrego Garcia's return. By upholding Judge Xinis's mandate to take all available steps to return Abrego Garcia, the appeals court emphasized limits on executive power to outsource detention and insisted on meaningful judicial review. (16 Apr 2025; 17 Apr 2025; 18 Apr 2025)

3. US District Judge Paula Xinis rebuked the administration and opened a fact-finding inquiry into noncompliance in the Abrego case. Ordering sworn explanations and discovery after "nothing has been done" to return Abrego Garcia showed a district court using contempt tools to enforce its orders against executive resistance. (15 Apr 2025; 16 Apr 2025)

4. US District Judge James Boasberg found probable cause to hold officials in contempt for deportations under a blocked policy. Concluding that officials willfully disregarded his order halting Alien Enemies Act deportations, and threatening a private prosecutor, asserted that executive actors remain subject to judicial sanctions. (16 Apr 2025; 17 Apr 2025)

5. federal courts in multiple districts temporarily blocked deportations of Venezuelan migrants under the Alien Enemies Act. Injunctions from judges in Colorado, Nevada, and California paused removals to El Salvador, underscoring judicial checks on novel uses of an old statute for mass deportation. (12 Apr 2025; 14 Apr 2025; 16 Apr 2025)

6. federal district court in Boston blocked termination of a parole program for migrants from four countries. Preventing the shutdown of a program granting legal status and work authorization to over 500,000 migrants preserved existing rights while courts review the administration's attempt to reverse a prior policy. (14 Apr 2025; 15 Apr 2025)

7. federal courts blocked EPA efforts to claw back or freeze large Biden-era climate grants. District and appellate rulings that halted or scrutinized attempts to rescind climate funding highlighted judicial willingness to police abrupt policy reversals affecting long-term environmental programs. (15 Apr 2025; 16 Apr 2025)

8. federal courts temporarily blocked fast-track deportations to third countries without fear screenings. Orders barring rapid transfers of immigrants to non-home countries without a chance to claim fear of persecution preserved minimal due process protections against refoulement. (18 Apr 2025)

9. US District Judge Amy Berman Jackson blocked mass layoffs at the Consumer Financial Protection Bureau. Halting reduction-in-force letters to about 1,500 CFPB employees checked an executive attempt to effectively dismantle a congressionally created agency without formally abolishing it. (18 Apr 2025)

10. California Governor Gavin Newsom and Attorney General Rob Bonta filed a federal lawsuit challenging Trump's tariffs as unconstitutional. California's suit arguing that emergency trade powers cannot replace Congress's tariff authority tested separation of powers and sought judicial limits on unilateral economic measures. (16 Apr 2025)

11. NAACP sued the Trump administration over anti-DEI policies in schools. Challenging federal efforts to restrict diversity, equity, and inclusion initiatives invoked the Civil Rights Act to contest a shift in education policy that could narrow protections for students of color. (15 Apr 2025)

12. ACLU and Pentagon school students filed a lawsuit against Defense Secretary Pete Hegseth over book bans in military schools. The suit argued that removing books on race and gender from Pentagon school libraries violated students' First Amendment rights, testing judicial willingness to curb viewpoint-based censorship in federal education settings. (15 Apr 2025)

13. labor rights organizations sued the administration over cancellation of international labor rights programs. Groups argued that the Labor Department lacked authority to terminate congressionally authorized grants combating child labor abroad, asserting legislative control over appropriated funds and labor standards. (15 Apr 2025)

14. Protect Democracy sued the Office of Management and Budget over

removal of a federal spending tracker. Challenging OMB's deletion of apportionment data from public view sought to enforce statutory transparency requirements that enable Congress and the public to monitor executive spending. (15 Apr 2025)

15. environmental and consumer advocacy groups sued the administration over removal of federal climate and environmental justice webpages. The lawsuit contested the deletion of online tools and datasets tracking climate impacts and pollution, framing access to environmental information as essential for public health and accountability. (15 Apr 2025)

16. Center for Biological Diversity sued federal agencies over an oil-friendly green policy rollback order. Seeking records on how agencies planned to weaken environmental rules under a pro-oil executive order, the suit highlighted transparency and environmental governance concerns around regulatory rollbacks. (17 Apr 2025)

17. universities and civil society groups filed lawsuits challenging federal funding and visa policies affecting higher education. Universities sued over Department of Energy research funding cuts, while foreign students challenged mass visa revocations, collectively testing judicial protection of academic institutions from politicized federal actions. (14 Apr 2025; 17 Apr 2025)

18. US Supreme Court agreed to hear arguments on Trump's executive order limiting birthright citizenship. Taking up a challenge to an order restricting birthright citizenship put core constitutional guarantees of national membership and equal status under direct judicial review. (17 Apr 2025)

19. North Carolina Supreme Court and appellate courts issued rulings enabling challenges to hundreds of ballots and requiring proof of voter eligibility. State court decisions invalidating ballots and demanding post-election proof of residency for overseas and other voters risked disenfranchising eligible citizens and undermining confidence in final results. (15 Apr 2025; 18 Apr 2025)

20. North Carolina Board of Elections moved to restore ballots wrongly invalidated by court rulings. The board's decision to re-verify and reinstate improperly discarded ballots sought to correct judicially driven disenfranchisement and protect the integrity of the 2024 election results. (16 Apr 2025)

21. US House of Representatives passed the Save Act requiring proof of citizenship for voter registration. House approval of a federal proof-of-citizenship requirement and limits on mail and online registration advanced a nationwide framework that could make registration harder for many eligible voters. (18 Apr 2025)

22. Republican-controlled state legislatures introduced bills requiring documentary proof of citizenship to vote. Coordinated state-level proposals to demand citizenship documents for voting extended a restrictive model that disproportionately burdens naturalized citizens and low-income voters. (18 Apr 2025)

23. Department of Justice Civil Rights Division under Harmeet Dhillon revised mission statements to de-emphasize traditional civil rights enforcement. New guidance prioritizing voter fraud, protection of white people from discrimination, and enforcement of Trump's orders while sidelining the Voting Rights Act and Fair Housing Act reoriented a key enforcement arm away from protecting marginalized groups. (18 Apr 2025)

24. Department of Justice filed lawsuits against Maine to enforce a federal ban on transgender girls in girls' sports. Suing Maine's education authorities to compel exclusion of transgender girls from girls' sports used federal litigation to override state anti-discrimination protections and reshape Title IX interpretation. (16 Apr 2025; 17 Apr 2025)

25. Justice Department fired an immigration lawyer who admitted Abrego Garcia's deportation was wrongful. Removing the attorney who acknowledged in court that Abrego Garcia should not have been deported suggested retaliation against internal candor and discouraged officials from correcting unlawful actions. (15 Apr 2025)

26. Congressman Gerald Connolly demanded reversal of the Social Security Administration's freeze of the Enumeration Beyond Entry program. By launching oversight and questioning the legality and efficiency of the EBE freeze, a senior lawmaker used congressional tools to challenge an administrative change affecting immigrant access to Social Security numbers. (17 Apr 2025)

27. Federal Election Commission set filing deadlines for a Texas special congressional election. Publishing reporting schedules for candidates and committees in a special election maintained standardized transparency and compliance expectations for campaign finance in a mid-cycle contest. (18 Apr 2025)

28. federal courts handled multiple challenges to climate grant clawbacks with conflicting interim rulings. A district court's order to disburse climate grants and the DC Circuit's stay of that order illustrated institutional friction over how far the executive can go in reversing prior funding commitments. (15 Apr 2025; 16 Apr 2025)

29. federal judiciary oversaw high-profile defamation and capital punishment cases. The Palin v. New York Times retrial and a federal murder indict-

ment positioned courts at the center of debates over press protections and renewed federal death penalty policy. (14 Apr 2025; 17 Apr 2025)

Civil Rights and Dissent

1. Trump administration and State Department used immigration law and foreign policy tools to target activists and scholars for deportation or detention. Cases involving Mahmoud Khalil, Rumeysa Ozturk, Badar Khan Suri, Mohsen Mahdawi, and a Turkish PhD student showed immigration powers being applied to people with no criminal charges, often linked to pro-Palestinian speech. (12 Apr 2025; 13 Apr 2025; 14 Apr 2025; 15 Apr 2025; 17 Apr 2025)

2. US Immigration and Customs Enforcement and DHS wrongfully detained or deported individuals including US citizens and non-target migrants. Incidents involving a US-born citizen in Florida, a Massachusetts lawyer, and Venezuelan asylum seekers highlighted errors and overreach in enforcement that threatened basic protections for both citizens and noncitizens. (15 Apr 2025; 17 Apr 2025)

3. Trump administration used deportation and foreign prisons as tools against migrants and critics. Sending migrants and at least one innocent Salvadoran resident to El Salvador's mega-prison, and discussing exporting US citizens there, extended punishment beyond US legal safeguards and blurred lines between immigration and penal policy. (13 Apr 2025; 14 Apr 2025; 15 Apr 2025)

4. Department of Homeland Security and border agents conducted intrusive searches and polygraph campaigns targeting perceived dissenters and leakers. Border searches of a protester's lawyer's phone and widespread polygraphs of senior staff to find leakers signaled a security posture that treats legal advocacy and internal dissent as threats. (12 Apr 2025; 14 Apr 2025)

5. Trump administration pursued policies and litigation restricting transgender participation in sports. An executive order barring trans women from women's sports, House Title IX legislation, and DOJ suits against Maine collectively targeted transgender athletes' access to education and competition. (16 Apr 2025; 17 Apr 2025)

6. Trump administration issued an executive order and supported legislation requiring proof of citizenship to vote. Federal and state-level moves to require documentary proof of citizenship for registration and voting, justified by unsubstantiated fraud claims, risked disenfranchising eligible voters lacking paperwork, especially naturalized and low-income citizens. (18 Apr 2025)

7. Trump administration shifted DOJ Civil Rights Division priorities away from marginalized groups. New mission statements emphasizing voter fraud and protection of white people from discrimination while downplaying core civil rights statutes signaled a reorientation of federal enforcement away from historically disadvantaged communities. (18 Apr 2025)

8. Trump administration used immigration enforcement and notices in ways that threatened citizens and legal residents. Erroneous deportation notices to a US-born lawyer and detention of a US-born citizen under a state immigration law showed how aggressive enforcement regimes can spill over onto citizens' rights. (15 Apr 2025; 17 Apr 2025)

9. Trump administration advanced anti-DEI policies and book bans affecting students and service members. Removing hundreds of books on slavery, civil rights, and the Holocaust from Naval Academy and Pentagon school libraries, and facing NAACP litigation, narrowed access to critical perspectives for young people in federal institutions. (12 Apr 2025; 15 Apr 2025)

10. law enforcement and courts in Pennsylvania responded to an attempted firebombing of the governor's mansion with terrorism charges and denied bail. Charging Cody Balmer with terrorism and denying bail after an attack on Governor Shapiro's residence underscored the seriousness of political violence and the state's role in protecting elected officials. (13 Apr 2025; 14 Apr 2025; 15 Apr 2025; 16 Apr 2025)

11. local police at a Marjorie Taylor Greene town hall used a stun gun and arrests to manage protesters at a political event. Requiring ID and residency proof for entry, prescreening questions, and tasing protesters at a town hall blurred the line between event security and suppression of dissenting voices. (16 Apr 2025)

12. Harvard University leadership publicly rejected federal demands that conditioned funding on governance and speech changes. Harvard's refusal to alter its governance, DEI programs, and academic policies in exchange for federal funds asserted institutional autonomy and academic freedom against political pressure. (16 Apr 2025)

13. Representatives Alexandria Ocasio-Cortez and Bernie Sanders held a large rally in Idaho opposing Trump administration policies. Drawing 12,000 attendees in a conservative state demonstrated ongoing capacity for peaceful mass mobilization and grassroots opposition within formal democratic channels. (14 Apr 2025)

14. Trump administration and DHS targeted international students and universities with visa revocations and record demands. Mass termination of

student legal status and DHS threats to Harvard's student visa certification used immigration controls to pressure campuses and chilled participation by foreign students. (16 Apr 2025; 17 Apr 2025)

15. Trump administration pursued policies and rhetoric demonizing immigrants and transgender people. Early-term messaging that vilified immigrants and transgender individuals framed vulnerable groups as threats, laying groundwork for restrictive policies and social hostility. (12 Apr 2025)

16. US public health agencies under political influence reduced vaccination promotion and research amid a measles outbreak. Halting NIH funding for vaccine hesitancy research and canceling CDC flu campaigns during a large measles outbreak showed how political skepticism of vaccines can undermine basic public health protections. (12 Apr 2025)

17. Florida State University community and law enforcement experienced and responded to a campus mass shooting. A deadly shooting using a law enforcement officer's gun highlighted ongoing gun violence risks on campuses and the political choice to prioritize gun rights over regulatory responses. (16 Apr 2025)

18. Trump administration used proof-of-citizenship and deportation policies to stratify legal protections by identity and ideology. From deporting activists to third-country prisons to imposing documentary barriers to voting, the administration's approach increasingly tied core rights to origin, beliefs, and status rather than equal citizenship. (12 Apr 2025; 15 Apr 2025; 18 Apr 2025)

Economic Structure

1. Trump administration implemented and repeatedly modified sweeping tariffs and exemptions on imports. Rapidly changing universal and country-specific tariffs, including quiet exemptions for key electronics, created uncertainty for businesses and investors, contributing to capital flight and undermining predictable trade governance. (12 Apr 2025; 13 Apr 2025)

2. Trump administration imposed a 21% tariff on Mexican tomatoes. Tariffs on Mexican tomatoes, which supply most of the US market, raised consumer prices and strained cross-border agricultural trade, illustrating how trade tools can reshape everyday economic conditions. (14 Apr 2025)

3. Trump administration froze or threatened billions in federal funding and tax benefits to Harvard University. Freezing over $2 billion in grants and contracts and threatening Harvard's tax-exempt status weaponized federal financial levers against a single institution over ideological disputes, raising

risks of politicized resource allocation. (14 Apr 2025; 15 Apr 2025; 16 Apr 2025; 17 Apr 2025)

4. Trump administration deregulated the cryptocurrency industry while Trump family interests expanded in the sector. Halting SEC crypto enforcement and disbanding a DOJ crypto team, as Trump-linked firms grew, blurred lines between public regulation and private gain, heightening systemic and corruption risks. (14 Apr 2025)

5. Trump Media & Technology Group launched investment accounts designed to profit from Trump's policy agenda. Creating tariff-aligned investment products that benefit from presidential decisions embedded direct financial incentives for policy choices, deepening the fusion of governance and private enrichment. (15 Apr 2025; 16 Apr 2025)

6. Trump administration announced plans to cut one-third of the federal health budget and consolidate programs. Proposed deep health cuts, including major CDC reductions, would shrink federal capacity for disease control and shift burdens to states and individuals, altering the balance between public and private health provision. (16 Apr 2025)

7. Department of Justice terminated an environmental justice settlement with Alabama over sanitation failures. Ending federal oversight of Lowndes County's sewage crisis removed a mechanism that had forced state investment in basic infrastructure, leaving a poor, Black community more exposed to environmental and health harms. (14 Apr 2025)

8. Department of Government Efficiency and Trump administration attempted to embed federal staff in a justice-reform nonprofit and cut its funding. Trying to place Doge teams inside Vera Institute while canceling its government grants signaled efforts to control or punish civil-society organizations that depend on federal contracts for public-interest work. (16 Apr 2025)

9. Trump administration began firing most Consumer Financial Protection Bureau staff after a court allowed downsizing. Using a ruling that the CFPB could be shrunk, not abolished, to dismiss nearly 90% of staff effectively disabled a key consumer regulator while preserving its formal existence. (17 Apr 2025)

10. Trump administration froze federal funding to Harvard after it rejected mandated governance changes. Conditioning billions in research and education funds on ideological and governance concessions from a private university tied federal economic power to compliance with political demands. (14 Apr 2025; 15 Apr 2025; 16 Apr 2025)

11. Internal Revenue Service leadership under Trump planned to revoke Harvard University's tax-exempt status. Reported IRS plans to strip Harvard's nonprofit status in response to its defiance of administration demands raised

alarms about using tax enforcement as a political weapon against disfavored institutions. (17 Apr 2025)

12. Trump administration froze the Social Security Enumeration Beyond Entry program for noncitizens. Suspending automatic SSN issuance for authorized noncitizens forced in-person visits and increased administrative burdens, complicating legal work and tax participation for immigrants and straining SSA operations. (17 Apr 2025)

13. Trump administration announced termination of Head Start funding for early childhood programs. Proposing to end Head Start funding would dismantle a major federal support for low-income children's education and care, deepening inequality in early-life opportunities. (17 Apr 2025)

14. Federal Reserve Chair Jerome Powell refused to cut interest rates despite presidential pressure. Maintaining rates in the face of tariff-driven uncertainty and presidential attacks underscored the Fed's institutional independence, even as political pressure threatened to erode that norm. (16 Apr 2025; 17 Apr 2025; 18 Apr 2025)

15. Billy Long and donors with tax issues retired Long's campaign debt after his nomination to lead the IRS. Large donations from individuals with tax problems to pay off the IRS nominee's campaign debt raised concerns that regulatory decisions could be influenced by recent benefactors seeking favorable treatment. (16 Apr 2025)

16. Trump administration cut 139 State Department grants worth $214 million. Canceling a large slate of State Department grants reduced funding for diplomacy-related programs, potentially weakening civil-society partnerships and international initiatives tied to US foreign policy. (15 Apr 2025)

17. Trump administration deregulated federal office space and procurement rules via executive orders. Relaxing siting and procurement constraints in the name of "common sense" and efficiency could lower costs but also open more room for politically connected contractors and opaque real estate decisions. (15 Apr 2025; 16 Apr 2025)

18. Trump administration deregulated the seafood industry and sought trade advantages for US producers. Ordering regulatory review and a seafood trade strategy aimed to boost domestic producers, but also risked loosening environmental and labor safeguards in a sector with global supply chains. (17 Apr 2025)

19. Trump administration froze or clawed back climate and environmental grants until blocked by courts. Efforts to halt disbursement of billions in climate grants signaled a shift away from prior environmental commitments, using budget control to redirect policy priorities. (15 Apr 2025; 16 Apr 2025)

20. Trump administration restructured civil rights enforcement to de-emphasize disparate-impact cases. Eliminating disparate-impact liability reduced legal exposure for employers and institutions whose policies disproportionately harm protected groups, shifting economic and legal risk away from powerful actors. (17 Apr 2025)

21. Trump administration used tariffs and trade policy to create market volatility and capital flight. Tariff announcements and reversals contributed to a sell-off in US bonds and a weaker dollar, illustrating how unpredictable executive trade actions can destabilize financial markets and investment planning. (12 Apr 2025)

22. Trump administration and China triggered retaliatory Chinese restrictions on rare earth exports and Boeing purchases. Chinese responses to US tariffs, including halting rare earth exports and Boeing deliveries, exposed vulnerabilities in US supply chains and employment tied to confrontational trade policy. (14 Apr 2025)

23. Trump Media & Technology Group urged the SEC to investigate a hedge fund's short position in its stock. Calling for regulatory scrutiny of a hedge fund shorting Trump Media raised concerns that market oversight could be invoked to protect politically connected firms from normal trading activity. (17 Apr 2025)

24. Social Security Administration leadership placed a senior executive on leave after he objected to adding living immigrants to the deaths database. Removing an SSA official who resisted a plan that would have blocked thousands of immigrants from legally working suggested internal pressure to align administrative data practices with restrictive immigration goals. (12 Apr 2025)

25. federal agencies (EPA, FCC, Census, OSHA, DEA) undertook routine regulatory notices, approvals, and information collections. A series of technical actions—from air quality SIP approvals to workplace safety data renewals and telecom rate surveys—illustrated ongoing administrative governance that maintains environmental, labor, and communications standards. (14 Apr 2025; 15 Apr 2025; 16 Apr 2025; 17 Apr 2025; 18 Apr 2025)

Information, Memory, and Manipulation

1. Trump administration and White House blocked Associated Press journalists from White House access despite a court order. Refusing AP reporters entry to Oval Office events in defiance of an injunction undermined judicial authority and signaled willingness to punish outlets that resisted administration language demands. (13 Apr 2025; 14 Apr 2025; 15 Apr 2025)

2. President Trump called for CBS to lose its broadcasting license and urged FCC punishment over critical coverage. Pressuring regulators to fine or strip licenses from a major network for unfavorable reporting used state power to intimidate independent media and chill investigative journalism. (13 Apr 2025; 15 Apr 2025)

3. White House and FCC Chair Brendan Carr attacked public broadcasters and threatened Comcast over coverage of the Garcia case. Labeling NPR and PBS as propagandists and warning Comcast over "biased" reporting on deportations signaled a broader campaign to delegitimize and pressure outlets that scrutinize administration actions. (14 Apr 2025; 16 Apr 2025)

4. Trump administration replaced Covid.gov's public health content with a site promoting the lab-leak theory and attacking institutions. Transforming a practical Covid resource into a platform for a favored origin theory and criticism of Fauci, WHO, and NIH repurposed an official site to advance partisan narratives over neutral health guidance. (18 Apr 2025)

5. Trump administration removed federal climate and environmental justice webpages and data tools. Deleting online resources that tracked climate impacts and pollution reduced public access to evidence needed for local planning and advocacy, weakening transparency and long-term accountability. (15 Apr 2025)

6. Trump administration and Department of Education/Defense removed hundreds of books on race, civil rights, and the Holocaust from military-linked schools. Purging works on historical oppression from Naval Academy and Pentagon school libraries while leaving extremist texts intact reshaped official curricula to downplay injustice and critical perspectives. (12 Apr 2025; 15 Apr 2025)

7. Trump administration removed a public federal spending tracker website and related data. Taking down a site that detailed how Congress-appropriated funds were apportioned reduced real-time visibility into executive spending decisions, complicating oversight by Congress and the public. (14 Apr 2025; 15 Apr 2025)

8. Trump administration classified its deportation agreement with El Salvador and limited disclosure. Sealing the terms of a deal governing detention of US-directed deportees abroad shielded a controversial policy from scrutiny, hindering legal and historical assessment of its lawfulness. (15 Apr 2025)

9. Homeland Security Secretary Kristi Noem demanded records on Harvard's international students and threatened visa certification. Linking student visa program certification and DHS grants to disclosure of alleged

"dangerous" foreign students used information demands and funding threats to pressure a university's handling of dissent. (16 Apr 2025)

10. Trump administration administered polygraph tests to dozens of DHS and FEMA officials to find leakers. Using lie detectors on senior staff to identify sources of leaks signaled a surveillance-heavy approach to internal information control, likely deterring whistleblowing and candid communication. (12 Apr 2025; 14 Apr 2025)

11. Trump ally and administration figures allegedly sought favorable media coverage in exchange for avoiding lawsuits. Reports that a Trump ally suggested CNN could avert legal action by producing positive content indicated attempts to trade legal pressure for editorial compliance, undermining media independence. (15 Apr 2025)

12. Lamar Consolidated Independent School District banned the Virginia state flag and seal from an online curriculum over nudity concerns. Removing a state flag depiction from elementary materials on nudity grounds reflected a censorious approach that can narrow students' exposure to civic symbols and historical context. (18 Apr 2025)

13. White House social media team posted an edited New York Times front page misrepresenting a Supreme Court ruling. Altering a headline about Abrego Garcia to remove "wrongly" and add "who is never coming back" used official channels to spread a narrative contradicting a Supreme Court order, confusing public understanding of the case. (18 Apr 2025)

14. Trump administration attacked public broadcasters NPR and PBS as purveyors of "radical, woke propaganda". An official White House article denouncing public media as grifters delegitimized taxpayer-funded journalism and laid rhetorical groundwork for defunding or tighter political control. (14 Apr 2025)

15. Trump administration used removal of climate, environmental justice, and spending data to reshape public memory. Erasing online records of environmental harms and federal spending patterns limited future researchers' and citizens' ability to reconstruct policy choices and hold officials accountable. (14 Apr 2025; 15 Apr 2025)

16. Trump administration and allied officials misrepresented Supreme Court rulings and economic impacts of tariffs in public messaging. Claiming court victories where orders actually constrained the government, and downplaying tariff-driven market turmoil, reflected a pattern of selective or misleading information about legal and economic realities. (12 Apr 2025; 13 Apr 2025)

17. Trump administration closed the State Department's foreign disinformation monitoring hub. Eliminating the R/FIMI office under the banner of

fighting censorship reduced institutional capacity to track and counter foreign information operations that can distort democratic debate. (16 Apr 2025)

18. Trump administration used book bans and curriculum changes to narrow historical narratives in federal institutions. Coordinated removals of works on racism and civil rights from military schools and climate data from federal sites collectively steered official memory away from structural injustice and environmental risk. (12 Apr 2025; 15 Apr 2025)

CHAPTER 14
WEEK 14 (19 APR 2025 – 25 APR 2025): UNIVERSITIES AND BORDERS AS LEVERS

A near-still Democracy Clock masks a week in which the White House tightened control over courts, campuses, and civil rights while testing the limits of law.

This was a heavily structured week of democratic backsliding, focused on aggressive executive overreach, weaponization of law, and systematic assaults on pluralistic institutions. The administration intensified its campaign against universities through large funding freezes, coercive conditions on academic governance, and new accreditation and DEI rollback orders. Immigration enforcement and detention policies became more stringent: closure of key oversight offices, wrongful detentions of citizens, politicized targeting of student activists, and contempt rulings over deportations. Civil rights enforcement was fundamentally altered through the disparate-impact order and cuts to disability and Medicaid, deepening inequality and stratified citizenship. Within the government, restructurings at Interior and State Departments, DOGE's opaque data practices, and Musk and Hegseth's conduct indicated a speeding up of the capture and politicization of civil service and security agencies. Nevertheless, courts and civil society mounted significant resistance: multiple federal rulings blocked sanctuary-city defunding, voter documentation mandates, and deportations; Harvard and state attorneys general filed lawsuits; and nationwide protests and statements from university presidents showed organized resistance. Overall, the week's overall momentum heavily favored authoritarian consolidation, despite some pockets of institutional resilience.

Power and Authority

1. The Trump administration cut and froze over $2 billion in federal grants and contracts to Harvard University and threatened its tax-exempt status. By conditioning core research and institutional funding on ideological concessions and governance changes, the administration used fiscal power to coerce a private university, pressuring academic freedom and institutional autonomy. (19 Apr 2025; 20 Apr 2025; 21 Apr 2025)

2. The Trump administration expanded coal mining for data center energy while cutting miner health and safety agencies and delaying a silica dust rule. Executive promotion of coal extraction alongside weakened safety enforcement shifted risks onto workers and communities, prioritizing industrial output over regulatory protections and long-term public health. (19 Apr 2025)

3. The Trump administration pursued a campaign to restructure the Justice Department and FBI by removing career prosecutors and watchdogs. Targeting independent law enforcement and oversight personnel for removal weakened institutional checks on executive power and increased vulnerability to politicized justice. (19 Apr 2025)

4. President Trump considered firing Federal Reserve Chair Jerome Powell over interest rate policy. Threatening to remove the central bank chair for policy disagreements challenged Federal Reserve independence, risking politicization of monetary policy and economic management. (19 Apr 2025)

5. President Trump indicated he would ignore the Supreme Court's order to facilitate Kilmar Ábrego García's return from El Salvador. Openly rejecting a Supreme Court mandate on a wrongful deportation case signaled disregard for judicial authority and separation of powers in immigration enforcement. (21 Apr 2025)

6. U.S. Transportation Secretary Sean Duffy threatened New York with loss of federal transportation funding unless it halted Manhattan congestion pricing. Using federal funding leverage to coerce a state's transportation policy tested federalism norms and enabled selective punishment of disfavored jurisdictions. (21 Apr 2025)

7. Secretary of Defense Pete Hegseth and DHS Secretary Kristi Noem prepared a report to President Trump on whether to invoke the Insurrection Act at the southern border and reportedly declined to recommend it. Considering but stepping back from using military force for domestic border enforcement highlighted the availability of extraordinary powers and the importance of internal restraint. (21 Apr 2025)

8. Secretary of the Interior Doug Burgum signed an order consolidating

control of Interior's personnel and budget under a politically connected assistant secretary. Centralizing Interior's administrative authority in a political operative with energy ties reduced internal checks over public lands and resource policy and raised appointments-clause concerns. (23 Apr 2025)

9. The White House celebrated Earth Day by promoting expanded extraction of oil, gas, and minerals from federal lands and waters. Framing aggressive extraction on public lands as stewardship signaled executive prioritization of resource exploitation over environmental safeguards and long-term public interests. (23 Apr 2025)

10. President Trump issued a memorandum directing the attorney general to investigate alleged foreign and straw donations through ActBlue. Ordering a high-profile probe of a major opposition fundraising platform risked weaponizing federal law enforcement against political rivals under disputed factual claims. (24 Apr 2025)

11. President Trump issued an executive order eliminating disparate-impact liability from federal civil rights enforcement. Rolling back disparate-impact standards weakened tools to challenge systemic discrimination, narrowing civil rights protections for minorities and women across sectors. (23 Apr 2025)

12. President Trump issued an executive order strengthening probationary periods and easing removal of federal employees. Making it easier to dismiss probationary civil servants increased executive leverage over the bureaucracy and risked politicizing hiring and retention decisions. (24 Apr 2025)

13. President Trump issued an executive order to unleash offshore critical minerals and resources by expediting seabed permitting. Fast-tracking offshore mineral extraction under national security framing expanded executive discretion over environmental and industrial policy with limited public process. (24 Apr 2025)

14. President Trump issued an executive order to advance AI education for American youth. Creating a White House AI education task force centralized agenda-setting over emerging technology curricula, shaping future workforce skills and public understanding of AI. (23 Apr 2025)

15. President Trump issued an executive order to align federal workforce programs with reindustrialization and skilled trades. Directing agencies to reorient workforce programs toward targeted industrial goals concentrated federal influence over training priorities and labor-market interventions. (23 Apr 2025)

16. President Trump issued an executive order reforming higher education accreditation and targeting DEI-based standards. Recasting accreditation oversight to police diversity and equity criteria allowed the executive to

pressure universities' internal policies through control of eligibility for federal aid. (23 Apr 2025)

17. President Trump issued an executive order on school discipline to roll back equity-focused policies. Reframing discipline guidance against "equity ideology" risked weakening protections against discriminatory discipline practices, especially for students of color. (23 Apr 2025)

18. President Trump issued an executive order increasing enforcement of foreign funding disclosure at universities. Mandating stricter disclosure of foreign gifts and contracts expanded federal leverage over universities' international ties under a national security rationale. (23 Apr 2025)

19. President Trump issued an executive order establishing a White House initiative on HBCUs and a presidential advisory board. Centralizing HBCU policy in a White House initiative created new channels for support but also for political influence over historically Black institutions' priorities. (23 Apr 2025)

20. Secretary of Veterans Affairs Doug Collins ordered staff to report perceived anti-Christian bias through a new taskforce mechanism. Directing federal employees to flag "anti-Christian bias" institutionalized preferential attention to one faith identity, risking uneven treatment of religious expression and workplace rights. (22 Apr 2025)

21. Secretary of Health and Human Services Robert F. Kennedy Jr. proposed large cuts to disability-related education, research, and support services. Planned reductions in disability services would shrink federal support for a vulnerable population, deepening inequality in access to care and inclusion. (24 Apr 2025)

22. Secretary of Health and Human Services Robert F. Kennedy Jr. halted key autism research tied to DEIA programs. Stopping autism projects associated with diversity and accessibility initiatives curtailed scientific inquiry into disability and equity, narrowing evidence for inclusive policy. (24 Apr 2025)

23. The Trump administration terminated a civil rights settlement requiring Alabama to address sewage pollution in majority-Black Lowndes County. Canceling an environmental justice agreement left Black residents without promised sanitation remedies, weakening civil-rights enforcement against discriminatory infrastructure neglect. (24 Apr 2025)

24. The Trump administration announced plans to fast-track fossil fuel and mining permits under an asserted energy emergency. Drastically shortening permit timelines under an emergency declaration sidelined environmental review and public input, normalizing emergency powers for routine resource policy. (24 Apr 2025)

25. The Trump administration closed two federal oversight offices for

healthcare and conditions in immigration detention. Eliminating CRCL and the detention ombudsman removed key internal checks on ICE facilities, reducing accountability for abuses against detainees, especially disabled people. (25 Apr 2025)

26. Elon Musk and the Department of Government Efficiency asserted aggressive control over federal employees through weekly reporting demands and public clashes with Cabinet officials. Allowing a politically connected billionaire to direct civil servants outside normal chains of command blurred lines between public authority and private influence over the state. (25 Apr 2025)

27. The Trump administration reversed a policy that had revoked student visas over minor legal infractions after extensive litigation. Rolling back a harsh visa revocation rule under court pressure partially restored protections for international students, illustrating how legal challenges can constrain executive overreach. (24 Apr 2025)

28. The Trump administration ended pandemic-related school relief funding to help offset costs of extending 2017 tax cuts. Abruptly cutting nearly $3 billion in school relief to finance tax policy favored capital shifted fiscal burdens onto public education and low-income communities. (22 Apr 2025)

29. The Trump administration canceled access to COVID relief funds for schools, prompting a multistate lawsuit. Withdrawing previously available federal education funds without clear legal basis triggered state litigation and highlighted executive control over critical social spending. (22 Apr 2025)

30. Secretary of State Marco Rubio announced a sweeping reorganization of the State Department cutting staff and democracy-related offices. Planned reductions in bureaus focused on democracy, human rights, and global issues signaled a shift away from traditional diplomatic missions toward a leaner, more centralized foreign policy apparatus. (21 Apr 2025; 22 Apr 2025)

31. Secretary of State Marco Rubio withdrew from scheduled London peace talks after presenting a Ukraine peace plan as a final offer. Treating a controversial Ukraine settlement as non-negotiable and exiting talks reduced diplomatic flexibility and aligned U.S. posture more closely with Russian territorial claims. (24 Apr 2025)

32. President Trump publicly pressured Ukraine's president to accept a peace plan recognizing Russian claims over occupied territories. Urging acceptance of a settlement favoring Russian annexations undermined support for Ukraine's sovereignty and signaled tolerance for authoritarian aggression abroad. (24 Apr 2025; 25 Apr 2025)

33. President Trump requested that the Supreme Court reinstate a ban on

transgender individuals serving in the military. Seeking to revive a categorical ban on trans service members used military policy to restrict rights based on gender identity, challenging equal protection norms. (24 Apr 2025)

34. President Trump misrepresented the status of tariff negotiations with China despite denials from Chinese officials. Claiming nonexistent trade talks with China from the presidential podium blurred the line between official diplomacy and political narrative, complicating public understanding of foreign policy. (24 Apr 2025; 25 Apr 2025)

Institutions and Governance

1. The U.S. Supreme Court temporarily halted deportations of Venezuelan detainees under the Alien Enemies Act. Emergency orders blocking removals from Texas detention centers reinforced judicial oversight of executive immigration actions and protected detainees' access to legal process. (19 Apr 2025; 20 Apr 2025; 21 Apr 2025; 23 Apr 2025)

2. The U.S. Supreme Court unanimously upheld a lower court order requiring the government to facilitate Kilmar Ábrego García's return. Affirming a mandate to remedy a wrongful deportation underscored the Court's role in enforcing due process against executive resistance. (21 Apr 2025)

3. U.S. District Judge Paula Xinis ordered the Trump administration to facilitate García's return and provide daily compliance updates. Requiring detailed reporting on efforts to undo a wrongful deportation strengthened judicial tools for monitoring executive compliance with rights-protective orders. (23 Apr 2025)

4. U.S. District Judge James Boasberg found probable cause to hold the Trump administration in contempt for defying deportation orders. A contempt finding against the executive branch for ignoring court directives highlighted escalating institutional conflict over adherence to the rule of law. (21 Apr 2025; 23 Apr 2025)

5. The U.S. Supreme Court heard arguments on the constitutionality of the Preventive Services Taskforce under the ACA. Reviewing the structure of a body that mandates no-cost preventive care put judicial doctrine at the center of access to key health services. (21 Apr 2025)

6. U.S. District Judge William Orrick blocked the Trump administration from withholding federal funds from sanctuary jurisdictions. Enjoining funding threats against sanctuary cities reaffirmed limits on executive power to coerce local immigration policy through budgetary punishment. (24 Apr 2025)

7. U.S. District Judge Colleen Kollar-Kotelly blocked an executive order adding proof-of-citizenship requirements to the federal voter registration form. Striking down a presidential attempt to change federal registration rules protected congressional authority over elections and prevented a measure likely to disenfranchise many voters. (24 Apr 2025)

8. A federal judge ordered the Trump administration to restore Voice of America and other congressionally funded news services. Reinstating shuttered international broadcasters upheld Congress's power of the purse and limited unilateral executive dismantling of statutory media institutions. (21 Apr 2025)

9. Harvard University filed a federal lawsuit challenging the administration's funding freeze and control demands. By suing over conditions tying grants to governance and content changes, Harvard sought judicial protection for academic freedom and institutional independence from executive coercion. (22 Apr 2025)

10. Sixteen state attorneys general and Governor Josh Shapiro sued the Trump administration over termination of school relief funds. The multistate suit contested abrupt withdrawal of education funds as unlawful, using the courts to check executive budget maneuvers affecting public schools. (22 Apr 2025)

11. The Pentagon inspector general opened an investigation into Defense Secretary Pete Hegseth's use of Signal for sharing operational details. Launching an internal probe into potential mishandling of military information tested whether watchdogs can hold senior defense officials accountable despite political backing. (22 Apr 2025)

12. A federal immigration judge ruled Mahmoud Khalil eligible for deportation based partly on his political views. Treating a lawful resident activist as deportable for beliefs deemed contrary to U.S. foreign policy blurred lines between security adjudication and punishment of dissent. (23 Apr 2025)

13. A federal judge scheduled former congressman George Santos's sentencing hearing on fraud charges. Proceeding toward sentencing in a high-profile corruption case signaled that at least some political financial misconduct faces formal judicial consequences. (22 Apr 2025)

14. A federal court in New York sentenced former representative George Santos to over seven years in prison for donor fraud and identity theft. Imposing a substantial custodial sentence on a former member of Congress demonstrated meaningful accountability for egregious campaign-related fraud. (24 Apr 2025; 25 Apr 2025)

15. A federal jury in New York found the New York Times not liable in Sarah Palin's defamation retrial. Reaffirming the high 'actual malice' standard

preserved strong First Amendment protections for media commentary on public figures. (22 Apr 2025)

16. The U.S. Justice Department secured a $350 million settlement from Walgreens over unlawful opioid prescriptions. Resolving extensive opioid dispensing violations through a large civil settlement rather than criminal convictions illustrated how major corporate harms are often addressed via negotiated payments. (22 Apr 2025)

17. Attorney General Pam Bondi's Justice Department pursued the death penalty against Luigi Mangione in a high-profile murder case. Aggressively seeking capital punishment under a presidential crime agenda raised concerns about politicization of prosecutorial discretion and fair-trial safeguards. (25 Apr 2025)

18. The Federal Election Commission scheduled closed Sunshine Act meetings to discuss compliance, investigations, and civil actions. Holding nonpublic sessions on sensitive enforcement matters reflected the tension between transparency and confidentiality in election oversight. (24 Apr 2025)

19. The Federal Election Commission scheduled an open Sunshine Act meeting to consider advisory opinions and internal directives. Planning a public meeting on advisory opinions and guidance maintained some transparency around how federal campaign rules are interpreted and applied. (25 Apr 2025)

20. Representative Gerald Connolly requested investigations into DOGE's cross-agency data practices and potential Privacy Act violations. Calling for oversight of opaque data exfiltration by a new federal entity sought to enforce legal limits on government use of personal information. (22 Apr 2025)

21. Senator Chris Van Hollen publicly defended due process in the García case after visiting El Salvador. Using media appearances to highlight wrongful deportation and executive admissions of error exemplified legislative advocacy for rule-of-law constraints on immigration policy. (21 Apr 2025)

22. House Democrats traveled to El Salvador to advocate for Kilmar Ábrego García's release and challenge U.S. noncompliance. The delegation's diplomacy underscored congressional efforts to counter executive defiance of court orders and defend due process for deportees. (21 Apr 2025)

23. House Republicans advanced plans to reduce the federal share of Medicaid expansion funding. Proposed Medicaid cuts would shift healthcare costs to states and low-income residents, reshaping the social safety net through legislative budget choices. (21 Apr 2025)

24. The Republican-controlled Congress proposed slashing Medicaid by nearly one-third over a decade. Deep long-term Medicaid reductions threat-

ened access to care for millions of disabled and poor Americans, entrenching structural inequality through federal law. (24 Apr 2025)

25. Secretary of State Marco Rubio fired USAID official Peter Marocco involved in dismantling the agency. Removing a key figure in USAID restructuring reflected internal power struggles over the direction and capacity of U.S. development policy. (21 Apr 2025)

26. The Department of Government Efficiency claimed $160 billion in spending cuts on its website despite only $12.6 billion being verifiable. Inflating reported savings without documentation undermined fiscal transparency and distorted public understanding of federal budget performance. (24 Apr 2025)

27. The Department of Government Efficiency was implicated in accessing and deleting monitoring logs on secure NLRB data systems. Alleged tampering with NLRB systems and deletion of audit trails raised alarms about internal sabotage of labor oversight and record integrity. (22 Apr 2025)

28. The Trump administration announced plans to replace the SmartPay government expense system with a contract for Ramp, a politically connected firm. Shifting a core payment system to a company linked to top political allies blurred boundaries between public procurement and private patronage. (22 Apr 2025)

29. The National Institutes of Health began collecting private medical records from multiple databases for an autism study ordered by HHS leadership. Centralizing sensitive health data for a large autism registry without clear consent safeguards raised governance questions about privacy oversight in federal research. (25 Apr 2025)

Civil Rights and Dissent

1. U.S. Immigration and Customs Enforcement and DHS detained Indonesian student Aditya Wahyu Harsono after a secret visa revocation and appealed his bond. Revoking a valid student visa retroactively and keeping a noncitizen parent in custody highlighted opaque enforcement practices that destabilize families and chill lawful presence. (19 Apr 2025)

2. Border Patrol, ICE, and CBP officers wrongfully detained multiple U.S. citizens as suspected noncitizens in immigration sweeps and border checks. Arresting and holding citizens like Jose Hermosillo, Julio Noriega, and Bachir Atallah exposed systemic due process failures and profiling risks in immigration enforcement. (20 Apr 2025; 21 Apr 2025; 23 Apr 2025)

3. Florida's governor and law enforcement agencies directed participation

in ICE's 287(g) program and enrolled university police in immigration enforcement partnerships. Embedding campus and local police in federal immigration programs increased deportation risks for international students and blurred lines between education and enforcement. (21 Apr 2025)

4. ICE and an immigration judge kept Palestinian activist Mahmoud Khalil detained, denied his request to attend his child's birth, and found him deportable. Treating a lawful resident activist as a foreign policy threat and denying family contact underscored how immigration tools can be used to punish political expression. (22 Apr 2025; 23 Apr 2025)

5. ICE and DHS detained Tufts student Rümeysa Öztürk in harsh conditions without criminal charges. Holding a graduate student in punitive conditions despite no charges suggested use of immigration detention to intimidate campus activists and suppress dissent. (25 Apr 2025)

6. Democratic lawmakers visited ICE detention centers in Louisiana and condemned detentions of Khalil and Öztürk as violations of constitutional rights. Congressional visits framed the detentions as punishment for protected speech, spotlighting civil liberties concerns in immigration enforcement. (23 Apr 2025)

7. Democratic lawmakers from Massachusetts demanded the release of Tufts student Rümeysa Öztürk and investigation of detention conditions. Their advocacy emphasized that immigration detention should not be used as a tool of political repression and must meet basic human rights standards. (25 Apr 2025)

8. The Trump administration closed CRCL and the Immigration Detention Ombudsman offices overseeing detention conditions. Eliminating internal civil-rights and ombuds oversight left detainees with fewer avenues to challenge abuse, weakening protections for bodily security and due process. (25 Apr 2025)

9. The Trump administration sought Supreme Court reinstatement of a ban on transgender military service. Attempting to exclude transgender people from the armed forces used state power to restrict equal participation in a key public institution based on identity. (24 Apr 2025)

10. The Trump administration and DOJ dismissed an Alabama sewage settlement as illegal DEI and ended enforcement in a majority-Black county. Abandoning a civil-rights-based environmental remedy disproportionately harmed Black residents, signaling retreat from using law to address structural racism. (24 Apr 2025)

11. The Trump administration and HHS planned large-scale monitoring of autistic individuals' health records for a national registry. Creating a centralized autism registry from private records without clear consent safe-

guards raised fears of surveillance and stigmatization of disabled people. (24 Apr 2025)

12. The Trump administration and Congress advanced deep Medicaid cuts and disability service reductions affecting millions. Shrinking healthcare and support for disabled and poor residents restructured social rights, making access to basic services more contingent on wealth and status. (24 Apr 2025)

13. The Equal Employment Opportunity Commission texted Barnard College employees a survey about Jewish or Israeli identity and harassment experiences. Direct outreach to employees about religious identity in an active investigation raised privacy concerns even as it sought to probe potential antisemitic discrimination. (24 Apr 2025)

14. The U.S. Supreme Court temporarily blocked deportations from a Texas detention center due to inadequate notices and appeal information. Intervening over English-only notices and lack of challenge instructions protected detainees' minimal due process rights in expedited deportation proceedings. (23 Apr 2025)

15. U.S. District Judge William Orrick enjoined enforcement of funding penalties against sanctuary jurisdictions. The injunction shielded localities that limit cooperation with ICE from federal financial retaliation, preserving some space for local immigrant-protective policies. (24 Apr 2025)

16. U.S. District Judge Colleen Kollar-Kotelly blocked a proof-of-citizenship requirement for federal voter registration forms. Preventing new documentation hurdles protected many eligible voters—especially naturalized citizens and low-income residents—from disenfranchisement. (24 Apr 2025)

17. The state of Colorado implemented a law guaranteeing in-person voting access for eligible people held in jails and detention centers. Mandating in-jail voting hours significantly expanded ballot access for pretrial detainees and others not disenfranchised by felony convictions. (25 Apr 2025)

18. The Trump administration's antisemitism taskforce and universities conditioned restoration of federal funds on campus policy changes like mask bans and expanded arrest powers. Tying university funding to restrictive protest and security rules pressured institutions to curb expressive activity to avoid financial penalties. (20 Apr 2025)

19. The Trump administration threatened and in some cases withheld funds from multiple universities over governance and protest issues. Using federal grants as leverage to demand structural and disciplinary changes at universities risked chilling campus dissent and academic self-governance. (22 Apr 2025)

20. Over 150 U.S. college and university presidents signed a statement denouncing federal overreach and political interference in higher education. The joint letter represented a coordinated defense of academic freedom and institutional autonomy against escalating governmental pressure. (22 Apr 2025)

21. Nationwide protesters organized by the 50501 movement held over 700 demonstrations opposing Trump administration policies. Large, geographically broad protests signaled widespread civic mobilization against perceived executive overreach and threats to constitutional norms. (19 Apr 2025; 21 Apr 2025)

22. The Trump administration and HHS banned autism-related research and services tied to DEIA initiatives. Curtailing research and services framed as DEIA limited institutional attention to inequities affecting autistic and disabled people, narrowing the knowledge base for inclusive policy. (24 Apr 2025)

23. The FDA and RFK Jr.'s HHS leadership suspended federal quality control programs for dairy and food testing after staff cuts. Weakening food safety surveillance increased health risks, particularly for consumers with fewer resources to manage contamination hazards. (21 Apr 2025)

24. Milwaukee County Circuit Judge Hannah Dugan and federal law enforcement saw the judge arrested by the FBI for allegedly obstructing an ICE arrest. Charging a local judge over actions affecting an immigration arrest raised concerns about federal retaliation against judicial actors perceived as sympathetic to migrants. (24 Apr 2025)

25. An arsonist targeting Governor Josh Shapiro's residence carried out a firebomb attack on the Pennsylvania governor's home during Passover. The politically charged arson attack on a sitting governor's home underscored rising risks of violence against elected officials and minority communities. (23 Apr 2025)

26. The Trump administration and DOJ terminated a civil-rights-based sewage settlement in Lowndes County, Alabama. Abandoning enforcement left Black residents exposed to raw sewage and potential prosecution for noncompliance, deepening environmental and racial injustice. (24 Apr 2025)

Economic Structure

1. The Environmental Protection Agency reopened the comment period for the 2026 industrial stormwater NPDES general permit. Extending public comment on a nationwide stormwater permit maintained opportunities for

industry and communities to influence environmental compliance rules. (21 Apr 2025)

2. The Environmental Protection Agency updated the Federal Agency Hazardous Waste Compliance Docket with new facilities. Adding federal sites to the hazardous waste docket improved transparency about government pollution liabilities and regulatory oversight obligations. (21 Apr 2025)

3. The Federal Communications Commission sought comments on proposed changes to radio station community-of-license assignments. Reviewing license community changes affected local media markets and residents' access to broadcast information and services. (21 Apr 2025)

4. The Federal Communications Commission invited comment on information collection for robocall mitigation and TRACED Act compliance. Evaluating data requirements for robocall controls shaped regulatory burdens on carriers and protections for consumers from abusive calling practices. (21 Apr 2025)

5. The Food and Drug Administration rescheduled and amended procedures for an advisory meeting on extended-release opioid safety. Adjusting timelines and comment procedures for opioid oversight meetings influenced how expert input informs regulation of high-risk pain medications. (21 Apr 2025)

6. The Food and Drug Administration approved AMVUTTRA and TREMFYA using rare pediatric disease priority review vouchers. Using priority review vouchers to expedite pediatric treatments illustrated how regulatory incentives steer pharmaceutical innovation and market entry. (21 Apr 2025)

7. The Food and Drug Administration corrected guidance on lead levels in baby food and confirmed MOBIC tablets were not withdrawn for safety reasons. Clarifying regulatory records on food safety and drug status supported accurate industry compliance and consumer protection. (21 Apr 2025)

8. The Transportation Security Administration proposed revisions and extensions to multiple information collections on surface transportation security, screening partnerships, visitor vetting, training, airport security, speaker requests, and LEOSA credentials. Updating data requirements for transportation security programs affected how public and private operators comply with federal safety standards and oversight. (21 Apr 2025; 22 Apr 2025; 23 Apr 2025)

9. The Food and Drug Administration continued a voluntary quality management maturity assessment program for drug manufacturers. Encouraging firms to participate in quality maturity assessments aimed to raise

manufacturing standards and reduce supply disruptions for medicines. (23 Apr 2025)

10. The Food and Drug Administration approved EYLEA HD under a material threat medical countermeasure voucher and issued a voucher for EBANGA. Deploying countermeasure vouchers incentivized development of drugs for serious threats like Ebola, shaping preparedness markets and public health resilience. (23 Apr 2025)

11. The Food and Drug Administration opened a docket on using HL7 FHIR standards for real-world clinical study data submissions. Exploring standardized health data formats could modernize regulatory science and affect how patient data informs drug approvals. (23 Apr 2025)

12. The Environmental Protection Agency approved Connecticut's SIP revisions for 2015 ozone standards and finalized CSAPR allowance allocations. Implementing air quality plans and cross-state pollution allowances shaped industrial emissions constraints and interstate environmental equity. (22 Apr 2025)

13. The Environmental Protection Agency revised the format of Wisconsin's SIP materials and published notices of environmental impact statements. Improving SIP documentation and publicizing EIS availability supported clearer regulatory baselines and public participation in major federal projects. (22 Apr 2025; 25 Apr 2025)

14. The General Services Administration sought OMB approval to extend information collection for surplus property transfer forms. Maintaining documentation for surplus property transfers affected how public assets are redistributed to state agencies and nonprofits. (22 Apr 2025)

15. The Federal Communications Commission revised its schedule of application fees with a CPI-based increase and sought comments on Section 214 and emergency antenna information collections. Adjusting fees and paperwork for telecom authorizations influenced market entry costs and regulatory oversight of critical communications infrastructure. (23 Apr 2025; 25 Apr 2025)

16. The Occupational Safety and Health Administration corrected a control number and processed multiple NRTL recognition and expansion applications. Updating testing-lab recognitions and paperwork identifiers affected product safety certification capacity and international conformity assessment. (24 Apr 2025; 25 Apr 2025)

17. The Drug Enforcement Administration announced applications for importing and manufacturing controlled substances by Royal Emerald Pharmaceuticals and SpecGx LLC. Considering new controlled-substance import

and manufacturing registrations shaped legal supply chains for cannabis derivatives and potent drugs like fentanyl. (25 Apr 2025)

18. The Occupational Safety and Health Administration announced DEKRA, CSA, Intertek, TUV Rheinland, and UL applications to expand NRTL recognition, including overseas sites. Expanding recognized testing labs, including in Asia, affected global product safety oversight and the role of foreign facilities in U.S. compliance regimes. (25 Apr 2025)

19. The Occupational Safety and Health Administration processed DEKRA's NRTL expansion application including Shanghai sites. Allowing a U.S.-recognized lab to operate test sites in China further integrated international facilities into domestic safety certification systems. (25 Apr 2025)

20. The Occupational Safety and Health Administration corrected the OMB control number for the lead in construction standard information collection. Fixing paperwork identifiers ensured accurate tracking of compliance burdens for lead safety rules affecting construction workers. (24 Apr 2025)

21. The Food and Drug Administration continued a voluntary QMM program and opened a docket on HL7 FHIR for real-world data. These initiatives aimed to modernize pharmaceutical quality oversight and data interoperability, influencing regulatory efficiency and innovation incentives. (23 Apr 2025)

22. Cleveland Cliffs, GM, Volvo, and Howmet Aerospace announced layoffs and potential production halts citing Trump-era tariffs and uncertainty. Manufacturing job cuts and threatened shutdowns linked to tariff policy showed how trade decisions can erode industrial employment and worker security. (22 Apr 2025)

23. Ford Motor Company halted sales of some American-made cars to China due to tariff-related disruptions. Suspending exports to China highlighted how tariff escalations can reshape trade flows and widen bilateral trade imbalances. (22 Apr 2025)

24. The Philadelphia Federal Reserve reported sharp pessimism in its manufacturing survey amid tariff impacts. Surveyed gloom among manufacturers reflected broader economic uncertainty and reduced investment appetite under protectionist trade policies. (22 Apr 2025)

25. Twelve U.S. states filed lawsuits challenging the Trump administration's tariff policies. State litigation over tariffs underscored tensions between federal trade strategies and their inflationary, growth, and distributional effects on local economies. (23 Apr 2025)

26. Chinese importers canceled over 12,000 metric tons of U.S. pork purchases amid tariff disputes. Retaliatory cancellations hurt American

farmers and illustrated how geopolitical frictions can be targeted at politically salient industries. (24 Apr 2025)

27. Treasury Secretary Scott Bessent and former President Trump announced an expected trade deal with South Korea despite an existing FTA. Promoting a largely symbolic trade agreement suggested use of trade policy announcements for political messaging more than substantive economic change. (24 Apr 2025)

28. China's Commerce Ministry warned countries against trade deals with the U.S. that disadvantage China and promised reciprocal countermeasures. Beijing's warning highlighted the risk that U.S. trade pressure could trigger broader retaliatory dynamics affecting global supply chains. (20 Apr 2025)

29. The UK and U.S. governments negotiated a draft trade agreement trading tariff relief for changes to the UK digital services tax. The draft deal linked sectoral tariffs to digital tax policy, illustrating how trade negotiations can reshape national tax bases and industrial advantages. (22 Apr 2025)

Information, Memory, and Manipulation

1. Secretary of Defense Pete Hegseth shared sensitive details of U.S. strikes in Yemen in private Signal chats including family and associates. Discussing operational plans on unsecured channels with non-cleared participants jeopardized military secrecy and raised questions about elite impunity for security breaches. (20 Apr 2025; 21 Apr 2025; 22 Apr 2025)

2. Secretary of Defense Pete Hegseth had an unsecured internet line installed in his Pentagon office to access Signal and blocked websites. Bypassing Pentagon network protections to use personal communications tools created exploitable vulnerabilities at the heart of U.S. defense operations. (23 Apr 2025; 25 Apr 2025)

3. Secretary of Defense Pete Hegseth threatened criminal prosecutions of former DoD employees accused of leaking information. Publicly warning leakers of prosecution amid his own security controversies signaled a climate where exposing misconduct risks retaliation rather than protection. (21 Apr 2025)

4. President Trump and the White House denied reports of searching for a new defense secretary and labeled NPR coverage as fake news. Dismissing mainstream reporting as fabricated contributed to public confusion about defense leadership and eroded trust in independent journalism. (20 Apr 2025)

5. President Trump attacked judges on social media after adverse Supreme Court immigration orders. Personalized attacks on the judiciary

sought to delegitimize legal constraints and frame court decisions as partisan obstruction. (21 Apr 2025)

6. The Trump campaign used DOGE's claimed budget cuts to suggest Americans might receive $5,000 rebate checks in fundraising emails. Promising implausible rebate checks based on unsubstantiated savings figures exploited fiscal misinformation to solicit political donations. (24 Apr 2025)

7. The Department of Government Efficiency inflated its reported spending cuts online without adding new documented reductions. Quietly increasing claimed savings totals without evidence turned an official data portal into a vehicle for misleading narratives about government efficiency. (24 Apr 2025)

8. The Department of Government Efficiency was reported to have exfiltrated and obscured personal data from other agencies, including the NLRB. Cross-agency data grabs and deletion of monitoring logs suggested emerging use of state IT access for opaque surveillance and record manipulation. (22 Apr 2025)

9. The Trump administration shut down Voice of America and related news services until ordered by a court to restore them. Attempting to disband congressionally mandated broadcasters showed willingness to defund independent public media in favor of more controllable information channels. (21 Apr 2025)

10. President Trump called on Rupert Murdoch to fire Fox News's pollster after an unfavorable approval rating. Pressuring a media owner to remove a pollster over results he disliked exemplified efforts to shape coverage and undermine independent polling. (23 Apr 2025)

11. The Trump administration framed ActBlue as a conduit for foreign and straw donations in a presidential memorandum. Casting a major opposition fundraising platform as inherently suspect without public evidence contributed to a narrative that delegitimizes political rivals as corrupt. (24 Apr 2025)

12. President Trump misstated the existence of ongoing tariff negotiations with China contrary to Chinese officials' statements. Publicly asserting nonexistent talks blurred factual baselines in foreign economic policy, complicating accountability for trade outcomes. (24 Apr 2025; 25 Apr 2025)

13. The National Institutes of Health and HHS aggregated private medical records into an autism study database under RFK Jr.'s direction. Building a large health-data repository without transparent governance raised fears that sensitive information could be repurposed beyond research aims. (25 Apr 2025)

14. The Trump administration and HHS banned DEIA-linked autism research and recast civil-rights settlements as illegal DEI initiatives. Labeling equity-focused work as unlawful DEI sought to delegitimize and curtail lines of inquiry that document structural injustice and marginalized experiences. (24 Apr 2025)

15. The Federal Communications Commission sought comments on information collection for the Wireless E911 Coordination Initiative. Maintaining accurate data on emergency call centers supported reliable public safety communications and crisis response. (22 Apr 2025)

16. The Federal Communications Commission invited comments on information collections for Section 214 transfers and emergency antennas. These notices shaped how much information carriers and broadcasters must provide when altering critical infrastructure, affecting transparency in network changes. (25 Apr 2025)

17. The Trump administration and DOGE used overlapping crises and opaque data claims around tariffs, budget cuts, and university funding to advance contested policies. Simultaneous controversies over trade, spending, and higher education created an information environment where scrutiny of any single issue was harder to sustain. (22 Apr 2025; 24 Apr 2025)

CHAPTER 15
WEEK 15 (26 APR 2025 – 2 MAY 2025): EMERGENCY RULE AS ROUTINE GOVERNANCE

In Trump's fifteenth week back in office, emergencies, executive orders, and data systems quietly rewired law, citizenship, and information into tools of regime protection.

This was an exceptionally intense week of efforts to strengthen authoritarian control. The executive branch used emergency powers, executive orders, and agency influence to overhaul key rules on immigration, climate, education, civil service, and media funding, often bypassing or weakening legislative and judicial checks. Immigration enforcement and the Alien Enemies Act were stretched toward collective punishment and secretive detentions, while courts and some state actors provided important but limited resistance. Project 2025–focused actions—reclassifying civil servants, dismantling the Department of Education, ending DEI and environmental justice initiatives, and subordinating independent regulators—directly threaten institutional independence. At the same time, the administration increased control over information: cutting funding to NPR/PBS, launching a White House propaganda website, weakening journalist protections, and inserting disinformation into school curricula. Economic policy—tariffs, favoritism toward fossil fuels, and selective deregulation—shifted public risk and crises toward insiders' profits. A few court rulings and state efforts modestly reinforced the rule of law, but they were overshadowed by systematic efforts to normalize emergency governance, politicize laws, and divide citizens along ideological and ethnonational lines.

Power and Authority

1. Trump administration threatened and froze federal funding to universities over pro-Palestinian protests. By tying federal funds to how universities handle pro-Palestinian activism, the administration used financial leverage to shape campus speech and governance, pressuring institutions to align with its political preferences. (26 Apr 2025)

2. Republican members of Congress passed a budget framework enabling deep social spending cuts and tax extensions. The budget framework set up one-party passage of large cuts to safety-net programs and tax extensions, shifting fiscal priorities in ways that can entrench inequality and weaken social protections without broad consensus. (26 Apr 2025)

3. President Donald Trump declared a national border emergency to enable troop deployment and hardline immigration policies. The border emergency declaration expanded executive latitude to use military resources and aggressive enforcement at the border, normalizing emergency powers for long-term immigration policy. (30 Apr 2025; 1 May 2025)

4. President Donald Trump issued executive orders ending birthright citizenship for some US-born children. The orders attempted to narrow constitutional birthright citizenship, directly challenging the Fourteenth Amendment and creating a more stratified system of legal status based on parentage. (30 Apr 2025; 1 May 2025)

5. President Donald Trump issued pardons and commutations for January 6 defendants and ordered related cases dropped. By pardoning January 6 participants and halting prosecutions, the president weakened accountability for an attack on the transfer of power and signaled tolerance for allied political violence. (30 Apr 2025; 1 May 2025)

6. President Donald Trump signed executive orders banning gender transitions for minors and restricting transgender participation in sports and the military. These orders curtailed access to gender-affirming care and participation in public institutions for transgender youth and adults, narrowing equal protection for a targeted group through executive power. (30 Apr 2025; 1 May 2025)

7. President Donald Trump withdrew the United States from the Paris climate agreement and related global climate mechanisms. Leaving the Paris accord and associated climate funds reduced US participation in multilateral climate governance, weakening cooperative checks on domestic environmental policy choices. (30 Apr 2025; 1 May 2025; 2 May 2025)

8. President Donald Trump invoked emergency economic powers to impose sweeping tariffs, including a 145% tariff on Chinese goods. Using

emergency authorities to unilaterally impose high tariffs concentrated trade power in the executive branch, sidelining Congress's traditional role in tariff policy and increasing economic leverage over domestic actors. (28 Apr 2025; 29 Apr 2025; 1 May 2025; 2 May 2025)

9. President Donald Trump issued numerous executive orders restructuring federal agencies, civil service protections, and regulatory oversight. Orders to reclassify civil servants, subordinate independent regulators to the White House, review and eliminate advisory bodies, and expand DOGE's reach shifted long-term administrative power toward loyalists and the presidency. (1 May 2025)

10. President Donald Trump signed executive orders reshaping federal climate and energy policy toward fossil fuel expansion. By declaring an energy emergency, boosting drilling, coal, deep-sea mining, and halting enforcement of state climate laws, the president used executive tools to entrench fossil fuel interests over environmental and public health concerns. (1 May 2025; 2 May 2025)

11. President Donald Trump issued executive orders targeting undocumented immigrants' access to federal benefits and preparing mass detention at Guantánamo Bay. Ending federal benefits for undocumented immigrants and planning a large migrant detention facility at Guantánamo Bay deepened a tiered system of rights and expanded coercive tools against noncitizens. (1 May 2025)

12. President Donald Trump created a Religious Liberty Commission and expanded the White House Faith Office's policy role. Establishing a federal commission to advise on religious liberty, closely tied to the White House Faith Office, increased the role of favored religious perspectives in shaping national policy. (1 May 2025)

13. President Donald Trump ordered investigations and funding threats against universities and school systems over diversity and race-focused programs. Federal investigations into Harvard Law Review and Chicago's Black Student Success Plan, coupled with broader DEI rollbacks, used central power to chill race-conscious initiatives in education. (29 Apr 2025; 1 May 2025)

14. President Donald Trump directed the Department of Justice to investigate ActBlue and created a DOJ weaponization working group. Ordering an ActBlue probe and framing investigations of Trump as political persecution repurposed federal law enforcement to target opponents and delegitimize independent scrutiny. (27 Apr 2025; 2 May 2025)

15. President Donald Trump used pardon power to erase over $1 billion in debts and penalties for white-collar offenders and a crypto firm. Mass

pardons that canceled large financial penalties for wealthy individuals and a cryptocurrency exchange signaled that proximity to presidential favor can nullify serious economic sanctions. (2 May 2025)

16. President Donald Trump signed executive orders cutting federal funding for NPR and PBS. Defunding public broadcasters through executive order weakened independent, publicly funded news sources and increased executive influence over the media landscape. (1 May 2025; 2 May 2025)

17. President Donald Trump ordered dismantling of the Department of Education and elimination of federal DEI initiatives. Moves to dismantle the Education Department and end diversity programs restructured federal involvement in schooling and civil rights, centralizing ideological control while reducing institutional capacity. (30 Apr 2025; 1 May 2025; 2 May 2025)

18. President Donald Trump reclassified tens of thousands of civil service roles as political appointments. Reinstating Schedule F–style reclassification allowed mass replacement of career officials with loyalists, undermining a neutral civil service and concentrating operational control in the executive. (1 May 2025; 2 May 2025)

19. President Donald Trump shifted more disaster relief costs to states, tying aid to immigration compliance. By moving disaster costs onto states and linking relief to immigration enforcement, the order used federal fiscal tools to pressure disfavored jurisdictions' policy choices. (2 May 2025)

20. President Donald Trump fired National Security Adviser Mike Waltz and reassigned him as UN ambassador nominee. Removing a national security adviser over a messaging scandal but then nominating him as UN ambassador illustrated personalized control over key security and diplomatic posts, with limited accountability for mishandling sensitive information. (30 Apr 2025; 2 May 2025)

21. President Donald Trump publicly attacked judges and courts for blocking his policies. Rhetorical attacks on "radical-left judges" for halting executive actions sought to delegitimize judicial review and pressure courts to defer to presidential preferences. (30 Apr 2025)

22. Representative Clay Higgins called for the arrest of judges in public statements. A sitting member of Congress urging arrests of judges for ideological reasons contributed to a climate of intimidation around the judiciary and weakened respect for judicial independence. (27 Apr 2025)

23. Secretary of Defense Pete Hegseth issued a provocative social media warning to Iran over support for the Houthis. A senior defense official's unilateral threat on social media blurred lines between formal war powers and personal messaging, risking escalation without clear congressional authorization. (30 Apr 2025)

24. President Donald Trump used AI systems to help draft executive orders and policy justifications. Reliance on AI to generate executive orders and tariff justifications introduced opaque, machine-mediated reasoning into binding legal texts, complicating accountability for policy choices. (1 May 2025)

25. President Donald Trump blamed former President Biden for current economic downturn during a Cabinet meeting. Using an official Cabinet setting to shift responsibility for economic contraction onto a predecessor shaped public narratives about accountability for policy-driven shocks like tariffs. (1 May 2025)

26. President Donald Trump hosted a National Prayer Day event emphasizing a Christian identity for the nation. Framing national greatness as contingent on being "One Nation Under God" and highlighting a White House Faith Office blurred church–state boundaries and elevated favored religious narratives in governance. (30 Apr 2025)

27. President Donald Trump authorized sanctions against the International Criminal Court and withdrew from UN human rights bodies and WHO. Sanctioning ICC staff and exiting UN human rights and health institutions reduced external checks on US conduct and signaled retreat from multilateral accountability frameworks. (1 May 2025)

28. President Donald Trump renamed major geographic features such as the Gulf of Mexico and Mount Denali. Renaming prominent landmarks by executive order used symbolic power to recast national geography, reflecting an effort to imprint partisan narratives on shared civic reference points. (1 May 2025)

29. President Donald Trump ordered declassification of MLK and JFK assassination files. Directing release of high-profile historical records increased transparency around past political violence, potentially strengthening public trust in official accounts of major events. (1 May 2025)

30. President Donald Trump created a sovereign wealth fund and strategic bitcoin reserve through executive orders. Launching a sovereign wealth fund and a bitcoin reserve by executive action reoriented national investment strategy and digital asset policy with limited legislative input or debate. (1 May 2025)

31. President Donald Trump ordered development of an American missile defense shield dubbed a next-generation Iron Dome. Mandating plans for a large-scale missile defense system committed defense resources and strategy through executive direction, shaping long-term security posture without clear public deliberation. (1 May 2025)

32. President Donald Trump made English the official language of the

United States and tightened language rules for truck drivers. Declaring English the official language and enforcing English proficiency for commercial drivers raised barriers for non-English speakers' access to services and employment, reinforcing linguistic hierarchies in civic life. (28 Apr 2025; 1 May 2025)

33. President Donald Trump ended federal funding for UNRWA and withdrew from the UN Human Rights Council. Cutting support for Palestinian refugees and leaving the UN Human Rights Council reduced US backing for multilateral human rights and humanitarian mechanisms, affecting vulnerable populations' protections. (1 May 2025)

Institutions and Governance

1. Harvard University sued the Trump administration over threats to cut federal funding. Harvard's lawsuit challenged federal attempts to condition billions in funding on compliance with contested directives, asserting institutional autonomy and judicial review over executive pressure on universities. (27 Apr 2025)

2. US Department of Justice Civil Rights Division leadership removed voting section managers and ordered dismissal of active voting rights cases. Purging the DOJ voting unit's leadership and cases sharply reduced federal enforcement against voter discrimination, weakening a key institutional safeguard for fair elections. (28 Apr 2025)

3. Judge Royce Lamberth ordered restoration of appropriated funds to Radio Free Europe. By ruling that the executive cannot refuse to spend congressionally appropriated funds, the court reinforced legislative control over the purse and checked unilateral impoundment. (28 Apr 2025)

4. US federal courts blocked or limited the Trump administration's use of the Alien Enemies Act for deportations. District and appellate rulings, along with a Supreme Court stay, curtailed efforts to use an 18th-century wartime law for mass deportations, affirming statutory limits and due process for immigrants. (29 Apr 2025; 30 Apr 2025; 1 May 2025; 2 May 2025)

5. US Supreme Court Justice Ketanji Brown Jackson publicly warned that administration rhetoric was intimidating the judiciary. A sitting justice's speech describing coordinated attacks and threats against judges highlighted institutional concern that political leaders were undermining judicial independence and the rule of law. (2 May 2025)

6. Democratic state attorneys general mounted legal challenges to Trump executive orders across multiple domains. Coordinated lawsuits from blue-state attorneys general sought to check executive overreach on issues like

immigration and regulation, using federal courts as a counterweight to presidential power. (30 Apr 2025)

7. federal appeals court upheld an injunction blocking DOGE access to Social Security records. By preventing DOGE from obtaining sensitive Social Security data, the court limited a new executive department's reach into personal information and preserved existing privacy safeguards. (30 Apr 2025)

8. Trump administration filed an emergency appeal to the Supreme Court seeking DOGE access to Social Security records. The emergency appeal aimed to rapidly expand a politically directed department's access to nationwide personal data, testing judicial willingness to constrain new surveillance powers. (2 May 2025)

9. US Department of Justice under Attorney General Pam Bondi halted prosecutions under the Foreign Corrupt Practices Act and closed its cryptocurrency unit. Pausing FCPA enforcement and shutting a crypto crime unit signaled a retreat from policing complex financial misconduct, especially where it implicated powerful business interests. (1 May 2025; 2 May 2025)

10. Trump administration dropped federal investigations and lawsuits against 89 corporations that had donated to Trump's inaugural fund. Ending dozens of corporate cases involving major donors weakened deterrence for corporate misconduct and suggested enforcement priorities were influenced by political contributions. (28 Apr 2025)

11. US Department of Justice sued Michigan and Hawaii to block their climate lawsuits against oil companies. Federal suits arguing that the Clean Air Act preempts state climate litigation sought to shield fossil fuel firms from state-level accountability and narrowed states' policy space. (2 May 2025)

12. Puerto Rico government voluntarily dismissed its climate lawsuit against major oil companies. Dropping a climate damages case after DOJ's preemption actions illustrated how federal interventions can chill subnational efforts to hold powerful industries accountable. (2 May 2025)

13. US Senate Republicans blocked Democratic measures to challenge Trump's tariff authority. By voting down efforts to rein in emergency-based tariffs, Senate leaders preserved broad unilateral trade powers for the president and limited legislative oversight of economic policy. (1 May 2025)

14. House Republican leadership used procedural rules to prevent votes on resolutions challenging Trump's tariff emergency. House leaders' procedural maneuvering to block debate on the tariff emergency further insulated executive trade decisions from congressional scrutiny. (1 May 2025)

15. House Republicans blocked a Democratic investigation into Defense

Secretary Pete Hegseth's use of Signal. Embedding a rule to bar resolutions of inquiry about Hegseth's communications limited Congress's ability to investigate potential mishandling of sensitive information by a senior official. (29 Apr 2025)

16. federal judiciary issued rulings scrutinizing executive retaliation against law firms and limiting DOGE access to records. Judicial skepticism of security-clearance retaliation against law firms and injunctions against DOGE data access showed courts acting as a partial check on politicized use of administrative tools. (27 Apr 2025)

17. federal courts intervened in individual immigration detention cases to enforce due process and free speech protections. Orders releasing Mohsen Mahdawi and blocking Javier Salazar's deportation underscored judicial willingness to curb executive detention when it chilled speech or bypassed fair procedures. (30 Apr 2025)

18. US Department of Education and Oklahoma officials advanced a new social studies curriculum through a rushed, opaque approval process. Last-minute changes, limited review time, and pressure for an immediate vote on Oklahoma's standards weakened procedural safeguards meant to ensure educational content is vetted and accurate. (1 May 2025)

19. Trump administration cut staffing and shifted priorities within the DOJ Civil Rights Division. Reassigning or losing over 250 attorneys and refocusing the Civil Rights Division on voter fraud and limiting transgender rights sharply reduced federal capacity to enforce core civil rights laws. (1 May 2025)

20. USDA and State of Maine settled litigation over frozen child nutrition funds tied to trans athlete policies. Restoring Maine's nutrition funding in exchange for dropping suit preserved program access but left unresolved the broader question of conditioning federal aid on state civil rights policies. (2 May 2025)

21. President Donald Trump signed only five measures into law in his first 100 days of the second term. A sparse legislative record contrasted with extensive executive action, underscoring a governing strategy that relies on unilateral tools rather than negotiated statutes. (30 Apr 2025)

22. Senators Adam Schiff and Elizabeth Warren requested an ethics inquiry into President Trump's $TRUMP cryptocurrency contest. The senators' appeal to the Office of Government Ethics sought institutional review of a scheme that appeared to monetize presidential access, testing remaining guardrails against self-dealing. (28 Apr 2025)

23. federal agencies and advisory boards sought nominations for key scientific and ethics advisory committees. EPA and FDA calls for experts to

serve on advisory boards and review human studies and air standards showed ongoing use of expert bodies to inform regulation, even amid broader politicization. (30 Apr 2025; 1 May 2025)

24. Trump administration fired Doug Emhoff and other Biden-era appointees from the US Holocaust Memorial Museum board. Removing prior administration figures from a key memory institution's board allowed the White House to reshape oversight of Holocaust remembrance in line with its own political agenda. (1 May 2025)

25. Senate Judiciary and Finance Committees scrutinized controversial nominations for US Attorney and CBP Commissioner. Hearings questioning Ed Martin's and Rodney Scott's records highlighted the Senate's role in vetting nominees whose past actions raised concerns about law enforcement impartiality and abuse. (30 Apr 2025)

26. federal courts and regulators oversaw multiple technical regulatory processes and debarments in communications and education programs. FCC suspensions from the E-Rate program and various EPA and FDA comment processes reflected routine, rules-based governance that maintains program integrity despite higher-level politicization. (29 Apr 2025; 30 Apr 2025)

Civil Rights and Dissent

1. FBI and federal authorities arrested Wisconsin Judge Hannah Dugan for allegedly obstructing immigration enforcement. Arresting a sitting state judge amid an immigration crackdown raised concerns that federal law enforcement was being used to intimidate the judiciary and chill local resistance to deportation policies. (26 Apr 2025)

2. ICE and DHS conducted deportations and detentions that separated US citizen children and families, including medically vulnerable minors. Rapid deportations of parents and children, sometimes without medication or legal access, demonstrated an enforcement approach that subordinated family unity and child welfare to removal targets. (26 Apr 2025; 27 Apr 2025; 28 Apr 2025)

3. ICE and ORR targeted unaccompanied immigrant children and their sponsors for deportation or prosecution using shared data. Using welfare checks and data-sharing to locate children and sponsors for enforcement blurred child protection and immigration control, raising fears of backdoor family separation. (28 Apr 2025)

4. ICE and DOJ prosecuted migrants for entering a military buffer zone along the US-Mexico border. Charging migrants for crossing a new military-

patrolled buffer zone expanded criminalization of border crossing and blurred lines between military and civilian law enforcement. (30 Apr 2025)

5. Trump administration and El Salvador authorities detained and deported Venezuelan migrants under opaque conditions, leading to enforced disappearances. The disappearance and imprisonment of Venezuelan migrants after US detention, with families kept uninformed, reflected severe due process failures and cross-border human rights concerns. (29 Apr 2025)

6. Trump administration used the Alien Enemies Act to detain and deport Venezuelan immigrants alleged to be gang members. Invoking an 18th-century wartime law against a specific nationality for alleged gang ties stretched legal authority and stigmatized an entire immigrant group as security threats. (30 Apr 2025; 1 May 2025; 2 May 2025)

7. Trump administration ended birthright citizenship and froze refugee admissions through executive orders. Limiting automatic citizenship and suspending refugee resettlement redefined who can belong and seek protection in the US, entrenching a more exclusionary citizenship regime. (30 Apr 2025; 1 May 2025)

8. Trump administration banned gender-affirming medical care for minors and restricted transgender participation in public life. Federal bans on youth gender transitions and trans participation in sports and the military curtailed bodily autonomy and equal access to institutions for transgender people. (30 Apr 2025; 1 May 2025)

9. US Health and Human Services Department released a report urging therapy over medical treatment for youth with gender dysphoria. An HHS report contradicting major medical associations' guidance on gender dysphoria provided federal backing for restricting gender-affirming care, influencing state policies and access. (1 May 2025)

10. Trump administration ended diversity, equity, and inclusion programs across government and pressured institutions to roll back DEI. Terminating DEI initiatives and linking funding to compliance with anti-DEI directives reduced institutional tools for addressing discrimination and supporting marginalized groups. (30 Apr 2025; 2 May 2025)

11. US Department of Education investigated Chicago's Black Student Success Plan for alleged race discrimination. A federal probe into a program aimed at improving outcomes for Black students, with funding threats attached, risked chilling targeted efforts to remedy racial disparities in education. (1 May 2025)

12. Yale University revoked recognition of a student group that organized a protest against an Israeli minister. Deregistering a student group over a protest encampment signaled institutional willingness to sanction pro-Pales-

tinian activism, narrowing space for campus political expression. (27 Apr 2025)

13. FBI and local police raided homes of pro-Palestinian students in Michigan and seized electronics. Law enforcement raids tied to alleged vandalism were perceived by activists as part of a broader pattern of criminalizing pro-Palestinian organizing, potentially chilling student dissent. (27 Apr 2025)

14. Swarthmore College suspended students involved in a pro-Palestinian protest encampment without full process. Interim suspensions and campus bans for student protesters, imposed before full conduct hearings, raised due process and free expression concerns in campus governance. (2 May 2025)

15. Kennedy Center board appointed by Trump administration canceled LGBTQ Pride events planned for World Pride Festival. Canceling Pride programming at a major national arts venue reduced public visibility for LGBTQ communities and signaled official disfavor toward queer expression. (26 Apr 2025)

16. Trump administration ended the Pentagon's Women, Peace and Security program. Terminating a congressionally mandated program to integrate gender perspectives into security policy rolled back efforts to include women's voices in defense decision-making. (28 Apr 2025; 29 Apr 2025)

17. Trump administration used the Alien Enemies Act and deportation powers in the Kilmar Ábrego García case despite a prior court order. Deporting Ábrego García in defiance of a 2019 court order and then justifying it with domestic abuse allegations raised serious questions about respect for judicial rulings and due process. (28 Apr 2025; 1 May 2025)

18. ICE agents conducted a mistaken raid on a US citizen family in Oklahoma City, seizing property. A botched raid that left a citizen family without phones or savings highlighted risks of aggressive immigration enforcement tactics spilling over onto non-targeted residents. (2 May 2025)

19. Illinois Governor J.B. Pritzker and national protesters called for and organized mass protests against Republican and Trump policies. State-level leaders and nationwide rallies mobilized large-scale peaceful dissent against federal cuts and civil rights rollbacks, demonstrating continued capacity for civic resistance. (29 Apr 2025; 30 Apr 2025)

20. Democratic leaders Hakeem Jeffries and Cory Booker held a 12-hour sit-in at the US Capitol to protest GOP budget cuts. A high-profile sit-in by senior lawmakers used nonviolent protest to spotlight proposed reductions in social programs, blending institutional roles with extra-parliamentary dissent. (28 Apr 2025)

21. Trump administration used English-only and sanctuary-city orders to

penalize jurisdictions and workers tied to immigration policies. Mandating English proficiency for drivers and threatening to cut funds to sanctuary jurisdictions leveraged regulatory and fiscal tools to pressure immigrants and local governments. (28 Apr 2025; 1 May 2025)

22. Trump administration ended federal benefits for undocumented immigrants and barred certain workers from loan forgiveness based on immigration-related activities. Linking access to benefits and loan forgiveness to immigration status and perceived ties to foreign groups created new penalties for association and advocacy around migration. (1 May 2025)

23. Trump administration withdrew from the World Health Organization and cut funding to UNRWA. Leaving WHO and defunding UNRWA reduced support for global health and refugee protections, indirectly affecting the rights and welfare of vulnerable populations worldwide. (1 May 2025)

24. Trump administration terminated the Women, Peace and Security program and reshaped military DEI policies. Rolling back gender-focused defense initiatives and DEI efforts in the military narrowed inclusion and signaled reduced institutional commitment to equal opportunity in security forces. (28 Apr 2025; 30 Apr 2025; 1 May 2025)

Economic Structure

1. Trump administration implemented sweeping tariffs and reciprocal tariff policies affecting major trading partners. Broad tariffs on China, Mexico, Canada, steel, aluminum, autos, and reciprocal duties reshaped trade flows, raised consumer costs, and concentrated trade decision-making in the executive branch. (26 Apr 2025; 27 Apr 2025; 28 Apr 2025; 29 Apr 2025; 1 May 2025; 2 May 2025)

2. Trump administration imposed extremely high tariffs on imported solar panels from several Asian countries. Tariffs exceeding 3,000% on solar panels from Vietnam, Cambodia, and Malaysia sharply increased renewable project costs, discouraging clean energy investment while favoring fossil fuel competitors. (2 May 2025)

3. Trump administration closed the de minimis tariff loophole for low-value imports, heavily impacting Chinese exporters. Ending duty-free treatment for small shipments altered e-commerce trade patterns and increased customs burdens, particularly on Chinese-origin goods, as part of a broader tariff escalation. (1 May 2025; 2 May 2025)

4. Trump administration halted disbursement of bipartisan infrastructure funds and froze many renewable energy permits. Stopping infrastructure spending and blocking renewable permits disrupted long-term investment in

public works and clean energy, privileging short-term ideological goals over stable economic planning. (27 Apr 2025; 2 May 2025)

5. President Donald Trump issued executive orders boosting fossil fuel extraction and exempting the sector from some tariffs. Easing restrictions on drilling, coal plants, and exports while shielding fossil fuel firms from tariff burdens advantaged a politically connected industry over environmental and economic diversification goals. (1 May 2025)

6. Trump administration withdrew a salmonella safety rule for poultry after industry lobbying. Rolling back stricter salmonella controls at industry request prioritized corporate cost concerns over public health protections in the food supply. (28 Apr 2025)

7. Department of Government Efficiency and Elon Musk expanded DOGE's role in federal contracting, payments, and regulatory rewrites. Centralizing contract and payment oversight under DOGE and using AI to rewrite regulations shifted core economic governance toward a quasi-private, less accountable structure aligned with favored business interests. (27 Apr 2025; 28 Apr 2025; 1 May 2025; 2 May 2025)

8. Trump administration ended prosecutions under the Foreign Corrupt Practices Act for a defined period. Pausing FCPA cases reduced legal risk for companies engaged in foreign bribery, weakening a key tool against transnational corruption and altering incentives for corporate behavior abroad. (1 May 2025; 2 May 2025)

9. President Donald Trump and family monetized political access through the $TRUMP cryptocurrency contest and the Executive Branch club. Offering dinners, White House tours, and elite networking to top token holders and club members turned proximity to presidential power into a purchasable commodity, blurring public office and private profit. (28 Apr 2025)

10. Trump administration dropped investigations into 89 corporations and closed DOJ's cryptocurrency enforcement unit. Ending numerous corporate cases and shuttering a crypto crime unit signaled that certain financial and corporate offenses would face reduced scrutiny, especially where politically connected actors were involved. (28 Apr 2025; 2 May 2025)

11. Trump administration withdrew from global climate initiatives and climate finance mechanisms. Halting US climate initiatives and leaving international climate funds ceded leadership to other powers and weakened coordinated responses to climate-related economic risks. (26 Apr 2025; 1 May 2025; 2 May 2025)

12. Trump administration used tariffs and enforcement to reshape supply chains, prompting Chinese rare earth export controls. Tariff escalation

contributed to Chinese export controls on rare earths, exposing US dependence on foreign critical minerals and highlighting vulnerabilities in industrial policy. (27 Apr 2025)

13. UPS announced layoffs of about 20,000 workers and closure of 73 facilities amid tariff-driven volume declines. Large-scale job cuts and facility closures at UPS illustrated how trade policy shocks translated into concentrated employment losses in logistics and related sectors. (28 Apr 2025; 1 May 2025)

14. US Bureau of Economic Analysis reported a 0.3% GDP contraction in Q1 2025 linked to tariff timing. The first GDP decline in three years, partly driven by pre-tariff buying surges and subsequent slowdowns, signaled macroeconomic costs of abrupt trade policy changes. (1 May 2025)

15. US Department of Labor recorded an unexpected rise in unemployment claims to the highest level since February. Rising initial and continuing jobless claims pointed to labor-market stress, likely exacerbated by tariff-related disruptions and broader economic uncertainty. (30 Apr 2025)

16. Republican policymakers proposed work requirements for Medicaid and SNAP and maintained a low federal minimum wage. Keeping the minimum wage at $7.25 while adding work requirements to benefits risked pushing vulnerable people off essential programs without improving employment outcomes. (30 Apr 2025)

17. President Donald Trump proposed ending federal taxation on tips instead of raising the minimum wage. Exempting tips from federal income tax offered limited help to the lowest-paid workers and risked entrenching a tipped-wage model that keeps base pay low and incomes unstable. (30 Apr 2025)

18. Trump administration withdrew environmental justice orders and closed related federal offices. Eliminating environmental justice initiatives and grants removed targeted support for communities facing disproportionate pollution burdens, reinforcing inequities in environmental risk. (1 May 2025)

19. Trump administration ended federal benefits for undocumented immigrants without specifying programs. A broad order to cut unspecified benefits for undocumented people threatened access to basic services and deepened economic precarity for already marginalized residents. (1 May 2025)

20. US Department of Agriculture prepared a bailout request for farmers harmed by tariffs. Planning a farmer bailout to offset tariff-driven bankruptcies shifted some trade-policy risks from policymakers and agribusiness onto taxpayers. (27 Apr 2025)

21. Trump administration pressured Amazon to abandon plans to display

tariff impacts on prices. Presidential pressure on a major retailer to avoid showing tariff costs to consumers limited market transparency around policy-driven price increases. (28 Apr 2025)

22. Trump administration withdrew from global leadership roles and favored autocratic regimes over democratic allies. A foreign policy tilt away from democratic alliances toward autocrats altered the geopolitical environment for trade, investment, and rule-based economic cooperation. (30 Apr 2025)

23. US economic commentators and libertarian lawmakers criticized Trump's tariffs and advocated for free trade and state-capacity reforms. Public critiques by libertarians and economists highlighted internal right-of-center opposition to protectionist policies and called for more efficient, less politicized economic governance. (30 Apr 2025)

24. FDA, EPA, FCC, TSA and DEA conducted numerous technical rule-makings and information collections affecting health, environment, and communications. Ongoing regulatory notices on chemicals, fuels, drugs, food safety, and spectrum showed the administrative state continuing routine oversight and public comment processes despite high-level political turbulence. (28 Apr 2025; 30 Apr 2025; 1 May 2025; 2 May 2025)

Information, Memory, and Manipulation

1. Attorney General Pam Bondi and US Department of Justice rescinded protections for journalists' sources and allowed subpoenas and jailing in leak cases. Rolling back DOJ rules that shielded reporters from compelled source disclosure increased legal risks for investigative journalism and could deter whistleblowers from exposing misconduct. (26 Apr 2025; 2 May 2025)

2. President Donald Trump publicly attacked New York Times reporter Peter Baker on Truth Social. Personal insults against a prominent White House correspondent for critical coverage contributed to a hostile environment for independent reporting on presidential actions. (26 Apr 2025)

3. White House Press Office hosted alternative press briefings featuring right-wing influencers and propagandistic questions. Inviting ideologically aligned media figures to shape briefings while sidelining critical outlets helped construct a more controlled, partisan information environment around the presidency. (28 Apr 2025)

4. Trump administration launched the White House Wire website to publish exclusively positive coverage of the president. Creating a government-hosted news-style site aggregating favorable stories and official content

blurred lines between public information and propaganda, competing with independent journalism. (1 May 2025)

5. President Donald Trump signed executive orders cutting federal funding for NPR and PBS and the FCC opened investigations into them. Defunding and investigating public broadcasters on grounds of bias threatened the financial stability and independence of key noncommercial news and educational outlets. (1 May 2025; 2 May 2025)

6. Trump administration and Oklahoma education officials advanced a new curriculum emphasizing Christianity and debunked 2020 election fraud claims. Embedding Christian nationalist narratives and false election claims into state standards used public education to normalize partisan myths and religious bias in civic instruction. (1 May 2025)

7. Trump administration dismissed hundreds of contributors to the National Climate Assessment and cut climate science agencies. Firing NCA contributors and slashing NOAA and FEMA climate capacity undermined the production of authoritative climate data that informs public understanding and policy. (29 Apr 2025; 1 May 2025)

8. US Health and Human Services Department under Robert F. Kennedy Jr. announced changes to vaccine testing and surveillance that conflicted with scientific consensus. Proposed placebo-controlled trials for established vaccines and altered surveillance frameworks risked sowing doubt about vaccine safety and weakening evidence-based public health messaging. (30 Apr 2025)

9. President Donald Trump made false claims about a deported man's gang tattoos despite evidence of photo manipulation. Insisting on debunked tattoo evidence in an interview to justify a controversial deportation showed willingness to rely on falsified imagery to shape public perceptions of security threats. (1 May 2025)

10. US Department of Justice created a weaponization working group to portray investigations of Trump as political persecution. Institutionalizing a narrative that accountability efforts are partisan attacks reframed oversight as illegitimate, undermining trust in neutral law enforcement. (2 May 2025)

11. Trump administration renamed the Gulf of Mexico and Mount Denali through executive order. Changing long-established geographic names by decree used symbolic acts to reshape national memory and identity in line with current leadership's preferences. (1 May 2025)

12. Trump administration fired Doug Emhoff and others from the Holocaust Memorial Museum board. Removing prior appointees from a key historical institution's board allowed the administration to influence how Holocaust memory and lessons are curated for the public. (1 May 2025)

13. Trump administration withdrew environmental justice and climate reporting requirements, reducing public climate information. Rescinding environmental justice orders and missing UN greenhouse gas reporting deadlines limited public access to data on pollution and emissions, weakening informed debate. (1 May 2025)

14. Trump administration and DOGE used AI to draft executive orders and analyze regulations with limited transparency. Algorithmic drafting of legal texts and regulatory rewrites introduced opaque, machine-driven inputs into public policy, complicating citizens' ability to trace responsibility for decisions. (1 May 2025; 2 May 2025)

15. Chinese officials and contractors stole and resold surveillance data collected by the state. The illicit sale of state surveillance data in China illustrated how expansive monitoring systems can be abused, undermining privacy and trust in government data stewardship. (1 May 2025)

16. Indian political parties used deepfakes in election campaigns to influence voters. The routine use of deepfake videos in Indian elections showed how synthetic media can be deployed to mislead voters and erode confidence in authentic political communication. (1 May 2025)

17. Federal Communications Commission held open meetings and sought comment on multiple information collection and broadcasting rules. FCC proceedings on children's programming, numbering, LPFM, and spectrum sharing reflected ongoing procedural avenues for public input into media and communications policy. (29 Apr 2025; 30 Apr 2025; 2 May 2025)

18. President Donald Trump declassified assassination records related to JFK, RFK, and Martin Luther King Jr. Ordering release of long-classified assassination files increased transparency about historic political violence, potentially strengthening public understanding of past abuses. (1 May 2025)

19. Trump administration pressured Amazon not to display tariff impacts and spun economic data to deflect blame. Discouraging a major retailer from labeling tariff costs and publicly blaming predecessors for downturns shaped how citizens perceive the causes of economic hardship. (28 Apr 2025; 1 May 2025)

CHAPTER 16
WEEK 16 (3 MAY 2025 – 9 MAY 2025): STRATIFIED RIGHTS AS ROUTINE GOVERNANCE

With the clock frozen at 7:59 p.m., immigration, media, and the civil service are quietly retooled to sort who is protected, heard, and expendable.

This was a heavily disruptive week for democratic erosion, as the executive branch reinforced its power across media, civil service, immigration, and regulatory areas while courts and some state actors offered partial resistance. The most intense pressures targeted information and media pluralism (VoA shutdown and OAN outsourcing, NPR/PBS defunding, FCC's CBS investigation, Bondi's rollback of leak protections), depoliticization of the civil service (DOGE firings, EPA and NIH purges, hiring freeze, dismantling of safety and consumer agencies), and immigration enforcement (massive ICE buildup, deputization of other agencies, detention policies, self-deportation programs). Crony capitalism and emoluments grew through Trump family crypto and Gulf business deals, large institutional investments in Trump Media, and regulatory influence over mergers and DEI initiatives. Meanwhile, federal courts in North Carolina and in the Öztürk case, state policies in New York and Hawaii, and active lawyers defending the rule of law provided significant counter-pressures. Overall, this week demonstrates an administration using chaos, symbolic nationalism, and targeted law enforcement to solidify a patronage-driven, media-orchestrated presidency, even as institutional safeguards are strained but not yet broken.

Power and Authority

1. Tom Homan threatened to have Wisconsin governor Tony Evers arrested over ICE guidance. The threat to arrest a sitting governor for advising state workers to seek legal counsel before cooperating with ICE signaled an aggressive use of federal immigration power to intimidate state officials and chill policy dissent. (3 May 2025)

2. President Donald Trump pardoned Proud Boys leader Enrique Tarrio. Pardoning a leader convicted of seditious conspiracy for his role in the January 6 attack weakened accountability for political violence against democratic institutions and signaled leniency toward loyalist extremists. (3 May 2025)

3. President Donald Trump announced plans for a large military parade on his birthday. Ordering a massive military parade tied to the president's birthday and national founding symbols used state military power for personal glorification, blurring lines between civic commemoration and leader cult. (3 May 2025)

4. President Donald Trump directed the reopening and expansion of Alcatraz prison for violent offenders. Ordering agencies to reopen Alcatraz as a high-profile prison used punitive symbolism and incarceration policy to project toughness on crime, raising concerns about spectacle-driven criminal justice. (5 May 2025; 6 May 2025)

5. Secretary of Health and Human Services Robert F. Kennedy Jr. shifted federal public health focus away from vaccination toward alternative treatments. Redirecting HHS emphasis from proven vaccines to unproven alternatives undermined evidence-based public health authority and risked weakening population immunity against preventable diseases. (5 May 2025)

6. President Donald Trump questioned whether everyone in the United States is entitled to due process. Publicly expressing uncertainty about universal due process rights signaled a willingness to treat constitutional protections as optional, especially in the context of immigration enforcement. (5 May 2025)

7. President Donald Trump issued an executive order restricting funding for foreign gain-of-function biological research. Halting federal support for risky biological research abroad and demanding oversight of unfunded work expanded executive control over high-risk science in the name of security and transparency. (5 May 2025)

8. President Donald Trump issued an executive order easing regulation to promote domestic production of critical medicines. Directing agencies to relax environmental and regulatory constraints for drug manufacturing

strengthened executive influence over industrial policy and raised questions about balancing supply security with safeguards. (5 May 2025)

9. President Donald Trump asserted broad foreign-affairs authority to justify opaque deportation flights to El Salvador. Invoking expansive foreign-affairs powers and a recent Supreme Court ruling to defend secretive deportation operations normalized emergency-style discretion with limited transparency or oversight. (6 May 2025)

10. President Donald Trump announced a 100% tariff on foreign films and later walked it back. Floating and then softening a sweeping tariff on foreign films as a security measure illustrated erratic use of trade powers that can unsettle markets and cultural exchange while obscuring true policy intent. (4 May 2025; 5 May 2025; 6 May 2025)

11. President Donald Trump publicly refused to rule out using military force to seize Greenland. Suggesting possible military action to claim Greenland, a territory of a NATO ally, challenged norms against territorial aggression and raised concerns about unilateral use of U.S. force. (3 May 2025; 4 May 2025)

12. Secretary of Defense Pete Hegseth ordered a 20% reduction in four-star generals and admirals. Mandating deep cuts to senior military ranks without clear justification restructured command in ways that could weaken professional military leadership and increase susceptibility to politicization. (4 May 2025; 5 May 2025; 7 May 2025)

13. Secretary of Defense Pete Hegseth halted weapons shipments to Ukraine without proper authorization. Unilaterally pausing approved military aid to Ukraine, later reversed, showed a senior official exercising significant war-related discretion outside normal decision channels, complicating foreign commitments. (5 May 2025; 7 May 2025)

14. Secretary of Defense Pete Hegseth declared an end to so-called wokeness in the military in a speech to troops. Framing diversity, climate policy, and vaccine mandates as threats to the armed forces signaled top-down cultural enforcement within the military that could marginalize some service members and politicize service norms. (5 May 2025)

15. President Donald Trump implemented a federal hiring freeze despite critical staffing shortages. Freezing hiring across the federal government, including air traffic control, used executive authority to shrink the civil service even where shortages threaten safety and service delivery. (8 May 2025)

16. Trump administration halted an independent review of air traffic control oversight after a deadly collision. Stopping an outside expert panel's safety review following a fatal crash prioritized political control over trans-

parent investigation, weakening accountability for aviation risks. (8 May 2025)

17. Federal Aviation Administration under the Trump administration approved a fivefold increase in SpaceX launches from Texas despite prior damage. Authorizing many more SpaceX launches while finding no significant environmental impact suggested regulatory deference to a politically connected firm over local environmental and safety concerns. (8 May 2025)

18. White House removed National Transportation Safety Board vice chair Alvin Brown. Ousting the NTSB vice chair, an independent safety official, raised fears of politicizing transportation accident investigations and weakening an important check on executive agencies. (8 May 2025)

19. Trump administration began dismantling the Consumer Product Safety Commission. Moving to dismantle the CPSC reduced federal capacity to police unsafe consumer products, shifting risk to the public and limiting an independent constraint on corporate practices. (8 May 2025)

20. President Donald Trump rescinded federal workplace nondiscrimination guidance protecting gender identity. Revoking guidance that recognized gender identity in federal workplace nondiscrimination narrowed protections for LGBTQ employees and signaled official rejection of prior civil rights interpretations. (9 May 2025)

21. White House blocked Defense Secretary Pete Hegseth's choice of chief of staff and imposed its own pick. Overruling the defense secretary's staffing choice and installing a White House-selected chief of staff increased presidential control over Pentagon decision-making and internal gatekeeping. (9 May 2025)

22. President Donald Trump established the National Center for Warrior Independence for homeless veterans. Creating a large veterans' housing center while directing agencies to redirect funds from services for undocumented immigrants tied social welfare for veterans to cuts for a disfavored group, reinforcing stratified rights. (9 May 2025)

23. President Donald Trump issued an executive order to reduce overcriminalization in federal regulations. Ordering agencies to review and limit regulatory crimes and favor civil enforcement aimed to curb strict-liability offenses, potentially improving fairness but also constraining tools for policing corporate misconduct. (9 May 2025)

Institutions and Governance

1. Trump administration announced plans to cut thousands of jobs at the CIA and other intelligence agencies. Large planned staff reductions at intelligence

agencies, combined with elimination of DEI programs, risked weakening analytic capacity and diversity in institutions central to national security decision-making. (3 May 2025)

2. U.S. Department of Agriculture and the state of Maine reached a settlement restoring previously frozen school funds. Restoring federal education funds frozen over Maine's transgender sports policy reaffirmed legal process requirements and limited the administration's ability to punish states for policy disagreements. (3 May 2025)

3. U.S. Court of Appeals for the DC Circuit stayed a lower court order reinstating Voice of America employees. Allowing the administration's dismantling of USAGM to proceed pending appeal kept over 1,000 VoA staff off the job and deferred judicial protection for a key public broadcaster. (3 May 2025)

4. Judge Beryl Howell permanently struck down Trump's executive order targeting Perkins Coie. Invalidating an order that barred a specific law firm from federal work and buildings reinforced constitutional protections against retaliatory use of executive power to punish disfavored legal advocates. (3 May 2025)

5. Justice Ketanji Brown Jackson publicly warned about political attacks on judges. A sitting Supreme Court justice's remarks underscored how sustained political attacks on the judiciary threaten judicial independence and public confidence in courts as neutral arbiters. (3 May 2025)

6. Trump administration reached a settlement in principle with Ashli Babbitt's family. Settling a high-profile civil suit over a January 6 rioter's death risked signaling special consideration for movement allies and complicating accountability for law enforcement actions during the insurrection. (3 May 2025)

7. U.S. Department of Labor experienced mass resignations and major cuts to international labor grants. Loss of about 20% of Labor Department staff and hundreds of millions in labor grants weakened enforcement of worker protections and reduced U.S. support for labor rights abroad. (3 May 2025)

8. Federal Aviation Administration faced severe air traffic controller shortages causing major delays at Newark. Chronic understaffing and technology failures at a major airport exposed how weakened federal capacity can endanger transportation safety and public confidence in regulatory oversight. (3 May 2025; 4 May 2025)

9. President Donald Trump appointed Alina Habba as interim U.S. Attorney for New Jersey. Installing a controversial loyalist as interim chief

federal prosecutor raised concerns about politicized law enforcement and the use of key legal posts as patronage. (3 May 2025)

10. President Donald Trump appointed Sid Rosenberg to the U.S. Holocaust Memorial Council. Naming a radio host with a record of racist remarks to a Holocaust remembrance body risked undermining the institution's moral authority and politicizing historical memory. (3 May 2025)

11. U.S. Senate and House Republicans blocked a resolution to repeal Trump's tariffs and delayed further consideration. A tied Senate vote broken by the vice president and a House rule delaying action preserved controversial tariffs, highlighting executive leverage over trade and partisan limits on congressional checks. (4 May 2025)

12. Supreme Court of the United States intervened in reinstatement of mass-fired federal workers. High court involvement in DOGE-related firings, including rehiring then re-dismissing workers, contributed to instability in the civil service and uncertainty about legal protections for public employees. (4 May 2025; 5 May 2025)

13. U.S. Office of Special Counsel dropped its inquiry into mass firings of probationary federal workers. Ending an investigation into potentially unlawful dismissals after leadership changes weakened an internal watchdog and reduced avenues for challenging politicized personnel purges. (4 May 2025)

14. Federal court in North Carolina ordered certification of Allison Riggs as winner of the state supreme court race. By blocking retroactive ballot disqualifications and compelling certification, the court protected thousands of votes and upheld stable election rules against partisan manipulation. (5 May 2025; 6 May 2025; 7 May 2025)

15. Supreme Court of the United States allowed Trump's ban on transgender military service to take effect pending litigation. Permitting enforcement of a ban on transgender service members while cases proceed endorsed a discriminatory policy that reshapes who can serve in the armed forces. (5 May 2025; 6 May 2025)

16. Michigan Attorney General Dana Nessel dismissed charges against seven pro-Palestinian protesters while pursuing other cases. Dropping some protest-related charges amid questions about bias, while continuing others, highlighted prosecutorial discretion's role in shaping the legal consequences of campus activism. (5 May 2025)

17. Federal judges criticized Department of Justice lawyers for poor performance defending Trump policies. Judicial complaints about inadequate arguments and noncompliance from DOJ attorneys suggested institu-

tional degradation within the department and reduced capacity to defend or test executive actions. (5 May 2025)

18. Hawaii Legislature and Governor Josh Green approved a bill raising tourist taxes to fund climate resilience. Using targeted taxes to finance environmental protection showed a state leveraging fiscal policy to address climate risks and public goods, independent of federal direction. (5 May 2025)

19. Federal district court and appeals court ordered transfer and then release of detained Turkish student Rümeysa Öztürk. Rulings that moved and then freed a student detained after writing an op-ed affirmed that immigration enforcement cannot be used to punish protected speech and must respect due process. (7 May 2025; 8 May 2025)

20. Senator Susan Collins and the Senate Appropriations Committee held a hearing challenging administration cuts to biomedical research and health agencies. A senior Republican appropriator publicly rebuking executive branch defiance of appropriations language signaled congressional resistance to unilateral health and science funding cuts. (7 May 2025)

21. Secretary of Homeland Security Kristi Noem refused to affirm that the Constitution guarantees due process to everyone. Declining to acknowledge universal due process rights before an appropriations subcommittee echoed the president's stance and raised alarms about executive respect for constitutional limits. (7 May 2025)

22. Trump administration sought a massive multiyear funding increase for ICE via budget reconciliation. Proposing tens of billions to expand ICE detention, transport, and staffing would make immigration enforcement the most heavily funded U.S. law enforcement function, entrenching a powerful internal security apparatus. (7 May 2025)

23. U.S. intelligence agencies issued a memo disputing Trump administration claims about Venezuela-gang ties. An official assessment contradicting White House justifications for invoking the Alien Enemies Act highlighted internal resistance to politicized intelligence used to support harsh migration policies. (7 May 2025)

24. FBI Director Kash Patel failed to submit the FBI budget on time and appeared disengaged from duties. Missing a statutory budget deadline and reports of limited engagement suggested weakened leadership at a key law enforcement agency, complicating congressional oversight and institutional performance. (7 May 2025; 8 May 2025)

25. Trump administration deputized thousands of federal officers from other agencies to assist ICE. Expanding immigration enforcement by cross-designating agents from DEA, FBI, IRS and others blurred agency

missions and concentrated coercive power in service of deportation goals. (7 May 2025)

26. Trump administration required headquarters approval for releasing detained immigrants, causing overcrowding. Centralizing release decisions for detainees increased detention lengths and pushed facilities beyond funded capacity, heightening human rights concerns and reducing local discretion. (7 May 2025)

27. House Committee on Education and the Workforce held hearings on campus antisemitism targeting university leaders. Congressional hearings criticized as politically motivated put pressure on universities to police speech and protest, using oversight powers in ways that may chill academic freedom. (6 May 2025; 7 May 2025)

28. Trump administration froze and threatened to revoke billions in federal funding and tax benefits for Harvard University. Conditioning Harvard's research grants and tax status on compliance with administration demands over campus protests weaponized federal levers to coerce a private university's policies. (6 May 2025)

29. Trump administration announced deep staffing and budget cuts at the Environmental Protection Agency. Reducing EPA staff to 1980s levels, dissolving its research office, and forcing staff to reapply for fewer jobs undermined independent environmental science and enforcement capacity. (6 May 2025)

30. Department of Government Efficiency (DOGE) faced multiple lawsuits alleging illegal consolidation of personal data. Privacy Act suits over DOGE's mass aggregation of citizen data challenged a powerful new data hub that could enable expanded surveillance with weak safeguards. (8 May 2025)

31. American Bar Association sued Donald Trump over termination of federal grants. The ABA's lawsuit contested the administration's move to cut its federal funding, testing whether the executive can financially punish a major professional body over policy disagreements. (9 May 2025)

32. Indiana Governor Mike Braun and state legislature enacted a law threatening nonprofit hospitals' tax-exempt status over high prices. Linking hospital tax exemptions to pricing benchmarks created a novel state tool to discipline powerful health systems and potentially reshape nonprofit accountability. (9 May 2025)

33. Los Angeles County Superior Court scheduled a resentencing hearing for the Menendez brothers. Reopening sentencing in a decades-old high-profile murder case reflected evolving judicial approaches to long-term incarceration and claims of abuse, with implications for precedent and public trust. (9 May 2025)

Civil Rights and Dissent

1. Swarthmore Borough Police and Swarthmore College administration disbanded a pro-Palestinian encampment and arrested nine activists. Calling in local police to clear a campus encampment and arrest protesters over divestment demands highlighted how institutional rules and law enforcement can constrain student protest. (3 May 2025)

2. Approximately 1,500 lawyers and supporters protested outside Manhattan federal courthouse in defense of rule of law. A large demonstration by legal professionals underscored organized civil society resistance to perceived attacks on judicial independence and constitutional norms. (3 May 2025)

3. Michigan Attorney General Dana Nessel dropped charges against University of Michigan pro-Palestinian encampment protesters. Ending prosecutions of some campus protesters amid allegations of bias reduced immediate legal pressure on demonstrators but left questions about selective enforcement and remaining cases. (5 May 2025)

4. University of Washington and law enforcement agencies arrested more than two dozen pro-Palestinian protesters occupying a campus building. Clearing an occupied engineering building with arrests and property-damage charges showed how universities and police respond to disruptive protest tactics tied to foreign policy demands. (6 May 2025)

5. Federal court and ICE detained and then ordered the transfer and release of Turkish student Rümeysa Öztürk. Detaining a student after an op-ed and then releasing her on First Amendment and due process grounds illustrated both the vulnerability of noncitizen speech and the judiciary's role in protecting it. (7 May 2025; 8 May 2025)

6. New York Police Department and Columbia University arrested dozens of pro-Palestinian protesters occupying the main library. Authorizing police to clear a library occupation and arrest about 75 activists over divestment demands highlighted escalating use of law enforcement to manage campus political conflict. (8 May 2025)

7. Federal agents and Newark Mayor Ras Baraka arrested the mayor during a protest outside an ICE detention center. Charging a sitting mayor with trespassing while he protested ICE operations and asserted local jurisdiction raised serious concerns about federal suppression of local officials' dissent. (8 May 2025)

8. Trump administration expanded deportation flights to El Salvador including legally residing migrants. Deporting people who were legally present and compliant with immigration rules, justified by disputed security

claims, showed how enforcement can strip rights from targeted groups. (6 May 2025)

9. Trump administration offered cash and airfare for undocumented immigrants to self-deport. A self-deportation program that downplayed long reentry bans used financial inducements and ambiguous messaging to encourage vulnerable residents to relinquish their place in U.S. society. (7 May 2025)

10. General Services Administration rescinded federal workplace nondiscrimination guidance on gender identity. Rolling back recognition of gender identity in federal nondiscrimination guidance weakened protections for transgender employees and signaled official endorsement of narrower civil rights coverage. (9 May 2025)

Economic Structure

1. Former President Donald Trump imposed a 25% import tax on auto parts affecting repair costs. Tariffs on auto parts risked raising repair and maintenance costs for consumers, illustrating how trade policy choices can function as regressive taxes and reshape industrial incentives. (3 May 2025)

2. U.S. Commerce Department released Q1 2025 GDP data that was widely misinterpreted as imports harming growth. Official framing and media repetition of a misleading narrative about imports subtracting from GDP risked distorting public understanding of trade and justifying protectionist policies. (3 May 2025)

3. Federal Communications Commission Commissioner Brendan Carr opposed a Verizon-Frontier merger over Verizon's DEI policies. Conditioning merger approval on rollback of corporate DEI programs used regulatory power to pressure private entities on internal equity policies, intertwining culture-war aims with market oversight. (4 May 2025)

4. Freight Technologies announced plans to buy $20 million of Trump Crypto to influence trade policy. A logistics firm's large purchase of a president-branded cryptocurrency to sway trade decisions exemplified how financial instruments tied to officeholders can become channels for policy influence. (4 May 2025)

5. President Donald Trump announced a 100% tariff on foreign films as a national security measure. Proposing to double the cost of all foreign films framed cultural imports as security threats, with major implications for global trade, cultural exchange, and domestic media markets. (4 May 2025; 5 May 2025)

6. World Liberty Financial and MGX (Abu Dhabi government-owned)

facilitated a $2 billion Binance investment using a Trump family stablecoin. A foreign state-owned investor's use of a Trump-family crypto product in a major deal raised concerns that foreign governments can buy goodwill and access through the president's private ventures. (5 May 2025)

7. Trump Organization and Dar Global announced a Trump-branded hotel and tower project in Dubai. Launching a new luxury project with a Saudi-linked firm while Trump is in office deepened entanglements between U.S. foreign policy interests and the president's private real estate brand. (5 May 2025)

8. Trump Organization, Dar Global, and Qatari Diar entered a $5.5 billion deal to build a Trump golf club in Qatar. Partnering directly with a Qatari government-owned company appeared to violate Trump's ethics pledge and exemplified foreign governments channeling money into the president's businesses. (5 May 2025; 6 May 2025)

9. Paramount Global leadership altered DEI policies and sought to settle Trump lawsuit amid merger talks. Adjusting corporate diversity initiatives and litigation strategy to ease FCC approval for a merger showed how regulatory leverage and presidential lawsuits can reshape corporate governance. (6 May 2025)

10. Secretary of the Treasury Scott Bessent evaded answering who ultimately pays tariffs during a House hearing. Refusing to acknowledge consumer costs of tariffs obscured the distributional impact of trade policy and hindered informed public debate about economic burdens. (7 May 2025)

11. Trump administration offered $1,000 and airfare to undocumented immigrants who self-deport. Paying undocumented residents to leave, while downplaying long reentry bans, used financial incentives and incomplete information to encourage departures that may permanently sever community ties. (7 May 2025)

12. New York Governor Kathy Hochul enacted middle-class tax cuts and inflation refund checks. State-level tax relief and direct payments aimed to cushion residents from inflation, illustrating how subnational fiscal policy can counter national economic shocks. (6 May 2025)

13. New York State government approved free school meals for all public school students. Guaranteeing universal free school meals reduced food insecurity and household costs, expanding a key social welfare program at the state level. (6 May 2025)

14. Trump administration imposed broad tariffs on Chinese goods, affecting firms like Mattel and Ford. Escalating tariffs on U.S.–China trade forced major companies to raise prices and reconfigure supply chains,

demonstrating how trade wars can reverberate through consumer markets and industrial planning. (6 May 2025)

15. Trump administration imposed global and sector-specific tariffs on multiple trading partners on "Liberation Day". A sweeping 10% global tariff plus higher rates on steel, aluminum, and autos jolted markets and signaled a willingness to use trade shocks as a political tool. (8 May 2025)

16. Elon Musk's Department of Government Efficiency implemented deep cuts to USAID funding and staff. Slashing USAID budgets and staff, leading to expiring medicines and halted HIV programs, weakened U.S. support for global health and stability in vulnerable regions. (8 May 2025)

17. Institutional investors significantly increased holdings in Trump Media despite losses. Large investments in a loss-making company closely tied to the president raised concerns that capital is being deployed to buy political favor rather than economic value. (8 May 2025)

18. Trump administration cut thousands of NIH employees including National Cancer Institute staff. Firing large numbers of NIH researchers, on top of earlier mass dismissals, undermined federal biomedical research capacity and long-term public health innovation. (5 May 2025)

19. Trump administration fired thousands of probationary federal workers and eased rules for dismissing them. Mass firings orchestrated through DOGE and an order expanding discretion to terminate probationary staff destabilized the civil service and made it easier to purge perceived ideological opponents. (4 May 2025)

20. Trump administration blocked federal research grants and aid to Harvard University. Freezing billions in research funds to pressure Harvard over protest-related demands used economic leverage to discipline an academic institution's governance and speech environment. (6 May 2025)

21. Trump administration terminated numerous NEA grants and proposed eliminating the agency. Canceling arts grants and seeking to abolish the NEA, while steering remaining funds toward projects aligned with the president's vision, reduced support for diverse cultural expression. (4 May 2025)

22. Trump administration cut EPA budget and dissolved its Office of Research and Development. Eliminating a core EPA science office and forcing staff to compete for fewer roles weakened environmental research and increased the risk of policy capture by regulated industries. (6 May 2025)

23. Trump administration proposed a 25% cut to NASA's budget while funding Mars initiatives. Slashing NASA's overall budget while prioritizing Mars projects shifted resources away from broader scientific missions, potentially weakening U.S. space leadership and basic research. (8 May 2025)

Information, Memory, and Manipulation

1. President Donald Trump issued an executive order cutting NPR and PBS off from federal funding. Blocking public broadcasters from CPB funds threatened the viability of noncommercial news and educational programming, especially in rural areas reliant on federal support. (4 May 2025)

2. President Donald Trump signed an executive order dismantling USAGM and shutting down Voice of America. Taking VoA off the air and placing 1,300 staff on leave silenced a longstanding U.S. international broadcaster and concentrated control over state-funded foreign news. (7 May 2025)

3. Voice of America leadership under USAGM contracted One America News to provide newsfeed and video services. Replacing VoA's own journalists with content from a hard-right outlet shifted a government-funded broadcaster toward partisan narratives and away from its neutral mandate. (7 May 2025)

4. Patsy Widakuswara filed a lawsuit challenging Trump's order defunding Voice of America. A VoA bureau chief's suit argued that cutting congressionally approved funding violated press freedom and separation of powers, testing judicial protection for government journalists. (5 May 2025)

5. Federal Communications Commission under Chairman Brendan Carr opened a news distortion investigation into CBS News after a 60 Minutes interview. Launching an unprecedented content-based probe that could threaten CBS's license used broadcast regulation to pressure a critical outlet, chilling editorial independence. (6 May 2025)

6. Bill Owens and Paramount Global leadership saw a 60 Minutes producer resign after corporate intervention in Trump coverage. A senior producer's resignation following owner review of Trump stories highlighted how corporate and political pressures can shape news content even without formal censorship. (6 May 2025)

7. Attorney General Pam Bondi rolled back protections for the press in leak investigations. Weakening safeguards for journalists in leak probes expanded the government's ability to surveil and punish sources and reporters covering sensitive national security issues. (7 May 2025)

8. Director of National Intelligence Tulsi Gabbard criticized the Wall Street Journal for reporting on Greenland intelligence activities. Accusing a major newspaper of politicizing and leaking classified information over Greenland spying stories framed investigative reporting as a threat to democracy and security. (7 May 2025)

9. TeleMessage and Smarsh suspended a secure messaging app used by officials after a suspected hack. A breach of an app used for sensitive govern-

ment communications exposed vulnerabilities in official messaging systems and raised questions about the security of national security discussions. (5 May 2025; 6 May 2025)

10. President Donald Trump posted an AI-generated image of himself as pope on official channels. Sharing an AI image depicting himself as pope during a papal transition used synthetic media for self-branding, offending some believers and illustrating how leaders can manipulate symbolism. (4 May 2025)

11. Former President Donald Trump publicly insulted Representative Jasmine Crockett with derogatory language. Using personal attacks against a Black congresswoman contributed to a hostile political discourse that delegitimizes opponents rather than engaging their arguments. (3 May 2025)

12. National Endowment for the Arts under Trump appointees terminated many grants and shifted priorities toward "American heritage" projects. Refocusing federal arts funding away from DEI initiatives toward projects aligned with the president's cultural vision narrowed publicly supported narratives and representation. (4 May 2025)

13. House of Representatives passed a bill to rename the Gulf of Mexico as the Gulf of America. Symbolically renaming a major body of water advanced nationalist branding through legislation, illustrating how political power can be used to reshape geographic memory. (4 May 2025; 8 May 2025)

14. Heather Cox Richardson and other reporters documented Trump family cryptocurrency ventures involving foreign nationals. Revelations that foreign nationals barred from campaign donations invested in Trump-linked crypto highlighted opaque financial channels that can circumvent campaign finance norms. (6 May 2025)

15. Bureau of Economic Analysis and major media outlets framed GDP data in ways that reinforced misconceptions about imports. Persisting in language that treats imports as a drag on GDP, and media echoing it, risked entrenching misunderstandings that can be exploited to justify protectionist or nationalist policies. (3 May 2025)

CHAPTER 17
WEEK 17 (10 MAY 2025 – 16 MAY 2025): CITIZENSHIP AS LEVERAGE

A week of near-static clock time in which law, borders, and money were quietly retooled to sort belonging and shield power from consequence.

This was an exceptionally heavy week of authoritarian pressure across multiple pillars of U.S. democracy. The most urgent threats center around the rule of law, immigration, and foreign influence. The administration openly considers suspending habeas corpus and due process for migrants, leverages the Alien Enemies Act, and directs DOJ to "name and shame" political opponents while preparing investigations of prosecutors who charged Trump. Immigration enforcement is linked with political repression: ICE misleads courts to raid student activists, DHS suggests classifying migrants as an "invasion," and the deployment of the National Guard for immigration issues is being considered. At the same time, a complex network of foreign money and arms deals—Qatar's $400 million jet, a $5.5 billion Trump-branded golf project, large Saudi and Qatari arms shipments, and sanctions relief for Syria tied to Trump-branded real estate—pushes emoluments and crony capitalism into focus. Civil society and the media face pressure through mass firings at Voice of America, exclusion of reporters from Air Force One, campus crackdowns, and new tools to revoke nonprofits' tax status. Courts and some states resist deportations, health budget cuts, and retaliation against grants, but overall, the structural pressure remains strongly negative.

Power and Authority

1. White House deputy chief of staff Stephen Miller suggested suspending the writ of habeas corpus. A senior White House official floated suspending habeas corpus, signaling willingness to curtail core constitutional protections against arbitrary detention in the name of security. (10 May 2025)

2. President Donald Trump planned to accept a $400 million luxury jet from the Qatari royal family for use as Air Force One and later his library. Trump's plan to accept a $400m jet from Qatar for presidential and later personal use blurred the line between public office and private enrichment, raising serious emoluments and foreign influence concerns. (10 May 2025; 11 May 2025; 12 May 2025; 13 May 2025; 14 May 2025)

3. President Donald Trump rarely attended in-person daily intelligence briefings during his second term. Trump's minimal participation in intelligence briefings reduced informed oversight of security agencies and weakened accountable decision-making on national security threats. (10 May 2025)

4. President Donald Trump implemented sweeping cuts to the federal government and pursued deportations sometimes in defiance of court orders. Trump's deep federal cuts combined with deportations that at times ignored court rulings strained state capacity and signaled disregard for judicial constraints on executive power. (12 May 2025)

5. President Donald Trump ended a 31-day bombing campaign against the Houthis in Yemen and declared victory. Halting the Yemen bombing campaign after limited success highlighted unilateral executive control over overseas military force with little public debate or congressional constraint. (13 May 2025)

6. President Donald Trump and Health Secretary Robert F. Kennedy Jr. announced an administration plan and executive order to tie U.S. drug prices to lower foreign prices. The administration used executive authority to reshape drug pricing, asserting strong centralized control over a major economic and public health domain normally shared with Congress and regulators. (11 May 2025; 12 May 2025)

7. President Donald Trump shut down the CBP One app used by migrants to schedule asylum appointments. Closing the CBP One app removed a key lawful channel for asylum processing, concentrating discretionary power at the border and increasing migrants' exposure to arbitrary enforcement. (13 May 2025)

8. President Donald Trump lifted nearly 50-year-old U.S. sanctions on Syria following Gulf consultations. Ending long-standing Syria sanctions in a context of prospective Trump-branded real estate deals raised concerns that

personal business interests were steering coercive foreign policy tools. (12 May 2025; 13 May 2025)

9. President Donald Trump promised Saudi Arabia $142 billion in advanced U.S. defense and security equipment. Trump's commitment to a massive Saudi arms package deepened security dependence on an authoritarian partner and tied U.S. defense policy to lucrative weapons exports. (13 May 2025; 14 May 2025)

10. President Donald Trump publicly questioned whether people in the U.S. have a right to due process. Trump's televised doubt about the constitutional right to due process undermined public understanding of a core safeguard against arbitrary state power. (16 May 2025)

11. Department of Justice weaponization working group head Ed Martin announced a policy to publicly name and shame political opponents who cannot be charged. DOJ's new practice of publicly stigmatizing uncharged political targets repurposed prosecutorial authority into a tool of reputational punishment outside normal legal process. (15 May 2025)

12. Director of National Intelligence Tulsi Gabbard fired the National Intelligence Council chair and deputy after a report contradicted Trump's claims on Venezuela. Removing top intelligence analysts for producing findings at odds with presidential narratives signaled political control over intelligence and discouraged independent threat assessment. (15 May 2025)

Institutions and Governance

1. California Fish and Game Commission began a mandatory review of Channel Islands marine protected areas. The commission's review of marine protections illustrated routine regulatory governance balancing ecological stewardship with economic interests through a structured public process. (10 May 2025)

2. Representatives Dina Titus and Ilhan Omar introduced the Evidence-Based Drug Policy Act of 2025 to ease research limits on Schedule I substances. The bill sought to remove statutory barriers to studying Schedule I drugs, strengthening evidence-based policymaking over ideologically driven restrictions. (10 May 2025)

3. House Judiciary Committee Republicans summoned former special counsel prosecutor Jay Bratt to testify about Trump prosecutions. Calling a former special counsel prosecutor to defend charging decisions signaled partisan pressure on prosecutorial independence and ongoing efforts to reframe accountability as persecution. (10 May 2025; 14 May 2025)

4. FBI Director Kash Patel appeared at a Senate budget hearing without a

required 2025 spending plan. The FBI director's failure to provide a timely budget plan hindered congressional oversight of a key law enforcement agency's priorities and resource use. (10 May 2025)

5. Senator Chris Murphy criticized Homeland Security for reckless spending that risked Anti-Deficiency Act violations. Murphy's warning that DHS spending could breach fiscal law highlighted tensions between aggressive enforcement agendas and statutory budget constraints. (10 May 2025)

6. President Donald Trump nominated Casey Means, an unlicensed physician with anti-vaccine views, as surgeon general. Selecting an unlicensed, anti-vaccine figure for surgeon general prioritized ideological loyalty over expertise in a role central to public health guidance. (10 May 2025)

7. President Donald Trump withdrew Ed Martin's nomination as U.S. attorney and reassigned him to powerful DOJ roles while nominating Jeanine Pirro. After opposition to a partisan U.S. attorney nominee, Trump placed him in influential non-confirmed DOJ posts and tapped a loyal media ally for the job, sidestepping Senate scrutiny. (10 May 2025)

8. House Energy and Commerce Committee Republicans proposed $880 billion in Medicaid cuts to help fund extension of 2017 tax cuts. The committee's plan to slash Medicaid for millions to finance tax cuts for higher earners reflected legislative priorities favoring fiscal relief for the wealthy over health coverage for low-income residents. (12 May 2025; 14 May 2025; 15 May 2025)

9. House Armed Services Committee members from both parties advanced a $150 billion increase in military spending as part of reconciliation. Bipartisan support for a large defense hike within reconciliation underscored how security budgets can expand with limited scrutiny even as social programs face cuts. (12 May 2025)

10. Federal courts approved multiple large patent-review-period determinations for drugs and biologics. FDA determinations on regulatory review periods for numerous drugs set the stage for extended patents, reinforcing the legal framework that grants pharmaceutical firms long market exclusivity. (12 May 2025; 14 May 2025)

11. House Ways and Means Committee Republicans drafted a reconciliation bill to extend Trump tax cuts while cutting social and climate programs. The reconciliation draft paired permanent tax relief for higher earners with deep reductions to Medicaid, SNAP, and climate incentives, entrenching a fiscal structure that favors capital over social protection. (14 May 2025)

12. House Republicans proposed a tax bill altering the child tax credit and excluding many low-income and undocumented families. By conditioning full child tax credits on higher earnings and Social Security numbers, the bill

would deny benefits to millions of poor and mixed-status families, embedding status-based inequality into the tax code. (14 May 2025)

13. Republican lawmakers sought authority to revoke tax-exempt status of nonprofits deemed terrorist-supporting in a major tax bill. A proposed power to strip nonprofits' tax status based on broad terrorism labels risked enabling partisan punishment of civil society groups critical of the government. (14 May 2025; 15 May 2025)

14. Health and Human Services Secretary Robert F. Kennedy Jr. testified in Congress defending deep health budget cuts and faced questions on vaccines. Kennedy's defense of large health cuts and evasiveness on vaccines highlighted how partisan budget priorities and skepticism of science can reshape federal health institutions. (14 May 2025; 15 May 2025)

15. House Republicans from New York formed a bloc to demand higher SALT deductions in exchange for supporting the budget bill. A small GOP faction leveraged the narrow House majority to seek tax relief for high-tax-state constituents, illustrating intra-party bargaining that can reshape national fiscal legislation. (14 May 2025)

16. House Budget Committee rejected a major reconciliation bill backed by Trump and GOP leadership. The committee's rejection of Trump's flagship spending bill exposed internal Republican divisions that temporarily slowed enactment of sweeping fiscal and immigration changes. (15 May 2025; 16 May 2025)

17. Senate Democratic leader Chuck Schumer placed a hold on Justice Department nominations over the Qatar jet gift. Schumer's blanket hold on DOJ nominees used Senate confirmation powers to demand transparency and constitutional justification for the Qatar aircraft arrangement. (13 May 2025)

18. Republican senators remained silent after Stephen Miller's suggestion of suspending habeas corpus. GOP senators' refusal to repudiate talk of suspending habeas corpus signaled weakening legislative resistance to extreme expansions of executive detention power. (13 May 2025)

19. Twenty Democratic-led states sued to block federal cuts to grants for jurisdictions limiting immigration cooperation. States turned to the courts to resist federal attempts to coerce local immigration policy through grant cuts, asserting federalism limits on executive punishment of disfavored jurisdictions. (13 May 2025)

20. Federal grand jury indicted Wisconsin Judge Hannah Dugan for allegedly obstructing an ICE arrest. Indicting a sitting state judge over courtroom handling of an immigration case raised alarms that federal prosecutors

were using criminal charges to intimidate the judiciary. (13 May 2025; 15 May 2025)

21. Judge Hannah Dugan moved to dismiss her indictment on constitutional and judicial immunity grounds. Dugan's motion argued that prosecuting her for courtroom decisions violated judicial independence, forcing courts to confront limits on executive power over judges. (15 May 2025)

22. Conservative judge J. Michael Luttig publicly warned that Trump was weaponizing the federal government and undermining the rule of law. A prominent conservative jurist's critique of Trump's use of state power lent cross-partisan credibility to concerns about erosion of legal constraints on the executive. (15 May 2025)

23. U.S. Supreme Court heard consolidated challenges to Trump's executive order restricting birthright citizenship. The Court's review of an order limiting citizenship for U.S.-born children of noncitizens put the constitutional scope of the 14th Amendment and presidential power over membership on the line. (14 May 2025; 15 May 2025)

24. U.S. Supreme Court blocked the Trump administration's attempt to deport alleged gang members without due process under the Alien Enemies Act. By requiring meaningful notice and legal challenge opportunities before deportation, the Court reaffirmed due process limits on emergency-style immigration removals. (15 May 2025; 16 May 2025)

25. Federal judge in South Dakota granted a preliminary injunction preventing deportation of Indian PhD graduate Priya Saxena. The injunction shielding a student from deportation over a minor traffic offense showed courts acting as a check on overbroad immigration enforcement. (16 May 2025)

26. Federal courts ordered the release of several international students detained for pro-Palestinian activism. Judges in multiple cases freed foreign students held over political speech, signaling judicial resistance to using immigration law as a tool to suppress campus dissent. (14 May 2025)

27. Federal judge rejected an injunction to stop IRS sharing immigrants' tax records with ICE. Allowing IRS-ICE data sharing to continue expanded the state's ability to repurpose confidential tax information for immigration enforcement, weakening privacy protections. (12 May 2025)

28. Judge Aileen Cannon dismissed the Mar-a-Lago classified documents case by ruling the special counsel unlawfully appointed. Throwing out the documents case on novel appointment grounds shielded Trump from trial and raised concerns that judicial doctrine was being stretched to favor a former president. (14 May 2025)

29. Appeals court allowed CREW to investigate Elon Musk's Department

of Government Efficiency. The ruling permitting watchdog scrutiny of a new government efficiency department supported transparency and external oversight of novel executive structures. (14 May 2025)

30. Federal judge temporarily blocked the administration from canceling ABA grants for domestic and sexual violence training. By halting grant cancellations seen as retaliation, the court protected funding for legal services and signaled limits on punishing organizations for their advocacy. (14 May 2025)

31. U.S. Department of Justice civil rights division leadership asked departing civil rights attorneys to stay or return amid mass exits and reassignments. DOJ's scramble to retain civil rights lawyers after politicized reshuffling revealed internal strain that could weaken enforcement of anti-discrimination laws. (14 May 2025)

32. Trump administration fired Shira Perlmutter, head of the U.S. Copyright Office, after an AI report. Removing the copyright chief soon after she issued a cautious AI report suggested political interference in a technical office expected to provide independent legal analysis. (12 May 2025)

33. House Appropriations subcommittee witnesses requested increased funding for judges' security amid rising threats. Judicial leaders' plea for more security funding underscored how escalating threats can endanger judges and, by extension, the independence of the courts. (15 May 2025)

34. House Homeland Security Committee held a hearing where DHS Secretary Kristi Noem refused to answer questions on deportations of U.S. citizens. Noem's stonewalling on wrongful deportations limited congressional oversight of DHS and obscured potential abuses in citizenship determinations. (15 May 2025)

35. Federal Election Assistance Commission sought public comment on voting system testing and financial reporting information collections. EAC's moves to refine data collection on voting systems and grant spending aimed to strengthen technical integrity and transparency in election administration. (15 May 2025; 16 May 2025)

36. Federal Election Commission announced a closed Sunshine Act meeting on personnel and civil matters. The FEC's notice of a closed meeting under Sunshine Act exceptions reflected routine governance of sensitive enforcement and personnel issues within election oversight. (15 May 2025)

37. Harvard Law School confirmed that a long-overlooked document is an original 1300 Magna Carta. Identifying an original Magna Carta in a U.S. archive highlighted enduring legal roots of rule-of-law and due process principles that underpin modern democratic institutions. (16 May 2025)

Civil Rights and Dissent

1. Federal judge in Vermont ordered the release of Turkish student Rümeysa Öztürk from immigration detention. The court found insufficient grounds for Öztürk's detention, reinforcing due process protections for immigrants targeted over political speech. (10 May 2025)

2. Newark Mayor Ras Baraka and Homeland Security agents clashed when Baraka was arrested while protesting outside an ICE detention facility. Arresting a sitting mayor at a peaceful protest against a private detention operator signaled federal readiness to criminalize local dissent over immigration policy. (10 May 2025)

3. Department of Homeland Security spokesperson threatened possible arrests of Democratic members of Congress for oversight visits to an ICE facility. DHS's threat to arrest lawmakers conducting oversight blurred lines between law enforcement and partisan intimidation, chilling legislative scrutiny of detention conditions. (10 May 2025)

4. Tennessee Highway Patrol and ICE conducted traffic-stop sweeps that led to 103 people being turned over to immigration authorities. The large-scale transfer of motorists to ICE after targeted stops raised concerns about racial profiling and the use of routine policing to feed immigration crackdowns. (10 May 2025)

5. New York City police and Columbia University arrested student protesters and briefly suspended student journalists covering Gaza protests. Arrests of campus protesters and suspensions of student reporters highlighted tensions between university order, free expression, and press freedom in political protests. (10 May 2025)

6. Pentagon leadership ordered military academies to disregard race, ethnicity, and sex in admissions while allowing athletic preferences. The directive to strip DEI considerations from academy admissions, while preserving athletic exceptions, threatened to reduce diversity in officer pipelines and reshape military representation. (10 May 2025)

7. Pentagon and Department of Defense Education Activity ordered removal of DEI and gender ideology books from military and base school libraries worldwide. Purging hundreds of books on diversity and gender from military-linked libraries narrowed the information environment for service members and families, curbing exposure to equality-focused ideas. (10 May 2025)

8. Trump administration ended Temporary Protected Status for Afghan nationals in the U.S. Terminating TPS for Afghans under Taliban rule

exposed thousands to possible return to unsafe conditions, reflecting a hard line on humanitarian protection. (12 May 2025)

9. Trump administration offered refugee status to a group of white South Africans despite a general suspension of refugee resettlement. Granting an exception for white South Africans while broader refugee programs were frozen suggested racially selective application of humanitarian protections. (11 May 2025)

10. House Energy and Commerce Committee and Capitol Police saw disability rights activists protesting Medicaid cuts arrested inside the Capitol. Arresting disabled protesters opposing Medicaid cuts inside Congress underscored how security rules can be used to suppress visible dissent over life-sustaining programs. (14 May 2025)

11. South Carolina Supreme Court upheld a six-week abortion ban against a challenge by Planned Parenthood. The unanimous ruling cemented one of the nation's earliest abortion cutoffs, sharply restricting reproductive autonomy and reinforcing a regional patchwork of rights. (14 May 2025)

12. Hasan Piker and U.S. Customs and Border Protection were involved in a secondary inspection where Piker was questioned about his political views. Border agents' questioning of a U.S. commentator about his opinions on Trump and Gaza suggested use of entry controls to intimidate critics and chill speech. (12 May 2025)

13. Trump administration ordered the FBI to shift one-third of its resources from white-collar crime to immigration enforcement. Redirecting FBI effort away from financial crimes toward immigration crackdowns prioritized policing vulnerable migrants over investigating elite wrongdoing. (12 May 2025)

14. Ben Cohen and U.S. Capitol Police clashed when Cohen was arrested for protesting Gaza blockade and Medicaid cuts during a Senate hearing. The arrest of a prominent business figure for a peaceful disruption at a hearing highlighted limits on protest inside Congress and the risks activists face when linking foreign policy and domestic welfare. (15 May 2025)

15. Trump administration fired nearly 600 Voice of America contractors, many foreign journalists, despite a court order. Mass firings at VOA gutted an independent U.S.-funded news outlet and left many journalists facing deportation, weakening both press freedom and protection for critics of authoritarian regimes. (16 May 2025)

16. State Department directed universities to report international students and scholars involved in certain protests deemed antisemitic or terrorist-related. Requiring universities to flag foreign students engaged in contentious

protests turned immigration status into leverage against campus speech and academic freedom. (16 May 2025)

17. Trump administration issued executive orders allowing deportation or exclusion of non-citizens based on political and cultural viewpoints, including broad definitions of antisemitism. New orders enabling immigration penalties for disfavored viewpoints weaponized entry and deportation powers against ideological expression, especially criticism of Israeli policy. (15 May 2025)

18. Homeland Security Secretary Kristi Noem suggested migrants could be deemed a rebellion or invasion to justify suspending habeas corpus. Framing migrant flows as an invasion to suspend habeas corpus signaled intent to strip basic court access from a targeted population under emergency rhetoric. (14 May 2025; 15 May 2025)

19. Trump administration sought to deport Venezuelan migrants accused of gang affiliation under the Alien Enemies Act. Using an 18th-century wartime statute to fast-track deportations of Venezuelans stretched emergency powers into immigration enforcement, raising due process and discrimination concerns. (13 May 2025)

20. Trump administration conducted ICE raids in Nashville that triggered an exodus of restaurant workers. High-profile ICE raids that emptied local workplaces illustrated how aggressive enforcement can destabilize communities and deter immigrants from participating in public life. (15 May 2025)

21. ICE agents obtained a search warrant under allegedly false pretenses to target Columbia students for pro-Palestinian activism. ICE's use of a misleading warrant to access student housing for arrests showed law enforcement tools being bent to suppress political activism under the guise of immigration enforcement. (16 May 2025)

22. U.S. Secret Service and DHS investigated former FBI Director James Comey over an Instagram post interpreted as a threat to Trump. Launching a threat investigation over ambiguous social media imagery by a Trump critic risked turning protective services into instruments for policing political expression. (14 May 2025; 15 May 2025; 16 May 2025)

23. Bruce Springsteen used a concert to denounce attacks on democratic principles and due process in the U.S. Springsteen's public criticism of deportations without due process and ideological pressure on institutions exemplified cultural figures mobilizing speech to defend democratic norms. (16 May 2025)

24. Omaha voters elected Democrat John Ewing as the city's first Black mayor over a Trump-aligned incumbent. Omaha's election of its first Black

mayor signaled local electoral pushback against Trumpism and modestly broadened representation in municipal leadership. (15 May 2025)

Economic Structure

1. House Republicans proposed changes to the federal retirement system to cut long-term costs. Plans to raise contributions and alter pensions for federal workers shifted fiscal burdens onto public servants, potentially weakening the attractiveness and independence of the civil service. (10 May 2025)

2. Columbia University and NewYork-Presbyterian Hospital agreed to a $750 million settlement with victims of gynecologist Robert Hadden. The large settlement and new safety policies represented institutional accountability for long-ignored abuse, showing civil litigation's role in checking powerful organizations. (10 May 2025)

3. Trump administration considered tariff exemptions for childcare and baby products after steep China tariffs. Contemplating carve-outs for baby goods after broad tariff hikes illustrated ad hoc trade policymaking that can create uncertainty for consumers and businesses. (10 May 2025)

4. President Donald Trump announced a 100% tariff on all foreign-produced movies. Imposing a blanket tariff on foreign films politicized cultural trade and risked retaliatory measures, with potential chilling effects on cross-border cultural exchange. (10 May 2025)

5. Trump Organization and foreign partners advanced 20 new Trump-branded real estate projects in nine countries during Trump's presidency. The rapid expansion of Trump-branded projects abroad while he held office deepened conflicts between private profit-seeking and impartial foreign policy. (10 May 2025; 13 May 2025)

6. U.S. Department of Energy announced elimination of 47 energy efficiency regulations for appliances. Rolling back appliance efficiency standards favored short-term industry savings over long-term consumer costs and environmental benefits, reflecting deregulatory capture. (12 May 2025)

7. President Donald Trump issued an executive order temporarily reducing tariffs on Chinese imports to 10–30% as part of trade talks. Trump's order to pause and lower China tariffs after earlier steep hikes exemplified volatile trade policy that unsettles markets and supply chains. (10 May 2025; 11 May 2025; 12 May 2025; 13 May 2025; 14 May 2025; 15 May 2025)

8. Food and Drug Administration expanded approvals for several natural color additives in foods. FDA's approvals of new food color additives reflected routine risk-based regulation that shapes manufacturing practices and consumer safety standards. (12 May 2025)

9. Federal procurement agencies issued Federal Acquisition Circular 2025-04 revising Buy American rules and technical FAR provisions. Updates to procurement rules and the list of domestically nonavailable articles adjusted how federal spending supports domestic industry and small businesses. (12 May 2025)

10. SpaceX and the U.S. Department of Defense secured a $6 billion Pentagon contract and emerged as frontrunner for the Golden Dome missile shield. The huge defense contract for SpaceX, amid concerns about weakened oversight, highlighted growing reliance on a politically connected private firm for core security infrastructure. (12 May 2025)

11. President Donald Trump proposed a $1.01 trillion military budget with deep cuts to non-defense discretionary spending. Trump's budget shifted federal priorities toward the military while slashing education, environment, and health, reinforcing a fiscal order that privileges defense and elites over social goods. (12 May 2025)

12. Environmental Protection Agency delayed PFAS reporting deadlines to 2026–2027. Extending PFAS reporting timelines gave industry more time to comply but also postponed data needed for regulating harmful chemicals affecting public health. (13 May 2025)

13. Trump administration cut an additional $450 million in federal grants to Harvard University. Large grant cuts to Harvard, which responded with a First Amendment lawsuit, suggested federal funding was being used to pressure an academic critic of administration policies. (13 May 2025)

14. Trump administration and Qatar approved a $2 billion U.S. arms sale to Qatar including advanced drones and munitions. The major arms sale to Qatar, alongside personal Trump business ties there, intertwined U.S. export policy with a partner linked to controversial groups and potential conflicts of interest. (13 May 2025)

15. Trump administration and Qatar signed a defense and aviation package including up to 210 Boeing jets and large defense investments. The $243 billion U.S.-Qatar package deepened economic and defense interdependence while the parallel Qatar jet gift raised questions about whether state deals were sweetened by personal benefits. (14 May 2025)

16. House Republicans and President Donald Trump backed a reconciliation bill allowing revocation of nonprofit tax-exempt status for alleged terrorist support. Empowering Treasury to strip nonprofits' tax status on vague terrorism grounds threatened to chill advocacy and concentrate economic leverage over civil society in the executive branch. (15 May 2025)

17. President Donald Trump nominated David Keeling, a critic of heat protections, to lead OSHA. Choosing an OSHA chief expected to weaken

heat safety rules signaled regulatory leadership aligned with employer interests over worker protections in a warming climate. (15 May 2025)

18. Moody's Rating Service downgraded the U.S. sovereign credit rating for the first time since 1917. The downgrade, citing widening deficits and weak revenues, increased borrowing costs and signaled market concern about the sustainability of current fiscal and tax policies. (15 May 2025)

19. Environmental Protection Agency announced a joint OTC–MANEVU meeting and proposed CERCLA settlements for the Mohawk Tannery site. EPA's regional air-quality meeting and Superfund settlements showed ongoing, if contested, use of federal tools to manage pollution and remediation responsibilities. (16 May 2025)

20. Environmental Protection Agency exempted l-arginine used in certain greenhouse pesticides from tolerance requirements. The pesticide tolerance exemption modestly reduced regulatory burdens for growers while relying on EPA's safety assessment to protect consumers and workers. (14 May 2025)

21. Drug Enforcement Administration processed multiple applications for controlled substance importation for research and distribution. DEA's handling of controlled-substance import applications balanced research and veterinary needs with diversion controls, illustrating routine but powerful gatekeeping over drug markets. (14 May 2025)

22. Food and Drug Administration requested information on revising infant formula nutrient requirements. FDA's review of infant formula standards opened the door to updated nutritional rules that could affect both child health and industry costs. (14 May 2025)

23. Jared Kushner's development firm and Serbian authorities saw a $500 million Trump International Hotel project in Belgrade halted after a forged demolition document was exposed. The halt of a major Trump-branded project over forged approvals highlighted governance and corruption risks when politically connected developers pursue foreign deals. (14 May 2025)

24. President Donald Trump repeatedly raised and then reduced tariffs on Chinese goods, including a spike to 145%. Frequent, dramatic tariff shifts on China created trade uncertainty, raised consumer prices, and showcased the executive's unilateral sway over global supply chains. (14 May 2025)

25. Popular business and political elites attended a Saudi lunch and investment forum with Trump and MBS despite prior Khashoggi concerns. Top U.S. executives' renewed engagement with Saudi leadership signaled that lucrative deals can outweigh human rights concerns in shaping corporate and diplomatic behavior. (14 May 2025)

26. Department of Government Efficiency cut staffing at Newark airport, contributing to a severe air traffic controller shortage. Aggressive staffing cuts

that left Newark with a fraction of needed controllers showed how austerity-driven reforms can compromise critical infrastructure and public safety. (15 May 2025)

Information, Memory, and Manipulation

1. White House communications office launched a government-run news website called White House Wire. Creating a presidential news outlet allowed the administration to bypass independent media and push unfiltered narratives under official branding. (10 May 2025)

2. White House posted AI-generated imagery and videos of deportation flights to promote its agenda. Using AI visuals and curated deportation footage for political messaging blurred lines between documentation and propaganda, shaping public perception of immigration policy. (10 May 2025)

3. Meidas and Zeteo sources describing White House travel practices reported that wire service reporters were excluded from Air Force One for Trump's Middle East trip. Barring wire reporters from Air Force One limited independent coverage of presidential diplomacy and signaled a preference for controlled media access. (12 May 2025)

4. Trump administration fired nearly 600 Voice of America contractors despite a court order to maintain strong news operations. The mass VOA firings weakened a key independent news outlet and suggested disregard for judicial directives protecting journalistic capacity. (16 May 2025)

5. State Department and DHS considered a reality TV show where immigrants would compete for U.S. citizenship. Entertaining a citizenship competition show trivialized naturalization and risked turning life-altering legal status into spectacle for political branding. (15 May 2025)

6. State Department directed universities to report foreign students involved in certain protests as potential security concerns. Linking campus protest participation to security reporting obligations pressured universities to monitor and potentially discipline political expression by international students. (16 May 2025)

7. Trump administration and Pentagon ordered removal of DEI and gender-related books from military and base school libraries. The book purge curated which histories and identities are visible in military education, erasing perspectives on equity and inclusion from official memory spaces. (10 May 2025)

8. Trump administration fired the head of the U.S. Copyright Office after she issued a cautious AI report. Removing a key knowledge official following

an unwelcome AI analysis signaled that expert assessments of emerging technologies would be shaped by political preferences. (12 May 2025)

9. FAA Chief Operating Officer Tim Arel refused in a congressional hearing to disclose how many air traffic controllers had quit or been fired. Withholding basic staffing data from Congress limited public insight into aviation safety risks and undermined transparent oversight of a critical agency. (14 May 2025)

10. Noahpinion and other commentators reported allegations that a $400 million Qatari jet gift to Trump reflected corruption and foreign influence. Public reporting on the Qatar jet allegations highlighted the role of independent analysis in surfacing potential corruption when official justifications remain opaque. (14 May 2025)

11. U.S. Environmental Protection Agency published a notice of availability for multiple Environmental Impact Statements. Making EIS documents publicly available supported informed participation in environmental decisions and maintained transparency in major project reviews. (16 May 2025)

12. U.S. intelligence community released an assessment concluding that Saudi Crown Prince Mohammed bin Salman approved Jamal Khashoggi's killing. The assessment formally attributing Khashoggi's murder to MBS underscored tensions between documented human rights abuses and ongoing U.S.-Saudi cooperation. (14 May 2025)

13. President Donald Trump and allies claimed credit for an India-Pakistan ceasefire that was negotiated without U.S. involvement. Trump's false assertion of brokering a South Asian ceasefire illustrated the use of misleading foreign policy narratives to bolster his image. (10 May 2025)

14. Department of Homeland Security and FBI investigated James Comey over an Instagram post interpreted as an assassination threat. Treating ambiguous imagery as a potential threat from a prominent critic risked conflating dissent with violence and could deter outspoken commentary. (14 May 2025; 15 May 2025; 16 May 2025)

15. Department of Homeland Security confirmed use of a hacked TeleMessage app for internal communications. CBP's reliance on a compromised messaging app exposed sensitive enforcement communications to potential interception, undermining secure and accountable record-keeping. (10 May 2025)

CHAPTER 18
WEEK 18 (17 MAY 2025 – 23 MAY 2025): INEQUALITY AS OPERATING SYSTEM

A reconciliation megabill, weaponized borders, and captured institutions hardwire hierarchy into law while the Democracy Clock's hands barely seem to move.

This week marks a concentrated push toward authoritarian governance, centered on three main areas: a broad redistribution of fiscal power upward, aggressive uses of immigration and law enforcement as weapons, and a coordinated attack on independent institutions. The passage of the One Big Beautiful Bill and related budget moves embed inequality into tax and spending policies, cut Medicaid and SNAP, and significantly increase deportation and detention capabilities. At the same time, the administration normalizes immunity for January 6 offenders while targeting protesters, immigrants, and oversight advocates. Executive actions and judicial decisions—such as terminating TPS, dismantling consent decrees, politicized appointments, and Supreme Court rulings that grant the president control over independent agencies—undermine checks and civil service neutrality. Efforts to control information and shape narratives—involving mandated election lies in Oklahoma schools, press intimidation, and scandals of foreign influence—further weaken truth enforcement. Although courts and some state actors oppose certain excesses, the overall trend is a steady shift towards a unified, patronage-based state with stratified citizenship and depleted social protections.

Power and Authority

1. President Donald Trump issued mass pardons for January 6 participants. Trump's unconditional pardons and commutations for over 1,500 January 6 defendants weakened accountability for an attack on the transfer of power, signaling tolerance for political violence against democratic institutions. (19 May 2025; 20 May 2025)

2. President Donald Trump announced the Golden Dome national missile defense project. Trump's launch of the costly Golden Dome missile shield concentrated long-term security spending and authority in the executive, expanding military infrastructure with limited legislative or public scrutiny. (20 May 2025; 21 May 2025)

3. President Donald Trump accepted a jumbo jet from Qatar for use as Air Force One. Acceptance and defense of a Qatari aircraft as an Air Force One replacement blurred constitutional limits on foreign gifts and raised concerns about foreign leverage over the presidency. (17 May 2025; 18 May 2025; 20 May 2025; 21 May 2025; 22 May 2025)

4. President Donald Trump threatened Walmart over tariff-related price increases. Trump's demand that Walmart absorb tariff costs rather than raise prices showed the executive using informal pressure on private firms to manage political fallout from trade policy. (17 May 2025; 20 May 2025)

5. President Donald Trump announced sweeping new tariffs on many countries. Trump's broad tariff package against allies and rivals alike reoriented trade policy around unilateral executive decisions, triggering price spikes and market turmoil with limited deliberation. (18 May 2025; 20 May 2025)

6. President Donald Trump proposed steep new tariffs on EU goods and Apple products. Trump's threat to impose punitive tariffs on EU imports and iPhones unless production moved to the U.S. used trade powers to coerce corporate and allied government behavior. (22 May 2025)

7. President Donald Trump ordered a historic funding surge for immigration enforcement. A new law doubling CBP and ICE budgets and vastly expanding detention capacity entrenched a militarized immigration regime with large discretionary power over non-citizens. (22 May 2025)

8. President Donald Trump announced investigations into Biden's autopen use and pardons. Plans to probe Biden's autopen signatures and pardons signaled use of executive investigative tools to delegitimize a predecessor and political rival rather than address systemic abuses. (18 May 2025; 20 May 2025)

9. Department of Homeland Security Secretary Kristi Noem revoked

Harvard University's foreign exchange student program. DHS's immediate revocation of Harvard's authority to enroll foreign students weaponized immigration controls against a single institution, threatening academic freedom and international mobility. (21 May 2025; 22 May 2025)

10. Department of Homeland Security Secretary Kristi Noem floated a reality show where immigrants compete for citizenship. Noem's discussions of a citizenship reality show trivialized naturalization and framed immigrant rights as entertainment, undermining equal treatment norms in immigration policy. (17 May 2025)

11. President Donald Trump used a White House crypto gala to court major investors. Trump's high-dollar crypto dinners at his golf club, using presidential trappings, blurred lines between public office and private fundraising, giving wealthy investors privileged access. (21 May 2025; 22 May 2025)

12. President Donald Trump pressured Vietnam on tariffs while Trump Organization pursued a tower deal. Simultaneous U.S.–Vietnam tariff talks and negotiations over a new Trump Tower in Ho Chi Minh City intertwined foreign policy with the president's family business interests. (18 May 2025)

13. President Donald Trump pursued a Russia–Ukraine ceasefire tied to future trade. Trump's ceasefire push in Ukraine, framed around post-war trade with Russia and threats of sanctions, highlighted a personalized diplomacy style that may sideline broader democratic and human-rights concerns. (18 May 2025)

14. President Donald Trump used a White House meeting to promote a 'white genocide' narrative to South Africa's president. Trump's presentation of debunked 'white genocide' claims to President Ramaphosa imported extremist narratives into official diplomacy, risking racialized foreign policy and distorted threat perceptions. (21 May 2025)

15. Federal Aviation Administration temporarily capped flights at Newark airport. The FAA's interim cap on Newark flights concentrated operational discretion in the agency to manage infrastructure and staffing shortfalls, affecting mobility and commerce in a major hub. (20 May 2025)

16. Department of Veterans Affairs leadership and the Department of Government Efficiency implemented staffing cuts and closures across VA facilities. Mass layoffs, contract cancellations, and unit closures at VA hospitals under DOGE guidance degraded veterans' access to care and illustrated executive willingness to shrink core public services. (23 May 2025)

17. Federal Emergency Management Agency leadership acknowledged unpreparedness for hurricane season and shifted responsibility to states. FEMA's admission that it was not ready for hurricane season and intent to

return duties to states signaled federal retreat from disaster response obligations. (17 May 2025)

18. Federal Emergency Management Agency failed to deliver timely aid after major tornadoes. Prolonged FEMA inaction in tornado-hit Mississippi and St. Louis left communities without federal relief for months, undermining trust in national emergency support. (19 May 2025; 20 May 2025; 21 May 2025)

19. Transportation Security Administration replaced references to gender with sex in its regulations. TSA's terminology change from 'gender' to 'sex' across rules implemented an executive directive that may narrow recognition of gender diversity in federal identification and screening systems. (21 May 2025)

Institutions and Governance

1. House Republican leadership advanced and passed the One Big Beautiful Bill through the House. House Republicans pushed through a reconciliation megabill that extends Trump-era tax cuts, slashes Medicaid and SNAP, funds mass deportations and a border wall, and curbs courts' contempt powers, reshaping fiscal and institutional balances. (17 May 2025; 18 May 2025; 19 May 2025; 20 May 2025; 21 May 2025; 22 May 2025; 23 May 2025)

2. Moody's Investors Service downgraded the U.S. sovereign credit rating. Moody's downgrade of U.S. debt, citing dysfunction and deficit-expanding policies, increased borrowing costs and signaled market concern over the sustainability of current fiscal governance. (17 May 2025; 18 May 2025; 19 May 2025; 21 May 2025)

3. Consumer Financial Protection Bureau leadership moved to dismantle the CFPB and rescind key consumer protections. Efforts to fire most CFPB staff, pull back guidance shielding borrowers from medical-debt harms, and fire safety commissioners weakened a central consumer watchdog and shifted power toward lenders. (19 May 2025)

4. U.S. Supreme Court allowed Trump to terminate Temporary Protected Status for Venezuelans. By granting an emergency request to end TPS for roughly 350,000 Venezuelans, the Court enabled abrupt status loss for a large immigrant group and signaled deference to harsh executive immigration policy. (19 May 2025)

5. U.S. Supreme Court restored a censured Maine lawmaker's voting rights. The Court's order reinstating Laurel Libby's voting rights after a state-house censure asserted federal power over internal legislative disci-

pline, raising questions about separation of powers and emergency relief standards. (20 May 2025)

6. U.S. Supreme Court stayed lower-court rulings protecting independent agency heads from removal. By granting a stay in Trump v. Wilcox and related orders, the Court allowed Trump's firings of NLRB and MSPB members to stand, advancing a unitary-executive view that weakens independent oversight bodies. (22 May 2025)

7. U.S. Supreme Court deadlocked on public funding for a religious charter school. A 4–4 split left in place a lower-court ruling blocking Oklahoma's Catholic virtual charter school, temporarily preserving church–state separation in public education funding without setting national precedent. (22 May 2025)

8. Federal judiciary blocked Trump administration efforts to dismantle federal agencies and programs. Judges halted attempts to dissolve the U.S. Institute of Peace, downsize agencies and lay off civil servants, dismantle the Education Department, and cancel desegregation grants, preserving key institutional capacities. (19 May 2025; 21 May 2025; 22 May 2025)

9. Federal judiciary temporarily blocked DHS from revoking visas and status for international students. Court orders pausing DHS moves against Harvard's foreign students and broader international student status protected thousands from sudden deportation and checked executive retaliation against universities. (22 May 2025)

10. Federal judiciary ruled the administration violated court orders in South Sudan deportations. Judges found that deporting men to South Sudan without required process breached prior injunctions, ordered their return or review, and raised the prospect of contempt for officials, reinforcing judicial checks on immigration enforcement. (21 May 2025; 22 May 2025; 23 May 2025)

11. Federal judiciary blocked or reversed questionable prosecutions and agency firings. Courts dismissed trespass charges against Newark's mayor, reversed firings of Privacy and Civil Liberties Oversight Board members, and rejected unusual restitution for a Jan. 6 rioter, curbing politicized uses of law. (20 May 2025; 21 May 2025)

12. U.S. Department of Justice Civil Rights Division ended negotiations over police reform settlements in Minneapolis and Louisville. DOJ's decision to walk away from consent-decree talks with Minneapolis and Louisville reversed prior federal efforts to address systemic police abuses, weakening a key civil-rights enforcement tool. (21 May 2025)

13. U.S. Department of Justice leadership scrapped the FBI's internal FISA compliance auditing unit. Eliminating the FBI office that monitored adher-

ence to surveillance rules reduced internal checks on intelligence powers, heightening risks of unlawful spying and politicized targeting. (20 May 2025)

14. U.S. Department of Justice leadership reoriented the Civil Rights Division and triggered mass resignations. Policy shifts that focused civil-rights enforcement on alleged anti-white discrimination led about 70% of DOJ Civil Rights Division staff to resign, sharply reducing federal capacity to protect vulnerable groups. (21 May 2025)

15. Trump administration and Department of Government Efficiency attempted large-scale layoffs and reclassification of civil servants. Plans to reclassify tens of thousands of federal employees into easily fired 'policy/career' roles and to downsize agencies threatened the neutrality and stability of the civil service. (18 May 2025; 22 May 2025)

16. U.S. Department of Justice pursued or considered high-profile settlements in January 6 and Ashli Babbitt cases. DOJ's willingness to pay millions to Ashli Babbitt's family while mass pardons proceeded reflected a complex mix of legal risk management and political messaging around the Capitol attack. (18 May 2025; 19 May 2025; 20 May 2025)

17. U.S. Department of Justice charged Rep. LaMonica McIver over an ICE facility oversight visit. Charging a sitting member of Congress with assaulting officers during an oversight trip to an ICE facility raised concerns that criminal law was being used to chill legislative scrutiny of executive detention practices. (19 May 2025; 20 May 2025; 21 May 2025)

18. House and Senate oversight committees held contentious budget and confirmation hearings with cabinet officials. Senators pressed DHS, HHS, State, and IRS nominees on habeas corpus, public-health funding, childcare cuts, human-rights cases, and tax-law misuse, exposing gaps between official claims and agency actions. (20 May 2025; 21 May 2025)

19. Senate and White House confirmed Charles Kushner as U.S. ambassador to France. Confirming a previously convicted and pardoned Trump associate as ambassador underscored the use of diplomatic posts as rewards for loyalty, raising questions about merit and independence in foreign service. (19 May 2025; 20 May 2025)

20. U.S. Department of Justice launched a criminal investigation into Andrew Cuomo's COVID-19 testimony. A DOJ probe into whether Andrew Cuomo misled Congress about nursing-home deaths highlighted the use of federal criminal process to revisit pandemic decisions with significant political overtones. (20 May 2025; 21 May 2025)

21. Federal Election Commission canceled multiple open meetings under the Sunshine Act. The FEC's repeated cancellations and reschedulings of open meetings reduced opportunities for public observation of enforcement

deliberations in a key election-oversight body. (20 May 2025; 22 May 2025; 23 May 2025)

22. Election Assistance Commission announced a vacancy on its Technical Guidelines Development Committee. The EAC's notice of a vacancy on the committee that shapes voting-system standards highlighted ongoing turnover in a body central to election technology integrity. (23 May 2025)

23. U.S. Congress used the Congressional Review Act to nullify EPA and NPS rules. Congressional disapproval resolutions overturning hazardous-air-pollutant and motor-vehicle rules showed legislators directly rolling back environmental protections through oversight of agency rulemaking. (23 May 2025)

24. Senate Democrats questioned Paramount over potential improper settlement with Trump. Senators' inquiry into whether Paramount's efforts to settle Trump's CBS lawsuit were tied to regulatory approvals spotlighted possible use of litigation and mergers to influence media coverage. (20 May 2025)

25. U.S. Department of Justice referred Kennedy Center finances for criminal review. A DOJ referral alleging financial misconduct at the Kennedy Center introduced potential criminal scrutiny into a major cultural institution amid claims of political motivation. (19 May 2025)

26. U.S. Department of Justice sought to dismiss charges against an MS-13 leader in favor of deportation. DOJ's move to drop criminal charges against an MS-13 leader to expedite deportation raised concerns about trading judicial accountability for diplomatic or political objectives. (23 May 2025)

27. Federal judiciary blocked dismantling of the Department of Education and reinstated staff. A judge's order halting efforts to break up the Education Department and rehiring fired employees preserved federal oversight of national education policy against executive downsizing. (22 May 2025)

28. Federal judiciary rejected DOJ's attempt to pay restitution to a January 6 rioter. A judge's refusal to authorize $63,000 in restitution to a Jan. 6 defendant clarified that such payments require congressional approval, limiting executive discretion in compensating aligned actors. (20 May 2025)

29. U.S. Department of Justice investigated alleged insider trading by senior officials before tariff moves. A request to probe whether Attorney General Pam Bondi and others traded on advance tariff knowledge highlighted risks that economic policy is being used for private gain inside government. (20 May 2025)

30. U.S. Department of Justice investigated Chicago and Harvard for alleged anti-white discrimination. Civil-rights probes into Chicago and Harvard Law Review for supposed anti-white bias signaled a reorientation of

enforcement priorities that may dilute protection for historically marginalized groups. (21 May 2025)

Civil Rights and Dissent

1. Georgia Attorney General Chris Carr pursued RICO prosecutions against Cop City protesters. Charging 61 Cop City opponents under Georgia's RICO law risked criminalizing loosely connected protest activity and chilling organized dissent against police expansion. (18 May 2025)

2. U.S. Department of Justice and Immigration and Customs Enforcement conducted aggressive immigration enforcement including court-house arrests and deportations to unsafe or third countries. ICE arrests at immigration courts, deportations of Bhutanese Nepali refugees into stateless limbo, and flights routing migrants to South Sudan and other conflict zones showed enforcement practices that endangered due-process and human-rights protections. (19 May 2025; 20 May 2025; 21 May 2025; 23 May 2025)

3. Immigration and Customs Enforcement and GEO Group denied a detained Palestinian activist a contact visit with his newborn. ICE's refusal to allow Mahmoud Khalil to hold his infant son, despite standards permitting such visits, highlighted punitive detention conditions and family-separation dynamics in immigration custody. (21 May 2025)

4. Trump administration terminated Temporary Protected Status for Venezuelan immigrants. Ending TPS for hundreds of thousands of Venezuelans, including many Trump supporters, stripped lawful status and heightened deportation risk for a large diaspora community. (19 May 2025)

5. Trump administration planned to repatriate immigrants to conflict zones using foreign aid funds. A proposal to spend $250 million in foreign aid to return Ukrainians, Haitians, and others to conflict areas used development resources to facilitate removals into danger. (20 May 2025)

6. Trump administration fast-tracked admission of white South African refugees while restricting others. Expedited entry for white South Africans fleeing alleged discrimination, contrasted with harsh treatment of other refugee groups, underscored a racially selective approach to humanitarian protection. (21 May 2025)

7. Oklahoma State Superintendent Ryan Walters mandated teaching of 2020 election fraud claims and Bible-based U.S. history. New curriculum rules requiring instruction in debunked 2020 fraud narratives and Bible-centered history politicized public education and blurred church–state boundaries. (17 May 2025)

8. California appeals court halted a school district's vague ban on critical

race theory. By pausing Temecula Valley's CRT ban, the court protected educators from unclear restrictions that chilled teaching about race and civil-rights history. (20 May 2025)

9. Federal judge in Georgia blocked deportation of a Venezuelan man to El Salvador over due-process concerns. The order preventing removal of a Venezuelan man to El Salvador underscored judicial willingness to intervene when deportations risked violating basic procedural rights. (21 May 2025)

10. Federal courts ordered the return or protection of deported Venezuelan nationals. Appeals and district courts requiring the government to facilitate return or halt deportation of Venezuelans emphasized due-process obligations in removal proceedings. (19 May 2025; 20 May 2025)

11. U.S. Department of Justice moved to cancel police reform consent decrees in Minneapolis and Louisville. Seeking to end court-enforced reform agreements after findings of civil-rights violations signaled a retreat from federal oversight of abusive policing in Black communities. (21 May 2025)

12. U.S. Department of Justice investigated Chicago for alleged anti-white discrimination. A Title VII probe into Chicago for supposed anti-white bias reflected a reorientation of civil-rights enforcement that may deprioritize longstanding patterns of discrimination against minorities. (21 May 2025)

13. U.S. Department of Justice investigated Harvard and Harvard Law Review over race-conscious practices. Federal investigations into Harvard's alleged race-based decisions threatened to chill diversity initiatives and academic autonomy in higher education. (21 May 2025)

14. ICE and federal prosecutors charged and detained Columbia student Mahmoud Khalil after pro-Palestinian advocacy. The detention and prosecution of a lawful permanent resident and activist, amid evidence contradicting flight claims, raised fears that immigration powers were being used to suppress campus speech. (21 May 2025)

15. Federal judge in Louisiana blocked cancellation of an education desegregation grant. A temporary order preserving funds for desegregation work in southern schools protected ongoing efforts to remedy racial inequities in education. (21 May 2025)

16. New Orleans Catholic archdiocese and bankruptcy court reached a clergy abuse settlement with survivors. A proposed $180–230 million settlement for decades of abuse claims, including document disclosure requirements, sought to compensate victims while raising questions about adequacy and institutional accountability. (22 May 2025)

17. Atlanta police and city officials faced a lawsuit over degrading treatment of a woman during a SWAT raid. A suit alleging an Atlanta officer left a woman topless in a squad car for hours during a Cop City-related raid chal-

lenged qualified immunity and highlighted abuses in protest-adjacent policing. (23 May 2025)

18. Immigration and Customs Enforcement conducted mass arrests at immigration courts nationwide. Coordinated ICE arrests in and around immigration courts in multiple cities discouraged attendance at hearings and undermined access to legal processes for non-citizens. (21 May 2025)

19. ICE and DHS deported Bhutanese Nepali refugees to countries where they lacked citizenship. Deporting long-settled Bhutanese Nepali refugees to Bhutan, then leaving some stranded in India and Nepal, created statelessness and raised serious human-rights concerns. (21 May 2025)

20. U.S. Department of Justice moved to cancel consent decrees with Minneapolis and Louisville police. Seeking to end federal oversight agreements after high-profile police killings signaled a shift away from structural remedies for systemic racism in policing. (21 May 2025)

21. Representative Nancy Mace used a House hearing to air personal abuse allegations. Mace's use of official proceedings to accuse her ex-fiancé and others of abuse, now subject to defamation litigation, tested the boundaries of legislative privilege and personal grievance in oversight forums. (21 May 2025)

22. Louisiana State Senate passed an anti-grooming bill targeting child sexual abuse. A unanimously passed bill criminalizing grooming behaviors toward minors sought to close gaps in child-protection law while raising implementation questions after amendments. (21 May 2025)

23. New Orleans Catholic archdiocese and insurers agreed to disclose abuse-related documents as part of settlement. Non-monetary terms requiring public release of abuse files aimed to enhance transparency and help prevent future misconduct in a powerful religious institution. (22 May 2025)

24. Federal courts and civil-rights advocates preserved desegregation funding and blocked dismantling of education oversight. Judicial orders protecting desegregation grants and the Education Department's structure maintained federal tools for addressing racial inequities in schools. (21 May 2025; 22 May 2025)

Economic Structure

1. House Republicans and President Donald Trump advanced a reconciliation bill that redistributes tax and spending benefits upward. Analyses showed Trump's reconciliation bill would add trillions to the debt, cut Medicaid and SNAP, increase uninsured rates, and shift after-tax gains to the wealthiest,

structurally deepening inequality. (17 May 2025; 18 May 2025; 19 May 2025; 20 May 2025; 21 May 2025; 22 May 2025)

2. Trump administration cut IRS enforcement resources by nearly a third. A 31% cut to IRS enforcement was projected to enable large-scale tax evasion by high earners, weakening rule-of-law in taxation and shifting the burden onto compliant taxpayers. (17 May 2025)

3. Trump administration rescinded methane waste emissions charges for oil and gas systems. Revoking the waste emissions charge for petroleum and gas operators removed a key economic incentive to curb methane pollution, easing compliance costs for industry at the expense of climate oversight. (19 May 2025)

4. Trump administration cut USAID contracts, leaving food aid unused. Reductions in USAID contracts left food for millions rotting in warehouses and reduced income for U.S. farmers, signaling deprioritization of humanitarian aid and rural economic support. (17 May 2025)

5. State of Oregon and county governments diverted addiction treatment funds to law enforcement uses. Oregon counties' use of treatment grants to hire prosecutors and buy police equipment shifted resources from public health to punishment, undermining voter-backed drug policy reforms. (19 May 2025)

6. Trump administration and Congress maintained broad tariffs that raised consumer prices and hurt exporters. Persistent universal and China-specific tariffs increased costs for U.S. firms and consumers, eroding trade stability while being justified as leverage in negotiations. (18 May 2025; 20 May 2025)

7. Major corporations including AT&T, Comcast, T-Mobile, Uber, and United Airlines endorsed a bill that sharply cuts SNAP benefits. Companies publicly aligned with anti-hunger efforts backed legislation slashing food assistance, illustrating how corporate lobbying can override stated social-responsibility commitments. (22 May 2025)

8. Verizon and federal regulators ended corporate DEI programs and scrubbed related public commitments. Verizon's termination of DEI policies and removal of DEI content, reportedly tied to FCC approval of a major acquisition, showed regulatory leverage being used to reshape corporate equity practices. (20 May 2025; 21 May 2025)

9. Trump administration cut federal grants to Harvard over alleged discrimination. Grant cuts to Harvard for supposed bias against white and Asian applicants signaled willingness to use federal funding to pressure universities over diversity and hiring policies. (21 May 2025)

10. President Donald Trump hosted high-priced crypto investor events

tied to his personal token. Crypto-themed dinners where attendees spent hundreds of millions on a Trump-linked token, some under regulatory investigation, highlighted how personal financial ventures intersected with political access. (22 May 2025)

11. Trump administration considered re-privatizing Fannie Mae and Freddie Mac. Plans to strip Fannie Mae and Freddie Mac of quasi-sovereign status risked credit downgrades and higher mortgage costs, potentially destabilizing housing finance for political or ideological goals. (22 May 2025)

12. California Insurance Commissioner approved a large emergency homeowners' insurance rate hike. Authorizing a 17% interim rate increase for State Farm in wildfire-prone California shifted climate-related risk costs onto homeowners while attempting to keep a major insurer solvent. (21 May 2025)

13. Trump administration signed executive orders to accelerate a nuclear energy 'renaissance'. A suite of nuclear-focused executive orders streamlined NRC processes, expanded testing and deployment, and sought to rebuild the nuclear industrial base, prioritizing rapid energy expansion with altered regulatory safeguards. (23 May 2025)

14. Environmental Protection Agency and other regulators approved multiple state air and water plans and hazardous-waste program revisions. EPA approvals of state SIPs, drinking-water primacy revisions, and hazardous-waste programs in several states adjusted environmental responsibilities between federal and state governments. (19 May 2025; 23 May 2025)

15. Environmental Protection Agency renewed and sought comment on multiple contractor and emissions information collections. EPA's ICR renewals on contractor conflicts, hazardous remediation, and cross-state air pollution maintained data flows needed for environmental enforcement and oversight of federal contracting. (23 May 2025)

16. Food and Drug Administration convened public processes on drug fees, generics, and safety guidance. FDA meetings and guidances on PDUFA, GDUFA, chemotherapy risks, and specific generics aimed to sustain drug-review capacity and transparency in pharmaceutical regulation. (19 May 2025; 20 May 2025; 21 May 2025)

17. General Services Administration updated travel and procurement-related information collections and rescinded old bulletins. GSA's rescission of outdated travel bulletins and requests for comment on contractor forms and construction-manager data reflected ongoing adjustments to federal administrative procedures. (19 May 2025; 22 May 2025)

18. Drug Enforcement Administration processed applications to import controlled substances for research and distribution. DEA import applications for psilocybin-related compounds and Schedule II drugs showed

controlled-substance regulation adapting to expanding research and pharmaceutical supply chains. (20 May 2025)

19. Occupational Safety and Health Administration extended approval for asbestos information collection in shipyards. OSHA's extension of asbestos-related reporting requirements maintained worker-safety oversight while modestly reducing estimated paperwork burdens. (20 May 2025)

20. San Francisco Mayor Daniel Lurie announced regulatory reforms to ease permitting for small businesses. San Francisco's move to simplify permits and cut fees for storefronts and homeowners aimed to reduce bureaucratic barriers and support local economic vitality. (23 May 2025)

21. California, Michigan, Texas, Indiana, and other state and federal agencies implemented targeted environmental and agricultural regulatory changes. EPA and FDA actions on air plans, pesticide tolerances, animal feed additives, and emissions budgets adjusted sector-specific rules with implications for industry compliance and public health. (19 May 2025; 20 May 2025; 23 May 2025)

Information, Memory, and Manipulation

1. President Donald Trump renewed false claims that the 2020 election was rigged and amplified conspiracy content. Trump's posts alleging a stolen 2020 election and sharing 'Clinton body count' material further entrenched disinformation that undermines confidence in electoral legitimacy and public discourse. (17 May 2025)

2. Trump administration and communications team used aggressive narrative-control tactics and influencer access to shape coverage. The White House's strategy of flooding media with sound bites, privileging right-wing influencers, and sidelining critical outlets aimed to dominate information flows and marginalize independent scrutiny. (17 May 2025)

3. White House and Trump legal team threatened legal action against critical media outlets. Threats to sue Business Insider's parent and ABC News over unfavorable stories exemplified the use of litigation intimidation to chill investigative reporting. (17 May 2025)

4. Department of Homeland Security spokesperson Tricia McLaughlin falsely accused House Democrats of assaulting ICE officers. McLaughlin's televised claim that Democrats 'bodyslammed' ICE officers, contradicted by video, spread official disinformation to discredit congressional oversight. (17 May 2025)

5. President Donald Trump questioned the accuracy of Joe Biden's cancer diagnosis. Casting doubt on Biden's prostate cancer diagnosis during a

briefing injected personal health misinformation into political debate, eroding norms around truthful communication about opponents. (19 May 2025)

6. Department of Homeland Security and Secret Service investigated James Comey over an ambiguous social-media post. A multi-agency probe into Comey's '8647' Instagram post, interpreted by some as a threat to Trump, illustrated how security resources can be deployed against perceived critics based on tenuous evidence. (17 May 2025)

7. Defense Secretary Pete Hegseth restricted press access inside the Pentagon. New rules confining reporters to a limited area and requiring escorts for movement within the Pentagon curtailed routine access to defense officials and information, citing leak concerns. (23 May 2025)

8. President Donald Trump verbally attacked reporters from NOTUS and NBC during public events. Trump's insults toward journalists, calling them 'idiot' or telling them to get a 'real job,' reinforced a pattern of delegitimizing independent media in front of supporters. (20 May 2025; 21 May 2025)

9. CBS News and Wendy McMahon saw its president depart amid a Trump-related lawsuit. The resignation of CBS News's president during litigation over a Kamala Harris interview highlighted how legal and political pressure can destabilize newsroom leadership. (19 May 2025)

10. Chicago Sun-Times and content partners published an AI-generated reading list containing fake books. Use of AI to generate a summer reading list that included nonexistent titles exposed weaknesses in editorial controls and raised concerns about AI's role in news content. (21 May 2025)

11. Verizon scrubbed diversity, equity, and inclusion content from its website. Verizon's removal of DEI webpages, documented via web archives, attempted to rewrite its public record on equity commitments amid political and regulatory pressure. (20 May 2025)

12. Director of National Intelligence chief of staff ordered edits to an intelligence assessment on Venezuela. Instructions to alter an intelligence product to avoid political fallout for senior officials suggested politicization of analytic work and potential distortion of the record. (20 May 2025)

13. House Republicans and oil companies exposed internal documents on fossil-fuel sponsorship of cultural institutions. Subpoenaed communications showed oil firms using sponsorships of museums and youth groups to burnish reputations and influence opinion during the climate crisis. (20 May 2025)

14. House Republican leadership delayed installation of a Capitol plaque honoring January 6 officers. Stalling a congressionally approved plaque for officers who defended the Capitol impeded formal recognition

of their role and contributed to contested memory of the attack. (19 May 2025)

15. Trump administration and Oklahoma education officials institutionalized election-fraud narratives in school curricula. Mandating classroom discussion of alleged 2020 'discrepancies' embedded discredited claims into civic education, shaping future voters' understanding of electoral legitimacy. (17 May 2025)

16. Trump administration and Oklahoma education officials required Bible instruction as part of U.S. history in public schools. Requiring Bible teaching in public-school history courses advanced a religiously inflected national narrative, challenging church–state separation and pluralistic civic education. (17 May 2025)

17. Trump administration and DHS revoked Harvard's ability to enroll international students citing 'anti-American' activity. Framing Harvard's alleged conduct as anti-American while stripping its authority to host foreign students used national-loyalty rhetoric to justify punitive action against an academic institution. (22 May 2025)

18. Federal Communications Commission convened its Communications Security, Reliability, and Interoperability Council. An announced CSRIC meeting to discuss communications security and reliability provided a public forum on infrastructure resilience and standards. (23 May 2025)

19. Federal Communications Commission implemented rule changes for FM digital broadcasting. Allowing asymmetric digital sideband power and simplified notifications aimed to encourage broader adoption of digital radio while adjusting regulatory burdens. (23 May 2025)

20. Congress and the President enacted the TAKE IT DOWN Act regulating online content removal. The TAKE IT DOWN Act created new rules for taking down certain online content, altering the balance between platform accountability and speech protections in the digital sphere. (19 May 2025)

21. Centers for Disease Control and Prevention and HHS leadership gave conflicting accounts about federal support for lead poisoning prevention. Senators' revelations that CDC had denied assistance to Milwaukee schools despite assurances of ongoing funding highlighted discrepancies that can obscure the true state of public-health programs. (21 May 2025)

22. HHS Secretary Robert F. Kennedy Jr. downplayed responsibility for childcare and ALS research funding cuts. Kennedy's evasive testimony about who ordered cuts to childcare grants and ALS research obscured accountability for decisions affecting vulnerable populations. (21 May 2025)

23. DHS Secretary Kristi Noem misdefined habeas corpus during Senate

testimony. Noem's assertion that habeas corpus is a presidential power to remove people from the country reflected a troubling misunderstanding of a core constitutional safeguard. (20 May 2025; 21 May 2025)

24. Senators and Secretary of State Marco Rubio clashed over human-rights commitments and visa policies. Senators' criticism of Rubio for visa revocations and renditions to El Salvador highlighted concerns that foreign-policy messaging no longer aligns with prior U.S. human-rights rhetoric. (20 May 2025; 21 May 2025)

25. Chicago Sun-Times and partner syndicates relied on AI for content without adequate editorial review. The AI-generated reading list incident underscored how automation in newsrooms can introduce fabricated information if not paired with robust human oversight. (21 May 2025)

CHAPTER 19
WEEK 19 (24 MAY 2025 – 30 MAY 2025): INSTITUTIONS AS INSTRUMENTS OF LOYALTY

A week of near-static clock time but deepening campaigns to bend immigration, universities, media, and law itself toward executive preference and profit.

This week reveals how an executive-centered project is evolving into a broad challenge to liberal democracy. Trump's rapid pace of executive orders, floated suspension of habeas corpus, and aggressive use of clemency for allies deepen the sense that law is being weaponized rather than serving as a limit. Immigration becomes the main testing ground: daily arrest quotas, the planned Office of Remigration, visa freezes, and Supreme Court approval to end parole and TPS all create a system that stratifies legal status based on origin and ideology. At the same time, universities and public media are targeted as rivals of authority—Harvard faces financial penalties and surveillance, NPR and PBS are defunded, while courts temporarily protect some of these institutions. Trade and foreign policy lean toward personal and crony interests, exemplified by Vietnam's Trump projects and Boeing's treatment. Yet, the judiciary, state attorneys general, universities, parents, and mass protests present strong resistance, blocking some orders and exposing overreach. Overall, the week increases pressure on executive dominance, politicization of civil service, control of information, and citizen stratification, while courts and civil society continue to serve as active, if challenged, counterbalances.

Power and Authority

1. President Donald Trump signed an executive order targeting DEI programs at military academies. The order led to the disbanding of student clubs and the removal of materials at service academies, narrowing inclusion and representation within the officer corps and signaling ideological control over military education. (24 May 2025)

2. Federal Emergency Management Agency denied North Carolina's request for full hurricane debris removal funding. Refusing previously promised disaster aid to a hard-hit state showed how federal relief can be used selectively, weakening equal protection and trust in central government support. (24 May 2025)

3. President Donald Trump announced a 50% tariff on European Union goods and threatened tariffs on Apple products. Unilaterally imposing steep tariffs and threatening targeted levies concentrated trade power in the presidency, bypassing normal legislative deliberation and destabilizing economic relations. (24 May 2025)

4. President Donald Trump was accused of blending personal business interests with foreign policy decisions. Allegations that foreign policy was shaped around Trump's financial interests undermined the idea that state power serves the public rather than private gain. (26 May 2025)

5. President Donald Trump pardoned former sheriff Scott Jenkins convicted of fraud and bribery. Using clemency to free a corrupt law-enforcement official signaled that loyalty and connections can override judicial accountability, weakening deterrence for public corruption. (26 May 2025; 27 May 2025; 28 May 2025)

6. President Donald Trump floated suspending the writ of habeas corpus. Considering suspension of habeas corpus, a core safeguard against arbitrary detention, directly threatened individual liberty and the constitutional balance between branches. (27 May 2025)

7. President Donald Trump pardoned reality TV personalities Todd and Julie Chrisley convicted of fraud and tax evasion. Granting clemency to well-known financial criminals with political ties reinforced perceptions that wealthy, connected offenders can escape consequences through presidential favor. (27 May 2025; 28 May 2025)

8. President Donald Trump commuted the sentence of former Chicago gang leader Larry Hoover and granted clemency to other political figures. High-profile commutations and pardons for serious offenders and ex-officials highlighted discretionary use of clemency that can appear inconsistent with

the administration's punitive stance toward marginalized groups. (28 May 2025; 29 May 2025)

9. President Donald Trump issued numerous pardons to allies, January 6 participants, and corruption defendants. A broad wave of pardons for politically aligned or financially connected individuals weakened the rule of law by signaling that proximity to power can nullify legal judgments. (28 May 2025)

10. President Donald Trump signed a record 152 executive orders since returning to office. Reliance on an unprecedented volume of executive orders shifted policymaking from Congress to the presidency, eroding checks and balances and normalizing rule by decree. (27 May 2025)

11. President Donald Trump delivered partisan speeches at West Point and Arlington National Cemetery. Injecting partisan attacks into military and memorial ceremonies blurred the line between commander-in-chief duties and campaigning, pressuring apolitical institutions to align with the ruling party. (27 May 2025)

12. President Donald Trump targeted DEI initiatives and trans rights, prompting corporate withdrawal from Pride sponsorships. Federal hostility toward LGBTQ+ inclusion chilled corporate support for Pride events, narrowing public space for minority expression and signaling state disfavor toward these communities. (29 May 2025)

13. President Donald Trump posted a QAnon-linked meme portraying himself as on a mission from God. Using conspiracy-coded religious imagery to rally supporters personalized political authority and encouraged a cultic view of leadership over institutional accountability. (29 May 2025)

14. President Donald Trump pressured Federal Reserve Chair Jerome Powell to lower interest rates. Directly urging the central bank to cut rates for political reasons challenged the norm of monetary policy independence that protects economic management from partisan cycles. (28 May 2025)

15. President Donald Trump ended Elon Musk's formal role leading the Department of Government Efficiency while keeping him as an informal adviser. Maintaining informal influence for a powerful businessman after a controversial stint in government blurred boundaries between private interests and public administration. (30 May 2025)

Institutions and Governance

1. U.S. House of Representatives passed a tax-and-spending bill funding the 'Golden Dome' missile defense system. Authorizing hundreds of billions for a

long-term missile shield committed vast public resources to a single defense project, shaping future budget priorities and oversight needs. (24 May 2025)

2. Republican lawmakers in the House threatened to block Trump's spending bill over national debt concerns. Intra-party resistance to the president's flagship spending plan exposed fiscal and procedural tensions that could affect budget stability and legislative bargaining power. (25 May 2025)

3. California legislature advanced significant amendments to the California Environmental Quality Act. Streamlining CEQA to ease construction aimed to address housing shortages but also reduced environmental review leverage that communities use to influence development decisions. (25 May 2025)

4. Multiple U.S. states advanced reforms allowing single-stair apartment buildings. Building-code changes to permit denser housing sought to expand supply and affordability, illustrating how state regulation shapes urban living conditions and economic opportunity. (25 May 2025)

5. Texas legislature advanced a bill allowing housing in former commercial zones. Requiring cities to accept housing in commercial areas limited local anti-development tactics, shifting land-use authority toward the state to address housing scarcity. (25 May 2025)

6. Federal judiciary security committee considered creating an armed security force independent of the Justice Department. Judges exploring their own security force reflected deep mistrust of executive-controlled protection and concern that political leaders could manipulate judicial safety. (25 May 2025; 27 May 2025)

7. U.S. District Court for the District of Massachusetts issued a temporary restraining order blocking the policy revoking Harvard's ability to enroll foreign students. The order checked an executive attempt to punish a university, underscoring the judiciary's role in defending institutional autonomy and due process. (25 May 2025)

8. National Public Radio and Colorado public radio stations filed a federal lawsuit challenging an executive order cutting their funding. Public broadcasters turned to the courts to contest retaliatory defunding, testing constitutional protections for independent media against executive pressure. (26 May 2025; 27 May 2025; 28 May 2025)

9. Federal judge in South Sudan deportation case rejected the administration's request to delay or rescind an order protecting deportees. By insisting that deported men remain in U.S. custody for fear interviews, the court reinforced due-process limits on executive immigration actions. (26 May 2025)

10. Federal judges issued at least 177 rulings temporarily pausing Trump administration initiatives. A large number of injunctions against firings and

civil-rights rollbacks showed courts actively constraining executive overreach across multiple policy areas. (27 May 2025)

11. Trump administration publicly refused to comply with judicial orders in the Kilmar Abrego Garcia immigration case. Defying court directives on a deported asylum seeker challenged judicial authority and signaled that executive preferences could trump legal rulings. (27 May 2025)

12. President Donald Trump attacked judges in a social media post, calling them 'USA hating' and blaming them for crime. Vilifying judges as enemies undermined public confidence in an independent judiciary and framed legal checks as threats to national safety. (27 May 2025)

13. U.S. District Court blocked Trump's executive order targeting the law firm WilmerHale as unconstitutional retaliation. Striking down an order aimed at a disfavored law firm protected legal actors from direct executive punishment for prior work, reinforcing First Amendment and rule-of-law norms. (27 May 2025; 28 May 2025)

14. U.S. District Court ruled that Elon Musk must face a lawsuit over his role in the Department of Government Efficiency. Allowing states' Appointments Clause challenge to proceed signaled judicial scrutiny of unconventional power centers embedded in the executive branch. (27 May 2025; 28 May 2025)

15. Trump administration filed an emergency appeal to the Supreme Court seeking to lift due-process protections in deportation cases. The appeal sought to ease deportations to third countries by weakening court-ordered safeguards, testing how far emergency litigation can erode immigrant rights. (27 May 2025)

16. Democratic state attorneys general prepared and filed numerous lawsuits anticipating unconstitutional Trump policies. Coordinated state-level legal strategies formed a key institutional counterweight to federal overreach, using courts to defend civil rights and administrative norms. (27 May 2025)

17. Federal judges blocked Trump's executive order cutting funds to NPR and PBS as alleged retaliation. Judicial review of the funding ban underscored that executive attempts to punish critical media must withstand constitutional scrutiny. (27 May 2025)

18. Harvard University and allied college leaders sued the Trump administration over demands and sanctions targeting the university. Harvard's lawsuit, backed by hundreds of academic leaders, challenged executive pressure on campus speech and enrollment, defending academic freedom through institutional litigation. (28 May 2025)

19. U.S. District Judge Paula Xinis denied the administration's request for

more time in the Garcia rendition lawsuit. Refusing a delay and criticizing the government's justification reinforced judicial expectations that the executive comply promptly with court processes in rights-sensitive cases. (28 May 2025)

20. Federal courts ruled that most of Trump's 'Liberation Day' tariffs were unconstitutional overreaches of emergency powers. Trade judges found that the president exceeded statutory and constitutional authority in imposing broad tariffs, reasserting Congress's primary role over taxation and trade. (28 May 2025; 29 May 2025; 30 May 2025)

21. Trump administration filed emergency appeals to keep contested tariffs in place pending higher court review. Seeking stays after losing in lower courts allowed the executive to preserve its tariff regime despite rulings against it, illustrating how appeals can blunt judicial checks. (28 May 2025)

22. U.S. Court of Appeals granted temporary pauses on rulings blocking Trump's tariffs. Stays that kept tariffs active pending appeal showed higher courts' willingness to tolerate contested emergency-based trade measures while legal battles continue. (29 May 2025)

23. Virginia legislature passed a constitutional amendment to codify abortion rights, pending further approval. Moving to entrench abortion rights in the state constitution shifted a contested liberty question from ordinary statutes to higher-order law subject to voter ratification. (30 May 2025)

24. U.S. Supreme Court allowed the Trump administration to revoke Temporary Protected Status and related protections for hundreds of thousands of migrants. By green-lighting TPS and parole rollbacks, the Court enabled sweeping executive changes to migrants' legal status, with limited immediate recourse for those affected. (30 May 2025)

25. U.S. District Court in Boston stopped a deportation flight to South Sudan for violating an earlier order. Halting the flight reaffirmed that the executive must honor court-mandated opportunities for deportees to challenge removal, even in complex multi-country transfers. (30 May 2025)

26. Federal judge ordered the administration to release over $12 million to Radio Free Europe/Radio Liberty. Compelling disbursement of previously appropriated funds protected an independent broadcaster from executive withholding, reinforcing congressional control over spending. (30 May 2025)

27. Federal Election Commission scheduled a closed Sunshine Act meeting on civil actions and proceedings. The FEC's closed meeting on litigation matters reflected routine but opaque oversight of campaign-finance enforcement, with limited public visibility into decisions affecting elections. (30 May 2025)

28. U.S. Supreme Court granted a stay in Noem v. Doe allowing DHS to terminate special parole programs. The emergency stay prioritized execu-

tive immigration prerogatives over a lower-court order, immediately altering the legal footing of hundreds of thousands of parole recipients. (30 May 2025)

Civil Rights and Dissent

1. Federal Judge Brian Murphy ordered the Trump administration to return a wrongly deported gay asylum seeker. Requiring the government to facilitate a deportee's return underscored judicial enforcement of due process and protection for LGBTQ+ asylum seekers against unlawful removal. (24 May 2025)

2. Immigration enforcement officers in Alabama detained a U.S. citizen filming a worksite raid after dismissing his Real ID as fake. Wrongfully arresting a citizen who documented arrests highlighted risks of civil-rights violations and retaliation during aggressive immigration operations. (24 May 2025)

3. Trump administration revoked humanitarian parole for a critically ill 4-year-old Mexican girl. Canceling life-saving parole for a child receiving U.S. medical care illustrated the human cost of hardline immigration policies on vulnerable individuals. (24 May 2025)

4. Patriot Front held a white nationalist march in Kansas City. The continued public activity of an extremist group underscored persistent threats to minority safety and the challenge of balancing assembly rights with countering hate. (24 May 2025)

5. Trump administration revoked Harvard's ability to enroll foreign students and demanded information on their protests and coursework. Linking enrollment privileges to surveillance of foreign students' speech and activism threatened academic freedom and chilled campus dissent. (25 May 2025)

6. Georgia police officer and ICE under state 287(g) law wrongfully arrested an undocumented student who was then jailed for weeks. Local participation in federal immigration enforcement led to prolonged detention and potential deportation, illustrating how such agreements endanger immigrant communities. (25 May 2025)

7. Trump administration planned to require social media vetting for all foreign student visa applicants and paused new interviews. Mandating broad social-media screening for students expanded surveillance of non-citizens and threatened privacy and academic exchange. (26 May 2025)

8. Trump administration ordered U.S. embassies to halt scheduling student visa interviews worldwide. Freezing new student visa appointments

abruptly cut off educational pathways and signaled a broader effort to restrict international academic mobility. (27 May 2025; 29 May 2025)

9. Trump administration attempted to cap foreign student enrollment at elite universities like Harvard. Proposed limits on international students framed them as displacing Americans, politicizing admissions and stratifying access by nationality. (29 May 2025)

10. Trump administration cut Harvard's SEVP certification and then temporarily reversed the ban while demanding justification. Suspending and conditionally restoring Harvard's ability to host foreign students used immigration tools to pressure a specific institution's policies and speech. (28 May 2025)

11. Federal Judge Allison Burroughs expanded an injunction protecting Harvard's enrollment of international students. The injunction shielded foreign students and the university from abrupt policy shifts, reinforcing judicial oversight of politically motivated immigration sanctions. (29 May 2025)

12. Idaho and Montana legislatures enacted bans on LGBTQ+ flags during Pride month at public institutions. Prohibiting Pride flags at government sites restricted symbolic expression of LGBTQ+ identity and signaled official disapproval of a minority community. (29 May 2025)

13. Utah legislature banned LGBTQ+ flags at government buildings and schools with daily fines. Utah's explicit flag ban, backed by financial penalties, curtailed visible support for LGBTQ+ rights in public institutions and emboldened similar measures elsewhere. (29 May 2025)

14. Parents group 'We're Oklahoma Education' (WOKE) used a state opt-out law to withdraw children from a politicized social studies curriculum. Parents leveraged a law intended for conservative causes to resist election conspiracies and Christian nationalism in classrooms, asserting community control over civic education. (29 May 2025)

15. Parents, grandparents, and teachers in Oklahoma filed a lawsuit challenging the rushed approval of the new social studies curriculum. The suit argued that opaque adoption of a conspiracy-laden curriculum violated transparency rules, using courts to defend evidence-based education. (29 May 2025)

16. Oklahoma State Superintendent Ryan Walters mandated a social studies curriculum including 2020 election conspiracies and Christian nationalism. Imposing ideologically skewed standards on all public schools politicized civics instruction and risked indoctrinating students with false narratives. (29 May 2025)

17. Trump administration canceled a $600 million contract with Moderna

for a bird flu vaccine. Walking away from a major pandemic-preparedness investment reduced future vaccine access, potentially exposing the public to greater health risks in a future outbreak. (29 May 2025)

18. Trump administration issued 'Merit Hiring Plan' guidelines discouraging consideration of race or gender and emphasizing loyalty. Redefining merit to exclude diversity and screen for willingness to 'faithfully serve' the executive politicized federal hiring and threatened equal-opportunity norms. (29 May 2025)

19. Trump administration and Secretary Marco Rubio planned an Office of Remigration to repurpose refugee functions toward deportation. Reorienting a humanitarian bureau toward tracking and removing migrants institutionalized a deportation-focused approach aligned with far-right 'remigration' rhetoric. (30 May 2025)

20. U.S. Supreme Court allowed termination of a program letting over 500,000 migrants live and work in the U.S. temporarily. Ending large-scale parole protections exposed hundreds of thousands of people to removal, deepening stratification of legal status by origin. (30 May 2025)

21. Trump administration secured Supreme Court permission to revoke Temporary Protected Status for Venezuelan, Cuban, Haitian, and Nicaraguan migrants. Rolling back TPS for specific nationalities heightened vulnerability for long-settled communities and signaled a more exclusionary approach to humanitarian relief. (30 May 2025)

22. Grassroots movement 50501 organized nationwide decentralized protests against authoritarianism and oligarchy. Sustained protests across all states demonstrated broad civic mobilization against perceived democratic erosion and concentrated tech-political power. (28 May 2025)

23. Fox Takedown protest movement staged protests at Fox News stations over its role as a propaganda arm. Targeting a major network for alleged misinformation reflected public efforts to hold media institutions accountable outside formal regulation. (28 May 2025)

24. Purge Palantir movement protested Peter Thiel and Palantir's surveillance work. Demonstrations against a surveillance contractor highlighted fears that data tools are being used to entrench authoritarian policies and monitor dissent. (28 May 2025)

25. Tesla Takedown movement organized showroom protests and boycotts targeting Tesla and Elon Musk. Economic boycotts and protests against a politically influential CEO illustrated how citizens use market pressure to contest perceived technocratic authoritarianism. (28 May 2025)

26. Federal and local law enforcement reported declines in U.S. mass shootings and violent crime rates. Lower levels of lethal violence improved

baseline public safety, even as political rhetoric emphasized crisis to justify expanded coercive powers. (25 May 2025)

27. Plaintiff Misti Leon filed the first wrongful death lawsuit against major oil companies over climate-related harm. Linking a heatwave death to fossil fuel firms' conduct opened a new legal front for climate accountability with implications for environmental justice. (29 May 2025)

28. Harvard University and Tamara Lanier settled a lawsuit over daguerreotypes of enslaved people, transferring them to a museum. Relocating historic images of enslaved individuals to an African American museum addressed contested ownership and advanced efforts to reckon with slavery's legacy. (29 May 2025)

29. Youth plaintiffs sued the Trump administration over executive orders promoting fossil fuels and curbing climate science. Young Americans argued that pro-fossil fuel orders violated their constitutional rights to life and liberty, using courts to contest environmental rollback. (29 May 2025)

Economic Structure

1. Trump administration extended the deadline for imposing 50% tariffs on EU trade to July 9, 2025. Delaying but not rescinding steep tariffs kept businesses and allies in a state of uncertainty, using trade threats as leverage in negotiations. (25 May 2025)

2. Trump administration ordered all federal agencies to cut contracts and grants with Harvard University. Canceling roughly $100 million in federal agreements punished a single university over ideological disputes, weaponizing procurement and research funding against perceived critics. (26 May 2025; 27 May 2025)

3. President Donald Trump threatened a 25% tariff on iPhones unless production moved to the United States. Targeting a specific company's supply chain with punitive tariffs blurred the line between national trade policy and pressure on individual firms. (26 May 2025)

4. Environmental Protection Agency submitted an Acid Rain Program information collection request for OMB review. Continuing data collection for the Acid Rain Program sustained regulatory capacity to monitor emissions and enforce environmental standards affecting public health. (27 May 2025)

5. Federal Communications Commission held an open meeting on telecom certification, foreign control, and spectrum use. The FCC's agenda on certification oversight and foreign network control addressed vulnerabili-

ties in communications infrastructure central to economic and national security. (27 May 2025)

6. OMB and federal procurement agencies sought extensions for multiple Federal Acquisition Regulation information collections. Maintaining reporting on payments, travel, service contracting, government property, and value engineering preserved transparency and cost control in federal contracting. (27 May 2025)

7. Elon Musk's company xAI acquired social media platform X. An AI firm taking over a major social network concentrated data and influence in a single private actor, raising questions about market power and information control. (27 May 2025)

8. Boeing and the Trump Justice Department reached a non-prosecution agreement over 737 MAX crashes after a prior deferred prosecution. Allowing Boeing to avoid trial after deadly crashes, despite earlier violations, signaled lenient treatment for a powerful corporation implicated in major safety failures. (27 May 2025)

9. Boeing and Trump administration officials maintained close political and contracting ties, including large aircraft deals. Extensive donations, lobbying, and high-value contracts between Boeing and the administration blurred lines between procurement decisions and political patronage. (27 May 2025)

10. Vietnamese government and Trump family businesses fast-tracked approvals for a Trump golf resort and tower, allegedly bypassing local laws. Accelerated approvals and land coercion for Trump-branded projects suggested foreign policy and trade considerations were intertwined with the president's private ventures. (24 May 2025; 25 May 2025)

11. Environmental Protection Agency approved alternative test methods for air emission standards. Authorizing new measurement methods gave regulated industries more flexibility while preserving oversight of pollution that affects communities and ecosystems. (28 May 2025)

12. Federal Communications Commission launched a matching program with Arizona to verify eligibility for Lifeline and ACP. Data-matching to confirm low-income eligibility aimed to reduce fraud while sustaining subsidized connectivity for vulnerable households. (28 May 2025)

13. Federal Communications Commission sought public comment on multiple information collections affecting cable, radio, equipment, and broadband over power lines. Reviewing paperwork requirements for communications providers balanced regulatory oversight with burdens on industry, shaping how infrastructure is documented and monitored. (28 May 2025)

14. Governor Josh Green of Hawaii signed legislation increasing taxes on

vacation stays to fund climate mitigation. Using tourism taxes to finance climate resilience shifted environmental costs toward visitors and created a dedicated revenue stream for public adaptation projects. (28 May 2025)

15. Travel and tourism analysts reported a sharp decline in international tourism to the United States linked to policy perceptions. Falling foreign visitor spending highlighted how trade and immigration stances can damage economic sectors reliant on international openness. (28 May 2025)

16. Trump Media & Technology Group raised $2.5 billion to purchase Bitcoin as a corporate treasury asset. Amassing a large Bitcoin position while its controlling figure influences crypto policy raised concerns about market manipulation and regulatory capture. (28 May 2025)

17. Truth Social and Index Technologies Group launched investment accounts designed to profit from Trump administration policies. Creating financial products explicitly tied to presidential decisions fused public policy with private investment strategies that benefit the president's company. (28 May 2025)

18. Environmental Protection Agency established pesticide residue tolerances for florylpicoxamid on several crops. Setting residue limits balanced agricultural productivity with consumer safety, shaping how chemical risks are managed in the food supply. (29 May 2025)

19. Food and Drug Administration classified several medical devices and diagnostic tests as class II with special controls. Reclassifying devices such as genetic tests, drug level assays, BPH systems, Zika reagents, and fertility tests aimed to speed innovation while maintaining safety standards. (29 May 2025; 30 May 2025)

20. Food and Drug Administration confirmed the effective date for allowing myoglobin as a color additive in meat analogues. Finalizing approval for a new color additive affected food manufacturing practices and labeling, with implications for consumer perception and safety oversight. (29 May 2025)

21. Food and Drug Administration issued draft and final guidance on electronic submissions and Q-Submission processes for medical devices. Modernizing device submission procedures aimed to streamline regulatory review, potentially lowering barriers for innovators while preserving scrutiny. (29 May 2025)

22. Food and Drug Administration extended the comment period on opiate alkaloid contamination in poppy seeds. Seeking more input on opiate thresholds in food products supported evidence-based regulation of a subtle but important public-health risk. (29 May 2025)

23. Food and Drug Administration revoked Emergency Use Authoriza-

tions for four COVID-19 diagnostic devices at manufacturers' request. Ending EUAs for certain tests marked a shift in pandemic regulatory posture and affected which diagnostics remain available in the market. (29 May 2025)

24. Food and Drug Administration debarred Quality Poultry and Seafood, Inc. from importing food for five years. Banning a convicted importer from the U.S. market enforced food-safety laws and signaled consequences for fraud in global supply chains. (29 May 2025)

25. National Archives and Records Administration announced a FOIA Advisory Committee meeting on statutory reform and implementation. The advisory meeting supported ongoing refinement of transparency rules that govern public access to federal records. (29 May 2025)

26. Food and Drug Administration issued multiple guidance and determinations on drug products, color additives, and postmarketing commitments. Regulatory actions on drug withdrawals, patent review periods, color additive changes, postmarketing studies, and NDA withdrawals shaped pharmaceutical market dynamics and safety oversight. (30 May 2025)

27. Environmental Protection Agency published a notice of availability for multiple Environmental Impact Statements. Making EIS documents publicly available enabled scrutiny of major infrastructure and energy projects that carry long-term environmental and economic consequences. (30 May 2025)

28. Environmental Protection Agency announced a Pesticide Program Dialogue Committee public meeting. The PPDC meeting provided a forum for stakeholders to influence pesticide regulation, which affects agriculture, health, and environmental justice. (30 May 2025)

29. Environmental Protection Agency received requests to voluntarily cancel certain pesticide registrations. Processing voluntary cancellations adjusted the mix of approved pesticides, with implications for environmental risk and farming practices. (30 May 2025)

30. Health policy analysts reported that U.S. health care costs have stabilized as a share of GDP. Evidence that health spending growth has leveled off suggested prior reforms improved affordability, affecting household finances and fiscal space. (30 May 2025)

31. Education analysts reported that higher education tuition has fallen in real terms since the pandemic. Declining inflation-adjusted tuition, driven by enrollment drops, modestly improved access to college and challenged narratives of ever-rising costs. (30 May 2025)

32. Economists observed accelerated productivity growth in U.S. service sectors since 2008. Rising service productivity, aided by technology adoption, pointed to potential for higher living standards and fiscal capacity without proportional cost increases. (30 May 2025)

Information, Memory, and Manipulation

1. White House stopped publishing and removed official transcripts of President Trump's speeches. Eliminating a searchable transcript archive reduced transparency and impaired the public's ability to verify and analyze presidential statements over time. (24 May 2025)

2. Trump allies and administration officials described using government power to pressure universities over perceived bias and discrimination. Boasting about leveraging state power to reshape campus policies signaled a willingness to subordinate academic independence to partisan agendas. (24 May 2025)

3. UK Home Office released data showing a record rise in U.S. citizens applying for British residency. Migration statistics highlighted how political polarization and policy shifts influence individuals' decisions to leave or avoid the United States. (24 May 2025)

4. Islamic State propagandists used Trump's international tariffs in recruitment narratives about Western decline. Framing U.S. trade wars as evidence of collapsing Western power showed how domestic economic policies can be repurposed in extremist messaging abroad. (26 May 2025)

5. Trump administration rewarded or punished media companies, law firms, and universities based on loyalty. Conditioning access and benefits on institutional alignment with the president's views threatened independent judgment in key knowledge and legal sectors. (27 May 2025)

6. Health and Human Services Secretary Robert F. Kennedy Jr. released a 'Make American Healthy Again' report criticized for errors and nonexistent sources. Publishing a flawed flagship health report undermined confidence in official information and risked misinforming policy debates. (28 May 2025)

7. Trump administration temporarily reversed its plan to bar Harvard from admitting international students while demanding justification. The partial retreat, under court pressure, still framed foreign students as suspect and kept Harvard under heightened scrutiny, chilling academic openness. (28 May 2025)

8. Health and education researchers reported strong learning gains from AI tutors in Nigeria. Evidence that AI tutoring can dramatically boost learning suggested new tools for expanding educational access, with implications for civic knowledge. (25 May 2025)

9. Cities such as Dallas and Santa Monica implemented YIMBY reforms like upzoning and deregulation to spur housing. Local zoning reforms aimed to address housing crises, illustrating how municipal policy choices shape economic inclusion and urban development. (25 May 2025)

10. Trump administration sought lists and data on Harvard's foreign students while criticizing their numbers. Publicly demanding information on international students portrayed them as a problem group and risked stigmatizing foreign scholars. (25 May 2025)

11. Trump administration planned mandatory social media screening for all Harvard-bound visa applicants. Requiring consular officers to scrutinize applicants' online speech to visit one university fused immigration vetting with ideological monitoring of academic visitors. (30 May 2025)

12. PBS filed a lawsuit challenging an executive order targeting its federal funding. PBS's suit contested what it viewed as retaliatory defunding, defending public broadcasting's independence from direct political reprisal. (30 May 2025)

13. Trump administration opposed a G7 proposal to lower the price cap on Russian oil exports. Blocking a tighter oil price cap limited economic pressure on Russia, affecting the information environment around Western resolve and sanctions efficacy. (26 May 2025)

14. German Chancellor Merz and Western allies lifted range restrictions on weapons supplied to Ukraine and endorsed strikes on Russian territory. Expanding Ukraine's ability to hit targets in Russia altered the conflict narrative and signaled a stronger Western commitment to Ukrainian defense. (25 May 2025)

15. President Donald Trump publicly criticized both Vladimir Putin and Volodymyr Zelensky over the Ukraine conflict. Trump's comments framed the war as a failure of multiple leaders and suggested it would not have occurred under him, shaping partisan narratives about foreign policy competence. (25 May 2025)

16. Trump administration closed the State Department's office of analytic outreach and cut research staff. Eliminating a unit that connected diplomats with outside experts reduced the diversity of information feeding foreign-policy decisions. (28 May 2025)

17. Trump administration used tariffs and self-interested Middle East deals in ways that fed extremist propaganda. Policies framed as transactional and self-serving were repurposed by ISIS to argue that Western powers are corrupt and in decline. (26 May 2025)

18. Oklahoma State Superintendent Ryan Walters installed a curriculum embedding election conspiracies and Christian nationalism in public schools. Rewriting social studies standards to include false election claims and sectarian narratives reshaped civic memory and normalized disinformation in education. (29 May 2025)

19. Trump administration campaigned against DEI and trans rights,

contributing to corporate withdrawal from Pride sponsorships. Official rhetoric and policy pressure discouraged corporate support for LGBTQ+ events, influencing how public culture remembers and recognizes minority struggles. (29 May 2025)

20. President Donald Trump fired National Portrait Gallery director Kim Sajet over her support for DEI. Removing a museum leader for diversity work signaled political control over cultural institutions and the stories they choose to display. (30 May 2025)

21. Trump administration canceled a major Moderna bird flu vaccine contract, affecting future preparedness. Abandoning a pandemic-preparedness contract also shaped public understanding of the administration's priorities regarding science and health risk. (29 May 2025)

22. Federal Bureau of Investigation leadership reopened investigations into the 2023 White House cocaine incident and Dobbs draft leak. Revisiting politically sensitive cases signaled a focus on past controversies that could be used to shape narratives about prior administrations and institutions. (26 May 2025)

23. Deputy FBI Director Dan Bongino announced investigations into the January 6 pipe bomber and COVID-19 origins. High-profile probes into unresolved events aimed to address public demands for answers but also risked being framed through partisan lenses. (28 May 2025)

24. FBI and Justice Department officials were implicated in claims of an illegal NSA wiretap during a Pentagon leak investigation. Allegations of warrantless surveillance in an internal leak probe, later discredited, eroded trust in official narratives about investigative methods. (27 May 2025)

25. Kenner Police Department and Louisiana authorities announced arrests in a scheme to drug and rob victims including a Telemundo reporter. Publicizing arrests in a high-profile crime case demonstrated law-enforcement responsiveness but also shaped media narratives about safety and vulnerability. (30 May 2025)

26. FBI investigated an AI-enabled impersonation of White House Chief of Staff Susie Wiles. The deepfake-style impersonation exposed how synthetic media can be used to solicit favors and money, threatening secure communication at the top of government. (30 May 2025)

CHAPTER 20
WEEK 20 (31 MAY 2025 – 6 JUN 2025): SURVEILLANCE AS EVERYDAY GOVERNANCE

In a week of near-still clock time, immigration raids, data centralization, and partisan clemency showed power consolidating quietly inside a more permissive order.

This was an exceptionally intense week of authoritarian structural pressure, with the executive branch aggressively consolidating power while weakening multiple safeguard mechanisms. Trump's team signaled a willingness to bypass Congress on spending and civil service purges, politicized immigration and law enforcement against political opponents and protesters, and normalized sweeping travel bans and mass deportations. The House advanced the "Big, Beautiful Bill," incorporating deep social cuts, deregulatory favors, and even non-reviewable mining leases, showing how legislation is used to entrench crony capitalism and rollback environmental protections. Courts had mixed outcomes: some rulings protected migrants and free speech, but the Supreme Court repeatedly used emergency orders to approve data collection and union-hostile measures, and to shield industries like guns from accountability. Control of information and memory politics intensified through attacks on NPR/PBS, censorship of VA scientists, erasures of history, and conspiratorial presidential messaging. Across issues like immigration, reproductive rights, veterans' care, science agencies, and FEMA/NOAA, policy choices systematically shifted risk and hardship onto vulnerable groups while maintaining elite advantages, revealing a regime that views inequality and institutional chaos as tools of governance rather than unintended consequences.

Power and Authority

1. President Trump announced and signed orders doubling tariffs on steel and aluminum imports to 50%. By sharply raising metal tariffs via executive action, the president unilaterally reshaped trade conditions with limited congressional input, concentrating economic decision-making power in the executive and testing checks on tariff authority. (31 May 2025; 2 Jun 2025)

2. President Trump ordered an investigation into former President Biden's competence and presidency. Ordering an executive-branch probe into a predecessor's mental fitness and decision-making weaponized investigative powers against a political rival, blurring lines between neutral oversight and partisan re-litigation of prior governance. (5 Jun 2025)

3. President Trump launched investigations into Joe Biden's pardons and clemencies. Targeting a former president's clemency decisions for special scrutiny risked turning prosecutorial discretion into a tool against political opponents, undermining the norm of even-handed treatment of presidential powers. (2 Jun 2025; 5 Jun 2025)

4. President Trump issued mass pardons and commutations for January 6 defendants and ordered related cases dropped. Granting sweeping clemency to January 6 offenders and halting prosecutions signaled tolerance of political violence on the regime's behalf, weakening deterrence and the rule of law around attacks on democratic institutions. (3 Jun 2025)

5. Trump administration fired or sidelined prosecutors handling January 6 cases and disbanded the Capitol siege section. Removing prosecutors who pursued January 6 cases and dismantling their unit undermined prosecutorial independence and signaled that accountability for insurrection-related crimes depends on political loyalty. (3 Jun 2025)

6. President Trump signed proclamations imposing a broad travel ban on nationals from 12 countries and restricting entry from seven more. Reviving and expanding nationality-based travel bans concentrated sweeping gatekeeping power in the executive, stratifying access to U.S. territory and family unity by origin under a security rationale with limited individualized review. (4 Jun 2025; 5 Jun 2025; 6 Jun 2025)

7. President Trump signed a proclamation suspending Harvard University from the student visa program and restricting foreign student visas. Targeting a single university's ability to host foreign students used immigration powers to punish a disfavored institution, pressuring academic independence and signaling that access to U.S. study can hinge on political alignment. (4 Jun 2025; 5 Jun 2025)

8. President Trump threatened to impose large fines on California over

trans athlete participation in sports. Threatening punitive federal fines against a state for allowing trans athletes in school sports leveraged national power to coerce state policy on civil rights, undermining state autonomy and equal protection norms. (3 Jun 2025)

9. President Trump publicly threatened to terminate Elon Musk's federal subsidies and contracts after political disagreements. Using the prospect of canceling major federal contracts as retaliation for criticism blurred the line between neutral procurement and personal vendetta, signaling that access to state resources depends on political loyalty. (5 Jun 2025; 6 Jun 2025)

10. President Trump ordered a large military parade to celebrate his birthday. Directing a personal military parade used state coercive symbols for leader glorification, normalizing personalized displays of force that can erode norms of civilian, institution-centered democratic culture. (2 Jun 2025)

11. President Trump issued an executive order reshaping federal cybersecurity policy and expanding AI-enabled defenses. Centralizing cybersecurity strategy and expanding AI-based defenses strengthened protection against foreign threats but also broadened executive control over digital infrastructure and data, with implications for surveillance and accountability. (6 Jun 2025)

12. President Trump issued executive orders to expand supersonic flight, tighten drone airspace control, and promote U.S. drone dominance. A trio of aviation and drone orders used unilateral authority to reset safety rules, expand commercial and security uses, and centralize control of airspace, increasing executive leverage over critical transport and surveillance technologies. (6 Jun 2025)

13. President Trump ended enforcement of federal emergency abortion guidance under EMTALA. Halting enforcement of emergency abortion protections narrowed federal guarantees for life-saving care, shifting life-and-death decisions toward state bans and signaling executive willingness to roll back established health rights. (2 Jun 2025; 5 Jun 2025)

14. President Trump directed the Justice Department to investigate Biden-era emergency abortion guidance. Framing prior emergency abortion protections as suspect policy and ending them recast federal health guarantees as partisan, weakening the expectation that core medical rights are insulated from political swings. (5 Jun 2025)

15. President Trump ordered the renaming of the USNS Harvey Milk and other ships to emphasize a "warrior culture". Stripping a Navy ship of Harvey Milk's name and similar moves used command authority to recast official symbols away from civil rights figures, narrowing whose histories are honored in state narratives. (3 Jun 2025)

16. President Trump announced plans to cancel significant federal funding and grants for California. Preparing to strip California of federal funds weaponized fiscal powers against a political adversary state, threatening residents' services to pressure state leaders and eroding norms of neutral intergovernmental support. (5 Jun 2025)

17. President Trump publicly promoted a conspiracy theory claiming Joe Biden was executed and replaced by clones. Amplifying an extreme conspiracy about a former president's death from the bully pulpit degraded shared reality and modeled disinformation as acceptable political communication, undermining informed consent in democratic governance. (31 May 2025; 2 Jun 2025)

18. Trump administration rescinded a Biden-era guidance requiring hospitals to perform emergency abortions where state bans apply. Revoking federal protection for emergency abortions in hostile states reduced national baseline rights to life-saving care, leaving access to depend more heavily on local politics and weakening uniform application of federal law. (2 Jun 2025)

19. Trump administration announced plans to transform the State Department's refugee bureau into an Office of Remigration. Reorienting a refugee-focused bureau toward facilitating migrant return signaled a structural shift away from protection toward removal, embedding a more exclusionary vision of membership into foreign and humanitarian policy. (31 May 2025)

20. Trump administration deployed National Guard and US Marines to Los Angeles to suppress mostly peaceful anti-deportation protests. Using military forces to police civilian demonstrations against deportations militarized domestic protest management, chilling dissent and blurring boundaries between civil law enforcement and armed forces. (3 Jun 2025)

21. Trump administration announced a broad travel ban that also trapped many veterans' translators abroad. Imposing a nationality-based travel ban that stranded translators who aided U.S. forces signaled that loyalty to the U.S. does not guarantee protection, undermining trust essential for future military partnerships. (6 Jun 2025)

Institutions and Governance

1. Office of Management and Budget Director Russell Vought signaled plans to use impoundment and executive tools to cut federal jobs and spending without full congressional approval. Proposing to bypass Congress on major workforce and budget cuts challenged the legislature's power of the purse and suggested a readiness to revive constrained

impoundment tactics to centralize fiscal control in the executive. (1 Jun 2025)

2. U.S. Court of International Trade ruled that President Trump's "Liberation Day" tariffs were unconstitutional without congressional authorization. By striking down unilateral tariffs as beyond presidential authority, the trade court reinforced Congress's constitutional role over taxation and trade, modestly checking executive overreach in economic policy. (31 May 2025; 5 Jun 2025)

3. Federal appeals court temporarily paused a lower-court ruling that had blocked many of Trump's tariffs. Allowing contested tariffs to remain in force during appeal preserved executive leverage over trade while legal challenges proceed, illustrating how interim judicial decisions can sustain disputed policies. (31 May 2025)

4. U.S. Supreme Court allowed the Trump administration to end humanitarian parole for about 500,000 migrants during ongoing litigation. Letting parole terminations proceed before final review exposed hundreds of thousands to deportation, showing how emergency high-court decisions can reshape lives and immigration policy before full merits consideration. (31 May 2025)

5. U.S. Supreme Court agreed to hear a case on nationwide injunctions affecting Trump's efforts to restrict birthright citizenship. Taking up a challenge to courts' ability to issue nationwide injunctions in birthright citizenship disputes opened the door to narrowing judicial tools that currently check sweeping executive actions. (1 Jun 2025)

6. U.S. Supreme Court ordered the government to facilitate the return of a wrongfully deported Maryland resident. Requiring the administration to bring back a deported resident underscored the judiciary's capacity to correct executive abuses in immigration enforcement and to enforce due process after the fact. (1 Jun 2025)

7. U.S. Supreme Court upheld President Trump's firing of National Labor Relations Board chair Gwynne Wilcox. Affirming the president's removal of an independent agency head strengthened the unitary executive model, potentially weakening the insulation of labor regulators from direct political control. (1 Jun 2025)

8. U.S. Supreme Court lifted an injunction to allow the Department of Government Efficiency access to Social Security data. Granting emergency access to vast Social Security records for an unelected efficiency unit expanded state and quasi-private reach into sensitive data, prioritizing administrative goals over privacy and union concerns. (6 Jun 2025)

9. U.S. Supreme Court granted a stay in a Social Security Administration

labor dispute, favoring management over unions. Allowing the SSA to proceed with contested employment practices during litigation tilted the balance toward agency leadership and away from union protections, weakening organized labor's leverage inside government. (6 Jun 2025)

10. U.S. Supreme Court dismissed Mexico's lawsuit against U.S. gunmakers under federal immunity law. By shielding gun manufacturers from Mexico's suit over cartel violence, the Court reaffirmed broad statutory immunity for a powerful industry, limiting cross-border accountability for weapons flows. (5 Jun 2025)

11. U.S. Supreme Court ruled unanimously that Catholic Charities is exempt from unemployment taxes under the First Amendment. Expanding religious exemptions from unemployment taxes adjusted the boundary between church and state, potentially encouraging more entities to seek faith-based carve-outs from generally applicable labor laws. (5 Jun 2025)

12. U.S. Supreme Court lowered the burden for majority-group plaintiffs in reverse discrimination cases. Making it easier for majority-group employees to bring discrimination claims could redirect civil rights litigation resources and reshape how equality law is used and perceived in workplace disputes. (5 Jun 2025)

13. U.S. Supreme Court allowed the Department of Government Efficiency to proceed with contested actions via emergency stay. Letting Doge continue disputed efficiency measures through an emergency order highlighted how the Court's shadow docket can accelerate structural changes in federal operations without full briefing or transparency. (6 Jun 2025)

14. U.S. District Judge Tanya Chutkan allowed 14 states' lawsuit against Elon Musk and the Department of Government Efficiency to proceed. Letting states challenge the legality of a Musk-led government unit preserved a key avenue for contesting novel delegations of state power to private actors. (31 May 2025)

15. U.S. District Court in Washington, DC ruled that migrants sent to an El Salvador prison must be allowed to challenge their deportations. Requiring a process for migrants exiled under an old wartime law reinforced judicial oversight of extraordinary deportation schemes and affirmed that even novel programs must allow legal challenge. (4 Jun 2025)

16. U.S. District Court in Boston ordered the return of a deported gay Guatemalan asylum seeker due to due process violations. Forcing DHS to bring back a wrongly deported asylum seeker underscored courts' role in correcting administrative misrepresentations and protecting vulnerable individuals from summary removal. (4 Jun 2025)

17. Federal Judge in Colorado temporarily halted deportation of the

family of the Boulder attack suspect. Blocking immediate removal of a suspect's family pending review emphasized that even in high-profile terrorism cases, due process protections extend to relatives seeking asylum. (4 Jun 2025)

18. Federal judge blocked the deportation of a Venezuelan man under the Alien Enemies Act for lack of due process. Stopping a deportation under a rarely used wartime statute highlighted judicial concern over expansive executive power in immigration, even while acknowledging broad statutory authority. (2 Jun 2025)

19. Federal appeals court ruled that San Diego's ban on group yoga classes in shoreline parks violated the First Amendment. Recognizing yoga instruction as protected speech limited local governments' ability to restrict peaceful expressive activities in public spaces under the guise of regulating commerce. (5 Jun 2025)

20. NPR and public radio stations filed a lawsuit challenging Trump's executive order cutting funding to allegedly biased media. Public broadcasters' suit argued that defunding based on perceived bias violates the First Amendment, testing whether the executive can financially punish critical outlets without judicial pushback. (1 Jun 2025)

21. Department of Homeland Security published and then removed a list of allegedly noncompliant sheriffs and sanctuary jurisdictions. Issuing a public shaming list of sheriffs over immigration cooperation, then retracting it under pressure, showed federal attempts to coerce local law enforcement alignment through reputational tools rather than formal process. (2 Jun 2025; 3 Jun 2025)

22. House of Representatives passed Donald Trump's One Big Beautiful Bill and related budget legislation with deep social cuts and AI preemption. Advancing a sprawling bill that extends tax cuts, slashes safety-net programs, and preempts state AI regulation illustrated Congress functioning as a vehicle for an executive-aligned agenda with limited deliberation. (1 Jun 2025; 2 Jun 2025; 3 Jun 2025; 4 Jun 2025; 6 Jun 2025)

23. Congressional Budget Office reported that Trump's tariffs and omnibus bill would raise inflation, slow growth, and increase deficits. Independent fiscal analyses contradicting administration claims provided a factual check on major economic policies, though political actors' misrepresentation of the findings highlighted pressures on neutral budget institutions. (3 Jun 2025; 5 Jun 2025)

24. House Oversight Committee Republicans sought testimony from Biden aides about his cognitive state and decision-making. Launching an inquiry into a former president's mental fitness risked turning congressional

oversight into partisan theater, potentially crowding out substantive policy scrutiny. (5 Jun 2025)

25. House Oversight Committee Democrats demanded release of all FBI and DOJ files related to the Jeffrey Epstein case. Pressing for long-promised Epstein records highlighted concerns that law enforcement may be shielding information about elite misconduct, and tested transparency commitments from top justice officials. (5 Jun 2025)

26. Senator Elizabeth Warren released a report detailing Elon Musk's wealth gains and alleged influence over federal decisions. Documenting how a powerful businessman's net worth and federal influence surged raised alarms about regulatory capture and the entanglement of public policy with private fortunes. (3 Jun 2025)

27. Newark Mayor Ras Baraka filed a civil rights lawsuit against federal officials over his arrest and prosecution. A sitting mayor's suit alleging false arrest and malicious prosecution by federal actors spotlighted potential misuse of justice powers against local elected officials and tested avenues for redress. (3 Jun 2025)

28. Federal Election Commission canceled its scheduled open meeting for June 5, 2025. Calling off a public FEC meeting reduced opportunities for transparent discussion of campaign finance and enforcement issues, modestly weakening open oversight of electoral rules. (2 Jun 2025)

29. Federal courts issued orders barring ICE from transferring Boston student Marcelo Gomes Da Silva and later clarifying his detention conditions. Judicial interventions in a high-profile student protester's case underscored courts' role in checking immigration enforcement and protecting due process for politically active noncitizens. (2 Jun 2025)

30. U.S. Justice Department allowed Dominion Voting Systems' defamation trial against Mike Lindell to proceed. The continuation of Dominion's suit against a prominent election denier showed that courts remain a venue for holding purveyors of election misinformation civilly accountable. (2 Jun 2025)

31. U.S. Justice Department Civil Rights Division sent a letter warning California schools that allowing trans girls in sports violates equal protection. Using federal civil rights enforcement to threaten schools over trans inclusion inverted traditional protections, signaling a willingness to reinterpret constitutional guarantees to restrict, rather than expand, marginalized students' rights. (2 Jun 2025)

32. Congressional caucuses formed new groups to advance "Abundance"-inspired legislation on green energy and public goods. Creating caucuses around an abundance agenda indicated some lawmakers' intent to use insti-

tutional channels to expand state capacity for public investment, countering broader trends of retrenchment. (2 Jun 2025)

33. Senator Angus King and Representative Jamie Raskin delivered speeches invoking Margaret Chase Smith's Declaration of Conscience to warn about executive overreach. By publicly recalling a historic stand against demagoguery, the lawmakers used institutional platforms to frame current power concentration as a constitutional crisis and to rally colleagues toward oversight. (1 Jun 2025)

34. House Oversight Committee Democrats moved toward subpoenaing Elon Musk over alleged drug use while serving in the administration. Pursuing testimony on a powerful insider's conduct signaled some willingness in Congress to scrutinize elite behavior, though the inquiry also intersected with factional political conflicts. (4 Jun 2025)

35. Federal courts allowed the Social Security Administration to proceed with contested employment actions in a union case. The Supreme Court's stay in the SSA union dispute enabled management to implement changes before full review, reflecting a judiciary increasingly deferential to agency leadership over organized labor. (6 Jun 2025)

Civil Rights and Dissent

1. Immigration and Customs Enforcement and Federal Protective Service officers entered Representative Jerry Nadler's office and handcuffed an aide during a claimed safety check. Detaining a congressional staffer in his office under dubious pretexts suggested federal enforcement tools being used to intimidate political opponents, chilling legislative independence. (31 May 2025; 2 Jun 2025)

2. Immigration and Customs Enforcement conducted a high-profile raid on a San Diego restaurant, detaining staff and using flash-bang grenades on protesters. Aggressive tactics at a workplace raid, including crowd-dispersal grenades, exemplified militarized immigration enforcement that can endanger bystanders and suppress community protest. (2 Jun 2025)

3. Senior ICE and DHS officials including Stephen Miller pressured ICE leadership to dramatically increase deportations beyond criminal cases. Internal demands to boost deportation numbers and expand targets beyond serious offenders prioritized quotas over discretion, heightening fear among immigrants and eroding trust in enforcement priorities. (2 Jun 2025; 3 Jun 2025; 4 Jun 2025)

4. Senior U.S. immigration officials ordered officers to increase warrantless "collateral" arrests of undocumented people encountered incidentally.

Encouraging collateral arrests without warrants expanded the pool of people swept into detention, stretching legal norms and intensifying the climate of insecurity for immigrant communities. (4 Jun 2025)

5. Trump administration ended humanitarian parole for hundreds of thousands of migrants from several countries. Terminating parole for about half a million people abruptly converted many into undocumented status, exposing them to detention and deportation and deepening a tiered system of rights based on origin. (31 May 2025)

6. Trump administration restored humanitarian parole for a four-year-old girl with a life-threatening illness after public outcry. Reinstating parole for a single high-profile child after backlash highlighted how life-or-death immigration decisions can hinge on media attention rather than consistent humanitarian standards. (2 Jun 2025)

7. Trump administration intensified a crackdown on pro-Palestinian campus protests, detaining and seeking to deport student activists. Using immigration enforcement against student protesters under the banner of combating antisemitism conflated dissent with bigotry, threatening free speech and academic freedom for noncitizens. (5 Jun 2025)

8. Immigration agents arrested international student Rümeysa Öztürk after she co-authored a Gaza op-ed. The street arrest of a student writer by masked immigration officers suggested political speech about foreign policy can trigger coercive action for noncitizens, chilling campus expression. (2 Jun 2025)

9. Federal judge blocked deportation of a Venezuelan man under the Alien Enemies Act for lack of due process. Judicial intervention in a wartime-law deportation underscored the tension between expansive security statutes and individual rights, especially for migrants labeled as potential enemies. (2 Jun 2025)

10. West Virginia county prosecutor suggested women should report miscarriages to police under the state's abortion ban. Encouraging police involvement in miscarriages blurred lines between healthcare and criminal investigation, heightening the risk that pregnancy loss could be treated as a crime. (5 Jun 2025)

11. Trump administration deployed National Guard and Marines to manage protests against deportations in Los Angeles. Bringing military forces into a largely civilian protest context escalated the state's response to dissent, potentially deterring lawful assembly through the threat of overwhelming force. (3 Jun 2025)

12. Cook County regional organized crime taskforce and partner agencies conducted a nationwide crackdown on organized retail theft, arresting

hundreds. A large, coordinated operation against retail theft illustrated robust law enforcement capacity, but also raised questions about proportionality and the focus of criminal justice resources. (4 Jun 2025)

13. Local authorities in Charlottesville, Virginia charged a traffic safety activist with vandalism for chalking a crosswalk at a dangerous intersection. Prosecuting a citizen for a chalk crosswalk after officials ignored safety requests suggested a punitive response to grassroots advocacy, potentially discouraging civic engagement. (4 Jun 2025)

14. Rev. William Barber and Moral Monday protesters were arrested in the Capitol Rotunda while protesting budget cuts to healthcare and social services. Arresting peaceful demonstrators inside the Capitol underscored how access to symbolic democratic spaces can be tightly controlled when protests challenge dominant fiscal agendas. (4 Jun 2025)

15. David Huerta, SEIU of California president was arrested and injured during an immigration raid at a Los Angeles garment factory. The arrest and hospitalization of a union leader at a raid, amid disputed official accounts, suggested labor organizers challenging enforcement priorities may face heightened physical and legal risks. (6 Jun 2025)

16. Louisiana legislature passed an anti-grooming law criminalizing manipulative pursuit of minors for sexual offenses. Creating a standalone offense for grooming aimed to prevent child abuse earlier in the cycle, expanding legal tools to protect minors while raising questions about definitional scope. (5 Jun 2025)

17. Federal prosecutors and courts indicted Kilmar Ábrego García on smuggling charges after his mistaken deportation and ordered return. Charging a previously wrongfully deported man upon his return blurred the line between correcting government error and pursuing potentially politicized prosecutions in a contentious immigration case. (6 Jun 2025)

18. Enrique Tarrio and other January 6 defendants filed a lawsuit against the federal government challenging their prosecutions. The suit by convicted January 6 participants contested the legitimacy of their prosecutions, reflecting ongoing efforts to reframe accountability for the Capitol attack as political persecution. (6 Jun 2025)

19. Senator Cory Booker publicly urged citizens to hold politicians accountable despite fear of Trump. Calling on the public to make officials fear electoral consequences more than presidential retaliation framed civic participation as a counterweight to authoritarian pressure within Congress. (1 Jun 2025)

20. West Virginia officials signaled that miscarriages might be scrutinized under strict abortion laws. Hints that pregnancy loss could trigger law

enforcement review deepened concerns that reproductive autonomy is being policed in ways that deter seeking medical care or reporting complications. (5 Jun 2025)

Economic Structure

1. Trump administration proposed deep Medicaid and ACA cuts projected to leave over 10 million people without coverage. Large reductions in Medicaid and ACA subsidies would shift health costs onto low-income households, weakening the social safety net and increasing economic precarity tied to illness. (31 May 2025; 3 Jun 2025)

2. Trump administration proposed a 42% cut to federal rental assistance programs serving over 10 million people. Slashing housing vouchers and Section 8 aid would likely increase homelessness and housing insecurity, especially for families with children, embedding deeper inequality into the housing system. (2 Jun 2025)

3. Trump administration proposed steep cuts to WIC nutrition benefits for women, infants, and children. Reducing basic food support for millions of low-income mothers and young children would worsen nutrition and health outcomes, using budget policy to shift hardship onto those with least power. (2 Jun 2025)

4. Trump administration proposed eliminating Preschool Development Grants for early childhood education. Ending federal support for state preschool systems would widen educational gaps by income and geography, undermining long-term equality of opportunity. (2 Jun 2025)

5. Trump administration proposed massive cuts to FEMA grants and signaled an intent to eliminate FEMA. Dismantling FEMA's grant programs and planning its eventual elimination would offload disaster risk onto states and individuals, weakening national capacity to respond to climate-driven emergencies. (4 Jun 2025)

6. Trump administration canceled nearly $4 billion in Building Resilient Infrastructure and Communities grants. Revoking pre-disaster resilience funding undermined local efforts to harden infrastructure against storms and floods, increasing future public costs and vulnerability. (4 Jun 2025)

7. Trump administration downsized FEMA staff and reduced training for state and local emergency officials. Allowing thousands of FEMA staff to leave and cutting training hollowed out federal disaster-response capacity, making communities more dependent on uneven local resources. (4 Jun 2025)

8. Trump administration cut staffing and proposed deep budget reductions for NOAA and the National Weather Service. Large staff and budget

cuts at NOAA and NWS degraded weather forecasting and hurricane preparedness, weakening a core public good that protects lives and property. (2 Jun 2025; 3 Jun 2025; 4 Jun 2025)

9. Trump administration proposed a 43% cut to the National Institutes of Health budget. Slashing NIH funding threatened to halt much university-based biomedical research, undermining long-term public health innovation and shifting scientific capacity toward private or foreign actors. (3 Jun 2025)

10. Trump administration proposed eliminating 80,000 VA jobs and canceling many veterans' service contracts. Mass VA staffing cuts and contract cancellations would push veterans toward private care and likely degrade service quality, effectively privatizing key aspects of veterans' healthcare. (2 Jun 2025; 6 Jun 2025)

11. Trump administration requested Congress rescind $9.4 billion in previously approved spending, including for NPR, PBS, and foreign aid. Seeking to claw back funds from public media and international aid reprioritized federal resources away from information and diplomacy, while signaling that appropriations can be revisited to punish disfavored programs. (3 Jun 2025; 4 Jun 2025; 5 Jun 2025)

12. House Republicans advanced the GENIUS Act to regulate stablecoins amid heavy crypto industry donations. Moving a stablecoin framework that could benefit a Trump-family-backed token after large crypto contributions illustrated how financial regulation can be shaped to favor politically connected ventures. (5 Jun 2025)

13. MGX, a UAE government-owned firm used the Trump-family-backed stablecoin USD1 to invest $2 billion in Binance. A foreign sovereign fund's use of a Trump-linked stablecoin for a major investment highlighted how private political families can profit from international finance flows intertwined with U.S. policy. (5 Jun 2025)

14. Organization for Economic Cooperation and Development reported that Trump's trade war is slowing U.S. and global economic growth. An international body's warning that tariffs are dampening growth and raising inflation underscored the broader economic risks of unilateral trade policies driven by political goals. (5 Jun 2025)

15. Trump administration paused implementation of its "Liberation Day" tariffs amid market and legal pressures. Temporarily shelving record-high tariffs after backlash showed how abrupt economic moves can be used as leverage, creating uncertainty that itself becomes a tool of political pressure. (5 Jun 2025)

16. Trump administration centralized federal personal data using Palantir technology under an executive order. Building a unified data infrastructure

across agencies increased efficiency but also concentrated sensitive information in ways that could enable surveillance or discriminatory targeting with limited oversight. (2 Jun 2025)

17. Trump administration threatened to cancel federal funding for California's high-speed rail project over alleged noncompliance. Using grant compliance findings to justify pulling billions from a major state infrastructure project risked politicizing federal investment decisions and undermining long-term public transit development. (4 Jun 2025)

18. Trump administration sought to rescind funding for NPR and PBS as "antithetical to American interests". Targeting public broadcasters for defunding based on perceived ideological bias used budget tools to reshape the media landscape, favoring commercial or aligned outlets over independent public service media. (3 Jun 2025)

19. House Republicans included a provision in reconciliation to grant Twin Metals mining leases near Boundary Waters with limited judicial review. Embedding a mining company's lease rights and shielding them from most lawsuits in a budget bill exemplified how legislation can be tailored to protect specific corporate interests from environmental and legal accountability. (6 Jun 2025)

20. Trump administration proposed budget cuts and structural changes that would reduce support for veterans' translators and pause refugee admissions. Restricting entry for allies who aided U.S. forces and pausing refugee admissions signaled that economic and security policy can disregard prior commitments, potentially undermining future cooperation abroad. (6 Jun 2025)

21. Trump administration proposed and enacted policies that reversed industrial growth in battery manufacturing and clean energy. Tariffs, subsidy rollbacks, and new fees discouraged domestic battery and EV investment, weakening the industrial base needed for both climate goals and modern defense capabilities. (3 Jun 2025)

22. China imposed export controls on rare earth materials to the United States. Chinese restrictions on rare earth exports exposed U.S. dependence on foreign supply chains for critical technologies, highlighting vulnerabilities in economic and security planning. (3 Jun 2025)

23. Major corporations withdrew or reduced sponsorships for Pride parades under political pressure. Corporate retreat from Pride sponsorships in response to political attacks on diversity initiatives reduced financial support for LGBTQ events, illustrating how culture-war pressure can reshape private-sector backing for civil society. (3 Jun 2025)

24. Companies including Oracle and Morgan Stanley cut ties with law

firms that complied with Trump's anti-media executive order. Corporate clients' decision to drop firms enforcing a controversial order signaled market resistance to perceived executive overreach, using economic leverage to defend rule-of-law norms. (2 Jun 2025)

25. U.S. labor market saw unemployment claims rise to an eight-month high amid tariff uncertainty. An uptick in jobless claims alongside tariff shocks suggested that trade policy volatility was feeding into labor market stress, with workers bearing the brunt of macroeconomic experimentation. (4 Jun 2025)

26. Bureau of Labor Statistics reported inflation data based partly on less precise methods due to staffing shortages. Reliance on rougher estimation techniques for key inflation metrics because of understaffing raised concerns about the accuracy of economic data that guides policy and public expectations. (4 Jun 2025)

27. Trump administration proposed limiting federal student loans and forgiveness for medical and professional programs. Capping federal loans and curbing forgiveness for graduate programs risked pushing aspiring doctors toward private debt or different careers, with long-term effects on healthcare access and class mobility. (1 Jun 2025)

28. Trump administration threatened to cancel government contracts with Musk's companies, prompting SpaceX to plan Dragon decommissioning. The feud over contracts and spacecraft decommissioning exposed how critical public services like ISS resupply depend on a few private actors whose business decisions are entangled with political disputes. (4 Jun 2025; 5 Jun 2025; 6 Jun 2025)

29. Trump administration proposed and enacted policies that would cut FEMA infrastructure grants and shift disaster costs to states. Rolling back federal disaster mitigation funding and planning FEMA's elimination would leave poorer states especially exposed to climate shocks, deepening regional inequality in resilience. (4 Jun 2025)

Information, Memory, and Manipulation

1. Department of Veterans Affairs political leadership required VA doctors and scientists to obtain political clearance before publishing or speaking publicly. Mandating political review of VA research communications curtailed scientific independence and limited veterans' and the public's access to unfiltered information about health risks and system capacity. (1 Jun 2025)

2. Pentagon leadership under Secretary Pete Hegseth locked briefing

room doors and effectively halted regular press briefings. Restricting Pentagon press access reduced transparency around military operations and policy, weakening a key channel for public oversight of the defense establishment. (31 May 2025)

3. President Trump amplified extreme conspiracy content claiming Joe Biden was executed and replaced by clones. The president's promotion of fantastical claims about a rival's identity normalized disinformation at the highest level, corroding shared factual baselines essential for democratic debate. (31 May 2025; 2 Jun 2025)

4. Homeland Security Secretary Kristi Noem accused Harvard of promoting Chinese Communist Party priorities and suggested students were spies. Baselessly portraying a major university and its students as aligned with a foreign adversary stoked xenophobia and undermined trust in academic institutions as spaces for independent inquiry. (1 Jun 2025)

5. Trump administration issued an executive order titled "Restoring Gold Standard Science" that empowered political appointees to suppress disfavored research. Framing prior pandemic science as politicized while granting new authority to silence inconvenient findings inverted the idea of scientific integrity, making evidence more vulnerable to partisan control. (3 Jun 2025)

6. Defense Department temporarily removed Jackie Robinson's biography from its website. Taking down material honoring a civil rights icon from an official site fit a broader pattern of selectively editing public history, raising concerns about politically motivated erasure. (2 Jun 2025)

7. Trump administration moved to cut federal funding to NPR and PBS and labeled them biased against American interests. Targeting public broadcasters for defunding based on content judgments threatened the financial viability of independent news and signaled preference for more compliant media ecosystems. (1 Jun 2025; 3 Jun 2025; 4 Jun 2025; 5 Jun 2025)

8. Trump administration centralized personal data across agencies using Palantir technology under a new executive order. Building a unified data platform increased the state's capacity to monitor individuals and patterns, raising fears that advanced analytics could be used to target opponents or marginalized groups. (2 Jun 2025)

9. FBI Director Kash Patel required employees to take polygraph tests to root out leakers amid staff purges. Expanding polygraph use in a climate of high turnover risked turning internal security tools into instruments for silencing dissent and discouraging whistleblowing within a key investigative agency. (2 Jun 2025)

10. Bureau of Labor Statistics acknowledged using less precise methods for inflation estimates due to staffing shortages. Reliance on rougher estima-

tion for core economic indicators, combined with political spin about fiscal impacts, undermined confidence in official statistics that anchor public debate and policy. (3 Jun 2025; 4 Jun 2025)

11. Trump administration used the Boulder rally attack suspect's immigration status to promote a broader deportation agenda. Highlighting one attacker's visa overstay to justify sweeping deportation policies framed immigrants as inherent security threats, shaping public memory of the incident toward punitive reforms. (3 Jun 2025)

12. Trump administration and Department of Government Efficiency secured Supreme Court permission to access sensitive Social Security records for efficiency drives. Granting a Musk-led unit broad access to Social Security data expanded the scope for algorithmic profiling and targeting of beneficiaries, with limited transparency about safeguards or uses. (6 Jun 2025)

13. National Archives and Records Administration invited public comment on proposed federal records schedules. Opening records disposition plans to public input supported transparency and helped guard against inappropriate destruction of documents with historical or accountability value. (5 Jun 2025)

14. Education Secretary Linda McMahon testified with uncertainty about whether teaching Black history and 2020 election facts violates DEI policies. Hesitation to affirm that teaching Tulsa, Ruby Bridges, or accurate election results is permissible signaled pressure on schools to self-censor core civic and historical content. (4 Jun 2025)

15. Trump administration renamed the USNS Harvey Milk and other ships to de-emphasize civil rights figures. Rebranding Navy vessels away from LGBTQ and other icons recast official commemorations, narrowing which struggles are honored in state symbolism and shaping collective memory. (3 Jun 2025)

16. Senator Joni Ernst responded to concerns about Medicaid cuts by saying "we are all going to die" and invoking Christianity. Deflecting fears about healthcare loss with fatalistic and religious rhetoric minimized policy consequences and used faith language to normalize reduced social protection. (3 Jun 2025)

17. Representative Mary Miller publicly disparaged a Sikh prayer in Congress after misidentifying the leader as Muslim. A lawmaker's inaccurate, intolerant comments about a minority faith leader amplified religious ignorance from an official platform, risking normalization of sectarian bias in civic spaces. (5 Jun 2025; 6 Jun 2025)

18. Trump administration used antisemitism rhetoric to justify detaining and deporting pro-Palestinian protesters. Invoking antisemitism to ratio-

nalize crackdowns on pro-Palestinian speech blurred genuine hate concerns with suppression of dissent, complicating public understanding of both. (5 Jun 2025)

19. Trump administration misrepresented deficit impacts of its budget bill despite contrary CBO findings. Claiming historic deficit reduction while independent analysis projected large increases showed willingness to distort fiscal facts, undermining informed democratic debate on budget choices. (3 Jun 2025)

20. Trump administration framed Harvard and foreign students as security risks while imposing visa bans. Pairing visa suspensions with rhetoric about espionage and foreign influence cast academic exchange as suspect, reshaping public narratives about universities and immigrants. (4 Jun 2025; 5 Jun 2025)

21. Trump administration used chaotic, overlapping policy moves across tariffs, immigration, social cuts, and media funding. Simultaneous shocks in trade, immigration raids, social spending, and media policy created a dense crisis environment that can overwhelm public attention and hinder coordinated opposition. (31 May 2025; 2 Jun 2025; 3 Jun 2025; 4 Jun 2025; 5 Jun 2025; 6 Jun 2025)

CHAPTER 21

WEEK 21 (7 JUN 2025 – 13 JUN 2025): EMERGENCY POWERS AS ROUTINE GOVERNANCE

In Los Angeles and beyond, immigration raids, troop deployments, and cultural decrees showed how emergency tools can be normalized as everyday management.

This week showcases a focused rise in authoritarian tendencies centered on immigration enforcement and militarized domestic governance. The Trump administration federalized and sent thousands of National Guard troops and active-duty Marines to Los Angeles despite state objections, used them near protests, and allowed at least one military detention of a civilian. ICE and DHS conducted warrantless raids, made mass arrests—including citizens and elected officials—denied legal counsel and congressional access, and employed aggressive crowd-control tactics against protesters and journalists. At the same time, the executive pushed to criminalize dissent, expand surveillance of immigrants and journalists, and use DOJ and FCC powers against media and political opponents. Attacks on independent institutions intensified with politicized appointments at HHS, EEOC, IRS, and cultural agencies; sidelining civil rights enforcement for LGBTQ workers; and efforts to control curricula, public broadcasting, and DEI-related research and grants. Courts and states offered notable resistance—blocking parts of Trump's election order, Alien Enemies Act deportations, and some deployments—but appellate stays and ongoing defiance show how far executive power is testing legal limits. Overall, the week applies heavy pressure on civil-military norms, the rule of law, and the information environment that sustains democratic accountability.

Power and Authority

1. President Trump ordered the deployment and federalization of National Guard troops to Los Angeles over state objections. Trump's unilateral activation and federalization of California's National Guard to police immigration protests, despite opposition from state leaders, expanded executive control over state military forces and blurred limits on domestic use of troops. (7 Jun 2025; 8 Jun 2025; 9 Jun 2025; 10 Jun 2025; 11 Jun 2025; 12 Jun 2025; 13 Jun 2025)

2. President Trump and Defense Secretary Pete Hegseth deployed and threatened further deployment of active-duty Marines to Los Angeles to support immigration enforcement. Sending 700 active-duty Marines, and threatening more, to back immigration raids and protest control in Los Angeles pushed military forces into civilian law enforcement roles normally constrained by law and custom. (7 Jun 2025; 8 Jun 2025; 9 Jun 2025; 10 Jun 2025; 11 Jun 2025; 12 Jun 2025; 13 Jun 2025)

3. President Trump publicly threatened protesters at his military parade with overwhelming force. Trump's warnings that parade protesters would face "very big" or "very heavy" force signaled willingness to use state violence against peaceful assembly, chilling dissent around a leader-focused military display. (9 Jun 2025; 10 Jun 2025; 11 Jun 2025)

4. President Trump called for the arrest of California Governor Gavin Newsom over immigration policy disputes. By urging federal officials to arrest a sitting governor for policy disagreements, Trump blurred lines between political conflict and criminality, pressuring law enforcement to target an elected rival. (8 Jun 2025)

5. President Trump issued a directive framing Los Angeles protests as a violent "Migrant Invasion" and ordered cabinet action to "liberate" the city. Labeling protests as an invasion and riots provided rhetorical cover for extraordinary enforcement and military measures, recasting dissent and immigrant presence as threats to national sovereignty. (9 Jun 2025)

6. President Trump labeled Los Angeles protests an insurrection and floated invoking the Insurrection Act. Describing protests as an insurrection and hinting at Insurrection Act use normalized treating domestic dissent as rebellion, lowering the bar for military intervention in civil life. (9 Jun 2025)

7. President Trump announced a National Garden of American Heroes and ordered restoration of contested monuments. Trump's monument initiatives sought to entrench a state-approved patriotic narrative in public spaces, privileging celebratory history over more critical or inclusive accounts of the past. (8 Jun 2025)

8. President Trump announced plans to restore Confederate names to

Army bases. Restoring Confederate base names used executive symbolism to honor a secessionist cause, complicating efforts to align military institutions with egalitarian democratic values. (10 Jun 2025)

9. President Trump seized control of the Kennedy Center's leadership to reshape its cultural direction. Removing and replacing Kennedy Center leadership for being "too woke" extended direct presidential influence over a major cultural institution, risking politicization of federally supported arts programming. (12 Jun 2025)

10. President Trump blocked California's gas-car phaseout and stricter vehicle emission rules via resolution. Overturning California's clean-car rules curtailed a state's ability to pursue ambitious climate policy, centralizing environmental authority in a deregulatory federal executive. (12 Jun 2025)

11. President Trump used executive power to target disfavored institutions and critics. Trump's pattern of using executive orders and agency pressure against media, universities, and states illustrated how presidential tools can be wielded to punish opposition rather than neutrally govern. (11 Jun 2025)

12. President Trump mobilized National Guard and Marines in Los Angeles as part of a broader immigration crackdown. Linking military deployments directly to immigration enforcement goals further fused border policy with domestic coercive power, making troop use part of a sustained campaign rather than an isolated emergency. (13 Jun 2025)

13. President Trump issued an executive order conditioning approval of Nippon Steel's acquisition of U.S. Steel on a national security agreement. By revising a prior block on a major foreign acquisition, Trump used CFIUS-linked authority to balance economic openness with security concerns, signaling how strategic industries can be governed through discretionary security reviews. (13 Jun 2025)

14. President Trump issued an executive order restructuring federal wildfire prevention and response programs. Centralizing wildfire management and ordering regulatory review altered how federal power is organized around climate-related disasters, with implications for accountability and local-federal coordination. (12 Jun 2025)

15. President Trump uninvited Senator Rand Paul from a White House congressional picnic. Using access to ceremonial White House events to reward or punish lawmakers reflected a personalized approach to presidential power that can chill intra-party dissent. (12 Jun 2025)

16. Treasury Secretary Scott Bessent signaled Trump would likely extend a pause on certain tariffs during negotiations. Extending a tariff pause as leverage in talks showed the executive's central role in managing trade shocks

that can affect domestic economic stability and political coalitions. (12 Jun 2025)

17. President Trump commented that current immigration enforcement was harming farmers and suggested policy changes. Acknowledging that aggressive deportations were hurting agricultural employers while promising adjustments highlighted how executive discretion over enforcement can reshape labor markets and workers' security. (13 Jun 2025)

Institutions and Governance

1. California Attorney General Rob Bonta and Governor Gavin Newsom sued the Trump administration over federalization of the California National Guard. California's lawsuit challenging Trump's Guard deployment sought judicial clarification of federal limits over state military forces, testing constitutional protections for state sovereignty and checks on executive power. (8 Jun 2025; 9 Jun 2025; 10 Jun 2025)

2. U.S. District Judge Charles Breyer and the Ninth Circuit Court of Appeals ruled Trump's federalization of California's National Guard unlawful then temporarily stayed that ruling on appeal. A district court found Trump's Guard deployment exceeded statutory and Tenth Amendment limits, but an appellate stay kept federal control in place, illustrating both judicial resistance and the fragility of constraints under rapid appeals. (12 Jun 2025; 13 Jun 2025)

3. federal courts in Texas and Massachusetts blocked Trump's use of the Alien Enemies Act and his proof-of-citizenship voting order. Judges halted deportations under the Alien Enemies Act and enjoined an executive order requiring proof of citizenship to vote, reinforcing that immigration and election rules must conform to statutory and constitutional limits. (9 Jun 2025; 13 Jun 2025)

4. Department of Justice indicted Representative LaMonica McIver for allegedly impeding immigration officers during oversight. Charging a sitting member of Congress over conduct tied to detention-center oversight blurred the line between neutral law enforcement and political retaliation, potentially chilling legislative scrutiny of executive agencies. (11 Jun 2025; 13 Jun 2025)

5. Department of Justice leadership issued a memo allowing rapid oral dismissal of immigration cases at DHS lawyers' request. Streamlining dismissals at DHS request shifted immigration court procedure toward executive convenience, risking uneven treatment and weakening formal safeguards for noncitizens' cases. (11 Jun 2025)

6. Director of National Intelligence Tulsi Gabbard fired the acting counsel to the intelligence community inspector general and installed a direct adviser. Removing the IG counsel and replacing the role with a loyal adviser undermined the independence of intelligence oversight mechanisms meant to check abuses within the national security apparatus. (9 Jun 2025)

7. Pentagon inspector general investigated Defense Secretary Pete Hegseth's aides over possible deletion of encrypted messages. A probe into whether senior defense aides were told to delete Signal messages raised concerns about evasion of records laws and the integrity of decision-making around sensitive military briefings. (7 Jun 2025; 9 Jun 2025)

8. Equal Employment Opportunity Commission acting chair Andrea Lucas halted processing and downgraded priority of gender identity discrimination claims. Directing the EEOC to sideline gender identity cases effectively suspended enforcement of protections for trans and nonbinary workers, weakening a key civil-rights enforcement institution by internal policy. (13 Jun 2025)

9. Health and Human Services Secretary Robert F. Kennedy Jr. dismissed all members of the CDC's vaccine advisory committee and moved to replace them. Firing 17 independent vaccine advisers and installing controversial replacements politicized a core scientific advisory body, risking that immunization policy would reflect ideology rather than evidence. (9 Jun 2025; 10 Jun 2025; 13 Jun 2025)

10. Senate of the United States confirmed Billy Long, a former congressman who once sought to abolish the IRS, as IRS commissioner. Confirming an IRS chief who previously advocated eliminating the agency raised doubts about his commitment to tax enforcement and the neutral administration of revenue laws. (12 Jun 2025)

11. Department of Homeland Security and ICE leadership denied members of Congress access to immigration detention facilities in Los Angeles and New York. Blocking lawmakers from inspecting detention sites during mass raids curtailed statutory oversight of federal custody conditions, weakening a key legislative check on executive enforcement. (7 Jun 2025; 9 Jun 2025; 10 Jun 2025)

12. Department of Justice under Attorney General Pam Bondi reversed limits on subpoenaing journalists' records to target leaks that "undermine" Trump's agenda. Expanding DOJ authority to seize reporters' records for leaks deemed harmful to the president's agenda turned national-security tools into instruments for policing political narratives. (10 Jun 2025)

13. Department of Justice pursued indictments and charges against protesters and local officials tied to immigration demonstrations. Federal

prosecutions of a union leader, a Newark mayor, and LA protesters for actions around ICE raids suggested selective enforcement that can deter civic oversight and protest. (9 Jun 2025; 13 Jun 2025)

14. House Republicans passed a rescissions bill to defund NPR and PBS. Moving to strip funding from public broadcasters over perceived bias used budgetary power to pressure independent media, threatening pluralistic information infrastructure. (12 Jun 2025)

15. Florida State Board of Education and senior state officials threatened a school superintendent with criminal prosecution unless 55 books were permanently removed. Using criminal threats to force book removals without local review bypassed legislative processes and weaponized state power to control school library content. (12 Jun 2025)

16. Florida legislature and State Board of Education advanced and then administratively revived failed bills to purge books with sexual content from schools. After a book-removal bill stalled in the Senate, state education officials sought to impose similar restrictions by rule, testing how far executive agencies can go in overriding legislative outcomes on speech. (12 Jun 2025)

17. Congress of the United States enacted multiple resolutions disapproving EPA rules that allowed California stricter vehicle pollution standards. Congress's use of the Congressional Review Act to overturn California-linked EPA waivers curtailed state-led environmental experimentation and reinforced federal primacy over emissions policy. (12 Jun 2025)

18. Congress and President Trump enacted the Aerial Firefighting Enhancement Act of 2025. New statutory support for aerial firefighting strengthened federal capacity to respond to wildfires, illustrating constructive legislative–executive cooperation on a public-safety function. (12 Jun 2025)

19. Congressman Mark Green accepted a private-sector job while remaining in Congress without disclosing his future employer. Green's decision to keep serving and voting while negotiating undisclosed outside employment raised conflict-of-interest concerns and highlighted weak enforcement of ethics rules for lawmakers. (11 Jun 2025)

20. Quinnipiac University Polling Institute reported low public approval for Trump and his administration's policies. Polling showing broad disapproval of Trump's performance and issue handling documented a legitimacy gap between executive actions and public sentiment, with implications for democratic accountability. (12 Jun 2025)

21. World Bank projected a sharp slowdown in U.S. economic growth linked to Trump's trade war. An international forecast tying lower U.S. growth to tariff policies underscored how executive trade decisions can struc-

turally weaken economic conditions that underpin democratic stability. (12 Jun 2025)

22. Senator Rand Paul and other Republicans criticized the $40 million cost and symbolism of Trump's military parade. Intra-party criticism of an expensive, leader-centric military parade signaled some institutional resistance within the president's party to using public funds for personal glorification. (12 Jun 2025)

23. Republican leadership in Congress and the White House advanced a budget reconciliation bill dubbed the "One Big, Beautiful Bill" despite public opposition. Pushing a reconciliation package that cuts Medicaid and is opposed by a majority of voters highlighted how fiscal policymaking can proceed with limited responsiveness to public preferences. (10 Jun 2025; 12 Jun 2025)

24. Representative Anna Paulina Luna claimed Chinese funding of "No Kings" protests and called for a committee investigation. Alleging foreign sponsorship of domestic protests without clear evidence and promising investigations risked delegitimizing dissent and justifying expanded surveillance under the banner of countering interference. (12 Jun 2025)

25. Louisiana Governor and legislature enacted anti-grooming legislation to strengthen protections against child sexual abuse. New state laws targeting grooming and clergy abuse expanded legal tools to protect minors, reflecting a use of legislative power to address longstanding accountability gaps. (12 Jun 2025; 13 Jun 2025)

Civil Rights and Dissent

1. Department of Homeland Security and ICE conducted large-scale, often warrantless immigration raids and detentions across Los Angeles and other areas. Mass raids at workplaces, homes, and public spaces, including arrests of people without criminal records and denial of basic needs, intensified fear in immigrant communities and raised serious due process concerns. (7 Jun 2025; 8 Jun 2025; 9 Jun 2025; 10 Jun 2025; 11 Jun 2025; 12 Jun 2025; 13 Jun 2025)

2. ICE and allied agencies dramatically increased daily arrest quotas and used aggressive tactics including flash-bang grenades. Stephen Miller's demand for 3,000 daily arrests and the use of military-style tactics against immigrants and protesters escalated enforcement beyond targeted public-safety goals toward numerical and symbolic displays of power. (8 Jun 2025; 9 Jun 2025; 11 Jun 2025)

3. ICE and DHS arrested and mistreated U.S. citizens and officials during immigration operations. Mistaken detention of a U.S. marshal, arrest of a

pregnant citizen, and arrests of mayors and union leaders during raids showed how aggressive enforcement can sweep in citizens and elected officials, eroding trust in equal protection. (8 Jun 2025; 9 Jun 2025)

4. ICE and CBP conducted immigration arrests at courthouses and during legal check-ins, prompting litigation. Arresting immigrants at courthouses and monitoring-program check-ins, and the resulting lawsuit, highlighted how enforcement at justice venues can intimidate asylum seekers and undermine access to courts. (9 Jun 2025; 11 Jun 2025)

5. Department of Justice and DHS used immigration and national security tools to target pro-Palestine speech and activists. Arrests of immigrants for pro-Palestine speech, detention of Mahmoud Khalil, and visa revocations for student protesters showed how security powers were applied to suppress particular political viewpoints. (10 Jun 2025; 11 Jun 2025)

6. USCIS and DHS announced social media surveillance of immigrants for "antisemitic activity" affecting visas. Monitoring immigrants' online speech for vaguely defined antisemitic content tied visa status to political expression, chilling lawful speech among noncitizens. (10 Jun 2025)

7. Trump administration and DHS transferred Medicaid enrollees' personal data, including immigration status, to DHS for enforcement. Sharing millions of Medicaid records with DHS repurposed health data for deportation efforts, undermining privacy expectations and deterring vulnerable populations from seeking care. (13 Jun 2025)

8. Trump administration planned to send thousands of undocumented immigrants to Guantanamo Bay without notifying home countries. Proposals to detain migrants at Guantanamo extended a symbol of extralegal detention into immigration policy, raising grave concerns about rights protections and international norms. (10 Jun 2025)

9. Trump administration and ICE used immigration enforcement to retaliate against political speech and criticism of Trump. Denying entry to a French scientist over critical messages and targeting immigrants for protest activity showed how border controls were leveraged to punish disfavored speech. (10 Jun 2025)

10. Department of Justice and President Trump revoked security clearances from law firms representing political opponents. Executive orders stripping clearances from firms that had represented Trump's adversaries threatened the independence of legal representation and signaled that defending opponents could carry professional penalties. (10 Jun 2025)

11. Los Angeles Unified School District implemented security perimeters and protocols to shield students and families from ICE at graduations. LAUSD's measures to keep immigration agents away from graduations

showed local institutions adapting to protect community participation in education from federal enforcement threats. (10 Jun 2025)

12. Southern Baptist Convention endorsed a resolution seeking repeal of same-sex marriage legalization and other conservative policies. The denomination's call to overturn Obergefell and oppose LGBTQ rights signaled organized religious pressure to roll back established civil rights protections. (10 Jun 2025)

13. Mayor Eric Adams of New York City signed an order adopting the IHRA definition of antisemitism for city agencies. Requiring agencies to use a definition that can encompass some criticism of Israel risked conflating political speech with antisemitism, potentially chilling advocacy and academic debate. (9 Jun 2025)

14. Equal Employment Opportunity Commission dismissed pending gender identity discrimination cases and removed nonbinary markers from forms. EEOC's retreat from gender identity enforcement left transgender and nonbinary workers with fewer avenues for redress, weakening practical protections against workplace discrimination. (13 Jun 2025)

15. Departments of Veterans Affairs and State banned pride flags and similar symbols in government offices and consular posts. Prohibiting pride flags in federal workplaces curtailed visible support for LGBTQ employees and communities, signaling official disfavor toward certain identities in public service. (10 Jun 2025)

16. Department of Defense and DoDEA ordered removal of DEI-related books and instruction from military academies and schools. Purging diversity and gender-related materials from military education narrowed the range of perspectives available to service members' families and future officers, aligning curricula with political directives. (10 Jun 2025)

17. Florida right-wing advocacy groups and state officials pursued book bans and reported librarians to law enforcement over contested materials. Coordinated campaigns to remove books on race, LGBTQ issues, and sex education, backed by threats of prosecution, pressured schools to censor content to avoid political and legal risk. (12 Jun 2025)

18. Trump administration and allied state officials censored DEI and gender-related terms from federal and state websites under executive orders. Removing hundreds of words and phrases from government sites to comply with anti-DEI orders limited public access to information about marginalized groups and ongoing policy debates. (10 Jun 2025)

19. Trump administration and EEOC reduced enforcement of LGBTQ and gender identity protections while promoting restrictive cultural policies. Combined agency actions against pride symbols, gender identity claims, and

DEI content signaled a broader governmental retreat from protecting LGBTQ rights in workplaces and public spaces. (10 Jun 2025; 13 Jun 2025)

20. Trump administration and allied agencies used funding and regulatory tools to pressure universities and schools to suppress dissenting views. Threats to cut funds, revoke tax status, or block grants for institutions that hosted protests or taught disfavored topics turned economic dependence into a mechanism for curbing academic and student speech. (10 Jun 2025)

21. Trump administration and ICE planned to send immigrants to Guantanamo and expanded detention in harsh conditions. Proposals and practices that moved immigration detention toward offshore or punitive models eroded distinctions between civil immigration custody and national-security incarceration. (10 Jun 2025; 11 Jun 2025)

22. Trump administration and state allies used religion-inflected rhetoric and policy to justify restrictions on LGBTQ and reproductive rights. Policies and resolutions framed in religious or moral terms, such as opposing same-sex marriage and limiting gender expression, leveraged faith narratives to constrain equal citizenship for targeted groups. (10 Jun 2025)

Economic Structure

1. Environmental Protection Agency under the Trump administration moved to eliminate greenhouse gas limits for power plants and weaken toxics standards. Draft plans to scrap power-plant climate rules and relax mercury and air toxics limits shifted regulatory benefits toward fossil-fuel operators at the expense of public health and climate goals. (9 Jun 2025; 11 Jun 2025)

2. Department of Education under the Trump administration threatened to revoke funding from schools teaching about systemic racism. Conditioning federal education funds on avoiding lessons about systemic racism used financial leverage to narrow curricula and discourage critical civic education. (10 Jun 2025)

3. Trump administration pulled federal grants from the American Bar Association after it criticized Trump. Canceling ABA grants in apparent retaliation for criticism weaponized funding decisions against a professional body central to legal standards and access to justice. (10 Jun 2025)

4. Trump administration froze grants and challenged tax-exempt status of Harvard University over ideological disputes. Targeting Harvard's funding and tax status for resisting demands on hiring and admissions pressured an academic institution to align with government-preferred viewpoints. (10 Jun 2025)

5. President Trump banned federal grant funding for projects using

"gender ideology" terms. An executive order barring grants tied to certain gender-related language used funding rules to steer research agendas and suppress disfavored lines of inquiry. (10 Jun 2025)

6. President Trump threatened and implemented funding cuts for universities that allowed "illegal protests". Cutting or threatening federal funds to universities over campus protests linked institutional budgets to suppression of student dissent, undermining academic freedom and protest rights. (10 Jun 2025)

7. Trump administration yanked funding from scientific research projects using disfavored terms. Defunding over a thousand grants based on language choices politicized science funding, discouraging research that conflicted with administration ideology. (10 Jun 2025)

8. Trump administration defunded NPR and PBS and sought to cut the Corporation for Public Broadcasting. Executive moves to strip public broadcasters of federal support threatened a key noncommercial news source, tilting the media ecosystem toward private and partisan outlets. (10 Jun 2025)

9. Trump administration retaliated against the Associated Press by restricting access after terminology disputes. Limiting AP's pool and travel access for using disfavored geographic terms used state-controlled access as an economic and informational lever against independent reporting. (10 Jun 2025)

10. Trump administration punished Harvard and other institutions financially for resisting speech and hiring directives. Using grant freezes, tax threats, and funding cuts to coerce universities into ideological compliance blurred the line between neutral grant-making and political patronage. (10 Jun 2025)

11. Trump administration pulled or threatened federal support from DEI-related Fulbright projects and international scholarships. Requiring State Department approval to screen Fulbright projects for DEI content constrained academic exchange and signaled that funding abroad depends on alignment with domestic culture-war priorities. (10 Jun 2025)

12. Trump administration revoked visas of hundreds of international students involved in pro-Palestine protests. Stripping student visas for political activism used immigration status as an economic and educational sanction against campus dissent, chilling international participation in U.S. civic life. (10 Jun 2025)

13. Trump administration canceled or threatened grants to NPR, PBS, ABA, and other institutions after criticism. A pattern of grant cancellations and defunding against critical institutions showed how federal spending decisions were being used to reward loyalty and punish dissent. (10 Jun 2025)

14. Trump administration used funding and regulatory threats to pressure schools and libraries over book content. Tying school funding and legal exposure to removal of certain books turned economic levers into tools for reshaping what students can read and learn. (12 Jun 2025)

15. Trump administration and allied officials accused medical journals of political bias and hinted at restricting government scientists' publishing. Casting medical journals as partisan and threatening to limit government scientists' ability to publish there risked politicizing scientific reputations and constraining evidence that informs regulation. (10 Jun 2025)

16. Trump administration suppressed and altered economic and climate-related data and cut staff at statistical agencies. Delaying, editing, and under-resourcing key economic and climate reports undermined the data infrastructure needed for informed fiscal and regulatory decisions. (11 Jun 2025)

17. Department of Government Efficiency (DOGE) gutted USAID operations under the banner of cutting waste. DOGE's hollowing out of USAID reduced U.S. development capacity and exemplified how ad hoc austerity bodies can be used to dismantle parts of the civil service. (11 Jun 2025)

18. Trump administration used immigration raids that disrupted food and labor markets, including at meat and farm facilities. Large workplace raids that removed many workers from food plants and farms exposed how enforcement choices can destabilize supply chains while leaving employers' structural dependence on vulnerable labor intact. (11 Jun 2025; 12 Jun 2025)

19. Biden administration implemented targeted tariffs on Chinese EVs, solar cells, and semiconductors. New tariffs on strategic Chinese imports aimed to protect domestic manufacturing capacity in key sectors, reshaping trade exposure and industrial policy. (11 Jun 2025)

20. Pentagon comptroller estimated the cost of federalizing the National Guard and deploying Marines to Los Angeles at $134 million. The high projected cost of domestic military deployments highlighted the fiscal burden of using armed forces for internal security rather than civilian policing or social programs. (11 Jun 2025)

21. Environmental Protection Agency and other regulators issued multiple technical rules, corrections, and information-collection notices affecting environmental and health programs. Routine EPA and CDC rulemakings on chemicals, fuels, grants, and surveillance systems adjusted regulatory baselines that shape environmental quality and public health infrastructure. (9 Jun 2025; 10 Jun 2025; 11 Jun 2025; 12 Jun 2025; 13 Jun 2025)

22. Federal Communications Commission finalized spectrum and paperwork rules and sought comment on multiple information collections. FCC

actions on spectrum sharing, foreign sponsorship disclosure, and paperwork relief shaped the communications market's structure and the regulatory load on providers and small businesses. (9 Jun 2025; 10 Jun 2025; 11 Jun 2025; 12 Jun 2025)

23. Centers for Disease Control and Prevention and FDA advanced numerous data-collection and user-fee processes for health programs. CDC and FDA notices on surveillance systems, block grants, and medical device fees maintained the administrative scaffolding for public health monitoring and regulation. (9 Jun 2025; 11 Jun 2025; 12 Jun 2025; 13 Jun 2025)

24. General Services Administration sought OMB approval to continue collecting qualitative feedback on agency services. GSA's request to extend a generic clearance for customer feedback aimed to improve federal service delivery, modestly strengthening administrative responsiveness. (13 Jun 2025)

Information, Memory, and Manipulation

1. ABC News suspended and then fired correspondent Terry Moran after critical comments about Trump officials. Moran's suspension and dismissal following administration outreach suggested that political pressure was influencing newsroom personnel decisions, undermining journalistic independence. (8 Jun 2025; 9 Jun 2025)

2. Department of Justice under Attorney General Pam Bondi expanded authority to subpoena journalists' records for leaks that "undermine" Trump's agenda. Broadening leak investigations to include stories that politically harm the president turned surveillance tools against watchdog reporting, threatening source confidentiality and press freedom. (10 Jun 2025)

3. Federal Communications Commission under Chairman Brendan Carr investigated and sued media outlets over content disfavored by Trump. Launching FCC actions against CBS and others for editing or diversity coverage used regulatory scrutiny to intimidate outlets whose narratives clashed with administration preferences. (10 Jun 2025)

4. Trump administration attempted to dismantle the U.S. Agency for Global Media and curtail Voice of America. Efforts to break up USAGM and constrain VOA threatened an important source of relatively independent U.S. international broadcasting, narrowing the range of state-supported global news. (10 Jun 2025)

5. Trump administration censored DEI and gender-related terms from federal websites in response to executive orders. Removing hundreds of words and phrases from agency sites obscured information about marginal-

ized groups and policy debates, reshaping the official record to fit ideological lines. (10 Jun 2025)

6. Trump administration retaliated against the Associated Press by limiting access after terminology disputes. Excluding AP reporters from pools and Air Force One for using standard geographic terms signaled that access to government information could depend on adopting preferred language. (10 Jun 2025)

7. Trump administration and allied officials accused medical journals of political bias and hinted at restricting government scientists' publishing. Portraying medical journals as partisan and threatening to limit official contributions undermined trust in peer-reviewed science and risked politicizing what evidence enters public debate. (10 Jun 2025)

8. Los Angeles Police Department and the White House issued conflicting accounts of protest violence in Los Angeles. LAPD's description of protests as peaceful directly contradicted White House claims of violent mobs, suggesting federal exaggeration of disorder to justify military deployments. (9 Jun 2025)

9. coalition of press and civil liberties organizations warned that federal officers may have violated journalists' First Amendment rights in LA. An open letter documenting deliberate targeting of reporters at protests highlighted how on-the-ground tactics can suppress coverage of contentious government actions. (9 Jun 2025)

10. Los Angeles law enforcement and federal officers shot and detained journalists covering immigration protests. Rubber bullets, pepper balls, and detentions used against reporters in LA protests physically impeded newsgathering and signaled that documenting state force carries personal risk. (11 Jun 2025)

11. Noahpinion and other commentators reported suppression and alteration of economic and climate data under Trump. Accounts of delayed deficit reports, climate assessment firings, and staff cuts at statistical agencies pointed to systemic manipulation of official data that informs democratic debate. (11 Jun 2025)

12. Trump administration and state allies used executive orders and state directives to reshape historical narratives and public memory. From monument restoration orders and Confederate base names to book bans and cultural-institution purges, authorities sought to entrench a triumphalist national story while marginalizing dissenting histories. (8 Jun 2025; 10 Jun 2025; 12 Jun 2025)

13. Smithsonian Institution Board of Regents rejected Trump's attempt to fire National Portrait Gallery director Kim Sajet. By asserting that personnel

decisions rest with Smithsonian leadership, the board preserved some institutional autonomy against direct presidential interference in cultural curation. (13 Jun 2025)

14. Health and Human Services Secretary Robert F. Kennedy Jr. replaced mainstream vaccine experts with figures known for controversial views. Installing advisers associated with vaccine skepticism at ACIP risked embedding misinformation within official guidance, complicating public understanding of immunization risks and benefits. (13 Jun 2025)

15. Right-wing groups Moms for Liberty and Citizens Defending Freedom organized campaigns to remove books and restrict classroom discussions on race and LGBTQ issues. Coordinated pressure on school boards and librarians to purge certain topics from curricula and shelves narrowed the informational environment available to students about democracy and inequality. (12 Jun 2025)

16. Trump administration and allies framed LA immigration protests as foreign-funded riots and an "invasion". Official rhetoric depicting protesters as foreign-backed rioters and an invading force recast domestic dissent as external threat, justifying militarized responses and delegitimizing opposition. (9 Jun 2025; 12 Jun 2025; 13 Jun 2025)

17. Trump administration and state education authorities used obscenity claims to label non-obscene books as pornography and demand removal. Misapplying obscenity labels to contested books allowed officials to bypass established First Amendment standards and remove materials without case-by-case legal scrutiny. (12 Jun 2025)

18. Trump administration and statistical agencies altered or delayed key economic and climate reports while cutting staff. Manipulating the timing and content of official data releases, alongside staff reductions, weakened the informational basis for democratic oversight of fiscal and environmental policy. (11 Jun 2025)

19. Federal Communications Commission implemented a foreign sponsorship identification rule for broadcast programming. Requiring broadcasters to disclose foreign government-sponsored content improved transparency about external influence in domestic media, aiding informed consumption. (10 Jun 2025)

20. Heather Cox Richardson and collaborators launched the "Journey to American Democracy" educational video series. A new public-history series aimed to broaden access to nuanced accounts of U.S. democratic development, countering simplified or revisionist narratives. (8 Jun 2025)

CHAPTER 22
WEEK 22 (14 JUN 2025 – 20 JUN 2025): CITIZENSHIP AS SORTING MECHANISM

A week of layered decisions that turned immigration, protest, markets, and memory into tools for ranking who belongs and who may be punished.

This week reveals an executive willing to use nearly every lever of state power—military, regulatory, immigration, public health, and information—to reinforce personal rule and punish opponents, while courts and civil society mount fragmented but genuine resistance. Immigration enforcement is openly politicized: ICE raids and SWAT-style deployments target "Democrat power centers," with elected officials and journalists being arrested or moved into ICE custody; meanwhile, DHS seeks to block congressional oversight of detention facilities. At the same time, Trump consolidates economic and media influence through control of U.S. Steel, crypto deregulation, and the dismantling of Voice of America, while enforcement against donors is loosened. Civil–military boundaries weaken as the National Guard and Marines are deployed despite state objections, and appellate courts uphold federal control. Public health capacity declines sharply due to mass layoffs, funding cuts, and politicized vaccine policies. In response, courts block some executive overreach (such as NIH and EPA grant cuts, passport restrictions, and actions by Education and DOJ), Congress advances war powers and anti-corruption legislation, and millions participate in "No Kings" protests. Overall, the structure shifts toward normalized emergency governance, stratified citizenship, and crony capitalism intertwined with state authority.

Power and Authority

1. President Trump issued executive orders targeting sanctuary cities for defunding and prosecution of officials. The orders sought to punish jurisdictions resisting federal immigration policy, using fiscal threats and criminal prosecution to pressure local officials and expand centralized executive control over immigration enforcement. (14 Jun 2025)

2. President Trump attempted by executive order to cancel birthright citizenship for children of undocumented immigrants. The order directly challenged the Fourteenth Amendment's citizenship guarantee, testing the limits of unilateral presidential power over constitutional rights and the status of millions of residents. (15 Jun 2025)

3. President Trump ordered ICE to focus mass deportations on Democratic-run cities he labeled "Democrat Power Centers". Directing immigration raids toward political opponents' jurisdictions politicized federal enforcement power, threatening equal protection and using deportation policy as a partisan weapon. (15 Jun 2025; 17 Jun 2025)

4. President Trump and senior aides set and then reversed limits on ICE workplace raids in agriculture, hotel, and restaurant sectors. The rapid policy whiplash on worksite raids, influenced by donor-heavy industries, showed executive enforcement priorities being driven by political and economic favoritism rather than stable rule-based governance. (14 Jun 2025; 15 Jun 2025; 16 Jun 2025; 17 Jun 2025)

5. President Trump announced a $5 million "Trump Card" program offering permanent U.S. residency. Creating an ultra-expensive residency track tied to the president's brand blurred lines between public immigration authority and private enrichment, and further stratified access to residency by wealth. (16 Jun 2025)

6. President Trump took a golden-share style veto and board influence over U.S. Steel. Securing permanent veto power over a major corporation's decisions concentrated economic authority in the presidency and raised concerns about fusing state power with a single leader's personal control. (18 Jun 2025)

7. President Trump threatened to withhold federal wildfire disaster aid from California over political disputes. Using disaster relief as leverage against a political rival state signaled willingness to condition life-saving federal support on political compliance, undermining equal treatment of states. (18 Jun 2025)

8. President Trump extended the TikTok divestiture and enforcement deadline by executive order despite statutory and judicial mandates. By

unilaterally delaying enforcement of a law upheld by the Supreme Court, the president signaled that executive preference could override both Congress and the judiciary in regulating major platforms. (18 Jun 2025; 19 Jun 2025)

9. President Trump ordered Michigan coal plants to remain open under a national energy emergency declaration. Forcing continued operation of aging coal plants against state clean-energy law used emergency powers to override state policy choices and favored fossil interests over environmental and ratepayer concerns. (20 Jun 2025)

10. President Trump publicly attacked Federal Reserve Chair Jerome Powell and called for his removal. Sustained personal attacks on the Fed chair for policy decisions threatened the perceived independence of monetary policy, risking politicization of central banking in service of short-term political goals. (18 Jun 2025; 19 Jun 2025)

11. President Trump called for a special prosecutor to investigate the 2020 presidential election as fraudulent. Renewed demands for criminal investigation of a settled election, based on false fraud claims, further undermined confidence in electoral legitimacy and normalized using prosecutorial power against political outcomes. (19 Jun 2025; 20 Jun 2025)

12. President Trump directed the Department of Energy to keep Michigan coal plants open despite planned closures. The directive overrode market and state regulatory decisions on plant retirement, centralizing control over energy infrastructure in the executive and weakening state-level climate governance. (20 Jun 2025)

Institutions and Governance

1. U.S. District Court Judge Charles Breyer and the Ninth Circuit Court of Appeals issued conflicting rulings over federal control of California National Guard units in Los Angeles. A district judge ordered Guard control returned to California's governor, but an appellate panel stayed the order, highlighting tensions over who controls state military forces during domestic deployments. (14 Jun 2025; 18 Jun 2025; 19 Jun 2025)

2. U.S. District Judge William Young ruled the Trump administration's termination of NIH research grants illegal and discriminatory. The court ordered restoration of over $1 billion in NIH grants, finding unlawful racial and LGBTQ discrimination, and reaffirming judicial checks on politicized defunding of science. (17 Jun 2025; 18 Jun 2025)

3. Federal courts blocked the Trump administration's termination of NIH and EPA grants and Education civil-rights firings. Judges halted cuts to NIH and EPA equity-related grants and mass firings at Education's Office for Civil

Rights, preserving capacity for scientific and civil-rights enforcement against executive overreach. (16 Jun 2025; 17 Jun 2025; 18 Jun 2025)

4. Federal courts issued rulings allowing transgender passport gender markers and blocking an "X" marker ban. By enjoining enforcement of a birth-sex-only passport rule and protecting "X" markers, judges defended transgender and nonbinary individuals' access to accurate federal identification against discriminatory executive policy. (17 Jun 2025)

5. U.S. Supreme Court upheld Tennessee's ban on gender-affirming care for minors. The decision narrowed equal-protection interpretations for transgender youth and signaled judicial deference to state restrictions on gender-affirming healthcare, reshaping civil-rights baselines nationwide. (18 Jun 2025)

6. U.S. Supreme Court allowed fossil fuel companies and states to challenge California's stricter vehicle emission standards. By granting standing to attack California's long-standing emissions waiver, the Court opened a path to weaken state-led climate regulation that has often driven national standards. (20 Jun 2025)

7. U.S. Supreme Court expanded Second Amendment protections in McDonald v. Chicago, limiting handgun bans. The earlier landmark ruling, referenced this week, constrained local gun-control authority and continues to shape state capacity to regulate firearms despite child mortality concerns. (20 Jun 2025)

8. Federal appeals court rejected Justice Department representation for Trump in the E. Jean Carroll defamation appeal. The court held that government lawyers could not defend the president in a personal defamation case, reinforcing boundaries between official duties and private legal exposure. (18 Jun 2025)

9. Federal judge temporarily blocked mass firings at the Education Department's Office for Civil Rights. The injunction preserved civil-rights enforcement staff from a politically driven purge, maintaining institutional capacity to investigate discrimination in education. (18 Jun 2025)

10. Federal judge blocked EPA's cancellation of $600 million in environmental justice grants. The ruling protected funding for underserved communities facing pollution burdens, checking an attempt to dismantle environmental justice programs through administrative action. (18 Jun 2025)

11. Federal judge temporarily blocked the Trump administration from removing Harvard from the student visa program. The order prevented a punitive move against a single university's ability to enroll international students, defending institutional autonomy and academic exchange from politicized immigration controls. (20 Jun 2025)

12. Federal judge ordered the release of Palestinian activist Mahmoud Khalil from ICE detention on bail. Finding that detention appeared punitive for political activism, the court limited executive use of immigration custody as a tool of retaliation, reinforcing due-process protections. (20 Jun 2025)

13. Federal judge blocked the administration from tying transportation grants to immigration enforcement cooperation. The ruling stopped the federal government from conditioning infrastructure funding on local participation in immigration crackdowns, preserving state and local policy autonomy. (19 Jun 2025)

14. U.S. District Judge Dana Sabraw ordered restoration of legal services for migrant families separated under prior policies. By enforcing a settlement requiring legal aid for separated families, the court compelled the administration to honor obligations to remedy past rights violations at the border. (18 Jun 2025)

15. Florida Attorney General James Uthmeier and U.S. District Court Judge Kathleen Williams clashed over enforcement of a blocked state immigration law, leading to a contempt finding. Uthmeier's defiance of a restraining order and the court's contempt ruling underscored a breakdown in respect for judicial authority over unconstitutional state immigration enforcement. (18 Jun 2025)

16. American Bar Association sued the Trump administration over executive orders targeting law firms. The ABA challenged orders it said were meant to intimidate lawyers from taking cases against the administration, defending the independence of the legal profession and access to counsel. (16 Jun 2025)

17. State coalitions and non-profits sued to reverse termination of DOJ violence-prevention grants. The lawsuit argued that cutting grants to violence-prevention groups endangered vulnerable communities and violated legal obligations, pressing courts to review politicized funding decisions. (16 Jun 2025)

18. Colorado jury and federal courts found Mike Lindell liable for defamation and ordered $2.3 million in damages. The verdict against a prominent election conspiracist demonstrated that courts can impose real costs for spreading false claims that endanger individuals and erode trust in voting systems. (16 Jun 2025)

19. Representative Thomas Massie and bipartisan co-sponsors introduced a War Powers Resolution to block unauthorized U.S. military action in Iran. The resolution sought to reassert Congress's constitutional authority over war-making, challenging unilateral presidential moves toward conflict with Iran. (16 Jun 2025; 17 Jun 2025; 20 Jun 2025)

20. Senators Jeff Merkley, Chuck Schumer, and Democratic colleagues

introduced the "End Crypto Corruption" bill to bar federal officials from profiting from crypto ventures. The legislation aimed to close ethics gaps exposed by Trump's crypto activities, limiting conflicts of interest between public office and speculative digital assets. (17 Jun 2025)

21. House Judiciary Committee Democrats released a report estimating taxpayer costs of Trump's pardons at over $1.3 billion. The report framed clemency decisions as imposing large public costs, supporting arguments for stronger oversight of presidential pardon power and its use to benefit allies. (17 Jun 2025)

22. Government Accountability Office found the Trump administration illegally froze funds for libraries, archives, and museums. GAO concluded that withholding congressionally appropriated cultural funds violated budget law, documenting executive disregard for spending mandates and threatening institutions that preserve public memory. (16 Jun 2025)

23. Department of Homeland Security issued guidance requiring 72 hours' notice for congressional visits to immigration detention facilities. The new rules, contrary to statute, restricted lawmakers' ability to conduct surprise inspections of detention sites, weakening real-time oversight of immigration enforcement conditions. (19 Jun 2025)

24. ICE and DHS officials denied New York Representatives Dan Goldman and Jerry Nadler entry to ICE facilities. Blocking pre-arranged visits by members of Congress further impeded legislative oversight of detention operations and compliance with federal standards. (19 Jun 2025)

25. Senate Republicans and Democrats held and largely boycotted a hearing on alleged Biden mental decline. The partisan hearing, framed as a constitutional crisis, illustrated how oversight forums can be used for political theater rather than substantive governance, while Democrats' boycott signaled institutional polarization. (18 Jun 2025)

26. Senators Mike Lee and Steve Daines advanced an amendment authorizing expedited sale of 258 million acres of public land. The measure would allow large-scale disposal of public lands without hearings, reducing public input and potentially shifting shared resources into private hands with limited accountability. (18 Jun 2025)

27. West Virginia Governor Patrick Morrisey ended state-sponsored Juneteenth events and holiday status for state workers. Rolling back official recognition of Juneteenth and DEI programs signaled state retreat from commemorating emancipation and supporting diversity, reshaping public civic observance. (18 Jun 2025)

28. Florida Attorney General James Uthmeier continued enforcing a blocked immigration law until held in contempt. Persisting with arrests

under an enjoined statute showed a state official treating court orders as optional, eroding the rule of law and immigrant protections. (18 Jun 2025)

29. Federal Election Commission announced filing dates for a Virginia special election and later canceled an open meeting. While the FEC maintained transparency on special-election reporting deadlines, canceling an open meeting reduced opportunities for public oversight of campaign-finance regulation. (16 Jun 2025; 20 Jun 2025)

30. Congress used the Congressional Review Act to overturn OCC and EPA rules on bank mergers and air-quality standards. The joint resolutions reshaped regulatory baselines for bank consolidation and air pollution, demonstrating legislative power to rapidly reverse agency rules with long-term structural effects. (20 Jun 2025)

31. Centers for Disease Control and Prevention solicited nominations for its Advisory Committee to the Director. Seeking outside experts for a key advisory body reflected ongoing efforts to maintain scientific input into public health governance despite broader politicization pressures. (16 Jun 2025)

32. President Trump and the Senate fired Nuclear Regulatory Commission chair Christopher Hanson and confirmed Rodney Scott as CBP commissioner. Removing an independent regulator without cause and elevating a CBP leader accused of a cover-up signaled preference for loyalists over independent oversight in critical safety and enforcement agencies. (16 Jun 2025; 18 Jun 2025)

33. Sergio Gor, White House Personnel Director refused to complete standard security clearance paperwork. A senior personnel official's refusal to undergo routine vetting undermined standard security protocols and suggested politicized distrust of established clearance processes. (16 Jun 2025)

34. House Judiciary Committee Democrats reported that Trump's pardons cost over $1.3 billion in lost fines and restitution. Quantifying the fiscal impact of clemency decisions highlighted how presidential pardons can shift accountability and financial burdens from offenders to the public. (17 Jun 2025)

35. Election Assistance Commission sought public comment on a national survey of election office staffing. Collecting standardized data on election staffing aimed to improve administrative capacity and identify vulnerabilities in how elections are run across jurisdictions. (17 Jun 2025)

36. Senator Tammy Duckworth pressed Defense Secretary Pete Hegseth on costs and effectiveness of Red Sea operations. Her questioning underscored congressional scrutiny of military spending and strategic outcomes, reinforcing legislative oversight of defense policy. (20 Jun 2025)

Civil Rights and Dissent

1. Immigration and Customs Enforcement leadership under Stephen Miller ordered a sharp increase in migrant arrests, including non-criminal immigrants, with daily quotas. Quotas and broadened targeting of non-criminal immigrants expanded detention, strained oversight, and raised due-process concerns, especially in communities with little criminal activity. (14 Jun 2025; 15 Jun 2025)

2. Immigration and Customs Enforcement planned deployment of SWAT-style special response teams to Democratic-led cities ahead of protests. Using militarized immigration units to prepare for domestic protests in opposition jurisdictions blurred lines between immigration enforcement and crowd control, chilling dissent. (14 Jun 2025)

3. Texas Department of Public Safety evacuated the state capitol after credible threats against lawmakers attending an anti-Trump rally. Threats forcing evacuation of a legislative building underscored rising risks of political violence that can disrupt representative functions and intimidate officials. (14 Jun 2025)

4. Unknown assailant Vance Boelter and law enforcement carried out and was later charged for the politically motivated assassination of Minnesota lawmakers. The killing of Rep. Melissa Hortman and wounding of Sen. John Hoffman, followed by federal and state charges, highlighted the acute threat of targeted political violence to democratic representation. (14 Jun 2025; 15 Jun 2025; 16 Jun 2025; 17 Jun 2025)

5. Minnesota congressional delegation issued a bipartisan statement condemning the shootings of state lawmakers. The unified condemnation reaffirmed that political violence is incompatible with democratic norms and called for protecting public officials' safety across party lines. (15 Jun 2025)

6. Florida Governor Ron DeSantis stated that drivers could legally run over protesters if they felt threatened. The remark risked encouraging vehicular violence against demonstrators and undermined the right to peaceful assembly by framing protest crowds as legitimate targets. (15 Jun 2025)

7. Los Angeles Police Department used teargas, foam bullets, and mounted officers to disperse anti-Trump protesters. Declaring an unlawful assembly and deploying force against largely peaceful demonstrators raised concerns about disproportionate policing of dissent and protest rights. (15 Jun 2025)

8. No Kings protest organizers and participants held nationwide demonstrations opposing Trump's perceived abuses of power. With roughly five million participants at over 2,000 events, the No Kings protests represented a

massive civic mobilization in defense of constitutional limits and against authoritarian tendencies. (14 Jun 2025; 15 Jun 2025)

9. Protesters and peacekeepers in Salt Lake City were involved in a fatal shooting during a No Kings protest. The death of a demonstrator and injury of an armed individual during a protest confrontation illustrated the dangers of firearms at political gatherings and the complexities of non-state security roles. (15 Jun 2025)

10. Los Angeles District Attorney Nathan Hochman and federal prosecutors filed state and federal charges against individuals involved in protests against ICE raids. Felony assault, firearm, and curfew charges, alongside federal cases, raised questions about whether criminal law was being used to chill protest against immigration enforcement. (17 Jun 2025; 19 Jun 2025)

11. Los Angeles Dodgers organization denied ICE agents access to Dodger Stadium parking lots during heightened raids. Refusing federal agents entry signaled local resistance to immigration crackdowns and support for immigrant communities' sense of safety in civic spaces. (18 Jun 2025; 19 Jun 2025)

12. Journalists, legal observers, and protesters filed a lawsuit against DHS and Secretary Kristi Noem alleging protest suppression and excessive force. The suit claimed federal forces violated First Amendment rights during demonstrations, seeking judicial limits on the government's use of force against protest and press. (18 Jun 2025)

13. NAACP announced it would not invite President Trump to its national convention. Breaking with tradition by excluding a sitting president signaled organized civil-rights opposition to his policies and rhetoric, and a refusal to legitimize them symbolically. (17 Jun 2025)

14. State and local governments and corporate sponsors scaled back or canceled Juneteenth celebrations amid DEI rollbacks. Reductions in official and corporate support for Juneteenth events weakened public commemoration of emancipation and civil-rights history, reflecting a broader retreat from diversity initiatives. (18 Jun 2025; 19 Jun 2025)

15. Florida Attorney General James Uthmeier and state law enforcement continued arrests under a blocked immigration law until held in contempt. Persisting with unconstitutional arrests targeted immigrants despite a court order, undermining legal protections and signaling that civil liberties could be overridden by executive will. (18 Jun 2025)

16. Trump administration canceled all scheduled asylum appointments at the U.S.-Mexico border obtained via CBPOne. Nullifying 30,000 asylum appointments stranded families in precarious conditions and signaled that even legal pathways could be revoked unilaterally, eroding trust in asylum procedures. (19 Jun 2025)

17. Immigration and Customs Enforcement and local police conducted aggressive raids in Los Angeles and Lake Worth Beach targeting workplaces, churches, schools, and parishes. Sweeping operations in sensitive locations, including detentions of U.S. citizens, fueled fear, family separation, and allegations of racial profiling in immigrant communities. (16 Jun 2025; 18 Jun 2025; 19 Jun 2025)

18. ICE agents detained Oregon vineyard manager Moises Sotelo-Casas outside a church and transferred him without notifying family or counsel. The arrest of a long-time community figure at a church and opaque transfer practices highlighted due-process and humanitarian concerns in immigration enforcement. (19 Jun 2025)

19. ICE and FBI agents arrested New York City Comptroller and mayoral candidate Brad Lander at immigration court, then dropped charges. Detaining an opposition-aligned elected official while he accompanied an immigrant, on disputed assault claims later abandoned, suggested use of federal power to intimidate political critics of enforcement practices. (17 Jun 2025; 19 Jun 2025)

20. ICE officers detained U.S. citizen Adrian Martinez during a patrol in Pico Rivera. The detention of a citizen by immigration authorities underscored risks of mistaken or abusive enforcement that can strip individuals of liberty without proper basis. (17 Jun 2025)

21. Federal and state law enforcement pursued and charged Vance Boelter with federal and state offenses for stalking and murdering Minnesota officials. Robust prosecution of the assassin demonstrated that, despite rising political violence, institutions still moved to hold perpetrators accountable for attacks on elected officials. (17 Jun 2025)

22. Trump administration and immigration authorities expanded travel-ban considerations to dozens of additional countries. Contemplating adding 36 countries, including many in Africa, to the travel ban further restricted mobility based on nationality and religion, reinforcing stratified access to the U.S. (14 Jun 2025)

23. Federal judge denied release of Palestinian activist Mahmoud Khalil despite prolonged detention without charge. Continuing to hold a green-card holder on alleged immigration misstatements, amid claims of retaliation for activism, raised concerns about using detention to chill political expression. (14 Jun 2025)

24. Trump administration and state officials implemented and defended policies that deter undocumented immigrants from seeking medical care during outbreaks. Immigration crackdowns that make at-risk populations

fear reporting illness undermined outbreak detection and disproportionately endangered marginalized communities. (20 Jun 2025)

Economic Structure

1. Environmental Protection Agency dropped an enforcement case against private prison operator Geo Group after political donations. Ending a case that could have imposed millions in fines for toxic disinfectant use at an immigration facility raised concerns that regulatory enforcement was being softened for politically connected firms. (14 Jun 2025)

2. Target Corporation rolled back diversity, equity, and inclusion initiatives after Trump's inauguration. A major retailer's retreat from DEI under political pressure illustrated how corporate commitments to inclusion can be reversed when the political climate shifts, affecting workplace equity norms. (15 Jun 2025)

3. President Trump and Canadian Prime Minister Mark Carney publicly clashed over a tariff-based U.S.-Canada trade approach. Trump's preference for simple tariffs over more complex trade arrangements signaled a continued tilt toward unilateral, transactional trade policy with implications for cross-border economic stability. (15 Jun 2025)

4. President Trump and Commerce Secretary Howard Lutnick announced a U.S.-U.K. Economic Prosperity Deal via executive order. The deal restructured tariffs and quotas in key sectors like autos and aerospace, using executive authority to reshape trade flows and industrial advantages between the two countries. (16 Jun 2025)

5. Trump administration loosened cryptocurrency regulations and halted or paused multiple fraud cases. Rolling back crypto enforcement, including cases involving Trump-linked actors, weakened investor protections and suggested regulatory capture in a volatile financial sector. (17 Jun 2025)

6. Securities and Exchange Commission dismissed its civil lawsuit against Binance after listing a Trump family cryptocurrency. Dropping a major case over investor protections and trading controls following political entanglements raised fears that securities enforcement was being bent to favor regime-aligned platforms. (17 Jun 2025)

7. Trump Organization launched the "Trump Mobile" cellular service amid Trump's tariff threats against Apple. The new branded telecom venture, coinciding with presidential pressure on a major competitor, highlighted potential conflicts between public power and private profit-making. (16 Jun 2025; 17 Jun 2025)

8. Department of Veterans Affairs removed anti-discrimination protec-

tions for veterans and staff based on political beliefs and union activity. Stripping explicit protections risked politicizing access to VA services and employment conditions, weakening safeguards for staff and veterans with disfavored views. (16 Jun 2025)

9. Environmental Protection Agency and Department of Justice directed staff to halt enforcement against fossil fuel companies in parts of the Midwest. Pulling back on pollution enforcement for oil and gas operators shifted environmental and health risks onto communities while benefiting a powerful industry. (18 Jun 2025)

10. Department of Justice planned to cut two-thirds of staff inspecting federally licensed gun dealers. Slashing inspection capacity threatened enforcement of background-check and sales rules, potentially increasing illegal gun access and weakening public-safety regulation. (18 Jun 2025)

11. Amazon and Verizon withdrew corporate support and DEI commitments tied to Juneteenth celebrations. Major firms' retreat from Juneteenth and DEI, partly linked to regulatory bargaining, showed how corporate backing for racial equity can be traded away in pursuit of mergers and political favor. (18 Jun 2025)

12. Office of the Comptroller of the Currency and Congress had a bank-merger review rule overturned by a joint resolution. Congress's disapproval altered how bank mergers are evaluated, with implications for consolidation, competition, and systemic financial power. (20 Jun 2025)

13. Environmental Protection Agency and Congress saw an EPA air-quality reclassification rule overturned via joint resolution. Reversing the rule changed compliance obligations for major polluters, affecting air-quality protections and the balance between environmental health and industrial costs. (20 Jun 2025)

14. Chinese government and state-controlled banks maintained heavy manufacturing subsidies and redirected lending from real estate to industry, fueling price wars. China's industrial policy of subsidized overproduction and redirected credit created deflationary pressures and intense competition, illustrating how state-driven economics can destabilize markets. (20 Jun 2025)

15. Trump administration and corporate donors selectively exempted certain migrant workers from deportation while intensifying raids elsewhere. Shielding undocumented labor in donor-heavy sectors while targeting other workers entrenched a two-tier system where economic and political clout shaped exposure to enforcement. (15 Jun 2025; 17 Jun 2025)

16. Trump administration halted $11.4 billion in CDC Covid funding and canceled a $766 million H5N1 vaccine contract with Moderna. Pulling back large-scale public health investments weakened disease surveillance and

vaccine development capacity, trading long-term resilience for short-term ideological or fiscal goals. (20 Jun 2025)

17. Trump administration terminated or constrained multiple public health and environmental programs through budget and staffing cuts. Cuts to wildfire preparedness agencies, CDC bird-flu teams, and related programs eroded the state's ability to manage environmental and health risks, shifting burdens onto localities and individuals. (19 Jun 2025; 20 Jun 2025)

18. Federal Reserve and President Trump clashed publicly over interest-rate policy. Trump's denunciations of the Fed for not cutting rates pressured an institution meant to operate independently, risking politicized monetary decisions that could distort economic management. (18 Jun 2025; 19 Jun 2025)

19. Environmental Protection Agency approved and adjusted multiple air-permit and hazardous-waste decisions affecting industrial facilities. EPA actions on permits, sanctions deferrals, and waste classifications in several states shaped the regulatory environment for industry, balancing economic activity with pollution controls. (16 Jun 2025; 17 Jun 2025; 18 Jun 2025; 20 Jun 2025)

20. Food and Drug Administration and other federal agencies issued numerous patent-review determinations, guidance documents, and information-collection notices. Routine regulatory actions on drug patents, medical devices, food safety, and training shaped market exclusivity, compliance burdens, and the pace of generic competition in health-related sectors. (16 Jun 2025; 18 Jun 2025; 20 Jun 2025)

21. Office of Management and Budget and procurement agencies sought extensions of multiple federal acquisition and cost-accounting information collections. Maintaining reporting requirements for indirect costs, contract terminations, and quality assurance preserved transparency and accountability in federal contracting, albeit with administrative burdens. (16 Jun 2025)

22. Federal Communications Commission invited comment on several information-collection efforts and paperwork reductions. FCC reviews of data requirements for telecom services and small businesses aimed to balance regulatory oversight with reduced administrative burdens, affecting how communications markets are monitored. (16 Jun 2025; 18 Jun 2025)

23. General Services Administration advanced environmental review and siting decisions for a border port of entry and a new federal courthouse. The decisions shaped long-term federal infrastructure at the border and in Hartford, with implications for access to justice, trade flows, and local development. (20 Jun 2025)

Information, Memory, and Manipulation

1. Pentagon rapid response team under Defense Secretary Pete Hegseth used official social media accounts to promote partisan messages and attack critics. Deploying government communication channels for personal and political advocacy blurred the line between public information and propaganda, undermining trust in defense communications. (15 Jun 2025)

2. Katie Miller and the White House pressured the Social Security Administration commissioner not to contradict Trump's false claims about scam calls. Efforts to align agency statements with presidential misinformation compromised the independence of a key benefits agency and distorted public understanding of fraud risks. (16 Jun 2025)

3. Rightwing media figures and social media influencers spread misinformation portraying the Minnesota lawmaker assassin as a leftist and blaming Democrats. False narratives about the killer's ideology, amplified by high-profile accounts, distorted public understanding of the attack and weaponized tragedy for partisan gain. (17 Jun 2025)

4. Senator Mike Lee posted and then deleted social media claims mischaracterizing the Minnesota assassin as a Marxist. A sitting senator's widely viewed false posts about a political killing illustrated how elected officials can fuel disinformation that deepens polarization and mistrust. (17 Jun 2025)

5. Trump administration terminated 639 Voice of America and USAGM employees, effectively dismantling much of U.S. international broadcasting. Mass layoffs at VOA and its parent agency sharply reduced independent U.S. news capacity abroad, shifting information power toward administration-aligned outlets and narratives. (20 Jun 2025)

6. Centers for Disease Control and Prevention officials resigned or were fired over concerns about politicized vaccine and surveillance decisions. The departure of key CDC leaders, citing lack of confidence in objective data use, signaled erosion of scientific integrity in public health decision-making. (16 Jun 2025; 17 Jun 2025)

7. HHS Secretary Robert F. Kennedy Jr. fired members of the CDC's vaccine advisory committee and reduced CDC staffing. Removing experienced advisors and staff from vaccine programs weakened institutional memory and raised fears that ideology, not evidence, would guide immunization policy. (16 Jun 2025)

8. Trump administration issued a stop-work order for the LGBTQ-focused national suicide prevention hotline. Shuttering specialized support for LGBTQ callers reduced tailored mental health resources for a vulnerable

group, reflecting policy choices about whose crises merit dedicated attention. (18 Jun 2025)

9. Trump administration and State Department required foreign students and scholars to provide access to their social media for visa screening. Mandating review of applicants' online speech for signs of hostility to U.S. policies raised privacy concerns and risked ideological vetting of academic visitors. (18 Jun 2025)

10. Australian writer Alistair Kitchen and U.S. border authorities saw Kitchen denied entry and deported after questioning about his protest coverage and views. Turning away a foreign journalist over his reporting and political opinions suggested use of border controls to police speech and exclude critical voices. (19 Jun 2025)

11. Trump administration froze and illegally withheld federal funds for libraries, archives, and museums. The unlawful funding freeze, later flagged by GAO, threatened institutions that preserve historical records and public access to knowledge, aligning budget tactics with control over memory. (16 Jun 2025)

12. President Trump removed the MLK bust from the Oval Office and replaced Hillary Clinton's portrait with his own. Altering symbolic displays in the White House to downplay civil-rights and political rivals' imagery reflected an attempt to reshape the visual narrative of national leadership. (15 Jun 2025; 18 Jun 2025)

13. Defense Secretary Pete Hegseth and the Pentagon ordered a "passive approach" to Juneteenth messaging and withheld related web content. Suppressing official recognition of Juneteenth within the military communications apparatus diminished institutional acknowledgment of emancipation and racial history. (19 Jun 2025)

14. Defense Secretary Pete Hegseth renamed a Navy vessel previously honoring LGBTQ+ pioneer Harvey Milk. Removing Milk's name from a ship during Pride Month rolled back symbolic recognition of LGBTQ service and recast military honors along more exclusionary ideological lines. (15 Jun 2025)

15. Pollsters and media reported declining public support for Trump's immigration policies. Polling showing majority disapproval of deportation policies highlighted a gap between executive actions and public opinion, informing democratic accountability debates. (15 Jun 2025)

16. Trump administration and CDC cut $11.4 billion in Covid funding and fired bird-flu response officials, eroding surveillance. Dismantling key surveillance and response capacities reduced the flow of reliable public health data, impairing informed decision-making and public communication during outbreaks. (20 Jun 2025)

17. President Trump and allied media continued to claim the 2020 election was fraudulent and demanded a special prosecutor. Persistent false narratives about a "stolen" election kept disinformation at the center of political discourse, undermining trust in electoral institutions and future results. (19 Jun 2025; 20 Jun 2025)

18. Federal Communications Commission sought comment on information collection for radio astronomy coordination in Puerto Rico. The notice aimed to manage spectrum use to protect scientific observations, balancing communication needs with preservation of research infrastructure. (18 Jun 2025)

CHAPTER 23
WEEK 23 (21 JUN 2025 – 27 JUN 2025): SECRECY AS WAR-MAKING METHOD

Unauthorized strikes, militarized immigration raids, and curated intelligence fused into a week where executive power acted first and explained, if ever, later.

This week delivers a sharp shock to several core pillars of American democracy. The most intense pressure stems from unilateral war efforts against Iran, driven by manipulated intelligence and followed by attempts to limit Congress's access to classified information. This campaign, along with domestic troop deployments against immigration protesters, normalizes emergency-style executive power and blurs the line between civil and military authority. Meanwhile, immigration enforcement is weaponized on a large scale: masked raids, record numbers of detentions, deaths and medical neglect in custody, expansion of private detention centers, and plans for large new camps like "Alligator Alcatraz" all suggest a system where the law is used as a tool of fear rather than a safeguard against state power. The Supreme Court's decisions to narrow nationwide injunctions and restrict Medicaid patients' ability to sue, along with a hard-right immigration docket, weaken judicial checks just as the executive branch and DOJ push openly against court orders. Information and knowledge systems are also targeted: mass firings at Voice of America, threats and investigations targeting journalists, politicization of vaccine and health science agencies, and pressure on universities and DEI initiatives. Despite this, there are pockets of resistance—federal judges criticizing ICE and DOJ abuses, lawsuits by states and civil society, and a high-profile progressive electoral victory in New York—but these efforts operate in an environment of rapid authoritarian drift.

Power and Authority

1. President Donald Trump ordered large-scale airstrikes on Iranian nuclear facilities without congressional authorization. Trump's unilateral bombing of Iranian nuclear sites, conducted without a declaration of war or clear imminent threat, concentrated war-making power in the executive and sidestepped constitutional checks on the use of force. (21 Jun 2025; 22 Jun 2025; 23 Jun 2025; 24 Jun 2025; 25 Jun 2025; 26 Jun 2025; 27 Jun 2025)

2. President Donald Trump publicly dismissed U.S. intelligence assessments on Iran's nuclear intentions. By rejecting his own intelligence community's finding that Iran was not building a nuclear weapon, Trump weakened evidence-based national security decision-making and opened space for policy driven by politics and foreign partners' claims. (21 Jun 2025; 22 Jun 2025; 23 Jun 2025; 24 Jun 2025)

3. President Donald Trump called for a special prosecutor to investigate baseless 2020 election fraud claims. Trump's renewed demand for a special prosecutor into already-discredited 2020 fraud allegations kept a false narrative of a stolen election alive, undermining confidence in electoral outcomes and justifying future restrictive measures. (21 Jun 2025)

4. President Donald Trump threatened Iran with greater retaliation for any response to U.S. strikes. Trump's public warning that any Iranian retaliation would be met with greater force escalated the risk of open-ended conflict driven by executive rhetoric rather than deliberative policy. (21 Jun 2025)

5. President Donald Trump revoked security clearances of several former senior officials. Stripping former national security officials of clearances during an international crisis reduced continuity of expertise and signaled willingness to use access to classified information as a political tool. (25 Jun 2025)

6. President Donald Trump removed Director of National Intelligence Tulsi Gabbard from a Senate Iran briefing team. Pulling the DNI from a key Iran briefing and substituting other loyal officials narrowed the range of information reaching senators and further politicized intelligence oversight. (25 Jun 2025)

7. President Donald Trump ordered deployment and federalization of National Guard and Marines to Los Angeles over state objections. Federalizing and deploying thousands of troops to Los Angeles to support immigration raids over state leaders' objections blurred civil–military lines and used federal force to control a disfavored jurisdiction. (21 Jun 2025; 23 Jun 2025)

8. President Donald Trump announced restrictions on classified information sharing with Congress after an intelligence leak. By curbing Congress's

access to classified assessments following a leak about Iran strikes, the administration weakened legislative oversight of war powers and centralized control over critical information. (25 Jun 2025; 26 Jun 2025)

9. President Donald Trump publicly attacked Rep. Thomas Massie for introducing a War Powers Resolution. Trump's attacks on a Republican lawmaker for questioning unauthorized military action signaled intolerance for intra-party oversight and discouraged congressional checks on executive war powers. (23 Jun 2025)

10. President Donald Trump called for cancellation of Israeli Prime Minister Benjamin Netanyahu's corruption trial. Urging that a foreign leader's bribery and fraud trial be canceled invited political interference in another country's judiciary and normalized viewing corruption prosecutions as illegitimate "witch hunts." (26 Jun 2025)

11. President Donald Trump called for regime change in Iran on social media. Openly advocating regime change in Iran without congressional debate or allied backing raised the stakes of U.S. involvement and framed foreign policy around leader preferences rather than stable doctrine. (22 Jun 2025)

12. President Donald Trump announced a ceasefire between Israel and Iran and then publicly rebuked Israel for violating it. Trump's personal announcement of a ceasefire and subsequent public scolding of Israel underscored how major conflict diplomacy was being run through his social media persona rather than institutional channels. (25 Jun 2025)

13. President Donald Trump terminated U.S. trade discussions with Canada over its Digital Services Tax. Halting trade talks with Canada in retaliation for its digital tax on U.S. firms used bilateral economic relations as a personal leverage tool, risking broader economic and diplomatic fallout. (26 Jun 2025)

14. President Donald Trump called for resettling Afrikaners while barring other refugees from travel-ban countries. Prioritizing resettlement of Afrikaners while excluding refugees from travel-ban nations embedded ideological and ethnic preferences into humanitarian policy, deepening stratified access to protection. (27 Jun 2025)

15. President Donald Trump publicly demanded defunding of Voice of America and firing of critical journalists. Calling for VOA to be defunded and for specific reporters to be fired used presidential influence to intimidate independent media and chill critical coverage of military and foreign policy. (25 Jun 2025)

16. President Donald Trump announced a news conference to defend Iran strikes and attack critical media coverage. Orchestrating a Pentagon news

conference explicitly to rebut negative reporting on Iran strikes further fused military communications with the president's political narrative management. (26 Jun 2025)

17. President Donald Trump called for a special prosecutor and continued to promote 2020 election fraud narratives. Sustaining false claims of a stolen 2020 election through demands for new investigations kept distrust in electoral institutions high and normalized using prosecutorial tools against political outcomes. (21 Jun 2025)

18. President Donald Trump used social media to pressure Israel to scale down an airstrike on Iran. Directly instructing a foreign ally via social media to alter its military plans highlighted personalized, ad hoc control over sensitive security decisions outside normal diplomatic processes. (24 Jun 2025)

19. President Donald Trump publicly attacked Rep. Alexandria Ocasio-Cortez and other lawmakers with derogatory language. Trump's demeaning attacks on opposition lawmakers on his platform further degraded norms of democratic discourse and framed critics as illegitimate rather than as coequal representatives. (24 Jun 2025)

20. President Donald Trump called for cancellation of Benjamin Netanyahu's trial as part of praising joint military actions. Linking Netanyahu's legal troubles to shared military achievements suggested that loyalty in security matters should shield leaders from corruption accountability, echoing similar domestic narratives. (26 Jun 2025)

21. President Donald Trump announced secretive negotiations to ease sanctions on Iran in exchange for nuclear limits. Engaging in largely undisclosed talks to trade sanctions relief for nuclear concessions, while publicly emphasizing military pressure, concentrated foreign policy choices in the executive with limited public or congressional input. (27 Jun 2025)

22. President Donald Trump renewed public claims that Iran's nuclear program had been completely destroyed. Persisting in overstated claims about the success of Iran strikes despite contrary intelligence entrenched a pattern of executive narratives overriding factual assessments in national security debates. (26 Jun 2025)

23. President Donald Trump publicly praised NATO Secretary General's private texts to bolster his standing. Releasing flattering messages from NATO's leader to support his image before a summit personalized alliance diplomacy and used selective disclosure to shape perceptions of international support. (24 Jun 2025)

24. President Donald Trump called for resettling Afrikaners while maintaining travel bans on other refugees. Favoring Afrikaner resettlement while excluding refugees from banned countries embedded ideological and racial

preferences into refugee policy, signaling unequal valuation of lives in humanitarian decisions. (27 Jun 2025)

25. President Donald Trump used social media to frame Iran strikes as comparable to historic atomic bombings. Invoking Hiroshima and Nagasaki to describe Iran strikes glorified military action and recast a contested operation as a defining national triumph, shaping public memory of the conflict. (26 Jun 2025)

26. President Donald Trump publicly claimed that 2020 election investigations were needed despite prior indictment for obstruction. Continuing to demand probes into the 2020 election even after being indicted for obstructing the vote count blurred lines between personal legal exposure and the state's investigative machinery. (21 Jun 2025)

27. President Donald Trump used social media to pressure Israel over ceasefire violations with Iran. Publicly chastising Israel for breaking a ceasefire via social media highlighted how major alliance management decisions were being conducted through personal channels rather than institutional diplomacy. (24 Jun 2025)

28. President Donald Trump announced that Israel and Iran had agreed to a ceasefire that was quickly violated. Trump's premature announcement of an Israel–Iran ceasefire, followed by renewed strikes, underscored the gap between presidential declarations and on-the-ground realities, complicating accountability for conflict outcomes. (25 Jun 2025)

Institutions and Governance

1. Members of Congress criticized Trump's Iran strikes as unconstitutional and pushed War Powers resolutions. Lawmakers from both chambers argued that bombing Iran without authorization violated the Constitution and advanced War Powers measures, highlighting institutional resistance but also the fragility of legislative checks on war powers. (21 Jun 2025; 22 Jun 2025; 23 Jun 2025)

2. U.S. House of Representatives voted to table impeachment articles against Trump over unauthorized Iran strikes. By shelving impeachment articles related to unauthorized military action, the House signaled limited appetite to use its strongest accountability tool against executive overreach in foreign policy. (24 Jun 2025)

3. Trump administration canceled and postponed classified briefings to Congress on Iran strikes. Canceling and delaying briefings on the Iran operation restricted Congress's ability to scrutinize the decision-making and effec-

tiveness of the strikes, weakening routine oversight of military actions. (23 Jun 2025; 24 Jun 2025)

4. Senate Parliamentarian Elizabeth MacDonough ruled that several GOP reconciliation provisions violated Senate rules. The parliamentarian's decisions striking Medicaid and court-limiting provisions from the budget bill preserved procedural constraints on what can be passed via simple-majority reconciliation. (23 Jun 2025; 25 Jun 2025; 26 Jun 2025; 27 Jun 2025)

5. Republican lawmakers called for firing the Senate parliamentarian after adverse rulings. Threats to remove the parliamentarian for enforcing reconciliation rules showed willingness to attack neutral procedural referees when they constrain partisan legislative goals. (26 Jun 2025)

6. Senate Majority Leader John Thune rejected efforts to overrule the parliamentarian and pledged to amend the bill instead. Thune's decision to respect the parliamentarian's ruling and adjust the budget bill rather than override it upheld internal Senate norms that buffer institutions from raw partisan pressure. (27 Jun 2025)

7. Senate leadership planned to vote on a major budget reconciliation bill by July 4 under White House pressure. Rushing a sweeping tax-and-spending package to meet a presidential deadline, partly to cover DHS overspending, illustrated how fiscal timelines can be driven by executive demands and agency crises rather than deliberation. (27 Jun 2025)

8. Republican-controlled House of Representatives passed Trump's large tax-and-spending bill and sent it to the Senate. House passage of a sprawling bill with deep Medicaid cuts and enforcement funding shifts set the stage for major structural changes to social spending and immigration capacity if enacted. (26 Jun 2025)

9. Congressional Democrats condemned the administration's withholding of information on Iran strikes. Democratic leaders' public objections to restricted briefings underscored the importance of information access for meaningful oversight, even as they lacked tools to compel fuller disclosure. (26 Jun 2025)

10. Department of Homeland Security and ICE required 72 hours' notice for congressional detention facility visits despite law allowing surprise inspections. Imposing advance-notice requirements on congressional visits to detention centers undermined statutory unannounced inspection rights and reduced real-time oversight of conditions and abuses. (25 Jun 2025)

11. Supreme Court of the United States allowed the administration to deport migrants to third countries pending litigation. By staying lower-court blocks and permitting deportations to non-origin countries, the Court

expanded executive discretion over removal policy while migrants' legal challenges proceed. (23 Jun 2025; 24 Jun 2025)

12. Supreme Court of the United States limited lower courts' ability to issue nationwide injunctions against federal policies. New rulings curbing nationwide injunctions, including in a birthright citizenship case, reduced lower courts' capacity to halt contested executive orders across the country, shifting power toward the presidency. (26 Jun 2025; 27 Jun 2025)

13. Supreme Court of the United States ruled that Medicaid patients cannot sue to enforce provider choice rights. By holding that Medicaid beneficiaries lack a private right to sue over provider exclusions, the Court made it harder for low-income patients to challenge state efforts to defund providers like Planned Parenthood. (26 Jun 2025)

14. Supreme Court of the United States upheld Texas's age-verification law for pornography websites. Affirming Texas's strict age checks for adult sites endorsed a model of online regulation that raises privacy and free-expression concerns while expanding state control over digital access. (27 Jun 2025)

15. Supreme Court of the United States affirmed the constitutionality of key Affordable Care Act preventive services provisions. Upholding ACA preventive-care mandates while confirming the health secretary's power over the task force preserved coverage but concentrated influence over scientific recommendations in a politically appointed official. (27 Jun 2025)

16. Supreme Court of the United States required schools to allow religious opt-outs from LGBTQ-themed classroom materials. Mandating opt-outs from LGBTQ-inclusive readings on religious grounds risked encouraging districts to preemptively remove such content, narrowing inclusive civic education through litigation pressure. (26 Jun 2025; 27 Jun 2025)

17. Department of Justice under President Trump sued the entire bench of Maryland federal judges over a deportation-delay order. Suing all Maryland federal judges for requiring a one-day pause before deportations directly challenged judicial authority and signaled hostility toward court-imposed limits on immigration enforcement. (24 Jun 2025; 26 Jun 2025)

18. Federal courts in New York ordered the return of a man deported in violation of a court order. By compelling the government to retrieve a deported man and explain its actions, appellate judges asserted that executive agencies must obey judicial stays in immigration cases. (24 Jun 2025)

19. Whistleblower Erez Reuveni and federal courts exposed and scrutinized DOJ official Emil Bove's alleged defiance of deportation court orders. Allegations that a top DOJ official urged ignoring deportation injunctions, now under judicial and public scrutiny, highlighted internal resistance to

rule-of-law erosion but also the vulnerability of whistleblowers. (24 Jun 2025; 25 Jun 2025)

20. Senate Judiciary Committee held a contentious confirmation hearing for DOJ official Emil Bove to a federal appeals court. Questioning Bove over alleged court-order defiance and politicized prosecutions underscored concerns that judicial appointments are being used to entrench executive-aligned legal theories. (25 Jun 2025)

21. Federal courts blocked Trump's order terminating collective bargaining rights for over one million federal employees. A temporary injunction preserving federal workers' bargaining rights checked an executive attempt to weaken organized labor within the civil service. (24 Jun 2025)

22. Coalition of states and the District of Columbia sued the Trump administration over cancellation of federal grants. States' lawsuit challenging unilateral grant cancellations sought to defend funding for safety, health, and research programs against executive budgetary maneuvers. (24 Jun 2025)

23. U.S. District Court Judge Tana Lin enjoined the administration from withholding EV charger infrastructure funds from most states. Blocking efforts to freeze billions in EV charger funds reinforced statutory spending commitments and limited the executive's ability to unilaterally stall a nationwide infrastructure program. (25 Jun 2025)

24. Federal courts and EPA handled multiple challenges to Trump emergency declarations and environmental deregulation. Lawsuits over an "energy emergency" and use of the Alien Enemies Act, along with mixed rulings, showed courts both constraining and enabling executive efforts to bypass normal environmental and immigration processes. (23 Jun 2025)

25. National Archives and Records Administration invited public comment on federal records disposition schedules. NARA's routine solicitation of comments on records schedules maintained a formal avenue for public input into which federal records are preserved or destroyed, supporting archival transparency. (24 Jun 2025)

26. Federal courts rebuked prosecutors over the hasty charging of Newark Mayor Ras Baraka. A magistrate judge's criticism of rushed trespass charges against a mayor signaled judicial concern about using federal criminal process to intimidate local officials engaged in oversight. (21 Jun 2025)

27. Federal courts criticized the administration for failing to comply with an injunction on Voice of America firings. A judge's rebuke over noncompliance with an order protecting VOA staff highlighted tensions between the judiciary and executive over politicized media purges. (23 Jun 2025)

28. Federal courts handled lawsuits over ICE arrests at courthouses and detention of a Honduran family. Litigation by a Honduran family and others

against ICE courthouse arrests tested whether courts will protect vulnerable immigrants from enforcement tactics that may chill access to justice. (25 Jun 2025; 27 Jun 2025)

29. Federal courts oversaw emergency motions to prevent deportation of Kilmar Abrego Garcia. Emergency filings to halt Abrego Garcia's deportation underscored how judicial intervention remains a last line of defense against abrupt removals that may bypass due process. (25 Jun 2025; 26 Jun 2025; 27 Jun 2025)

30. Federal courts awarded damages to a clergy abuse survivor under extended civil limitations law. A $2.4 million verdict for a clergy abuse survivor, enabled by a state law reviving old claims, showed courts can expand accountability for historic institutional wrongdoing. (27 Jun 2025)

31. Federal courts handled Gavin Newsom's defamation lawsuit against Fox News. Newsom's suit over allegedly deceptive editing by Fox raised questions about how courts will balance political speech protections with remedies for misinformation by major outlets. (25 Jun 2025; 26 Jun 2025; 27 Jun 2025)

32. Federal courts heard a copyright case on AI training using pirated and purchased books. A ruling that AI firms may train on lawfully purchased books without paying authors, while barring use of pirated copies, set an important precedent for how intellectual property is treated in AI development. (26 Jun 2025)

33. Senate Parliamentarian and GOP leadership navigated internal conflict over reconciliation rules without overruling procedural advice. Despite pressure from some Republicans to fire the parliamentarian, leadership's decision to work within her rulings preserved a key nonpartisan constraint on majority power in the Senate. (25 Jun 2025; 26 Jun 2025; 27 Jun 2025)

34. Federal courts and DOJ oversaw and contested DOJ's lawsuit against Maryland judges over deportation delays. The unprecedented suit against an entire district bench over a deportation-delay order highlighted escalating institutional conflict between the executive and judiciary on immigration control. (24 Jun 2025; 26 Jun 2025)

Civil Rights and Dissent

1. ICE and DHS under the Trump administration conducted intensified, often masked immigration raids and mass detentions across Los Angeles and other areas. Aggressive ICE operations, including masked agents, record detention levels, wrongful arrests of citizens, and daily arrest quotas, created a climate

of fear that chilled everyday life and access to services for immigrant communities. (21 Jun 2025; 22 Jun 2025; 23 Jun 2025; 24 Jun 2025; 25 Jun 2025; 26 Jun 2025; 27 Jun 2025)

2. ICE and DOJ detained and attempted to deport activists, long-term residents, and families with serious medical needs. Cases involving Mahmoud Khalil, a Honduran mother with a child with leukemia, and other vulnerable individuals showed immigration enforcement being used against activists and the medically fragile, raising grave human rights concerns. (21 Jun 2025; 22 Jun 2025; 23 Jun 2025; 27 Jun 2025)

3. Department of Homeland Security issued a national terrorism advisory citing Iran conflict and domestic tensions. A terrorism advisory tied to the Iran conflict raised concerns that heightened threat framing could justify expanded surveillance and restrictions on civil liberties at home. (22 Jun 2025)

4. ICE and federal prosecutors arrested and charged local officials and a New York City comptroller during immigration-related incidents. Arrests and charges against Newark's mayor, a U.S. representative, and NYC's comptroller during oversight or accompaniment of immigrants suggested federal power being used to intimidate elected officials who challenge enforcement tactics. (21 Jun 2025; 25 Jun 2025)

5. Department of Homeland Security announced plans to build new immigrant detention facilities in Florida, including Alligator Alcatraz. Expanding detention capacity with remote, high-security facilities entrenched a carceral approach to migration that isolates detainees from communities and oversight. (23 Jun 2025; 25 Jun 2025; 27 Jun 2025)

6. Department of Homeland Security terminated Temporary Protected Status for over half a million Haitians. Ending TPS for Haitians with a short grace period threatened mass loss of lawful status and potential return to unstable conditions, disproportionately affecting a vulnerable diaspora. (26 Jun 2025)

7. Trump administration and DOJ planned to dismiss large numbers of asylum claims and expand DHS prosecutorial authority. Plans to summarily dismiss asylum claims and shift prosecutorial power from U.S. attorneys to DHS threatened due process protections and concentrated enforcement discretion in a politicized department. (25 Jun 2025)

8. Emil Bove and DOJ leadership purged DOJ staff involved in January 6 prosecutions and sought leniency for a politically useful mayor. Firing prosecutors who pursued January 6 cases and attempting to drop charges against NYC's mayor in exchange for immigration cooperation showed law enforcement being reshaped to serve regime interests. (25 Jun 2025)

9. Federal immigration officers increasingly concealed their identities

with masks and casual clothing during operations. The growing use of masks and unmarked attire by immigration agents eroded transparency and made it harder for the public to distinguish lawful officers from impersonators, undermining trust and accountability. (25 Jun 2025)

10. Department of Education under the Trump administration declared California's trans-inclusive sports policies in violation of Title IX. Threatening enforcement against California for allowing trans athletes reframed civil rights protections as violations, signaling federal willingness to punish inclusive state education policies. (25 Jun 2025)

11. Supreme Court of the United States required schools to allow religious opt-outs from LGBTQ-themed instruction. Allowing parents to withdraw children from LGBTQ-inclusive lessons on religious grounds risked marginalizing queer narratives in public education and emboldening broader content-based opt-outs. (26 Jun 2025; 27 Jun 2025)

12. Supreme Court of the United States upheld Texas's age-verification law for pornography sites despite privacy concerns. Requiring users to submit IDs or transactional data to access adult content raised civil liberties and privacy issues, particularly around state tracking of lawful adult behavior. (27 Jun 2025)

13. Supreme Court of the United States allowed deportations to third countries and narrowed migrants' ability to challenge removals. High Court stays and rulings enabling deportations to non-origin countries with limited process expanded executive power over noncitizens while reducing judicial avenues for relief. (23 Jun 2025; 24 Jun 2025)

14. Representative Andy Ogles called for denaturalization and deportation of Zohran Mamdani after his NYC mayoral primary win. A sitting congressman's demand to strip a political opponent's citizenship based on ideology and smears weaponized denaturalization against democratic participation by minorities. (26 Jun 2025; 27 Jun 2025)

15. House Homeland Security Committee Democrats publicly condemned Ogles' denaturalization remarks as racist. Committee leaders' denunciation of calls to denaturalize Mamdani framed such rhetoric as incompatible with equal citizenship, signaling institutional pushback against ethnonationalist politics. (27 Jun 2025)

16. New York Police Department hate crimes taskforce investigated death threats and Islamophobic attacks against Zohran Mamdani. Police probes into threats against Mamdani highlighted how minority politicians face heightened risks of targeted violence that can deter diverse representation. (26 Jun 2025)

17. ICE and local law enforcement arrested protesters and activists

opposing Palantir's ICE contracts. Arrests at a protest targeting Palantir's deportation software underscored how civil disobedience against surveillance contractors can trigger criminal charges, potentially chilling dissent. (26 Jun 2025)

18. Activists and Capitol Police clashed during protests against Medicaid cuts at the Russell Senate Office Building. Arrests of protesters opposing Medicaid reductions illustrated how direct action is used to contest redistributive policy shifts, and how security responses can constrain such mobilization. (27 Jun 2025)

19. Department of Homeland Security and ICE detained a long-term Iranian resident and other Iranians amid U.S. strikes on Iran. Arresting Iranian nationals with long U.S. residence during a foreign conflict blurred lines between external security policy and domestic targeting of diaspora communities. (27 Jun 2025)

20. Supreme Court of the United States limited Medicaid patients' ability to sue over provider exclusions affecting Planned Parenthood. Restricting Medicaid beneficiaries' standing to challenge provider bans weakened a legal avenue for defending reproductive and low-income healthcare access. (26 Jun 2025)

21. Trump administration and DOJ explored agreements with dozens of countries to hold deported individuals, including in rights-abusing states. Seeking deportation agreements with 53 countries, many with poor human rights records, raised the risk that U.S. removals would consign people to abusive conditions abroad. (25 Jun 2025)

22. Trump administration planned to resettle Afrikaners while barring refugees from travel-ban countries. Selective resettlement of Afrikaners alongside continued exclusion of other refugees embedded ideological and racial preferences into asylum policy, undermining equal treatment norms. (27 Jun 2025)

23. Supreme Court of the United States curbed nationwide injunctions that had blocked Trump's birthright citizenship order. Limiting nationwide injunctions in a case involving birthright citizenship made it harder to secure broad judicial relief against policies that could stratify citizenship by heritage. (27 Jun 2025)

24. Supreme Court of the United States allowed DHS to proceed with contested immigration status policies pending litigation. Granting stays that let DHS implement disputed status policies while cases proceed shifted the balance toward enforcement-first outcomes for affected immigrants. (23 Jun 2025)

25. Supreme Court of the United States upheld Texas's age-verification

law for pornography websites despite First Amendment concerns. Endorsing strict age checks for adult content, despite dissenting free-speech and privacy concerns, expanded state power over online expression in ways that may chill lawful adult access. (27 Jun 2025)

26. Supreme Court of the United States affirmed ACA preventive services while empowering the health secretary over the task force. While preserving preventive coverage, the Court's decision to place the task force under the health secretary's direct control increased the risk that scientific standards could be reshaped by ideological appointees. (27 Jun 2025)

27. Supreme Court of the United States limited lower courts' ability to block Trump's birthright citizenship order nationwide. Restricting nation-wide injunctions in the birthright citizenship case allowed partial implementation of a policy that could undermine equal citizenship while challenges continue. (27 Jun 2025)

28. Supreme Court of the United States narrowed Medicaid patients' ability to sue over provider choice, affecting Planned Parenthood access. By limiting private enforcement of Medicaid provider-choice rights, the Court made it easier for states to exclude reproductive health providers from coverage without direct patient recourse. (26 Jun 2025)

29. Supreme Court of the United States curbed nationwide injunctions that had blocked Trump's executive orders. Ending broad injunctions against executive orders reduced a key tool civil rights groups had used to quickly halt policies affecting people nationwide, shifting litigation burdens onto dispersed plaintiffs. (27 Jun 2025)

30. Supreme Court of the United States allowed deportations to third countries with limited process. Permitting removals to conflict-ridden third countries without robust individualized review heightened the risk that migrants would be sent to danger with little judicial oversight. (23 Jun 2025; 24 Jun 2025)

31. Supreme Court of the United States upheld Texas's age-verification law for pornography websites. The Court's endorsement of Texas's ID-based access regime for adult sites set a precedent for intrusive verification schemes that may chill lawful expression and privacy. (27 Jun 2025)

32. Supreme Court of the United States affirmed ACA preventive services while centralizing control under the health secretary. By confirming the health secretary's power to appoint and remove preventive-services task force members, the Court increased the potential for politicized control over which services must be covered. (27 Jun 2025)

33. Supreme Court of the United States required schools to allow religious opt-outs from LGBTQ-themed readings. The ruling that schools must accom-

modate religious opt-outs from LGBTQ-inclusive materials risked encouraging districts to avoid such content altogether, narrowing representation in public education. (26 Jun 2025; 27 Jun 2025)

34. Supreme Court of the United States limited nationwide injunctions in a birthright citizenship case. Restricting nationwide injunctions in litigation over Trump's birthright citizenship order made it harder to secure broad protection for affected children while the policy's constitutionality is tested. (27 Jun 2025)

35. Supreme Court of the United States allowed deportations to third countries with limited judicial review. By permitting deportations to non-origin countries with minimal process, the Court expanded executive discretion over where migrants are sent, often to places with serious safety risks. (23 Jun 2025; 24 Jun 2025)

36. Supreme Court of the United States upheld Texas's age-verification law for pornography websites despite privacy concerns. The Court's approval of Texas's ID-based access regime for adult content set a precedent for intrusive verification schemes that may chill lawful expression and privacy. (27 Jun 2025)

37. Supreme Court of the United States affirmed ACA preventive services while centralizing control under the health secretary. By confirming the health secretary's power over the preventive-services task force, the Court increased the potential for politicized control over which services must be covered. (27 Jun 2025)

Economic Structure

1. Trump administration conducted Iran strikes that threatened closure of the Strait of Hormuz and raised global freight and energy risks. Military escalation with Iran, including threats to the Strait of Hormuz and rising freight rates and evacuations, exposed how unilateral security decisions can destabilize global trade and energy markets. (21 Jun 2025; 22 Jun 2025)

2. Senate Republicans advanced a budget reconciliation bill with historic Medicaid cuts and large deficit increases. The reconciliation package's deep Medicaid reductions and deficit expansion shifted fiscal priorities toward tax cuts and enforcement spending at the expense of low-income healthcare. (25 Jun 2025; 26 Jun 2025; 27 Jun 2025)

3. Senator Elizabeth Warren and Democratic colleagues pressed oil companies about lobbying for a tax break in the reconciliation bill. Senators' inquiries into fossil fuel firms' lobbying for a CAMT exemption highlighted

how targeted tax provisions can be shaped by corporate influence to shield specific industries. (26 Jun 2025)

4. Trump administration and Florida officials approved and funded a large migrant detention facility in the Everglades known as Alligator Alcatraz. Authorizing a 5,000-bed Everglades detention complex with substantial federal costs embedded long-term spending on carceral infrastructure as a response to immigration pressures. (25 Jun 2025; 27 Jun 2025)

5. Governor Ron DeSantis and the state of Florida seized county land under emergency powers to build the Alligator Alcatraz detention facility. Using emergency authority to take local land for a controversial detention project bypassed normal land-use and fiscal scrutiny, raising concerns about how emergency framing can redirect public resources. (27 Jun 2025)

6. ICE and CoreCivic contracted to convert a shuttered California prison into the state's largest immigrant detention center. Partnering with a private prison firm to expand detention capacity deepened reliance on for-profit incarceration to implement federal immigration policy. (26 Jun 2025)

7. Stephen Miller, White House deputy chief of staff held a significant financial stake in Palantir while it received a major ICE contract. Miller's Palantir holdings during a $30 million ICE surveillance contract raised serious conflict-of-interest concerns about insiders profiting from expanded enforcement spending. (24 Jun 2025; 25 Jun 2025)

8. Trump's media company announced a $400 million share buyback program. A large buyback by Trump's media firm suggested efforts to bolster share prices and investor confidence, intertwining the financial health of a partisan outlet with the political fortunes of its principal. (23 Jun 2025)

9. President Donald Trump publicly attacked Federal Reserve Chair Jerome Powell for not cutting interest rates. Trump's criticism of the Fed chair for maintaining rates risked undermining central bank independence and signaling that monetary policy should align with short-term political goals. (23 Jun 2025)

10. Zohran Mamdani, New York City mayoral candidate proposed expansive economic policies including rent freezes, higher taxes, and major public investments. Mamdani's platform of rent freezes, higher taxes on the wealthy, free buses, universal childcare, and large-scale housing construction outlined a redistributive urban economic model that could reshape local public goods. (24 Jun 2025)

11. California Legislature passed a major expansion of film and TV production tax credits. Boosting Hollywood tax incentives to $750 million annually used targeted credits to compete for industry investment and jobs,

illustrating how states deploy fiscal tools to shape economic geography. (27 Jun 2025)

12. DHS restored previously frozen counter-terrorism funding to several major cities. Reinstating security grants to cities after earlier freezes suggested that critical safety funding had been used as leverage in disputes with local governments. (26 Jun 2025)

13. EPA and other federal regulators issued multiple chemical, environmental, and Superfund decisions affecting industry compliance. EPA actions on mine permits, chemical risk evaluations, SNURs, and Superfund settlements shaped the regulatory burden on industry and the strength of environmental protections. (23 Jun 2025; 26 Jun 2025; 27 Jun 2025)

14. FDA and OSHA updated multiple medical device, drug, and workplace safety standards and guidance. New classifications, guidances, and testing-lab recognitions for drugs, devices, and hazardous chemicals adjusted regulatory expectations that affect innovation, safety, and industry costs. (24 Jun 2025; 26 Jun 2025)

15. FDA and Census Bureau sought public comment on numerous information collections for food, tobacco, and economic data. Requests for comment on data collections for food safety, tobacco, and construction and demographic surveys maintained statistical infrastructure that underpins economic and health policymaking. (27 Jun 2025)

16. DHS and FEMA committed substantial federal funds to new migrant detention capacity in Florida. Federal financing of a costly Everglades detention complex illustrated how immigration enforcement priorities can drive large, recurring public expenditures. (25 Jun 2025; 27 Jun 2025)

17. EPA tentatively approved New York's revised drinking water supervision program. EPA's approval of New York's updated drinking water rules aligned state standards with federal requirements, affecting compliance costs and public health protections. (26 Jun 2025)

18. California Legislature and Governor Gavin Newsom advanced a large film tax credit expansion expected to be signed into law. Expanding film tax credits to retain production in-state showed how subnational governments use fiscal incentives to compete for mobile capital and jobs. (27 Jun 2025)

19. EPA issued corrections and updates to ozone and air-quality regulatory materials. Technical corrections to ozone-protection rules and SIP materials ensured that enforceable environmental standards remained accurate, supporting predictable compliance for regulated entities. (26 Jun 2025; 27 Jun 2025)

20. DHS restored counter-terrorism grants to cities previously frozen in political disputes. Reinstating security grants after earlier freezes suggested

that vital public safety funding had been used as leverage in conflicts with local governments, intertwining security budgets with political alignment. (26 Jun 2025)

Information, Memory, and Manipulation

1. Trump administration contradicted U.S. intelligence and relied on disputed or foreign claims to justify Iran strikes. By sidelining its own intelligence community and leaning on Israeli claims to rationalize bombing Iran, the administration politicized intelligence and echoed patterns seen before the Iraq War. (21 Jun 2025; 22 Jun 2025; 23 Jun 2025; 24 Jun 2025)

2. President Donald Trump and senior officials insisted Iran's nuclear program was obliterated despite intelligence showing only limited damage. Trump and Defense Secretary Hegseth's claims of total success, contradicted by DIA assessments and IAEA statements, exemplified executive disinformation about war outcomes. (22 Jun 2025; 23 Jun 2025; 24 Jun 2025; 25 Jun 2025; 27 Jun 2025)

3. Defense Secretary Pete Hegseth and FBI launched a criminal leak investigation into the DIA Iran assessment and attacked media coverage. Investigating the leak of an intelligence report that contradicted the White House narrative, while accusing media of cheering against the president, targeted sources of independent information about the war. (25 Jun 2025; 26 Jun 2025; 27 Jun 2025)

4. Trump administration announced plans to restrict congressional access to classified information after the DIA leak. Citing leaks as justification to limit classified briefings to Congress concentrated control over war-related information in the executive and weakened legislative oversight. (25 Jun 2025; 26 Jun 2025)

5. Trump administration terminated 639 Voice of America employees as part of dismantling the U.S. Agency for Global Media. Mass firings at VOA gutted a major independent public broadcaster, reducing U.S. capacity to provide credible news abroad and opening space for more state-aligned messaging. (25 Jun 2025)

6. President Donald Trump called for defunding Voice of America and firing specific journalists critical of his Iran policy. Trump's demands to defund VOA and fire CNN's Pentagon correspondent for unfavorable reporting exemplified direct political pressure on independent media and individual reporters. (25 Jun 2025)

7. White House Press Secretary Karoline Leavitt publicly attacked CNN correspondent Natasha Bertrand for her Iran coverage. The press secretary's

denunciation of a specific reporter as pushing false narratives further personalized attacks on journalists covering national security. (26 Jun 2025)

8. Media Matters for America sued the FTC alleging retaliatory investigations for its reporting on extremist content. Claims that Trump appointees used regulatory powers to punish a watchdog group for criticizing social media platforms raised alarms about weaponizing oversight against critical civil society. (23 Jun 2025)

9. Governor Gavin Newsom filed a major defamation lawsuit against Fox News and Jesse Watters. Newsom's suit over an allegedly deceptive clip sought to hold a powerful outlet accountable for misinformation, testing how courts will police partisan editing in political coverage. (26 Jun 2025; 27 Jun 2025)

10. Vice President J.D. Vance misidentified Senator Alex Padilla as a convicted criminal during a news conference. Confusing a sitting senator with a notorious criminal name functioned as a smear that associated a political opponent with criminality in the public mind. (21 Jun 2025)

11. Homeland Security Secretary Kristi Noem threatened to revoke Harvard's SEVP certification over alleged extremism before a judge blocked it. Using immigration certification as leverage against a university for perceived ideological noncompliance, later halted by a court, showed how federal power can be aimed at academic speech. (23 Jun 2025)

12. Trump administration and DOJ expanded investigations and threats against universities over hiring and perceived extremism. New probes into university hiring and pressure that led to UVA's president resigning as part of a DEI settlement signaled a broader campaign to reshape academic institutions' values and leadership. (26 Jun 2025; 27 Jun 2025)

13. Health Secretary Robert F. Kennedy Jr. fired and replaced CDC vaccine advisory panels with ideological allies and promoted anti-vaccine narratives. RFK Jr.'s wholesale replacement of vaccine advisers with skeptics and subsequent thimerosal restrictions injected anti-scientific ideology into core public health decision-making structures. (24 Jun 2025; 25 Jun 2025; 26 Jun 2025; 27 Jun 2025)

14. CDC and HHS under RFK Jr. allowed a presentation citing a nonexistent study on vaccine harms. Featuring a fabricated study in an official CDC presentation undermined the credibility of public health communications and suggested weakened internal scientific vetting. (24 Jun 2025)

15. RFK Jr. and the U.S. government announced U.S. withdrawal of funding from global vaccine alliance Gavi. Cutting support for Gavi over alleged suppression of dissenting vaccine views aligned U.S. global health

policy with anti-vaccine narratives and weakened multilateral immunization efforts. (25 Jun 2025)

16. Pakistani journalist Jalil Afridi and ICE saw his brief detention and credential seizure after a State Department briefing. Detaining a foreign journalist and seizing his press credential without charges sent a chilling signal to reporters covering U.S. foreign policy and immigration. (24 Jun 2025)

17. President Donald Trump attacked Rep. Alexandria Ocasio-Cortez and other lawmakers on Truth Social with demeaning language. Using his platform to insult and belittle opposition lawmakers normalized treating political disagreement as personal vilification rather than democratic debate. (24 Jun 2025)

18. Trump administration pressured the University of Virginia president to resign as part of a DEI investigation settlement. Forcing UVA's president out to resolve a DOJ probe into diversity policies showed how legal pressure can be used to reshape university leadership and chill equity initiatives. (27 Jun 2025)

19. U.S. State Department and OMB moved to terminate most overseas pro-democracy programs funded by DRL. Plans to end nearly all DRL democracy grants would sharply reduce U.S. support for civil society and human rights abroad, reshaping America's narrative role in global democracy promotion. (26 Jun 2025)

20. President Donald Trump and NATO Secretary General Mark Rutte publicized private texts praising Trump ahead of a NATO meeting. Releasing selective praise from NATO's leader served as a public-relations tool to bolster Trump's image, illustrating how private diplomatic communications can be weaponized for domestic narratives. (24 Jun 2025)

21. National Archives and Records Administration sought public comment on records schedules for multiple agencies. NARA's open comment process on records retention helped maintain transparency over which government documents are preserved, even as other parts of the state faced accusations of secrecy and manipulation. (24 Jun 2025)

22. EPA published a notice of availability for multiple Environmental Impact Statements. Making EIS documents publicly available with comment periods supported informed debate over major projects, contributing to an open environmental record despite broader pressures on transparency. (27 Jun 2025)

23. Trump administration and DOJ used lawsuits and investigations against media and watchdogs to contest critical narratives. From Newsom's Fox suit to Media Matters' FTC case, litigation around media practices

reflected a contested information environment where courts are asked to referee political narratives. (23 Jun 2025; 25 Jun 2025; 26 Jun 2025; 27 Jun 2025)

24. RFK Jr. and HHS restructured vaccine and preventive health advisory bodies following a Supreme Court ruling. Leveraging new authority affirmed by the Court, RFK Jr. reshaped key health panels in ways that may align scientific guidance with his long-standing skepticism of vaccines. (27 Jun 2025)

25. President Donald Trump and Defense Secretary Pete Hegseth planned a news conference to defend Iran strikes and counter negative media narratives. Coordinating a high-profile briefing explicitly to rebut critical coverage of the Iran operation showed how military communications were being used to reinforce a contested political storyline. (26 Jun 2025)

26. Vice President J.D. Vance and Secretary of State Marco Rubio publicly contradicted intelligence assessments to support claims about Iran's nuclear ambitions. Senior officials' statements dismissing the intelligence community's view on Iran's nuclear intentions reinforced a pattern of political narratives overriding professional analysis. (23 Jun 2025)

27. RFK Jr. and the U.S. government withdrew funding from Gavi while promoting skepticism about vaccine safety. Defunding a key global vaccination partner on ideological grounds signaled a shift away from evidence-based global health cooperation toward politicized narratives about vaccines. (25 Jun 2025)

28. Trump administration and DOJ expanded investigations into universities' hiring and DEI practices. Federal scrutiny of university hiring and diversity policies, coupled with leadership changes, risked pressuring campuses to align curricula and staffing with administration ideology. (26 Jun 2025; 27 Jun 2025)

29. Trump administration moved to terminate most DRL-funded pro-democracy programs abroad. Cutting nearly all DRL democracy grants would reduce U.S. support for independent media and civil society overseas, reshaping how American power influences global narratives about governance. (26 Jun 2025)

30. President Donald Trump continued to promote debunked 2020 election fraud narratives while facing related indictments. Persisting in claims of a stolen election despite an indictment for obstructing the 2020 count entrenched disinformation about electoral legitimacy at the highest level of government. (21 Jun 2025)

CHAPTER 24

WEEK 24 (28 JUN 2025 – 4 JUL 2025): HARDWIRING INEQUALITY AS GOVERNANCE

A megabill, a compliant Court, and a militarized border quietly rewrote who counts, who pays, and who can still say no.

This week signifies a significant shift toward authoritarian rule, marked by the passage and signing of the One Big Beautiful Bill and a series of Supreme Court decisions that expand executive immunity and limit judicial oversight. Fiscal and social policies were aggressively reshaped to favor capital over labor and native-born citizens over immigrants, with deep, long-term cuts to Medicaid, SNAP, Planned Parenthood, and Medicare, while dramatically increasing ICE, detention facilities, and defense budgets. At the same time, the Court restricted nationwide injunctions and reaffirmed broad presidential immunity, greatly weakening courts as a check on power. Law enforcement and immigration authorities were openly weaponized against political rivals, local officials, journalists, and even judges, while DOJ directives on denaturalization and birthright citizenship tactics further divided citizenship itself. Control over information grew tighter through threats to CNN, efforts to compel sources, shutdowns of federal climate sites, and politically motivated appointments. Although some judicial and state-level opposition emerged over issues like asylum, TPS, HHS dismissals, and data-sharing, the overall trend points to a coordinated consolidation of executive power, exclusionary policies, and oligarchic control.

Power and Authority

1. President Trump announced plans to end birthright citizenship by executive order. Trump's stated intent to end birthright citizenship by executive order signaled a willingness to unilaterally redefine constitutional citizenship rights, testing limits on presidential authority over fundamental status questions. (28 Jun 2025)

2. President Trump ordered large-scale airstrikes on Iranian nuclear facilities. Trump's unilateral strikes on Iranian nuclear sites, undertaken without clear congressional authorization, concentrated war-making power in the executive and risked escalation without robust democratic oversight. (28 Jun 2025; 30 Jun 2025; 2 Jul 2025)

3. President Trump endorsed the No Tax Dollars for Riots Act targeting protest-related nonprofits. By backing a bill to strip federal funds and tax status from nonprofits involved in protests, Trump used federal leverage to chill organized dissent and penalize civil society groups critical of his policies. (28 Jun 2025)

4. President Trump criticized Netanyahu's corruption trial and threatened to suspend US aid to Israel. Trump's threat to withhold US aid unless Netanyahu's corruption trial was curbed showed willingness to use American state power to influence a foreign judiciary for political allies' benefit. (28 Jun 2025)

5. President Trump issued an executive order indemnifying and enhancing protections for law enforcement officers. Trump's order to provide legal resources and indemnification for officers, and to enhance penalties for crimes against them, strengthened state coercive power while weakening accountability for rights violations. (30 Jun 2025)

6. President Trump issued an executive order revoking major Syria sanctions and ending a national emergency. Revoking longstanding Syria sanctions and redefining the national emergency framework concentrated foreign economic policy decisions in the presidency, with limited contemporaneous legislative input. (30 Jun 2025)

7. Department of Justice under President Trump directed attorneys to prioritize denaturalization of certain naturalized citizens. DOJ's memo prioritizing civil denaturalization cases, where defendants lack a right to counsel, created a more precarious, second-tier citizenship vulnerable to executive-driven enforcement. (30 Jun 2025)

8. President Trump met with Republican holdouts to press them to support his budget megabill. Trump's direct lobbying of skeptical Republicans to back his reconciliation bill underscored the president's dominant

role in shaping legislative outcomes on core fiscal and social policy. (2 Jul 2025)

9. President Trump threatened to back primary challengers against Republicans opposing his budget bill. By threatening primary challenges to GOP lawmakers who opposed his megabill, Trump used personal political power to discipline legislators and narrow space for intra-party dissent. (2 Jul 2025)

10. President Trump withheld $6.8 billion in legally appropriated K–12 school funding. The administration's refusal to disburse congressionally mandated school funds asserted executive power over the purse, undermining statutory budgeting and disrupting educational services nationwide. (2 Jul 2025)

11. President Trump pressured House Freedom Caucus members to back the Senate budget bill without changes. Trump's successful effort to flip House Freedom Caucus members into supporting the Senate bill without amendments showed executive dominance over internal legislative bargaining. (2 Jul 2025)

12. President Trump promised to fix disliked bill provisions later via executive orders. Trump's assurance that he would later alter statutory provisions through executive orders encouraged legislators to rely on unilateral presidential action instead of transparent legislative revision. (2 Jul 2025)

13. President Trump called for investigations of political opponents and threatened arrest of Zohran Mamdani. Trump's demand to investigate DHS Secretary Mayorkas and threat to arrest mayoral candidate Zohran Mamdani for noncooperation with ICE exemplified use of state power to intimidate political adversaries. (2 Jul 2025)

14. President Trump suggested deporting US citizens who commit crimes. Trump's public suggestion that US-born citizens who commit crimes should be deported challenged core constitutional protections and blurred the line between citizenship and deportable status. (1 Jul 2025)

15. President Trump threatened to cut federal subsidies to Elon Musk's companies over political criticism. Trump's threat to revoke subsidies from Musk's firms in retaliation for criticism of his tax bill showed willingness to wield economic state power against disfavored business actors. (1 Jul 2025)

16. President Trump suggested deporting Elon Musk amid their political feud. Floating the idea of deporting Musk during a political dispute illustrated the president's readiness to frame immigration enforcement as a tool of personal retaliation. (1 Jul 2025)

17. President Trump visited and publicly promoted a massive new migrant detention facility in Florida. Trump's visit to the Everglades detention

complex, framed as a centerpiece of his immigration agenda, symbolized executive commitment to large-scale, punitive detention as a governing tool. (2 Jul 2025)

18. President Trump signed the One Big Beautiful Bill Act and related tax-and-spending legislation into law. By signing sweeping tax-and-spending laws that cut safety nets and massively expand enforcement powers, Trump locked core elements of his agenda into statute, reshaping state power and obligations. (3 Jul 2025; 4 Jul 2025)

19. President Trump launched a personal Trump Fragrances merchandise line while in office. Trump's launch of a high-priced fragrance line tied to his name raised concerns about using the presidency to market private goods, blurring boundaries between public office and personal enrichment. (30 Jun 2025)

20. President Trump admitted allowing Iran to bomb a US air base in retaliation for US strikes. Trump's admission that he permitted Iran to strike a US base highlighted highly personalized control over military risk decisions, with limited transparency or institutional checks. (30 Jun 2025)

21. President Trump announced talks to potentially reopen the federal prison on Alcatraz Island. Trump's claim that private prison developers were exploring reopening Alcatraz suggested further expansion of punitive incarceration capacity, potentially via private partners. (1 Jul 2025)

22. President Trump signed executive orders creating a Make America Beautiful Again conservation commission and changing national park policies. Trump's conservation-themed orders centralized agenda-setting over public lands, raising fees for nonresidents and revoking diversity directives while expanding executive influence over park access and symbolism. (3 Jul 2025)

Institutions and Governance

1. Representative Yassamin Ansari and co-sponsors advanced a War Powers Resolution to reassert congressional authority over Iran conflict. Ansari's co-sponsorship of a War Powers Resolution sought to reclaim Congress's constitutional role in authorizing war, pushing back against unilateral presidential military action. (28 Jun 2025)

2. US Senate voted down a resolution limiting Trump's ability to escalate war with Iran. The Senate's rejection of a war-powers limit on Trump preserved broad executive discretion over military escalation, weakening legislative checks on war-making. (28 Jun 2025)

3. US Senate advanced Trump's budget reconciliation megabill through

key procedural votes. Narrow procedural votes to advance Trump's megabill enabled sweeping fiscal and social changes via reconciliation, sidestepping the filibuster and compressing deliberation on major structural reforms. (28 Jun 2025; 29 Jun 2025; 30 Jun 2025)

4. Senate Parliamentarian ruled several budget bill provisions violated reconciliation rules. The parliamentarian's finding that certain targeted Medicaid and state provisions breached the Byrd rule underscored internal procedural limits on partisan budget maneuvers. (28 Jun 2025; 30 Jun 2025)

5. Senate Republicans bypassed the Senate Parliamentarian and GAO to advance Trump's megabill and revoke EPA waivers. By overruling the parliamentarian and GAO on reconciliation and Congressional Review Act procedures, Senate Republicans weakened nonpartisan guardrails that constrain majority power. (29 Jun 2025; 1 Jul 2025)

6. US Senate adopted a current policy baseline treating trillions in tax cuts as costless. The Senate's adoption of a baseline that assumes permanent tax cuts with no scored cost distorted budget accounting, easing passage of deficit-expanding policies without transparent tradeoffs. (29 Jun 2025)

7. House Freedom Caucus and leadership publicly criticized but ultimately advanced the Senate budget bill. Freedom Caucus leaders decried the bill's deficit impact yet moved it forward, illustrating how partisan loyalty can override stated fiscal principles in legislative practice. (29 Jun 2025; 30 Jun 2025)

8. US Senate passed Trump's budget reconciliation bill with Vice President Vance's tie-breaking vote. The Senate's tie-breaking passage of the megabill, despite internal dissent, showed a narrowly controlled chamber enacting far-reaching changes with minimal bipartisan support. (30 Jun 2025; 1 Jul 2025; 2 Jul 2025; 3 Jul 2025)

9. President Trump urged Senate Republicans to ignore the parliamentarian's budget ruling. Trump's call to disregard the parliamentarian framed procedural referees as obstacles to be overridden, eroding respect for internal legislative rule enforcement. (30 Jun 2025)

10. House Republican leadership kept a procedural vote open for hours seeking support for the budget bill. Extending a House vote for over two hours to flip members on the megabill highlighted procedural manipulation to secure outcomes rather than reflect settled majorities. (2 Jul 2025)

11. US House of Representatives adopted the Senate's budget bill without amendments after intense pressure. The House's decision to pass the Senate version unchanged, despite earlier promises of revisions, underscored how leadership and executive pressure can override normal bicameral negotiation. (2 Jul 2025; 3 Jul 2025; 4 Jul 2025)

12. Senator Hakeem Jeffries and House Democrats used an eight-hour floor speech to delay the tax-and-spending bill. Jeffries' record-length speech leveraged minority procedural tools to spotlight the bill's social impacts, illustrating how opposition can still use institutional mechanisms to inform the public. (3 Jul 2025)

13. Supreme Court of the United States limited federal courts' ability to issue nationwide injunctions against federal policies. By curbing nationwide injunctions, the Court reduced lower courts' capacity to uniformly block contested federal actions, likely producing fragmented rights protections across jurisdictions. (28 Jun 2025; 3 Jul 2025)

14. Supreme Court of the United States allowed partial enforcement of Trump's birthright citizenship executive order. The Court's refusal to fully block Trump's order limiting birthright citizenship enabled uneven application of a core constitutional protection while sidestepping the underlying rights question. (30 Jun 2025)

15. Supreme Court of the United States agreed to hear a challenge to coordinated campaign spending limits. By taking a case that could loosen limits on party–candidate coordinated spending, the Court positioned itself to further expand money's influence over elections. (30 Jun 2025)

16. Supreme Court of the United States declined to hear an anti-vaccine group's social media censorship lawsuit. The Court's decision not to review Children's Health Defense's claims left unresolved questions about government influence over platform moderation and free speech online. (30 Jun 2025)

17. Supreme Court of the United States was reported to have granted presidents absolute immunity for official acts. The Trump v. United States ruling granting absolute immunity for official acts dramatically weakened legal accountability for presidents, undermining the principle that no one is above the law. (2 Jul 2025)

18. US District Court and federal judiciary ruled Trump's asylum ban unlawful and blocked its enforcement. Judge Randolph Moss's decision striking down Trump's border asylum ban, echoed by another federal judge, reaffirmed statutory limits on presidential power over asylum access. (2 Jul 2025)

19. Coalition of state attorneys general sued the Trump administration over sharing Medicaid data with DHS for immigration enforcement. Twenty attorneys general challenged federal sharing of Medicaid data with DHS, defending privacy norms and seeking to limit health programs' use as immigration enforcement tools. (1 Jul 2025; 2 Jul 2025)

20. Democratic state attorneys general sued the Trump administration

over termination of school-based mental health funds. Sixteen attorneys general sued to restore over $1 billion in school mental health funding, asserting that the administration's cuts violated statutory commitments to student services. (30 Jun 2025)

21. Federal courts blocked Trump administration attempts to fire HHS staff and terminate Haitians' TPS. Judges temporarily halted mass HHS firings and the end of TPS for Haitians, showing courts still acting as a check on abrupt executive moves against civil servants and vulnerable immigrants. (1 Jul 2025)

22. Federal appeals court rejected the administration's effort to detain Georgetown scholar Badar Khan Suri during deportation fight. An appeals court's refusal to detain Suri pending deportation proceedings modestly constrained executive detention power in a high-profile academic's case. (1 Jul 2025)

23. US Supreme Court allowed deportation of eight men from a US base in Djibouti to South Sudan. By clearing deportations despite torture concerns, the Court narrowed protections for noncitizens facing removal to dangerous third countries, deferring to executive removal decisions. (3 Jul 2025)

24. US Supreme Court ruled parents may opt children out of LGBTQ+-themed lessons on religious grounds. The Mahmoud v. Taylor decision expanded parental opt-outs from inclusive curricula, complicating schools' ability to provide uniform civic and rights education. (3 Jul 2025)

25. US Supreme Court agreed to hear appeals on state bans of transgender students in girls' sports. By taking up Idaho and West Virginia's trans sports bans, the Court positioned itself to reshape federal protections against discrimination for transgender students. (3 Jul 2025)

26. Wisconsin Judge Hannah Dugan and FBI saw a sitting judge arrested by federal agents for alleged obstruction in an immigration case. The FBI's arrest of Judge Dugan for actions in her courtroom raised alarms about federal law enforcement encroaching on judicial independence in politically charged immigration disputes. (30 Jun 2025)

27. US Election Assistance Commission scheduled a public meeting on certification of a voting system under VVSG 2.0. The EAC's open meeting on voting system certification reflected ongoing institutional efforts to standardize and publicly vet election technology. (30 Jun 2025)

28. DeKalb County Board of Registration and Elections appointed election denier Gail Lee to the county elections board. Installing a known election denier on a key county board risked undermining public confidence in

election administration and opened the door to partisan interference in local processes. (2 Jul 2025)

29. Representative Marge Greene introduced a bill for a citizens-only census and redistricting. Greene's proposal to base apportionment on a citizens-only census would reduce representation for areas with many noncitizens, structurally shifting political power and voting weight. (2 Jul 2025)

30. Office of Special Counsel nominating authorities selected Paul Ingrassia, a conspiracy theorist, to lead the Office of Special Counsel. Choosing an official who spread conspiracy theories to head the OSC threatened the credibility and impartiality of a key federal ethics and whistleblower protection office. (2 Jul 2025)

31. Department of Justice allowed a former January 6 defendant to advise its weaponization working group. Bringing a January 6 defendant into a DOJ advisory role on alleged weaponization signaled politicization of internal justice oversight and blurred lines between accountability and grievance politics. (2 Jul 2025)

32. Senator Elizabeth Warren called for an investigation into possible bribery in Trump's settlement with Paramount. Warren's request for an antibribery probe into a large settlement between Trump and Paramount highlighted concerns that private legal deals may be used to purchase favorable treatment from powerful officials. (2 Jul 2025)

33. Homeland Security Secretary Kristi Noem failed to disclose an $80,000 payment from a dark-money group while governor. Noem's undisclosed payment from a dark-money fund that attacked local media raised red flags about transparency and conflicts of interest in a senior national security official's finances. (1 Jul 2025)

Civil Rights and Dissent

1. Immigration and Customs Enforcement and DHS conducted aggressive raids, detentions, and deportations affecting long-term residents and military families. ICE operations targeting veterans' relatives, long-term residents, and workers, often without serious criminal records, illustrated a punitive enforcement regime with broad collateral damage to families and communities. (28 Jun 2025; 30 Jun 2025; 1 Jul 2025; 2 Jul 2025; 3 Jul 2025; 4 Jul 2025)

2. Trump administration moved to terminate Temporary Protected Status for approximately 500,000 Haitians. Ending TPS for Haitians would strip legal status from hundreds of thousands of residents, exposing them to deportation despite longstanding ties to US communities. (28 Jun 2025)

3. Federal judge temporarily blocked termination of TPS for Haitians. A

court order halting TPS termination for Haitians provided temporary protection against mass deportations, illustrating judicial resistance to abrupt status revocations. (1 Jul 2025)

4. Trump administration and HHS shared Medicaid data with DHS for immigration enforcement, prompting a multistate lawsuit. Using Medicaid records to aid deportations blurred lines between health care and policing, risking deterrence from seeking care and undermining trust in public programs. (1 Jul 2025; 2 Jul 2025)

5. US District Court ordered Kilmar Abrego Garcia to remain in custody to prevent immediate deportation. A judge's order keeping Abrego Garcia in custody to avoid rapid deportation highlighted the tension between immigration enforcement speed and due process protections. (30 Jun 2025; 2 Jul 2025)

6. US government and ICE attempted to deport stateless Palestinian Ward Sakeik despite a court order, then released her. ICE's efforts to deport Sakeik in defiance of a federal order, followed by her eventual release, exposed serious compliance issues with judicial rulings in immigration cases. (2 Jul 2025; 4 Jul 2025)

7. Trump administration and RFK Jr. at HHS assumed direct control of CDC and reshaped vaccine advisory panels. With no CDC director in place, RFK Jr.'s dismissal of independent vaccine advisers and policy shifts raised concerns about politicized public health guidance and reduced expert oversight. (29 Jun 2025)

8. Trump administration terminated over $1 billion in school-based mental health funding, triggering litigation. Cutting bipartisan mental health funds created after Uvalde weakened school support systems and prompted states to sue to restore promised services. (30 Jun 2025)

9. Trump administration and Congress enacted a one-year Medicaid ban on Planned Parenthood and similar providers. Blocking Medicaid reimbursements to Planned Parenthood threatened closure of many clinics and reduced access to reproductive and general health care for low-income patients. (2 Jul 2025; 4 Jul 2025)

10. University of Pennsylvania blocked trans athletes from women's sports and erased Lia Thomas's records. UPenn's exclusion of trans women from women's sports and retroactive record erasure, under federal pressure, curtailed transgender students' participation and recognition in campus life. (1 Jul 2025)

11. US Supreme Court allowed deportation of noncitizens to South Sudan despite torture concerns. The Court's decision enabling deportations from a US base to South Sudan, over lower-court protections, narrowed safeguards against removal to potential persecution. (3 Jul 2025)

12. US Supreme Court expanded parental opt-outs from LGBTQ+-inclusive lessons in public schools. Allowing broad religious opt-outs from LGBTQ+-themed lessons risked fragmenting civic education and marginalizing queer students in classroom content. (3 Jul 2025)

13. US Supreme Court agreed to review state bans on transgender students in girls' sports. Taking up trans sports bans put the Court at the center of defining equal protection for transgender youth in education and athletics. (3 Jul 2025)

14. Catholic school in Louisiana fired a teacher for being in a same-sex marriage. Terminating a longtime teacher over his same-sex marriage highlighted ongoing conflicts between religious employment policies and LGBTQ+ equality in education workplaces. (29 Jun 2025)

15. EPA employees, scientists, and academics issued a mass declaration dissenting from Trump-era environmental policies. Over 600 EPA staff and scientists publicly warned that agency policies were undermining its health and environmental mission, exemplifying internal resistance to politicized regulation. (30 Jun 2025)

16. Protesters and local officials in Florida demonstrated against the Alligator Alcatraz immigration detention facility. Large protests against the Everglades detention complex challenged the expansion of harsh immigration detention and the use of emergency powers to fast-track controversial projects. (28 Jun 2025)

17. Democratic lawmakers were denied entry to inspect the Alligator Alcatraz detention center. Blocking members of Congress from entering a new immigration jail limited democratic oversight of detention conditions and potential rights abuses. (4 Jul 2025)

18. Representative Brian Fitzpatrick's constituents held a die-in protest at his office against the budget bill's healthcare cuts. Constituents' die-in dramatized the human stakes of Medicaid and health cuts, using peaceful protest to pressure a swing-district lawmaker on a pivotal vote. (2 Jul 2025)

19. Elon Musk announced a new political party and threatened to fund primary challengers over the budget bill. Musk's creation of the America Party and pledge to bankroll challengers against pro-bill Republicans showed how billionaire actors can reshape intra-party dynamics and electoral competition. (30 Jun 2025)

20. Zohran Mamdani and New York City voters saw Mamdani win the NYC Democratic mayoral primary via ranked-choice voting. Mamdani's primary victory under ranked-choice rules illustrated how alternative electoral systems can elevate candidates outside traditional party establishments. (1 Jul 2025)

21. Representative Marge Greene proposed a citizens-only census and redistricting bill. Greene's bill to exclude noncitizens from apportionment would diminish representation for diverse communities, entrenching unequal political voice based on citizenship status. (2 Jul 2025)

22. Alabama Law Enforcement Agency refused to release body camera footage in the police killing of Jabari Peoples. Withholding footage in a disputed police shooting limited public scrutiny and accountability, deepening mistrust in law enforcement investigations. (2 Jul 2025)

23. Chicago courts exonerated six men wrongfully convicted in a 1987 murder case. Vacating convictions tied to a detective with a pattern of misconduct highlighted systemic failures in policing and prosecution, while modestly restoring faith in post-conviction review. (2 Jul 2025)

24. US Supreme Court and lower courts blocked Trump's January asylum ban at the southern border. Courts' injunctions against Trump's asylum proclamation preserved statutory rights for border crossers and checked executive attempts to unilaterally suspend asylum access. (2 Jul 2025)

25. US Supreme Court granted presidents absolute immunity for official acts, affecting accountability for rights violations. The immunity ruling made it harder to hold presidents criminally liable for abuses of power, weakening a key backstop against rights-violating executive behavior. (2 Jul 2025)

26. US government and ICE detained and later released journalist Mario Guevara and photographer Job Garcia over protest coverage. The detention of a journalist and arrest of a photographer documenting ICE operations, followed by legal challenges, underscored risks faced by media workers covering enforcement actions. (1 Jul 2025; 3 Jul 2025)

27. EPA and Trump administration cut research staff while facing a Clean Water Act lawsuit over PFAS pollution. Shrinking EPA's research arm amid litigation over toxic sludge spreading weakened institutional capacity to investigate and address environmental health harms. (3 Jul 2025; 4 Jul 2025)

28. US government and ICE agents were filmed urinating on a Los Angeles school campus before a raid, prompting a district complaint. ICE agents' misconduct on school grounds, and the district's demand for investigation, highlighted tensions between federal enforcement and community standards protecting children. (4 Jul 2025)

Economic Structure

1. Trump administration and congressional Republicans advanced and enacted the One Big Beautiful Bill Act with major tax cuts and safety net reductions. The megabill permanently extended 2017 tax cuts, slashed

Medicaid, SNAP, and other supports, and expanded enforcement and defense spending, structurally redistributing resources upward and deepening inequality. (28 Jun 2025; 29 Jun 2025; 30 Jun 2025; 1 Jul 2025; 2 Jul 2025; 3 Jul 2025; 4 Jul 2025)

2. Senate Republicans included new taxes and penalties targeting renewable and advanced energy projects. Provisions taxing wind, solar, nuclear, geothermal, and storage projects, while adding credits for metallurgical coal, shifted federal energy policy toward fossil fuels and away from clean generation. (28 Jun 2025; 29 Jun 2025)

3. Congressional Budget Office and economic agencies reported that Trump's policies widened the trade deficit, weakened the dollar, and shrank GDP. Official data showing a larger trade deficit, a sharp dollar decline, and a 0.5% GDP contraction undercut administration claims of self-financing tax cuts and robust growth. (28 Jun 2025; 29 Jun 2025; 30 Jun 2025)

4. Federal Communications Commission suspended and postponed rules capping prison phone rates. By delaying implementation of price caps on prison calls and citing facility finances, the FCC preserved a system that extracts high fees from incarcerated people and their families. (30 Jun 2025; 1 Jul 2025; 3 Jul 2025)

5. US government and ICE allocated unprecedented funding for immigration jails, enforcement, and border wall construction. The megabill's $172 billion for immigration enforcement, including $45 billion for new jails and $50+ billion for wall projects, entrenched a carceral border regime with resources rivaling core justice institutions. (28 Jun 2025; 29 Jun 2025; 30 Jun 2025; 2 Jul 2025; 3 Jul 2025; 4 Jul 2025)

6. Trump administration withheld nearly $7 billion in federal school funding for multiple education programs. Freezing billions in K–12 and adult education funds disrupted services for vulnerable students and signaled willingness to use appropriations holdups as a policy weapon. (1 Jul 2025; 2 Jul 2025)

7. US Department of Labor under Trump announced plans to roll back over 60 worker protection regulations. Planned deregulation of minimum wage, overtime, farmworker union rights, and anti-discrimination rules would weaken labor standards and shift bargaining power further toward employers. (1 Jul 2025)

8. Occupational Safety and Health Administration revoked requirements to consult a construction safety advisory committee in rulemaking. OSHA's removal of mandatory consultation with its construction safety committee streamlined rule changes but reduced expert and worker input into safety standards. (1 Jul 2025)

9. Environmental Protection Agency finalized and adjusted multiple environmental and emissions rules and deadlines. EPA actions tightening some incineration standards while extending compliance for coatings and steel plants reflected a mixed regulatory posture balancing industry petitions with environmental protections. (30 Jun 2025; 2 Jul 2025; 3 Jul 2025)

10. Food and Drug Administration and related agencies issued numerous patent, guidance, and information-collection decisions affecting drugs and devices. FDA's determinations on patent review periods, guidance drafts, and data collections shaped market exclusivity and regulatory pathways for pharmaceuticals and medical devices. (2 Jul 2025; 3 Jul 2025)

11. Federal Communications Commission modernized broadband data collection certification and advanced paperwork changes. FCC's shift from professional engineer certification to experienced engineers and its paperwork revisions aimed to reduce compliance burdens while maintaining data quality for broadband and communications services. (1 Jul 2025; 2 Jul 2025; 3 Jul 2025)

12. Transportation Security Administration extended and revised information collections on service feedback and surface transportation security. TSA's information collection extensions supported ongoing oversight of transportation security training and stakeholder feedback, affecting regulatory compliance for rail and hazardous materials operators. (2 Jul 2025)

13. Office of Management and Budget and federal procurement agencies sought extensions of multiple contractor-related information collections. OMB and procurement agencies' submissions on fleet vehicles, change orders, commercial acquisitions, and private security contractors maintained data needed for oversight of federal contracting. (3 Jul 2025)

14. National Restaurant Association requested immigration enforcement relief due to labor shortages. The restaurant industry's plea for targeted relief from immigration crackdowns highlighted how aggressive enforcement policies can disrupt labor-dependent sectors and economic stability. (1 Jul 2025)

15. University of Pennsylvania and Trump administration agreed on guidelines barring trans athletes from women's sports and erasing Lia Thomas's records. UPenn's agreement to exclude trans women from women's sports and erase records under federal pressure showed how funding leverage can reshape institutional policies and recognition. (1 Jul 2025)

16. House of Representatives passed a budget increasing endowment taxes on wealthy universities. Raising the endowment tax from 1.4% to as high as 21% for institutions like Stanford significantly altered federal financing of higher education and research capacity. (30 Jun 2025)

17. Trump administration withheld Medicare funds and cut coverage for

legal immigrants through new law. A new law increasing the deficit while triggering large Medicare cuts, including terminating coverage for many legal immigrants, shifted health risks onto older and immigrant populations. (1 Jul 2025)

18. Environmental Protection Agency launched an animal adoption program amid deep cuts to its research arm. EPA's lab animal adoption program, occurring alongside plans to slash its research workforce, signaled a retreat from long-term scientific capacity in favor of short-term projects. (3 Jul 2025)

19. Federal agencies and courts faced a lawsuit over EPA's handling of sewage sludge and PFAS pollution. Litigation alleging EPA Clean Water Act violations over sewage sludge spreading sought to force stronger regulation of PFAS contamination affecting drinking water and public health. (4 Jul 2025)

20. Federal Reserve critics within the Trump administration called on Congress to investigate Fed Chair Jerome Powell for alleged bias. A top housing regulator's push to investigate and potentially remove the Fed chair over supposed political bias threatened central bank independence and could politicize monetary policy. (2 Jul 2025)

21. Lancet researchers and USAID policymakers reported that US foreign aid cuts could cause millions of additional global deaths. A Lancet study projected that Trump-era USAID reductions could lead to over 14 million extra deaths abroad, underscoring how US budget choices reshape global public health outcomes. (30 Jun 2025)

Information, Memory, and Manipulation

1. President Trump and Homeland Security Secretary Kristi Noem threatened CNN with prosecution over reporting on the ICEBlock app and Iran assessment. Threats to prosecute CNN for coverage of an ICE-tracking app and Iran intelligence signaled direct executive pressure on investigative reporting about security policy. (30 Jun 2025; 1 Jul 2025)

2. President Trump suggested forcing reporters to reveal anonymous sources about Iran intelligence. Trump's suggestion that journalists could be compelled to disclose sources threatened source confidentiality, a cornerstone of investigative reporting on national security. (29 Jun 2025)

3. Trump administration shut down the US Global Change Research Program's public climate website. Closing a key federal climate information portal curtailed public access to scientific data and reports, hindering informed debate on environmental policy. (1 Jul 2025)

4. Trump administration sent Harvard a letter accusing it of civil rights violations over antisemitism and threatening funding cuts. Federal threats to pull funding from Harvard over contested antisemitism claims risked using civil rights enforcement to pressure campus speech and governance decisions. (30 Jun 2025)

5. White House Press Secretary Karoline Leavitt falsely labeled Zohran Mamdani a communist and antisemite during a briefing. Smearing a mayoral candidate with baseless accusations from the White House podium weaponized official communications to delegitimize an opposition figure. (30 Jun 2025)

6. President Trump attacked Zohran Mamdani on social media as a "Communist Lunatic". Trump's online attacks on Mamdani framed a local candidate as an extremist enemy, contributing to a hostile information environment around elections. (2 Jul 2025)

7. Representative Derrick Van Orden posted and deleted a tweet celebrating millions losing Medicaid under the budget bill. Van Orden's quickly deleted tweet praising Medicaid losses revealed the bill's harsh intent while illustrating efforts to manage public backlash through message control. (2 Jul 2025)

8. Social Security Administration sent a misleading email overstating tax relief in Trump's bill. An SSA email wrongly claiming the bill eliminated taxes on Social Security benefits showed how official communications can be used to oversell policies and confuse beneficiaries. (4 Jul 2025)

9. Trump campaign and legal team dropped and refiled a lawsuit against Iowa pollster Ann Selzer in state court. Shifting a suit over unfavorable polling into state court suggested strategic forum shopping that can burden pollsters and chill independent election surveying. (30 Jun 2025)

10. Paramount and Donald Trump reached a $16 million settlement over a 60 Minutes interview with Kamala Harris. A large settlement with Trump over critical coverage raised concerns that costly litigation can pressure media outlets and influence future editorial decisions. (1 Jul 2025)

11. Alabama Law Enforcement Agency withheld body camera footage in a controversial police shooting case. Refusing to release footage in the Jabari Peoples shooting limited public access to key evidence, undermining transparency in a high-stakes use-of-force investigation. (2 Jul 2025)

12. Iran-linked hackers threatened to release stolen emails from Trump associates and White House staff. The threat to leak hacked emails underscored vulnerabilities in political communications and the potential for foreign actors to manipulate domestic narratives with stolen data. (30 Jun 2025)

13. US Global Change Research Program and Trump administration removed public access to federal climate reports and resources. Taking down a central climate research website effectively erased an accessible archive of government climate findings from public view. (1 Jul 2025)

14. EPA and Trump administration faced a lawsuit alleging Clean Water Act violations over PFAS-contaminated sludge spreading. The PFAS sludge lawsuit challenged EPA's regulatory stance and information practices around toxic contamination, pressing for more transparent and protective standards. (4 Jul 2025)

CHAPTER 25
WEEK 25 (5 JUL 2025 – 11 JUL 2025): IMMUNITY AS ARCHITECTURE OF POWER

A Supreme Court shield for presidents, a hollowed civil service, and militarized immigration enforcement converged to normalize emergency-style rule and partisan law.

This was a rupture-level week for American democracy, marked by an aggressive centralization of executive power, structural assaults on the civil service, and the weaponization of immigration and law enforcement. The Supreme Court's immunity decision and its approval of mass federal layoffs, combined with Trump's emergency-based tariff policies and unilateral foreign policy actions, significantly weakened the checks on presidential power. Parallel workforce purges at the State Department, NSC, NWS, FEMA, NASA, and other agencies drained professional expertise and reinforced politicized control. Immigration enforcement became a key arena of authoritarian tactics: militarized raids, deportations to third countries, TPS termination, dismantling of DHS watchdogs, and abusive detention practices collectively normalized rights violations for unpopular populations. Information and public health systems were also undermined through anti-science appointments, vaccine disinformation, and cuts to NOAA/NSF, even as disasters and diseases increased. A few judicial and legislative efforts—on birthright citizenship, Florida's immigration law, Planned Parenthood funding, and ICE raid restrictions—offered limited resistance but were overwhelmed by the overall authoritarian trend of the week.

Power and Authority

1. President Trump blocked over $6bn in congressionally approved funding for after-school and summer programs. By refusing to spend education funds appropriated by Congress, the president undercut legislative control of the purse and expanded unilateral discretion over core social programs. (6 Jul 2025)

2. President Trump fired NSA Director Gen Timothy Haugh and his deputy after receiving a loyalty list from an outside influencer. Removing senior intelligence leaders based on an activist's loyalty list blurred lines between formal authority and outside pressure, weakening professional control over national security. (6 Jul 2025)

3. President Trump fired six National Security Council staffers deemed disloyal by an outside influencer. Purging NSC staff on ideological grounds subordinated expert security advice to personal loyalty, eroding impartial decision-making in foreign and security policy. (6 Jul 2025)

4. President Trump pardoned supporters involved in the January 6 attack on the US Capitol. Granting clemency to participants in an attack on Congress weakened deterrence for political violence and signaled tolerance for assaults on the peaceful transfer of power. (6 Jul 2025)

5. President Trump ordered the Department of Justice to scrutinize and punish political opponents and critics. Directing prosecutors to target rivals and strip protections politicized law enforcement, undermining equal application of the law and chilling opposition activity. (6 Jul 2025)

6. President Trump imposed tariffs by declaring a national emergency, bypassing Congress. Using emergency powers to set trade policy sidestepped normal legislative processes, normalizing unilateral economic rule-making by the executive. (6 Jul 2025)

7. President Trump limited classified information shared with Congress. Restricting lawmakers' access to classified material weakened congressional oversight of national security and concentrated informational power in the executive branch. (6 Jul 2025)

8. President Trump took control of California's National Guard and deployed it against mostly peaceful immigration protests over state objections. Federalizing a state's guard to police protests against immigration raids over the governor's opposition expanded presidential control over domestic force and weakened state autonomy. (6 Jul 2025)

9. President Trump ordered a military strike on Iran without seeking congressional approval. Launching a strike without Congress's consent

bypassed the legislature's war powers, reinforcing a pattern of unilateral executive control over major military actions. (6 Jul 2025)

10. Health Secretary Robert F. Kennedy Jr. dismissed all members of a key CDC vaccine advisory panel and installed new members skeptical of vaccines. Replacing scientific advisors with vaccine skeptics politicized expert health guidance, weakening evidence-based decision-making on immunization policy. (7 Jul 2025)

11. Department of Homeland Security terminated Temporary Protected Status for tens of thousands of Honduran and Nicaraguan immigrants. Ending TPS for long-resident migrants revoked legal protections by executive decision, exposing a large group to deportation with limited legislative input. (7 Jul 2025; 8 Jul 2025)

12. Trump administration cut hundreds of staff positions at the National Weather Service, weakening flood and storm forecasting capacity. Large-scale NWS staffing cuts reduced the state's ability to warn the public about extreme weather, shifting risk onto communities while central authorities retained budgetary control. (7 Jul 2025; 8 Jul 2025)

13. FEMA leadership under DHS direction restricted communication between FEMA personnel and other officials during disaster response. Gagging FEMA staff during an emergency limited information flow to Congress and local authorities, impeding coordinated disaster response and external oversight. (7 Jul 2025)

14. Trump administration instructed DOJ not to enforce a TikTok ban for 75 days while reviewing the law. Temporarily declining to enforce a duly enacted law signaled selective executive obedience to statutes, blurring the line between enforcement discretion and disregard for legislation. (7 Jul 2025)

15. President Trump issued an executive order ending subsidies and tax credits for wind and solar energy. Unilaterally redirecting federal energy subsidies away from renewables shifted long-term economic and environmental policy without new legislation, concentrating agenda-setting in the presidency. (7 Jul 2025)

16. President Trump signed an executive order extending suspension of certain reciprocal tariffs until August 1, 2025. Adjusting tariff timelines by executive order underscored the president's growing unilateral control over trade measures that affect domestic prices and foreign relations. (7 Jul 2025)

17. Department of Veterans Affairs reversed plans for a massive reduction in force, scaling back projected layoffs. Pulling back from planned VA layoffs preserved some service capacity for veterans and showed internal resistance to broader efforts to shrink the civil service. (7 Jul 2025)

18. President Trump expanded the definition of presidential authority

over foreign affairs via executive order. Formally asserting near-exclusive presidential control of foreign policy narrowed Congress's role in external affairs and strengthened claims of inherent executive power. (8 Jul 2025)

19. President Trump suggested the federal government could take over governance of New York City and Washington, D.C. Floating federal takeovers of major cities if voters choose disfavored leaders threatened local self-government and hinted at using national power to override electoral outcomes. (8 Jul 2025; 9 Jul 2025)

20. President Trump publicly expressed hatred for Democratic lawmakers who opposed his budget bill. Presidential rhetoric vilifying opposition legislators contributed to a climate where political disagreement is cast as illegitimate, raising the stakes of partisan conflict. (6 Jul 2025)

21. President Trump revoked security clearances of several prominent political figures and a national security lawyer. Stripping clearances from critics and former officials appeared retaliatory, using access to classified information as a tool to punish dissent and limit their influence. (8 Jul 2025)

22. President Trump announced an investigation into conspiracy theories alleging government-caused Texas floods. Ordering an inquiry into baseless geoengineering claims lent official weight to conspiracy narratives, diverting state capacity from evidence-based risk management. (9 Jul 2025)

23. President Trump signed an executive order promoting AI use in education without educator input. Mandating AI integration in schools through executive action, in partnership with major tech firms, shifted education policy toward corporate-designed tools with limited democratic deliberation. (9 Jul 2025)

24. White House recruited 68 technology companies to support its AI education agenda via a public pledge. Enlisting large tech firms to shape classroom AI use deepened corporate influence over public education, raising questions about accountability for data and learning outcomes. (9 Jul 2025)

25. President Trump launched efforts to undermine birthright citizenship guaranteed by the Fourteenth Amendment. Challenging automatic citizenship for US-born children of undocumented parents attacked a core constitutional principle defining equal membership in the polity. (10 Jul 2025)

26. President Trump suggested states should decide whether to restrict access to birth control. Signaling openness to state-level limits on contraception invited uneven access to reproductive autonomy and potential erosion of nationally protected rights. (10 Jul 2025)

27. President Javier Milei of Argentina enacted sweeping deregulation and

privatization measures largely by executive order. Using executive decrees to weaken unions, ease firings, and privatize sectors concentrated economic rule-making in the presidency and reduced labor's institutional power. (10 Jul 2025)

28. Homeland Security Secretary Kristi Noem required personal approval for FEMA contracts over $100,000, delaying Texas flood response. Centralizing sign-off for disaster spending in a political appointee slowed life-saving deployments, illustrating how bureaucratic control can override operational expertise. (9 Jul 2025; 10 Jul 2025; 11 Jul 2025)

29. US State Department under President Trump announced plans to lay off about 15% of domestic staff as part of an America First restructuring. Planning large-scale diplomatic layoffs aligned foreign service staffing with ideological priorities, shrinking institutional capacity for independent diplomacy. (10 Jul 2025)

30. President Trump launched an assault on birthright citizenship in public and legal arenas. Sustained efforts to end birthright citizenship sought to redefine who counts as American, potentially creating a hereditary underclass lacking full political rights. (10 Jul 2025)

31. President Trump publicly defended Jair Bolsonaro during his trial for attempting to overturn Brazil's 2022 election. Backing a foreign leader accused of subverting an election signaled US sympathy for anti-democratic tactics abroad, weakening normative support for electoral accountability. (7 Jul 2025)

32. President Trump paused and then partially resumed weapons shipments to Ukraine amid stockpile claims. Halting and selectively resuming Ukraine aid introduced uncertainty into a key security commitment, giving the executive leverage over a partner's war effort without clear legislative guidance. (5 Jul 2025; 8 Jul 2025)

33. President Trump announced new tariffs and tariff timelines on multiple countries, including South Korea and Canada. Setting high tariffs on allies and key commodities by executive action used trade tools for political leverage, straining alliances and bypassing normal trade-negotiation channels. (7 Jul 2025; 8 Jul 2025; 9 Jul 2025; 11 Jul 2025)

34. President Trump announced an investigation into Brazil's social media regulations under US trade law. Using trade authorities to challenge another country's content-moderation policies intertwined economic power with disputes over speech rules abroad. (9 Jul 2025)

35. US State Department under President Trump began issuing termination notices to over 1,300 employees after Supreme Court cleared layoffs. Executing mass diplomatic layoffs following a favorable court ruling opera-

tionalized a political restructuring of the foreign service workforce. (11 Jul 2025)

Institutions and Governance

1. Florida Governor Ron DeSantis signed HB 1143 banning oil drilling near national estuarine research reserves in rural counties. The law strengthened environmental protections for sensitive waterways through state legislation, illustrating a legislature and governor using regulatory power to safeguard public resources. (5 Jul 2025)

2. Representative Marjorie Taylor Greene introduced a bill to criminalize intentional weather modification. Proposing felony penalties around speculative geoengineering reflected how conspiracy-driven ideas can enter the legislative agenda and distract from evidence-based climate policy. (5 Jul 2025)

3. Elon Musk filed to create a new political party called the America Party. Forming a new party by a wealthy tech figure could reshape electoral competition and party structures, testing how open the system is to new entrants. (5 Jul 2025)

4. Republicans in Congress and President Trump enacted a budget reconciliation law making 2017 tax cuts permanent and cutting Medicaid and SNAP. Using reconciliation to lock in regressive tax cuts and deep social spending reductions showed Congress operating as a vehicle for partisan fiscal restructuring with limited deliberation. (6 Jul 2025; 11 Jul 2025)

5. US Supreme Court limited the use of nationwide injunctions against federal policies. Curtailing nationwide injunctions reduced lower courts' ability to halt contested federal actions across the country, weakening a key check on executive overreach. (6 Jul 2025)

6. Gun Owners of America and allied groups filed a lawsuit arguing the new budget law renders the National Firearms Act unconstitutional. Challenging a longstanding gun-control statute on novel grounds sought to leverage recent legislative changes to weaken federal firearms regulation. (6 Jul 2025)

7. Department of Justice closed its investigation into Jeffrey Epstein without further disclosures, stating he died by suicide and no client list existed. Ending the probe while withholding many records fueled public suspicion about elite accountability and the transparency of high-profile investigations. (6 Jul 2025; 7 Jul 2025; 8 Jul 2025; 9 Jul 2025)

8. US Supreme Court ruled that a former president has broad immunity from criminal prosecution for official acts. Granting expansive immunity for

presidential conduct sharply limited legal accountability for abuses of office, elevating the presidency above ordinary criminal law constraints. (8 Jul 2025)

9. US Supreme Court stayed a preliminary injunction blocking Trump's federal workforce reduction executive order. Allowing a hiring freeze and mass layoffs to proceed during litigation empowered the executive to reshape the civil service before courts fully review the policy. (7 Jul 2025; 8 Jul 2025; 9 Jul 2025)

10. US Supreme Court lifted a lower-court order freezing mass layoffs at the State Department. Removing the block on State Department reductions in force cleared the way for large-scale diplomatic downsizing aligned with executive priorities. (11 Jul 2025)

11. US Supreme Court upheld a block on Florida's law criminalizing undocumented immigrants entering the state. By leaving in place an injunction against Florida's immigration crime law, the Court affirmed federal primacy over immigration enforcement and checked a state-level crackdown. (9 Jul 2025)

12. Federal courts temporarily blocked provisions defunding Planned Parenthood's Medicaid reimbursements. Judicial intervention preserved access to Medicaid-funded reproductive health services while constitutional challenges to the defunding measure proceed. (7 Jul 2025)

13. American Academy of Pediatrics and other medical organizations sued HHS and Secretary RFK Jr. over vaccine policy changes and advisory panel restructuring. Medical groups turned to the courts to contest politically driven vaccine decisions, testing whether administrative law can restrain anti-science governance. (7 Jul 2025; 9 Jul 2025)

14. American Association of University Professors and allied groups brought a federal lawsuit challenging deportations of foreign students for pro-Palestinian views. The case argued that using immigration powers to punish campus speech violated First Amendment principles, highlighting courts' role in protecting academic freedom. (7 Jul 2025)

15. Coalition of 18 states filed an amicus brief supporting a lawsuit against mass immigration raids in Los Angeles. State governments intervened in federal court to oppose aggressive raids, using institutional channels to contest enforcement tactics they view as unlawful. (7 Jul 2025)

16. US Department of Justice began handing over sensitive audio tapes in the Kiki Camarena murder case to defense counsel. Releasing long-held evidence in a historic DEA case reflected judicially supervised disclosure obligations, potentially reshaping understanding of past state actions. (6 Jul 2025)

17. US Department of Justice was accused by a whistleblower of

instructing lawyers to ignore court orders blocking deportations. Allegations that senior DOJ officials urged defiance of judicial orders raised serious concerns about internal respect for the rule of law within the executive's legal arm. (10 Jul 2025; 11 Jul 2025)

18. Mahmoud Khalil filed a $20m claim against DHS, ICE, and the State Department alleging false imprisonment and malicious prosecution. A Palestinian activist's damages claim over prolonged detention for political speech tested whether civil remedies can check alleged abuses of national security powers. (10 Jul 2025)

19. Federal judge Joseph LaPlante blocked Trump's executive order ending birthright citizenship and certified a nationwide class. The ruling halted enforcement of a major citizenship change and used class certification to preserve broad relief despite new limits on nationwide injunctions. (10 Jul 2025; 11 Jul 2025)

20. State of New Mexico sued the US Air Force over PFAS contamination from Cannon Air Force Base. A state's lawsuit against a federal military installation sought to compel environmental remediation, illustrating intergovernmental litigation as a tool for public health protection. (10 Jul 2025)

21. US Court of Appeals for the Eighth Circuit vacated the FTC's click-to-cancel consumer protection rule on procedural grounds. Striking down a rule that simplified subscription cancellations limited the FTC's ability to curb exploitative business practices, favoring regulated firms' procedural objections. (8 Jul 2025)

22. US Supreme Court issued decisions allowing deportations of migrants to third countries with which they had no ties. Authorizing third-country deportations expanded executive discretion in immigration removal, weakening traditional constraints tied to nationality and safe-return considerations. (11 Jul 2025)

23. Internal Revenue Service announced that churches can endorse political candidates without losing tax-exempt status. Reinterpreting the Johnson Amendment for churches opened a channel for tax-subsidized partisan activity by religious institutions, altering the regulatory boundary between faith and politics. (8 Jul 2025; 9 Jul 2025)

24. US Congress enacted the Alaska Native Village Municipal Lands Restoration Act of 2025. Restoring municipal lands to Alaska Native villages strengthened local self-governance and recognized Indigenous land rights through federal statute. (7 Jul 2025)

25. US Congress enacted the Alaska Native Settlement Trust Eligibility Act. Defining eligibility for Alaska Native settlement trusts aimed to bolster

economic self-determination for Native communities within a federal legal framework. (7 Jul 2025)

26. California Governor Gavin Newsom and legislature enacted CEQA streamlining bills AB 130 and AB 131 to speed housing approvals. State-level reforms to environmental review for housing projects sought to rebalance procedural safeguards with urgent needs for more housing supply. (7 Jul 2025)

27. Democratic Senators Alex Padilla and Cory Booker introduced a bill to bar ICE and other immigration agents from wearing masks and hiding identification. The proposal aimed to increase transparency and accountability in immigration enforcement by ensuring officers are identifiable during operations. (8 Jul 2025)

28. House Democrats led by Representative Jamie Raskin demanded DOJ release Epstein-related files mentioning Donald Trump and a withheld special counsel report volume. The oversight letter challenged perceived politicized secrecy at DOJ, pressing for transparency in matters involving potential presidential misconduct. (8 Jul 2025)

29. Federal Election Commission scheduled a closed Sunshine Act meeting on civil actions and proceedings. A closed FEC meeting on litigation matters highlighted the tension between confidentiality needs and public visibility into election-law enforcement decisions. (10 Jul 2025)

30. US Census Bureau sought public comment on extending the Special Census Program. Maintaining a mechanism for localities to request special censuses supports more accurate population data for representation and resource allocation. (11 Jul 2025)

31. Centers for Disease Control and Prevention requested approval to enhance emergency case-data collection and monitor an injury prevention program. Improving federal health data systems can strengthen evidence-based responses to crises and inform public health policy decisions. (10 Jul 2025)

32. Occupational Safety and Health Administration and FCC extended approvals and sought comments on multiple information-collection and safety programs. Routine renewals of regulatory data collections and safety standards maintained administrative oversight of workplace and communications sectors. (7 Jul 2025; 8 Jul 2025; 9 Jul 2025; 10 Jul 2025; 11 Jul 2025)

33. Environmental Protection Agency approved and updated multiple state air-quality implementation plans and related consent decrees. EPA's approvals of SIP revisions and consent decrees across several states reflected ongoing cooperative federalism in environmental governance. (7 Jul 2025; 8 Jul 2025; 10 Jul 2025)

34. Federal agencies (EPA, FDA, OSHA) issued technical corrections to

prior Federal Register notices and rules. Correcting docket numbers, rule text, and notice titles maintained the integrity of the regulatory record that courts and the public rely on. (9 Jul 2025)

35. Centers for Disease Control and Prevention and Food and Drug Administration solicited nominations for federal health advisory committees. Seeking outside experts for TB and tobacco advisory bodies is a routine mechanism for incorporating scientific input into federal health regulation. (11 Jul 2025)

36. Environmental Protection Agency announced availability of recent Environmental Impact Statements and EPA comments. Publishing EIS notices and EPA reviews supported public participation and interagency accountability in major federal projects. (11 Jul 2025)

37. Food and Drug Administration requested comments on identity certification requirements for FOIA and Privacy Act requests. Reviewing FOIA identity procedures balanced privacy protections with the public's ability to access government-held records. (11 Jul 2025)

38. Department of Homeland Security canceled a grant to improve communication between the National Weather Service and local officials during Texas floods. Revoking funding for weather-communication upgrades amid a deadly disaster undermined institutional learning and coordination for future emergencies. (11 Jul 2025)

39. Senator Ted Cruz ensured that a federal spending bill included deep cuts to weather forecasting and climate research funding. Legislative action to reduce NOAA and climate grants weakened scientific infrastructure needed for disaster preparedness and climate policy. (8 Jul 2025; 9 Jul 2025)

40. Representative Jared Moskowitz called for House investigations into delayed FEMA response to Texas floods. A congressional demand for oversight of FEMA delays sought to hold executive agencies accountable for disaster-management failures. (9 Jul 2025)

41. Miami City Commission voted to postpone 2025 municipal elections to 2026, extending current officials' terms. Unilaterally delaying local elections without voter approval extended incumbents' power and raised legal and democratic concerns about altering electoral calendars. (9 Jul 2025)

42. Texas Governor Greg Abbott announced plans to redraw congressional districts to favor Republicans in upcoming midterms. A redistricting push coordinated with national party goals highlighted how map-drawing can be used to entrench partisan advantage in the House. (10 Jul 2025)

43. President Trump and House Republicans used budget reconciliation to pass a sweeping fiscal bill despite public opposition. Relying on a fast-track process to enact unpopular structural changes to taxes and social programs

underscored Congress's role as a partisan instrument rather than a deliberative body. (11 Jul 2025)

44. President Trump nominated Emil Bove, a loyal DOJ prosecutor, to the US Court of Appeals for the Third Circuit. Elevating a politically aligned prosecutor with contested conduct to a lifetime appellate judgeship raised concerns about further politicization of the federal judiciary. (11 Jul 2025)

Civil Rights and Dissent

1. US district court and Trump administration allowed deportation of eight immigrants to South Sudan despite limited ties, following Supreme Court clarification. Proceeding with deportations to a dangerous third country underscored how legal changes can expose noncitizens to severe risks with limited judicial protection. (5 Jul 2025; 11 Jul 2025)

2. President Trump publicly praised ICE and used the term "remigration" amid allegations of racial profiling and excessive force. Endorsing hardline immigration enforcement with racially charged language normalized aggressive tactics against immigrant communities. (5 Jul 2025)

3. ICE agents detained a Canadian mother of three US-born children during her green card interview. Arresting a long-resident nonviolent immigrant at a legal-status appointment highlighted the precariousness of undocumented families seeking regularization. (6 Jul 2025)

4. ICE and CBP with National Guard support conducted a large, militarized raid in Los Angeles's MacArthur Park without reported arrests. A show-of-force operation in an immigrant neighborhood, broadcast on national TV, appeared designed to intimidate residents rather than target specific suspects. (7 Jul 2025; 8 Jul 2025; 9 Jul 2025)

5. ICE detained farmworker activist Alfredo Juarez Zeferino based on an old deportation order. Targeting a labor and immigrant-rights organizer for detention raised fears that enforcement tools are being used to suppress activism. (7 Jul 2025)

6. ICE and National Guard troops raided California cannabis farms, clashing with protesters and using chemical munitions. Deploying military-style force against farmworkers and demonstrators during immigration raids blurred lines between policing and warfare and endangered protest rights. (11 Jul 2025)

7. ICE agents in an unmarked SUV drove through protesters outside San Francisco Immigration Court and used force against the crowd. An ICE vehicle ramming protesters and agents using batons and pepper spray

against demonstrators illustrated dangerous escalation against people exercising assembly rights. (8 Jul 2025)

8. Trump administration and Florida officials deployed National Guard troops and Marines to operate and support immigration detention and enforcement. Using military personnel to run detention facilities and assist ICE blurred civilian-military boundaries and intensified the coercive environment facing migrants. (8 Jul 2025)

9. Trump administration dismantled DHS oversight offices responsible for monitoring immigration detention conditions. Eliminating civil-rights and ombudsman offices removed institutional channels for detainees to report abuse, weakening safeguards against mistreatment. (10 Jul 2025)

10. ICE operated overcrowded detention centers with poor conditions and limited oversight. Severe overcrowding, unsanitary conditions, and unrest in detention facilities reflected systemic rights violations against people held under immigration authority. (10 Jul 2025)

11. ICE arrested long-term resident Arpineh Masihi, a mother of four, in front of her family. Detaining a long-resident parent with US-born children dramatized the human cost of strict enforcement and its impact on family unity. (9 Jul 2025)

12. US Department of Justice sued California over policies allowing transgender athletes in girls' school sports. The federal lawsuit sought to restrict state inclusion policies, using civil-rights law to challenge protections for transgender students. (9 Jul 2025)

13. US Department of Justice issued subpoenas to clinics and doctors providing gender-affirming care to minors. Targeting providers of gender-affirming care with criminal-style subpoenas risked chilling lawful medical services for transgender youth. (9 Jul 2025)

14. ICE detained Imam Ayman Soliman after terminating his asylum status over alleged material support. Revoking asylum and detaining a religious leader based on disputed terrorism-support allegations highlighted the vulnerability of asylum seekers to broad security labels. (9 Jul 2025)

15. Gwinnett County solicitor and ICE dropped traffic charges against journalist Mario Guevara, who remained in ICE custody. Dropping weak charges while the journalist stayed detained by ICE raised concerns that immigration tools were used to suppress reporting on protests. (10 Jul 2025)

16. Senator Josh Hawley accused immigrant-rights group Unión del Barrio of aiding criminal conduct related to protest monitoring. Labeling a community group that tracks ICE activity as criminal support risked delegitimizing civic organizing around immigration enforcement. (11 Jul 2025)

17. Trump administration terminated TPS for Honduran and

Nicaraguan migrants, stripping legal status from long-term residents. Ending TPS for tens of thousands of people who built lives in the US destabilized families and communities with limited individualized review. (7 Jul 2025; 8 Jul 2025)

18. President Trump and Congress enacted work requirements for Medicaid recipients, partly to replace deported migrant farmworkers. Linking healthcare eligibility to work and framing beneficiaries as a labor pool for agriculture tied social rights to economic coercion. (9 Jul 2025)

19. US Supreme Court blocked enforcement of Florida's SB 4-C anti-immigration law. Preventing Florida from criminalizing undocumented entry into the state protected immigrants from an additional layer of punitive state-level sanctions. (9 Jul 2025)

20. US Supreme Court and federal courts blocked Trump's birthright citizenship order through class-action litigation. Judicial certification of a nationwide class and injunction preserved citizenship rights for children of undocumented parents while the policy is litigated. (10 Jul 2025; 11 Jul 2025)

21. US Supreme Court and lower courts issued decisions enabling deportations to third countries without migrants' ties. Allowing removals to unrelated third countries expanded the state's power over noncitizens' fates, often to places with serious safety concerns. (11 Jul 2025)

22. US Department of Justice and FBI launched criminal investigations into John Brennan and James Comey over past Russia probes. Investigating former intelligence leaders for their roles in election-interference inquiries risked deterring future officials from probing executive misconduct. (8 Jul 2025)

23. US Department of Justice subpoenaed providers of gender-affirming care under a memo equating it with female genital mutilation. Equating gender-affirming care with criminal mutilation framed a marginalized group's healthcare as inherently suspect, inviting prosecutions and stigma. (9 Jul 2025)

24. US Department of Justice sued California over transgender athlete participation in girls' sports. Using federal civil-rights enforcement to challenge inclusive sports policies pitted competing interpretations of equality against each other in court. (9 Jul 2025)

25. US Department of Justice and DHS were accused in a whistleblower complaint of defying court orders on deportations. Claims that officials ignored judicial stays in removal cases suggested that migrants' legal protections can be overridden by internal directives. (10 Jul 2025; 11 Jul 2025)

26. Popular Info reporting documented overcrowding and abuses in ICE detention centers nationwide. Reports of maggot-infested food, lack of water,

and escapes highlighted systemic human-rights concerns in the immigration detention system. (10 Jul 2025)

27. Florida officials and Trump administration opened the Alligator Alcatraz detention center with severe reported abuses. Operating a remote, harsh facility with inadequate shelter and sanitation exemplified punitive treatment of migrants far from public scrutiny. (10 Jul 2025)

Economic Structure

1. Trump administration prepared to reimpose steep tariffs after a 90-day pause, with limited new trade deals. Allowing high tariffs to snap back after a brief pause risked price shocks and uncertainty for businesses and consumers dependent on imported goods. (5 Jul 2025)

2. Treasury Secretary Scott Bessent defended lack of new trade deals and Medicaid cuts while downplaying tariff impacts. Framing social cuts as personal responsibility and minimizing tariff costs reflected a policy stance prioritizing fiscal austerity and trade confrontation over distributional concerns. (5 Jul 2025)

3. US government under President Trump enacted a reconciliation law permanently extending 2017 tax cuts and sharply cutting Medicaid and SNAP while boosting immigration enforcement funding. Locking in tax advantages for corporations and the wealthy while slashing safety-net programs and expanding enforcement budgets deepened structural inequality and redirected public funds toward coercive functions. (6 Jul 2025)

4. US government dramatically increased Pentagon spending, sending over half of discretionary funds to contractors. A Pentagon budget exceeding $1 trillion, heavily paid to private firms, entrenched a military-industrial structure where war-related spending dominates federal priorities. (8 Jul 2025)

5. Trump administration cut funding to NOAA and slashed the National Science Foundation budget by more than half. Severe reductions in climate and science funding weakened the knowledge base for managing environmental and technological risks, privileging short-term savings over long-term resilience. (8 Jul 2025)

6. Internal Revenue Service allowed churches to endorse political candidates while retaining tax-exempt status. Permitting tax-subsidized religious endorsements created an uneven playing field where some nonprofits can engage in partisan politics without losing fiscal privileges. (8 Jul 2025; 9 Jul 2025)

7. Trump administration considered issuing work visas to migrant farm-

workers to avoid harming the food supply. Balancing mass deportation rhetoric with pragmatic visa issuance for farm labor underscored the economy's dependence on migrant workers despite restrictive immigration policy. (8 Jul 2025)

8. President Trump and Commerce officials repeatedly delayed and re-dated implementation of broad new tariffs to August 1, 2025. Shifting tariff start dates and terms created uncertainty for global supply chains and signaled that major economic rules could change abruptly by executive decision. (7 Jul 2025; 11 Jul 2025)

9. Amazon inflated list prices and offered higher referral fees to media for Prime Day promotions. Manipulating reference prices and incentivizing favorable coverage blurred lines between journalism and advertising, undermining transparent market information for consumers. (8 Jul 2025)

10. American Federation of Teachers and major AI companies created a National Academy for AI Instruction funded by Microsoft, OpenAI, and Anthropic. Large corporate funding for teacher AI training embedded private platforms in public education, potentially aligning classroom tools with vendor interests. (9 Jul 2025)

11. OpenAI and Google offered students free access to ChatGPT and Gemini through educational partnerships. Providing free AI tools to students cultivated long-term user bases and normalized reliance on proprietary platforms in learning environments. (9 Jul 2025)

12. Centers for Disease Control and Prevention sought to expand emergency data collection and injury program monitoring under the Paperwork Reduction Act. Enhancing federal health data systems can improve targeting of resources and evaluation of public health interventions. (10 Jul 2025)

13. Environmental Protection Agency processed multiple state air-quality plans and new chemical submissions under the Clean Air Act and TSCA. Ongoing review of state plans and new chemicals maintained regulatory oversight of pollution and industrial substances affecting health and environment. (7 Jul 2025; 8 Jul 2025; 10 Jul 2025; 11 Jul 2025)

14. Federal Communications Commission revised regulatory fee structures and broadband support reporting requirements. Adjusting fee methodologies and reporting rules for space, satellite, and broadband providers influenced the cost and incentives for communications infrastructure deployment. (7 Jul 2025; 8 Jul 2025; 9 Jul 2025; 10 Jul 2025)

15. Occupational Safety and Health Administration extended approvals for multiple workplace safety information collections and testing-lab recognitions. Maintaining data requirements and lab recognitions under OSHA

programs supported enforcement of safety standards across industries. (9 Jul 2025; 11 Jul 2025)

16. Centers for Disease Control and Prevention implemented a change request to add data elements for emergency case reporting. Expanding standardized emergency data elements aimed to improve coordination among health departments during crises. (10 Jul 2025)

17. Florida officials and Trump administration opened a new immigration detention center in the Everglades with reported inhumane conditions. Investing in a remote, harsh detention facility expanded carceral infrastructure for migrants, channeling public funds into punitive confinement with limited oversight. (10 Jul 2025)

18. USAID and Trump administration implemented deep cuts to international aid programs projected to cause millions of deaths. Slashing global health and development funding shifted US engagement away from life-saving assistance, with severe consequences for vulnerable populations abroad. (7 Jul 2025)

19. President Javier Milei of Argentina implemented fiscal austerity, currency liberalization, and rent-control repeal leading to housing and poverty shifts. Aggressive austerity and deregulation in Argentina cut public spending, devalued the currency, and liberalized housing, redistributing risks and opportunities across society. (10 Jul 2025)

20. Trump administration recommended near-total cuts to democracy promotion programs while boosting military spending. Defunding democracy assistance in favor of defense outlays shifted US external spending away from supporting governance and toward hard power. (8 Jul 2025)

Information, Memory, and Manipulation

1. Texas officials and DHS criticized the National Weather Service and accused media of lying about deadly Texas floods. Blaming forecasters and alleging media deceit after catastrophic flooding shifted attention from policy-driven staffing cuts and undermined trust in independent information sources. (5 Jul 2025; 7 Jul 2025)

2. National Weather Service leadership cited budget cuts as the cause of severe staffing shortages during Texas floods. Linking vacant forecasting positions to funding decisions highlighted how resource choices shape the state's capacity to generate life-saving public information. (5 Jul 2025; 7 Jul 2025; 8 Jul 2025)

3. President Trump claimed an unpopular budget law was the "most popular bill ever signed". Insisting on overwhelming public support despite

contrary polling exemplified official misrepresentation of political reality to shape perceptions of legitimacy. (6 Jul 2025)

4. Robert F. Kennedy Jr. as HHS Secretary spread misinformation about measles vaccines and promoted unproven treatments and autism theories. Using a top health post to question vaccine safety and tout ineffective remedies undermined scientific consensus and contributed to a resurgence of preventable disease. (7 Jul 2025)

5. US health agencies and commentators reported a record surge in measles cases linked to vaccination policy changes and funding cuts. The spike in measles cases illustrated the real-world consequences of anti-vaccine messaging and weakened public health infrastructure. (7 Jul 2025)

6. Department of Justice and FBI issued an unsigned memo dismissing the existence of an Epstein client list and limiting evidence disclosure. An opaque memo closing off expectations of broader Epstein disclosures fueled conspiracy narratives and raised questions about selective transparency in elite cases. (7 Jul 2025; 8 Jul 2025; 9 Jul 2025)

7. Amazon used elevated referral fees to encourage media outlets to promote Prime Day as a major discount event. Financial incentives for coverage risked turning news outlets into marketing channels, distorting consumer understanding of actual deals. (8 Jul 2025)

8. Federal Communications Commission sought comments on an internal anti-harassment intake form information collection. Inviting feedback on harassment-reporting processes within the FCC reflected internal transparency about workplace governance, though not directly about public information. (9 Jul 2025)

9. Office of Government Information Services announced a public annual meeting on FOIA reviews and reports. A public OGIS meeting provided a forum to discuss federal information access practices, modestly reinforcing transparency norms. (7 Jul 2025)

10. Environmental Protection Agency published notice of Environmental Impact Statements and EPA comments for public review. Making EIS documents and EPA critiques available supported informed public debate over major environmental decisions. (11 Jul 2025)

11. Food and Drug Administration requested public comment on FOIA identity certification procedures. Reviewing how requesters verify identity for FOIA and Privacy Act access affected practical barriers to obtaining personal records from the agency. (11 Jul 2025)

12. Department of Homeland Security canceled a grant to improve NWS communication with local officials during ongoing flood response. Pulling support for better warning systems in the midst of a disaster hindered

efforts to improve future risk communication and public awareness. (11 Jul 2025)

13. President Trump and allies promoted narratives minimizing economic and social harms of tariffs and social cuts. Official messaging that downplayed inflation and hardship from tariffs and benefit cuts contributed to a skewed public understanding of policy tradeoffs. (5 Jul 2025; 6 Jul 2025; 8 Jul 2025)

14. Trump administration and Netanyahu government framed Trump's Middle East actions as peace-making, including a Nobel Peace Prize nomination. Presenting controversial military and diplomatic moves as grounds for a peace prize contributed to a narrative that recasts coercive policies as peace-making. (8 Jul 2025)

15. Popular Info and other outlets reported on AI companies' deep involvement in shaping US classroom tools and curricula. Coverage of AI-education partnerships highlighted how corporate-designed systems may influence what and how students learn, with limited civic oversight. (9 Jul 2025)

CHAPTER 26
WEEK 26 (12 JUL 2025 – 18 JUL 2025): DATA AND FORCE AS GOVERNANCE

In a week without a single shock, immigration raids, civil service purges, and curated secrecy deepened a regime of control over bodies, data, and memory.

This was a heavily structured week for democratic erosion, with mounting pressures on the rule of law, independence of civil service, immigration enforcement, and information integrity. The administration intensified its efforts to politicize the state: Schedule G and mass layoffs at Education and State, purges and retaliatory firings at DOJ, and ideological restructuring at NIH and VA all push the bureaucracy to prioritize loyalty over competence. Immigration policy hardened into a near-police-state system—ending bond hearings, expediting deportations, courthouse arrests, data sharing from Medicaid and IRS, and highly visible, lethal raids—thus solidifying a two-tier citizenship system. Meanwhile, Congress and the executive worked together to defund public broadcasting and foreign initiatives. The Epstein files saga highlighted issues of information manipulation and elite impunity: DOJ secrecy, retaliatory personnel moves, and partisan blocking of transparency clashed with cross-party demands and court-ordered unsealing. Some limited countermeasures—courts protecting certain immigrants and refugees, bipartisan efforts for Epstein transparency, and strong protest mobilization—offered modest but notable resistance to democratic decline.

Power and Authority

1. Homeland Security Secretary Kristi Noem required prior approval for large FEMA expenditures and contracts. Noem centralized control over FEMA spending above $100,000, potentially slowing emergency response and concentrating disaster-management power in a single political appointee. (12 Jul 2025)

2. Trump administration cut FEMA grant programs and allowed staff exodus. Cuts to FEMA grants and loss of experienced staff weakened federal disaster capacity, shifting risk to vulnerable communities while preserving centralized political control. (12 Jul 2025)

3. President Donald Trump authorized ICE agents to use "whatever means" necessary for self-protection and ordered arrests of protesters. Trump's directive expanded ICE's discretion to use force and target protesters, blurring lines between immigration enforcement and suppression of dissent. (12 Jul 2025)

4. President Donald Trump claimed he was considering revoking Rosie O'Donnell's citizenship. Trump's threat to strip a critic's citizenship, though legally baseless, signaled willingness to wield state power rhetorically against dissenters and constitutional guarantees. (12 Jul 2025; 13 Jul 2025)

5. Trump administration canceled a Biden-era civil rights settlement addressing Alabama sewage crisis. By voiding a settlement that required Alabama to fix a raw sewage crisis in a poor, Black county, the administration withdrew federal protection from marginalized residents facing environmental health harms. (13 Jul 2025)

6. Homeland Security Secretary Kristi Noem declined to renew FEMA call center contracts after Texas floods. Nonrenewal of FEMA call-center contracts sharply reduced answered disaster calls, weakening federal responsiveness while leaving the decision in a single cabinet official's hands. (13 Jul 2025)

7. Trump administration conducted mass layoffs at the State Department and closed the Bureau of Democracy, Human Rights, and Labor. Eliminating over 1,300 State Department jobs and shuttering a key human-rights bureau reduced professional diplomatic capacity and centralized foreign-policy influence in political hands. (13 Jul 2025)

8. Attorney General Pam Bondi announced DOJ guidance limiting nonessential multilingual services. Restricting multilingual DOJ services after declaring English the official language reduced access to justice for non-English speakers and signaled state preference for a dominant linguistic group. (14 Jul 2025)

9. President Donald Trump expanded ICE officers and detention facilities to intensify deportations. Trump's expansion of ICE staffing and detention infrastructure entrenched a large-scale deportation apparatus, deepening reliance on coercive tools in immigration policy. (15 Jul 2025)

10. Trump administration ordered destruction of emergency food supplies for children in Afghanistan and Pakistan. Incinerating nearly 500 metric tons of paid-for emergency food for children abroad prioritized security narratives over humanitarian obligations and squandered public resources. (14 Jul 2025; 15 Jul 2025)

11. Trump administration pursued harsh immigration enforcement including Title 42 expulsions and mass deportations. Use of emergency health powers and aggressive deportations framed immigration as a security crisis, normalizing extraordinary authority over migrants and asylum seekers. (15 Jul 2025)

12. President Donald Trump asked House Republicans whether he should fire Federal Reserve Chair Jerome Powell. Trump's public musing about firing the Fed chair threatened the central bank's independence, signaling potential political interference in monetary policy. (16 Jul 2025)

13. President Donald Trump issued an executive order creating Schedule G in the excepted service. Schedule G reclassified many policy roles as easily removable, enabling presidents to replace career officials with loyalists and weakening civil service neutrality. (17 Jul 2025; 18 Jul 2025)

14. Department of Veterans Affairs leadership banned LGBTQ+ pride flags at VA hospitals and closed an office probing racial disparities. The VA's rollback of DEI symbols and investigations signaled official disfavor toward LGBTQ+ and Black veterans' concerns, narrowing institutional support for equal treatment. (18 Jul 2025)

15. Department of Veterans Affairs leadership ended gender-affirming care for transgender veterans. Terminating gender-affirming care under executive direction stripped a vulnerable group of medically recognized treatment, using state power to enforce ideological boundaries on healthcare. (18 Jul 2025)

16. Department of Veterans Affairs leadership removed explicit anti-discrimination protections from hospital bylaws. Deleting language barring discrimination based on marital status or political views weakened formal safeguards for equal access to VA care and opened space for viewpoint-based bias. (18 Jul 2025)

17. Camp Mystic director Dick Eastland delayed evacuation after severe flood warning at Texas camp. Eastland's hour-long delay in ordering evacuation despite flood warnings contributed to 27 deaths, raising questions

about private authority and accountability in life-or-death decisions. (18 Jul 2025)

Institutions and Governance

1. Representatives Marc Veasey and Ro Khanna announced plans for measures demanding release of Epstein files. House Democrats prepared a resolution and amendment to force disclosure of Epstein-related records, using legislative tools to press for transparency in a politically sensitive investigation. (12 Jul 2025)

2. Los Angeles federal judge temporarily blocked ICE raids over racial profiling concerns. The court halted certain ICE operations, requiring adherence to reasonable-suspicion standards and limiting appearance-based targeting, reinforcing judicial checks on discriminatory enforcement. (12 Jul 2025)

3. President Donald Trump criticized DOJ's closure of Epstein file and urged focus on voter fraud and corruption. Trump's comments sought to redirect investigative priorities away from Epstein toward favored narratives, pressuring DOJ's agenda-setting in politically charged areas. (12 Jul 2025)

4. Department of Justice and FBI leadership decided not to release additional Epstein case information. By withholding further Epstein materials while denying existence of a client list, DOJ and FBI limited public scrutiny of a major scandal, fueling distrust and conspiracy narratives. (12 Jul 2025; 14 Jul 2025; 15 Jul 2025; 17 Jul 2025)

5. Attorney General Pam Bondi directed dismissal of charges against Dr. Michael Kirk Moore over vaccine fraud. Dropping charges mid-trial against a doctor accused of destroying vaccines and issuing fake cards signaled politicized leniency in pandemic-related enforcement. (12 Jul 2025; 13 Jul 2025)

6. Senate Homeland Security and Governmental Affairs Committee issued report detailing Secret Service failures in 2024 Trump assassination attempt. The bipartisan report documented serious protective lapses and led to agent suspensions, illustrating congressional oversight of executive security services. (13 Jul 2025)

7. Texas legislature failed to pass a bill creating a flood warning system. Legislative inaction on a flood warning system left communities more exposed to disasters, underscoring how policy neglect can undermine public safety infrastructure. (13 Jul 2025)

8. Senators Richard Blumenthal and Chris Murphy criticized DHS Secretary Kristi Noem's migrant transport and ad spending. Senators warned that Noem's high-profile spending could violate budget law,

asserting congressional authority over appropriations and agency priorities. (13 Jul 2025)

9. U.S. Agency for Global Media overseen by Kari Lake dismantled most of its operations and related foreign influence programs. Shrinking USAGM reduced U.S. capacity to project independent news and democratic narratives abroad, weakening a key soft-power institution. (13 Jul 2025)

10. Supreme Court of the United States granted a stay allowing Department of Education to proceed with large workforce reduction. The Court's emergency stay let the administration fire nearly half of Education's staff despite lower-court concerns, expanding executive leeway over statutory protections. (14 Jul 2025; 15 Jul 2025)

11. Department of Justice opposed Ghislaine Maxwell's appeal and defended her conviction. DOJ's stance to uphold Maxwell's sentence affirmed accountability for a central Epstein accomplice even as broader transparency remained contested. (14 Jul 2025)

12. Trump administration fired 17 immigration judges despite congressional funding for more positions. Terminating immigration judges contrary to appropriations intent undercut adjudicatory capacity and suggested political interference in case processing. (14 Jul 2025)

13. Trump administration appealed ruling that barred DHS from racial profiling in arrests. By seeking to overturn limits on race-based arrests, the administration challenged judicial efforts to constrain discriminatory enforcement practices. (14 Jul 2025)

14. U.S. Election Assistance Commission announced a public meeting on updated voting system guidelines. The EAC scheduled an open technical meeting on voting system standards, supporting transparent, expert-informed election administration. (14 Jul 2025)

15. House Rules Committee Republicans rejected Representative Ro Khanna's amendment to release Epstein files. Blocking Khanna's transparency amendment kept key Epstein records sealed, reinforcing partisan control over access to politically sensitive information. (14 Jul 2025; 15 Jul 2025)

16. Federal Election Commission canceled two scheduled open meetings. The FEC's cancellation of July public meetings reduced opportunities for public oversight of campaign finance and election-regulation decisions. (15 Jul 2025)

17. House Speaker Mike Johnson called for DOJ to release Epstein files while having voted to block related amendment. Johnson's public demand for Epstein transparency contrasted with his procedural vote against release, illustrating performative oversight amid substantive obstruction. (15 Jul 2025; 17 Jul 2025)

18. House Speaker Mike Johnson insisted Ukraine aid be tied to a border security package. Linking foreign aid to contentious immigration measures used legislative leverage to advance domestic enforcement priorities, complicating bipartisan security policymaking. (15 Jul 2025)

19. U.S. Senate considered and then passed a $9.4 billion rescissions package cutting public broadcasting and foreign aid. Senate approval of Trump's rescissions package retroactively endorsed unilateral spending cuts, slashing funds for public media and foreign assistance and shifting budget power toward the executive. (15 Jul 2025; 16 Jul 2025; 17 Jul 2025)

20. House Judiciary Committee Democrats demanded hearings with Pam Bondi and Kash Patel on Epstein case handling. Democrats sought public testimony from top law-enforcement officials about Epstein decisions, using oversight powers to probe potential cover-ups and politicization. (15 Jul 2025)

21. House Oversight Chair James Comer used digital signatures while investigating Biden's autopen use. Comer's reliance on digital signatures in an inquiry criticizing Biden's autopen highlighted partisan inconsistency in standards for executive documentation. (15 Jul 2025)

22. House Committee on Education and the Workforce held hearings on antisemitism at major universities. Repeated hearings grilling university leaders over campus antisemitism and DEI practices increased congressional pressure on academic governance and speech policies. (15 Jul 2025; 16 Jul 2025)

23. Louisiana state legislature and courts upheld a lookback law enabling clergy abuse lawsuits. Maintaining Louisiana's lookback window preserved survivors' ability to sue over historic clergy abuse, reinforcing access to justice despite institutional resistance. (16 Jul 2025)

24. Roman Catholic Archdiocese of New Orleans and U.S. Bankruptcy Court filed a settlement plan including a public archive of abuse files. The archdiocese's bankruptcy plan proposed hundreds of millions in payouts and a limited public archive of abuse records, balancing institutional survival with partial transparency. (16 Jul 2025)

25. U.S. Supreme Court denied an emergency application in Gomez v. United States. By declining emergency relief without noted dissent, the Court left a lower-court ruling in place, illustrating its gatekeeping role over urgent challenges. (15 Jul 2025)

26. Over 75 former judges urged the Senate Judiciary Committee to reject Emil Bove's appeals court nomination. Retired judges warned that Bove's alleged disregard for court orders made him unfit for the bench, spotlighting concerns about politicized judicial appointments. (15 Jul 2025)

27. Senate Judiciary Committee Republicans advanced Emil Bove's nomination despite Democratic walkout and whistleblower concerns. Pushing

Bove's nomination forward without hearing a whistleblower underscored majority willingness to prioritize partisan loyalty over thorough vetting. (17 Jul 2025)

28. Florida Supreme Court upheld a congressional map that reduced Black voters' influence. The court's approval of a DeSantis-backed map that dismantled a Black-influence district weakened minority representation and signaled judicial tolerance of partisan gerrymandering. (17 Jul 2025)

29. U.S. District Court for the District of Columbia received a class-action lawsuit challenging courthouse immigration arrests. Immigrants and advocates sued DHS and DOJ over arrests at immigration courts, arguing due process violations and seeking to curb enforcement tactics that chill access to hearings. (16 Jul 2025; 17 Jul 2025)

30. Coalition of 20 states sued the Trump administration over cuts to a FEMA resilience grant program. States challenged FEMA grant reductions for infrastructure resilience, asserting that federal retrenchment undermined lawful disaster-preparedness commitments. (16 Jul 2025)

31. Department of Justice requested a one-day sentence for former officer Brett Hankison in Breonna Taylor civil rights case. DOJ's call for minimal jail time for a convicted officer in a high-profile killing raised doubts about federal willingness to impose serious consequences for civil rights violations. (16 Jul 2025; 17 Jul 2025)

32. Congress enacted the Apex Area Technical Corrections Act. Passage of a technical corrections law illustrated routine legislative maintenance of statutory language and local governance arrangements. (15 Jul 2025)

33. Congress enacted the HALT Fentanyl Act. The new law expanded tools against fentanyl trafficking, strengthening federal criminal authority in response to a public health crisis. (16 Jul 2025)

34. Congress enacted the GENIUS Act to promote innovation and technology. The GENIUS Act established new federal support structures for technological development, shaping long-term economic and strategic capacity. (18 Jul 2025)

35. National Archives and Records Administration sought public comment on proposed federal records schedules. NARA's request for input on records disposition plans invited public oversight of which federal documents are preserved or destroyed. (17 Jul 2025)

36. Federal judge ordered the Trump administration to provide documents on cost-cutting efforts to a watchdog group. The court compelled disclosure about the Department of Government Efficiency's cuts, reinforcing judicial enforcement of transparency obligations. (14 Jul 2025)

37. Texas Governor Greg Abbott's office refused to release emails with

Elon Musk citing privacy concerns. Abbott's refusal to disclose correspondence with a powerful businessman limited public insight into potential private influence on state policy. (14 Jul 2025)

38. National Archives and Records Administration invited comments on records schedules for DOT and VA. By opening proposed records schedules to comment, NARA allowed stakeholders to weigh in on long-term retention of transportation and veterans' records. (17 Jul 2025)

Civil Rights and Dissent

1. Immigration and Customs Enforcement conducted raids at licensed cannabis farms using less-lethal munitions and tear gas. ICE raids at California farms injured workers and swept up hundreds, including a disabled veteran, illustrating militarized tactics against largely nonviolent laborers. (13 Jul 2025; 14 Jul 2025; 17 Jul 2025)

2. ICE Director Todd Lyons authorized rapid deportations to third countries with minimal notice. Lyons' memo allowed deportations with as little as six hours' notice and limited safety assurances, heightening risks of refoulement and undermining due process. (13 Jul 2025)

3. ICE and DHS detained hundreds at "Alligator Alcatraz," including many with no criminal record. Reports that over 250 detainees at a harsh Florida facility had no criminal record contradicted official claims and highlighted punitive detention of non-criminal migrants. (12 Jul 2025; 13 Jul 2025)

4. Democratic state lawmakers in Florida filed suit after being denied access to the Alligator Alcatraz detention facility. Lawmakers sued to enforce their statutory right to inspect detention centers, challenging secrecy around conditions for detained migrants. (14 Jul 2025)

5. Trump administration implemented policy ending bond hearings for many undocumented immigrants. A new policy barring bond hearings for immigrants who entered unlawfully shifted release decisions from judges to DHS, curtailing judicial oversight of detention. (14 Jul 2025; 15 Jul 2025)

6. Immigration and Customs Enforcement used Terminal Island as a staging ground for mass workplace raids in Los Angeles. ICE's use of a historically significant island to launch raids that detained nearly 2,800 people evoked past mass incarcerations and intensified fear in immigrant communities. (16 Jul 2025)

7. U.S. Immigration and Customs Enforcement arrested Mahdi Khanbabazadeh outside his child's preschool in Oregon. ICE's first confirmed arrest at an Oregon school under new rules allowing operations at sensitive

locations highlighted the psychological impact of enforcement on families. (15 Jul 2025; 17 Jul 2025)

8. U.S. Immigration and Customs Enforcement detained an Irish tourist for a minor visa overstay and held him for about 100 days. ICE's prolonged detention of a tourist who overstayed by three days, despite his consent to deportation, showed punitive use of detention beyond clear security needs. (15 Jul 2025)

9. Texas Attorney General Ken Paxton threatened to arrest Democratic legislators boycotting a redistricting session. Paxton's threat to jail absent lawmakers used criminal law to coerce participation in a partisan redistricting process, pressuring political opposition. (14 Jul 2025)

10. Department of Homeland Security agents testified about unusual orders to arrest pro-Palestinian students and academics. Agents' testimony that they were directed to target specific political viewpoints raised alarms about law enforcement being used against campus dissent. (15 Jul 2025)

11. Internal Revenue Service and ICE developed a system to share confidential tax data for deportation targeting. Plans to give ICE access to IRS tax data, including home addresses, blurred lines between tax administration and immigration enforcement, threatening privacy and trust. (15 Jul 2025)

12. Trump administration agreed to share Medicaid data on tens of millions of recipients with ICE. Using Medicaid records to locate migrants repurposed health data for enforcement, risking deterrence from care and expanding surveillance of vulnerable populations. (17 Jul 2025)

13. Trump administration reversed policy to make undocumented immigrants ineligible for bond hearings. A policy shift concentrating release authority in DHS officials reduced judicial checks on detention and increased executive control over immigrants' liberty. (14 Jul 2025)

14. Trump administration used masked, out-of-uniform ICE agents in mass deportation raids. Deploying masked agents without clear identification in communities intensified perceptions of secret-police tactics and eroded trust in lawful enforcement. (18 Jul 2025)

15. Texas Board of Elections voted to require additional data or purge nearly 100,000 voters. New ID requirements risked removing tens of thousands from voter rolls, disproportionately affecting marginalized groups under the banner of list maintenance. (14 Jul 2025)

16. Texas Republicans and President Donald Trump pursued mid-decade redistricting to gain five GOP seats. Coordinated efforts to redraw Texas districts mid-cycle aimed to entrench partisan advantage and dilute the influence of growing nonwhite populations. (14 Jul 2025; 15 Jul 2025; 17 Jul 2025)

17. California Governor Gavin Newsom threatened to pursue partisan

redrawing of California's congressional map. Newsom's floated plan to bypass an independent commission to counter Texas gerrymandering underscored escalating partisan map wars and pressure on neutral processes. (17 Jul 2025)

18. Federal appeals court temporarily blocked termination of Temporary Protected Status for Afghans. The court's injunction preserved legal status for about 12,000 Afghans, providing temporary protection against abrupt loss of residency. (14 Jul 2025)

19. Federal judge blocked a presidential proclamation banning vetted refugees. Judicial intervention stopped use of a proclamation to bar 80 vetted refugees, checking executive overreach in refugee admissions. (14 Jul 2025)

20. Federal court in Ohio granted a temporary restraining order preventing transfer of detainee Ayman Soliman. The TRO kept Soliman in-state pending a bond hearing, safeguarding his ability to contest asylum termination and deportation. (16 Jul 2025)

21. Department of Homeland Security and Department of Justice were sued in a class action over courthouse immigration arrests. The lawsuit argued that arresting immigrants at court hearings violated constitutional protections and chilled access to justice. (16 Jul 2025; 17 Jul 2025)

22. Baltimore city government and partners expanded community-based violence reduction and youth engagement programs. Baltimore's Safe Streets, GVRS, youth engagement, and school-based interventions reduced shootings and assaults, showing non-carceral strategies can enhance safety and civic trust. (16 Jul 2025)

23. Nationwide protesters honoring John Lewis held over 1,500 demonstrations for voting rights and justice. Mass protests under the banner "Good Trouble Lives On" mobilized citizens to defend voting rights and civil liberties amid contemporary controversies. (18 Jul 2025)

24. Indivisible organized online training sessions to prepare for community organizing and protests. Indivisible's "One Million Rising" trainings built grassroots capacity for sustained civic engagement and resistance to perceived democratic backsliding. (14 Jul 2025)

25. Representative Pramila Jayapal announced legislation to bar ICE from detaining and deporting U.S. citizens. Jayapal's proposal responded to wrongful detentions by seeking statutory safeguards against citizens being swept into immigration enforcement. (16 Jul 2025)

26. Trump administration deported five immigrants to Eswatini, a country with which they had no ties. Sending migrants to a third country unconnected to them underscored the arbitrariness and potential cruelty of certain deportation practices. (15 Jul 2025)

27. El Salvador President Nayib Bukele transferred 250 Venezuelan

migrants in a prisoner swap returning 10 U.S. citizens. The swap highlighted how migrants can be treated as bargaining chips in international negotiations, raising concerns about their rights and agency. (17 Jul 2025)

28. House Republicans approved a rescissions package defunding PBS, NPR, and foreign aid. House passage of deep cuts to public broadcasting and aid reduced support for independent information and global humanitarian programs. (18 Jul 2025)

29. Supreme Court of the United States struck down affirmative action in college admissions. The Court's ruling against race-conscious admissions reshaped access to elite education, prompting alternative selection methods and raising equity concerns. (18 Jul 2025)

30. Texas officials received death threats during flood response operations. Threats against local officials managing disaster response undermined their ability to act and contributed to a hostile environment for public service. (15 Jul 2025)

31. Los Angeles Times and animal rescues reported and responded to pet abandonment linked to ICE raids. Increased pet abandonment after immigration raids illustrated the broader social disruption and family fragmentation caused by aggressive enforcement. (12 Jul 2025)

32. Federal court and Biden administration extended Temporary Protected Status for Venezuelans. Extending TPS for nearly half a million Venezuelans provided legal stability and work authorization, contrasting sharply with contemporaneous restrictive policies. (15 Jul 2025)

Economic Structure

1. President Donald Trump announced 30% tariffs on goods from the EU and Mexico. Sharp tariff hikes on allied economies risked trade retaliation, higher consumer prices, and strain on cooperative economic alliances. (12 Jul 2025)

2. Trump administration imposed a 17% tariff on Mexican tomatoes. Tariffs on Mexican tomatoes, half of U.S. supply, threatened to raise food prices and entrench domestic producers, illustrating how trade tools can burden consumers. (14 Jul 2025)

3. Trump administration and Congress enacted a reconciliation bill cutting renewable energy support and LIHEAP. The energy bill removed incentives for renewables and low-income energy aid, increasing projected power costs and deepening energy insecurity for poorer households. (14 Jul 2025)

4. Centers for Disease Control and Prevention invited public comment on multiple public health data collection initiatives. CDC notices on infection

surveillance, research tools, tobacco campaigns, emergency use, devices, and electronic products sought input on data burdens while sustaining evidence-based regulation. (14 Jul 2025; 18 Jul 2025)

5. Federal Communications Commission finalized cable television rate deregulation and sought comment on paperwork reductions. By easing cable rate rules and paperwork, the FCC reduced regulatory burdens on operators, potentially affecting consumer prices and competition. (14 Jul 2025)

6. Food and Drug Administration set regulatory review periods enabling patent extensions for several biologics. FDA determinations for multiple high-value drugs shaped how long manufacturers can maintain market exclusivity, influencing drug prices and innovation incentives. (14 Jul 2025)

7. Food and Drug Administration approved gardenia blue as a food color additive and revoked obsolete food standards. FDA's approval of a new natural dye and removal of outdated standards updated food regulations, balancing industry flexibility with labeling and safety. (15 Jul 2025; 17 Jul 2025)

8. General Services Administration issued decisions on port-of-entry modernization and rescinded outdated management bulletins. GSA's port expansion and regulatory clean-up affected cross-border trade efficiency and federal asset management practices. (15 Jul 2025; 16 Jul 2025)

9. General Services Administration sought OMB review of acquisition-related information collections. GSA's requests on contract modifications, packing lists, and construction payrolls aimed to streamline procurement compliance while maintaining oversight of federal spending. (15 Jul 2025; 18 Jul 2025)

10. Environmental Protection Agency approved multiple state and territorial air-quality plans and pesticide tolerances. EPA approvals for emissions inventories, maintenance plans, and pesticide tolerances set environmental baselines that affect public health and industry operations. (16 Jul 2025; 17 Jul 2025; 18 Jul 2025)

11. Food and Drug Administration issued draft guidances on hepatitis B blood testing and cancer drug combinations. FDA's draft guidances updated expectations for blood safety and combination cancer therapies, shaping clinical practice and drug development pathways. (16 Jul 2025; 17 Jul 2025)

12. Drug Enforcement Administration received applications for bulk manufacture and import of controlled substances. DEA notices on new manufacturing and import registrations for controlled substances balanced research and pharmaceutical supply needs with diversion risks. (17 Jul 2025)

13. Federal Communications Commission updated FM allotments tables for radio broadcasting. FCC adjustments to FM channel allotments reflected

licensing changes and shaped future opportunities for local radio service. (17 Jul 2025)

14. Food and Drug Administration sought comment on revoking standards and evaluating youth tobacco campaigns. FDA's deregulatory move on obsolete food standards and evaluation of anti-tobacco messaging illustrated ongoing recalibration of consumer protection tools. (14 Jul 2025; 17 Jul 2025)

15. Former Congressman Alex Mooney and Capitol South blurred lines between consulting and lobbying for Christian Employers Alliance. Mooney's role as a "consultant" soon after leaving Congress highlighted how ex-lawmakers can influence policy while skirting formal lobbying bans. (15 Jul 2025)

16. Senate Republicans and the White House agreed to restore $400 million in proposed PEPFAR cuts. Reversing part of the rescissions package preserved key global HIV/AIDS funding, tempering broader retrenchment in foreign aid. (15 Jul 2025)

17. Trump administration lifted export controls on chip design software and certain AI chips to China. Relaxing tech export limits allowed major U.S. firms to resume AI-related sales to China, potentially boosting profits while weakening strategic leverage. (16 Jul 2025)

18. Department of Commerce halted development of a NOAA extreme rainfall prediction tool. Stopping work on a rainfall forecasting tool reduced federal capacity to anticipate extreme weather, undermining climate resilience planning. (16 Jul 2025)

19. Department of Transportation cut $4 billion in federal funding for California's high-speed rail project. Pulling major support from California's rail project weakened long-term infrastructure investment and signaled partisan use of federal funding levers. (16 Jul 2025)

20. Trump administration and CBS News arranged settlements directing up to $63 million to Trump's presidential library. Large settlement flows from media lawsuits to Trump's library raised concerns about private legal windfalls funding institutions tied to a political figure. (16 Jul 2025)

21. Trump Organization and SDC Imobiliare announced Trump Tower Bucharest and resumed foreign real estate deals. New foreign projects and lifted self-imposed deal bans deepened Trump's overseas business entanglements, creating potential conflicts with U.S. diplomatic and security interests. (17 Jul 2025)

22. Department of Housing and Urban Development planned to terminate seven major housing discrimination investigations. Ending large fair-housing probes curtailed federal enforcement against segregation and

discrimination, weakening protections for marginalized renters and buyers. (17 Jul 2025)

23. Internal Revenue Service moved to terminate its free Direct File tax tool after industry lobbying. Efforts to end the IRS's free filing service following meetings with tax software firms favored private vendors over low-cost public options for taxpayers. (17 Jul 2025)

24. Trump administration terminated seven HUD housing discrimination probes and cut climate tools while expanding border surveillance contracts. Combined HUD, NOAA, and border-surveillance decisions shifted federal resources from civil-rights and climate work toward security tech benefiting favored contractors. (15 Jul 2025; 16 Jul 2025; 17 Jul 2025)

25. Bureau of Labor Statistics and Trump administration cut economic data collection, increasing estimated price shares. Reductions in BLS data collection forced greater reliance on imputed prices, degrading the accuracy of inflation statistics that guide policy and markets. (18 Jul 2025)

26. Trump administration funded $6 billion expansion of US-Mexico border surveillance under OBBA. Massive investments in biometric towers and data systems at the border deepened reliance on private surveillance firms for core state functions. (15 Jul 2025)

27. California state government funded low-income housing targeted to ex-prisoners and institutionalized individuals. California's supportive housing initiative for ex-prisoners and others sought to address homelessness and reintegration, but faced potential local resistance to siting. (18 Jul 2025)

28. California government implemented a $20 minimum wage for fast food workers, affecting employment. Research showing job losses after California's fast-food wage hike highlighted trade-offs between higher pay and employment in low-wage sectors. (18 Jul 2025)

Information, Memory, and Manipulation

1. Secretary of Defense Pete Hegseth used Metallica's song without permission in a drone promotion video. The Pentagon's unauthorized use of copyrighted music in propaganda content raised questions about respect for intellectual property and messaging practices. (12 Jul 2025)

2. U.S. Agency for Global Media under Kari Lake dismantled most U.S.-backed international broadcasting operations. Curtailing USAGM reduced U.S. support for independent journalism abroad, weakening a counterweight to authoritarian media ecosystems. (13 Jul 2025)

3. NASA decided not to publish major climate change assessments on its

website. Withholding climate assessments from public view limited access to scientific evidence crucial for informed debate and policy. (14 Jul 2025)

4. Elon Musk amplified criticism of Trump over unreleased Epstein files. Musk's high-profile posts questioning Epstein file secrecy leveraged his platform to shape public narratives and pressure the administration. (14 Jul 2025)

5. Popular Information and other outlets reported on Trump's defense of Pam Bondi amid Epstein backlash. Coverage of Trump's defense of Bondi highlighted efforts to manage public perception of DOJ's opaque Epstein decisions. (14 Jul 2025)

6. Wired and other media reported that DOJ and FBI edited out minutes from Epstein cell surveillance video. Allegations of missing footage from "full raw" Epstein video undermined confidence in official evidence and record-keeping. (15 Jul 2025)

7. Trump administration sued three members of the Corporation for Public Broadcasting board after defunding PBS and NPR. Litigation against CPB board members, following funding cuts, increased pressure on public media governance and independence. (15 Jul 2025)

8. President Donald Trump posted unsubstantiated mortgage fraud allegations against Senator Adam Schiff amid tariff-driven inflation. Trump's attack on Schiff appeared aimed at diverting attention from rising prices linked to his tariffs, using personal smears to shift blame. (15 Jul 2025)

9. Trump administration sued Dow Jones, News Corp, Rupert Murdoch, and Wall Street Journal reporters for libel over Epstein coverage. Trump's multibillion-dollar libel suit against major media entities sought to punish reporting on his ties to Epstein, potentially chilling investigative journalism. (17 Jul 2025; 18 Jul 2025)

10. Trump administration sued three CPB members after attempts to fire them. Suing public broadcasting board members escalated conflict with independent media governance and could deter resistance to political interference. (15 Jul 2025)

11. CBS announced cancellation of The Late Show with Stephen Colbert. Ending a prominent political satire program altered the late-night media landscape, reducing a high-visibility venue for critical commentary. (17 Jul 2025)

12. Elon Musk used his platform to criticize Trump over Epstein controversy. Musk's public criticism of Trump on Epstein matters illustrated how powerful private platforms can challenge or reshape elite narratives. (17 Jul 2025)

13. President Donald Trump ranted on Truth Social calling Epstein backlash a "hoax" and attacking former supporters. Trump's posts framed criti-

cism over Epstein files as a hoax, seeking to delegitimize concerns and maintain control over the scandal's narrative. (16 Jul 2025)

14. Trump administration cut Bureau of Labor Statistics resources, increasing estimated inflation data. Budget cuts that forced BLS to estimate a much larger share of prices weakened the reliability of official economic data used by the public and policymakers. (18 Jul 2025)

15. National Archives and Records Administration sought public input on records schedules affecting federal archives. NARA's comment process on records schedules allowed public scrutiny of which government documents are preserved, influencing collective memory. (17 Jul 2025)

16. Department of Justice filed motions to unseal Epstein grand jury transcripts with redactions. DOJ's request to unseal grand jury materials, while protecting identities, partially opened a secretive process to public view in a high-profile case. (17 Jul 2025)

17. President Donald Trump ordered Attorney General Pam Bondi to release Epstein grand jury testimony. Trump's directive to release testimony marked a tactical shift toward disclosure under political pressure, though scope and completeness remained uncertain. (18 Jul 2025)

18. Governor Gavin Newsom filed a major defamation lawsuit against Fox News and Jesse Watters. Newsom's $787 million suit over alleged misreporting sought accountability but also exemplified powerful officials using costly litigation against media outlets. (18 Jul 2025)

19. Trump administration dismantled USAGM and, with Congress, cut public broadcasting funding. Combined executive and legislative actions to shrink USAGM, PBS, and NPR funding weakened independent public media at home and abroad. (13 Jul 2025; 16 Jul 2025; 17 Jul 2025; 18 Jul 2025)

20. Heather Cox Richardson and pollsters reported polling showing strong public support for immigration and pathways to citizenship. Poll data revealing broad pro-immigration sentiment highlighted a gap between public opinion and the administration's restrictive policies. (15 Jul 2025)

21. Trump administration cut economic and climate-related data tools while amplifying partisan narratives. Reductions in BLS and NOAA data capacity, alongside politicized messaging, increased the administration's ability to shape perceptions without robust empirical checks. (14 Jul 2025; 16 Jul 2025; 18 Jul 2025)

ARCHIVAL CLOSURE NOTE

This volume is part of the ongoing event log for the period it covers. *The Democracy Clock Event Log* records governance actions affecting democratic institutions in the United States during a specific historical window starting January 20, 2025, the date of the constitutional transition.

The archive is divided into fifty-two separate weekly entries, each representing a distinct period, recorded entirely before the next begins. This volume contains those weekly records for the section of the period it documents, without summaries, evaluations, or interpretive judgments.

No attempt is made here to evaluate the overall direction of the period or to draw conclusions from the record. Such analysis is outside the scope of an archival log and is covered in related analytical volumes within *The Democracy Clock* project.

Events that occur after this volume's last covered date are not included. Actions or effects extending beyond that point are only recorded if they are observable and verifiable within the designated weeks. This maintains consistency and integrity across volumes.

This volume serves as a sealed part of a larger, ongoing record. It can be cited, referenced, and studied over the long term on its own, and is meant to be read alongside the volumes that follow.

www.ingramcontent.com/pod-product-compliance
Lightning Source LLC
Chambersburg PA
CBHW081226080526
44587CB00022B/3842